Ethical Dilemmas in Islāmic Psychotherapy

G. Hussein Rassool

Ethical Dilemmas in Islāmic Psychotherapy

Balancing Faith, Culture, and Professional Ethics

Springer

G. Hussein Rassool
Centre for Islāmīc Studies and Civilisations
Charles Sturt University
Auburn NSW, Australia

ISBN 978-3-032-26514-2 ISBN 978-3-032-26515-9 (eBook)
https://doi.org/10.1007/978-3-032-26515-9

This Springer imprint is published by the registered company Springer Nature Switzerland AG
The registered company address is: Gewerbestrasse 11, 6330 Cham, Switzerland

Dedicated to Idrees Khattab Rassool Ibn Adam Ibn Hussein Ibn Hassim Ibn Sahaduth Ibn Rosool Ibn Olee Al Mauritiusy, and to Yashfeen Psychiatry & Psychotherapy.

Preface

Islāmic psychotherapy is more than a set of techniques; it is a deeply relational practice that interconnects ethical, cultural, and spiritual dimensions with the science of mental health. For Muslim clients, therapy is not only about alleviating psychological distress but also about attending to spiritual, moral, and cultural dimensions of life. Ethical dilemmas in Islāmic psychotherapy emerge from the complex intersection of religious, cultural, and psychological principles, presenting challenges that demand careful reflection and thoughtful resolution. Unlike conventional psychotherapy, which primarily operates within secular frameworks, Islāmic psychotherapy integrates spiritual and theological insights into the therapeutic process. While this integration offers clients profound opportunities for personal growth and alignment with faith, it simultaneously raises critical ethical questions: How can therapists respect the sacred while adhering to professional codes of practice? How can they navigate dilemmas around identity, morality, and cultural expectations without imposing personal beliefs or compromising client autonomy? How can universal ethical frameworks, often grounded in Western traditions, be reconciled with the rich moral and spiritual heritage of Islām? These questions are not theoretical, they arise daily in clinical practice, in the lived experiences of clients and the decisions therapists must navigate.

The purpose of this work is multifold. It is primarily focused on the ethical dilemmas and challenges inherent in Islāmic psychotherapy. The opening chapters provide context, offering an overview of Islāmic psychotherapy, its epistemological foundations, and its ethical framework. Ethical behaviour remains a foundational pillar of this work, positioning Islāmic psychotherapy as a coherent and ethically grounded paradigm rather than a loosely affiliated set of practices. The framework articulated in this book emphasises the integrative relationship between spiritual, moral, and psychological dimensions of human experience, recognising ethics as central to both therapeutic intent and clinical practice. Within this paradigm, ethical decision-making is understood as a dynamic process informed by classical Islāmic source, such as Qur'ânic principles, prophetic guidance, and scholarly tradition, while also engaging rigorously with contemporary professional and regulatory standards. This integrated approach provides a robust foundation for clinicians to navigate complex therapeutic contexts with integrity, cultural attunement, and professional accountability.

Islāmic psychotherapists navigate unique ethical challenges, including respecting client autonomy and informed consent in contexts where family and community expectations exert significant influence. Boundaries and multiple roles present further dilemmas. Practitioners may embody roles such as *tarbiyah* (educating), *irshād* (guiding), *tazkiya* (purifying), *da'wah* (preaching), *taṭbīb* (healing), *shifa* (curing), *wisāṭah* (mediation), *istiṭā'a* (empowering), *ra'ya* (caretaking), and *nasīha* (advising). While these roles support holistic spiritual, emotional, and social well-being, their integration within conventional psychotherapy can create tensions, including risks to confidentiality, role confusion, and potential conflicts of interest. Therapists must also navigate issues of competence, power, and collaboration. Without sufficient theological literacy, addressing clients' faith-based struggles can inadvertently cause harm, while overstepping into the role of religious authority can compromise professional boundaries and autonomy. Collaboration with community leaders or *Imāms*, though valuable, requires clearly defined roles to prevent contradictory guidance or undue influence. Additional challenges arise in reconciling Western-derived ethical frameworks with Islāmic moral principles. Mainstream professional codes do not always address issues salient in Muslim contexts, such as gender roles, sexuality, or religious guilt. Therapists must therefore balance professional standards with Islāmic ethical guidance, ensuring therapy remains spiritually sensitive, culturally responsive, and ethically coherent. Addressing these dilemmas is essential for safeguarding client well-being, maintaining therapeutic integrity, and fostering a practice that is both professionally responsible and spiritually grounded.

This book explores these issues in depth. Chaps. 1 through 3 provide theoretical and ethical foundations, examining the intersections of psychotherapy, spirituality, religion, and ethics, as well as the historical contributions of classical Islāmic scholarship. Chaps. 4 through 9 examine ethical dilemmas, boundary challenges, client diversity, and working with vulnerable populations, including survivors of trauma, refugees, and marginalised groups. Chaps. 10 through 12 address contemporary and applied challenges, including digital therapy, structured ethical decision-making, and clinical supervision. Chap. 13, is especially significant for its provision of a comprehensive, practice-oriented ethical framework that enables Muslim psychologists to address professional obligations, ethical decision-making, and culturally grounded care within diverse clinical and institutional contexts. The final chapter, Reflections and Future Directions, synthesises insights, identifies gaps, and outlines pathways for advancing Islāmic psychotherapy as an ethically and spiritually informed field.

A unique feature of this work is its emphasis on applied clinical practice. Case studies and reflective vignettes illustrate the complexity of ethico-clinical decision-making in real-world contexts, demonstrating both the challenges and opportunities of ethically integrating Islāmic values into psychotherapy. These examples highlight the importance of therapist self-awareness, cultural competence, and reflective supervision, showing how moral and spiritual insights guide practical decision-making. The book also addresses working with diverse client populations, including LGBTQ+ individuals, refugees, and clients facing societal or familial pressures, offering frameworks for culturally and spiritually sensitive practice. The integration of Islāmic perspectives does not seek to impose dogma but rather to provide ethically coherent, psychologically informed, and spiritually grounded guidance for practitioners.

The intended audience includes scholars, clinicians, counsellors, psychologists, and students interested in the ethical dimensions of Islāmic psychotherapy. By integrating classical Islāmic wisdom, Qur'ânic and Prophetic guidance, contemporary psychological theory, and applied case examples, the book offers a comprehensive resource for navigating the complex ethical, cultural, and spiritual challenges in therapeutic practice. Ultimately, it aims to equip practitioners to deliver holistic, ethically sound, and spiritually meaningful care that respects both client well-being and Islāmic ethical traditions.

It is my hope that this book contributes to a deeper understanding of ethical dilemmas in both mainstream and Islāmic psychotherapy, offering guidance for navigating the complex intersections of professional ethics, cultural values, and spiritual principles. By examining the challenges therapists face, ranging from confidentiality, dual roles, and informed consent to culturally sensitive issues and faith-based conflict, this book seeks to provide a framework that is ethically coherent, culturally responsive, and spiritually attuned. By integrating contemporary psychological science with the enduring wisdom of Islāmic ethical teachings, this book seeks to empower therapists to make morally informed decisions while guiding clients on their personal and spiritual journeys. Ultimately, it aspires to cultivate a practice of psychotherapy that is not only clinically effective but also ethically sound and spiritually grounded, serving the well-being of the *Ummah.*

Auburn NSW, Australia G. Hussein Rassool

Acknowledgements All Praise is due to Allāh and may the peace and blessings of Allāh be upon our Prophet Muhammad (ﷺ) his family and his companions.

I extend my heartfelt thanks to Bruno Fiuza, Editor of Behavioural, Health and Social Sciences at Springer, for his invaluable support and guidance throughout the development of this book. I would like to express my heartfelt gratitude to Dr. Saima Khan, Assistant Professor and Programme Leader in Psychology at Bath Spa University, UAE Campus, for her invaluable contribution in authoring Chaps. 6–8, which address key ethical and clinical considerations in Islāmic psychotherapy: Chap. 6: Confidentiality and Informed Consent: Ethical Practices in the Islāmic Therapeutic Context; Chap. 7: Balancing Autonomy, Individual Rights, and Community Values in Islāmic Psychotherapy; and Chap. 8: Navigating Faith, Ethics, and Care: Islāmic Psychotherapy with LGBTQ+ Clients. Her scholarly insight and thoughtful engagement with complex ethical issues have made a significant contribution to this work. In addition, I wish to acknowledge the contribution of Hanan Dover, Vice President of the International Association of Muslim Psychologists (IAMP) and Clinical and Forensic Psychologist for authoring Chap. 13, The Formulation and Application of an Ethical Framework for Muslim Psychologists: The IAMP Code of Ethics. Her work provides a vital foundation for ethical practice within the field. I also extend my sincere appreciation to the International Association of Muslim Psychologists (IAMP) for granting permission to reproduce the IAMP Code of Ethics and Expanded Ethical Guidelines (2026) in this publication.

I am deeply grateful to the past and current students of the following courses at Al-Balagh Academy: Islāmic Counselling and Psychology (Level 2), Addiction Counselling and Islāmic Psychology, Islāmic Marriage Counselling, and Mental Health, *Jinn* Possession, and Islāmic Psychology. Their dedication to learning and exploring the intricacies of Islāmic psychotherapy and counselling has profoundly shaped my knowledge and skills in this domain.

I owe immense gratitude to my beloved parents, who instilled in me the value of education. Their unwavering love and guidance have been fundamental in shaping who I am today, and I am truly thankful for their wisdom and encouragement. I am deeply grateful for the unwavering love and support of Mariam, Idrees Khattab Ibn Adam Ali Hussein Ibn Hussein Ibn Hassim Ibn Sahaduth Ibn Rosool Al Mauritiusy, Adam Ali Hussein, Yasmin Soraya, Nabila Akhrif, Reshad Hasan, Fatima Zohra Bennaoui, Isra Oya, Asiyah Maryam, Nusaybah Burke, Musa Burke, Dr. Najmul Hussein, and Mohammed Ali. Their presence in my life is a blessing, and I am forever indebted to them for their love, support, and inspiration.

I also wish to acknowledge the invaluable contributions of my teachers, who have played a crucial role in deepening my understanding of authentic Islām. Through their guidance and teachings, I have been able to follow the Creed of *Ahlus-Sunnah wa'l-Jamaa'ah*. I sincerely pray to Allāh to forgive me and accept my humble effort in writing this book. May He make it a source of benefit and fruitfulness for all those who find it useful and informative. I pray to Allāh to forgive me for any unintentional shortcomings in this book and to make this effort helpful and fruitful to any interested parties.

May this book serve as a means of guidance and understanding for those who seek knowledge and insight. Finally, whatever benefits and correctness you find within this book are out of the Grace of Allāh, Alone, and whatever mistakes you find are mine alone.

مَّآ أَصَابَكَ مِنْ حَسَنَةٍ فَمِنَ ٱللَّهِ ۖ وَمَآ أَصَابَكَ مِن سَيِّئَةٍ فَمِن نَّفْسِكَ ۚ

- *Whatever of good befalls you, it is from Allāh; and whatever of ill befalls you, it is from yourself.* (An-Nisā' 4:79, interpretation of the meaning).

بسم الله الرحمن الرحيم

Praise be to Allāh, we seek His help and His forgiveness. We seek refuge with Allāh from the evil of our own souls and from our bad deeds. Whomsoever Allāh guides will never be led astray, and whomsoever Allāh leaves astray, no one can guide. I bear witness that there is no god but Allāh, and I bear witness that Muhammad is His slave and Messenger. (*Sunan al-Nasa'i: Kitaab al-Jumu'ah, Baab kayfiyyah al-khutbah*).

- *Fear Allāh as He should be feared and die not except in a state of Islām (as Muslims) with complete submission to Allāh.* (Ali-'Imran 3:102, interpretation of the meaning).[1]
- *O mankind! Be dutiful to your Lord, Who created you from a single person, and from him He created his wife, and from them both He created many men and women, and fear Allāh through Whom you demand your mutual (rights), and (do not cut the relations of) the wombs (kinship) Surely, Allāh is Ever an All-Watcher over you).* (Al-Nisā' 4:1, interpretation of the meaning).
- *O you who believe! Keep your duty to Allāh and fear Him and speak (always) the truth).* (Al-Aĥzāb, interpretation of the meaning 33:70).
- *What comes to you of good is from Allāh, but what comes to you of evil, [O man], is from yourself.* (An-Nisā 4:79, interpretation of the meaning).

The essence of this book is based on the following notions:

- The fundamental of as a religion is based on the Oneness of God.
- The source of knowledge is based on the Qur'ān and hadīths.
- Empirical knowledge from sense perception is also a source of knowledge through the work of classical and contemporary Islāmic scholars and research.
- Islām takes a holistic approach to health: physical, psychological, social, emotional, and spiritual health cannot be separated.

---

[1] The translations of the meanings of the verses of the Qur'ān in this book have been taken from Saheeh International, The Qur'ān: Arabic Text with corresponding English meanings.

- Muslims have an Islāmic or Qur'ânic worldview different from the Western' oriented worldview.
- It is a sign of respect that Muslims would utter or repeat the words 'Peace and Blessing Be Upon Him' after hearing (or writing) the name of Prophet Muhammad (ﷺ).

Competing Interests The author has no competing interests to declare that are relevant to the content of this manuscript.

Contents

List of Figures

List of Tables

Chapter 1
The Intersection of Psychotherapy, Spirituality, Religion, and Ethics

1.1 Introduction

Psychotherapy is not merely a therapeutic discipline; it is also a profoundly ethical and moral enterprise. Every therapeutic encounter is shaped not only by clinical techniques and theoretical models but also by professional and personal values, moral reasoning, and ethical behaviour. At its core, psychotherapy is a relational process that requires therapists to confront questions such as: What is right or wrong in this situation? How should responsibility be shared between therapist and client? How can human dignity be protected and enhanced throughout the process of care and therapeutic interventions? Professional and personal values serve as the compass of the therapeutic journey and they influence how therapists define mental health, interpret client struggles, and envision healing. For example, a therapist's understanding of human dignity may shape how they respond to sensitive issues such as addiction, family conflict, or personal identity. Similarly, moral responsibility guides the therapist's commitment to avoid harm, maintain confidentiality, and act in the client's best interest. Ethical behaviour, meanwhile, provides the practical framework through which values and responsibilities are enacted in day-to-day clinical interactions. It encompasses respecting boundaries, safeguarding privacy, obtaining informed consent, and ensuring that interventions are carried out with empathy, sincerity, and compassion.

Spirituality, religion, and ethics therefore cannot be treated as peripheral to psychotherapy; rather, they function as integral forces that guide clinical decision-making, influence the therapeutic alliance, and ultimately affect treatment outcomes. Therapy does not unfold in a cultural or value-free vacuum as both therapists and clients enter the therapeutic space with deeply embedded worldviews, moral commitments, and spiritual orientations that shape their understanding of mental health, suffering, and healing. In the field of psychotherapy ethics, a wide range of moral issues intersect, including respect for self-determination and

G. H. Rassool, *Ethical Dilemmas in Islāmic Psychotherapy*,
https://doi.org/10.1007/978-3-032-26515-9_1

autonomy, assessment of decision-making capacity and freedom of choice, the use of coercion or constraint, medical paternalism, distinctions between health and illness, patients' insight into their condition and the need for therapy, preservation of dignity, as well as concerns related to under- or over-treatment, among others (Trachsel et al., 2019).

In recent decades, there has been a growing demand among Muslims for therapeutic approaches that integrate spirituality into the healing process. This perspective recognises that mental health is not solely a psychological or medical issue but also a spiritual one. Incorporating spirituality into therapy enables individuals to draw upon their faith as a source of resilience, coping, and inner strength (Rassool, 2024). Furthermore, such integration supports a holistic model of mental health care that addresses the interconnected dimensions of mind, body, and soul. Islāmic psychotherapy, in particular, has gained significant momentum as this approach integrates religious principles and spiritual insights from the Qur'ān, *Sunnah*, and the broader Islāmic intellectual tradition with contemporary therapeutic models. It provides Muslim clients with a framework that aligns with their faith, fostering trust, cultural relevance, and therapeutic effectiveness.

The integration of spirituality and religion into psychotherapy offers significant benefits, yet it also introduces complex ethical challenges. These issues are particularly pronounced in Islāmic contexts, where therapists must carefully balance adherence to professional ethical standards with fidelity to Islāmic moral and spiritual principles. Ethical dilemmas can arise, for instance, when clients hold personal beliefs or practices that diverge from established Islāmic teachings, placing the therapist in a position where respecting the client's worldview must be weighed against adherence to religious norms. Similarly, tensions may emerge when the professional expectation of therapeutic neutrality conflicts with the therapist's own faith commitments, complicating the separation of personal convictions from professional responsibilities. Furthermore, cultural and religious expectations within Muslim communities, such as the emphasis on family and communal obligations, may at times conflict with psychotherapy principles like individual autonomy, self-determination, or confidentiality. Additional ethical complexities appear in practical settings. These include maintaining professional boundaries in close-knit Muslim communities, safeguarding confidentiality where communal responsibilities are emphasised, or balancing multiple responsibilities when the therapist is perceived as a clinician, guide, companion, facilitator, and a spiritual adviser (*shaykh*). Other dilemmas involve decisions about incorporating spiritual practices such as *duʿāh*', *dhikr*, or Qur'ānic recitation into therapy; addressing sensitive issues like premarital relationships, addiction, or same-sex attraction; and handling differences in religious interpretation without imposing one's own theological approach. These challenges highlight the importance of cultural humility, ethical sensitivity, and reflective practice for Islāmic psychotherapists.

Such scenarios focus on the need for an integrated ethical framework that draws on both Islāmic principles and contemporary professional guidelines. This framework should enable therapists to provide care that is culturally competent, spiritually sensitive, and ethically sound, grounded in Islāmic values such such as *amānah* (trust), *raḥmah* (compassion), *ʿadl* (justice), and *iḥsān* (excellence). It is further informed by the *Maqāṣid al-Sharīʿah*—the higher objectives of Islāmic law, which aim to preserve faith, life, intellect, dignity, and well-being—and guided by *Qawāʿid Fiqhiyyah*, the overarching legal maxims that support ethical reasoning, harm reduction, and context-sensitive decision-making. Together, these principles align with universal ethical standards, including beneficence, non-maleficence, and respect for autonomy.

Accordingly, this chapter examines the intersection of psychotherapy, spirituality, religion, and ethics, with a particular focus on the following areas: ethics as the foundation of psychotherapy; the role of worldviews and values; spirituality, religion, and therapy; ethical dilemmas in Islāmic psychotherapy; and moving toward an integrated ethical framework.

1.2 Integrating Spirituality into Therapy

Historically, organised religion played a key role in shaping the practices of psychotherapy and counselling. In both Judeo-Christian and Islāmic traditions, spiritual guidance and informal counselling shared the goal of caring for individuals' souls. However, the emergence of a "soulless" approach to psychology in the nineteenth century reflected the adoption of the positivist Western scientific paradigm (Rassool, 2024). Despite earlier separation, contemporary therapeutic practices increasingly recognise the importance of integrating spirituality, understood as an individual's search for meaning, purpose, connectedness, and values, while remaining distinct from religion, which involves formal beliefs, doctrines, and institutional practices.

The integration of spirituality and psychotherapy has deep historical roots, with early pioneers emphasising the essential role of spiritual experience in psychological growth. Carl Jung highlighted the "religious function" of humans, arguing that spirituality aids in personality development and the lifelong process of individuation (Ellenberger, 2018; Jung, 2013). Existential psychologists like Viktor Frankl and Rollo May emphasised the human search for meaning, recognising the spiritual dimension of suffering and psychological health. Similarly, Erich Fromm's "Psycho-Spiritual Discourse" explored the intersection of psychology and religious beliefs, advocating for personal transformation through love, faith, and self-realisation, irrespective of theistic or non-theistic frameworks (Araullo, 2010; Fromm, 1950). Contemporary approaches, such as transpersonal psychology, further integrate spirituality by considering higher states of consciousness and spiritual experiences as central to human development (Wilber, 2000). Collectively, these perspectives highlight the vital interplay between spirituality and psychotherapy in fostering holistic well-being.

Spirituality and religion often serve as vital sources of strength and coping mechanisms for many individuals facing psycho-spiritual challenges. Clients often bring spiritual concerns into therapy: struggles with faith, guilt, or crises of meaning. Pargament (2011) highlights that integrating spirituality into therapy can improve results by addressing clients' spiritual needs, thereby enhancing resilience and overall mental health. Practices such as prayer, meditation, and religious rituals provide clients with additional coping strategies and a stronger sense of purpose. In psychotherapeutic practice, spirituality has been recognised as an important factor affecting client outcomes. Engagement in religious and spiritual (R/S) practices and communities has been associated with lower levels of depression, anxiety, suicidal thoughts and behaviours, post-traumatic stress disorder (PTSD), and substance misuse, as well as higher levels of life purpose, hope, optimism, and self-esteem (Oman, 2018; Smith-MacDonald et al., 2017). Research indicates that clients in mental health care consider their spiritual, religious, and belief-based practices to be important for their psychological well-being (Currier et al., 2020). There is also evidence to suggest that clients agree that it is important for their therapist to be able to discuss their religious or spiritual beliefs during mental health therapy (Oxhandler et al., 2021). The findings of research indicate that spiritual and religious beliefs can positively influence mental health outcomes, such as reducing symptoms of depression and anxiety, enhancing resilience, and fostering a sense of purpose and meaning in life (Vieten et al., 2023). Nevertheless, a key challenge remains in understanding how spirituality can be effectively applied in clinical settings to promote optimal psychosocial outcomes for clients (Blando, 2006).

Integrating spirituality and religion into therapy requires therapists to acknowledge and respect clients' spiritual worldviews while tailoring interventions in ways that resonate with their beliefs. This integration can take various forms, including incorporating spiritual discussions into sessions, utilising spiritual resources like sacred texts, and employing techniques that align with clients' spiritual values. Such an approach ensures that therapy is culturally sensitive and responsive to the diverse needs of clients. For Muslim clients, this process can involve faith-informed practices that align with Islāmic teachings in the form of Islāmic psychotherapy (See Chapter 2). Islāmic psychotherapy is an approach that embeds spiritual dimensions into the therapeutic process, recognising the significant role spirituality can play in an individual's mental health. This approach acknowledges the intrinsic human need for meaning, connection, and transcendence, and integrates these elements into conventional psychotherapeutic practices. Incorporating spirituality into therapeutic frameworks enables therapists to deliver more holistic and culturally sensitive care that acknowledges and draws upon clients' spiritual resources for healing and personal growth (Alexander et al., 2021). Importantly, this integration does not involve preaching or attempting to direct clients toward or away from particular religious or spiritual beliefs, as such practices would be ethically inappropriate (Richards et al., 2014). Rather, the focus is on respecting clients' spiritual orientations and supporting their autonomy in making informed choices about their psycho-spiritual concerns.

1.3 Ethics as the Foundation of Psychotherapy

The practice of psychotherapy is deeply embedded in ethical and moral considerations. Every aspect of clinical work, from assessment to intervention, requires careful attention to ethical principles, making decision-making both essential and inherently complex. Consequently, adherence to ethical principles is essential to ensure that therapeutic interventions are conducted appropriately and in the best interest of the client.

Ethics, a branch of philosophy, addresses moral issues and judgements. It is defined as "the moral principles that govern a person's behaviour or the conducting of an activity" (Oxford Dictionaries, 2024), encompassing rules of conduct based on concepts of what is morally "right" or "wrong" and "good" or "bad" according to established ethical guidelines. Ethical codes have been developed to establish professional standards, define expectations, and protect clients from potential harm. However, the predominant ethical frameworks and decision-making models are largely rooted in Western values, drawing on the Judeo-Christian tradition. These principles form the basis of international ethical guidelines, such as the Declaration of Helsinki, as well as codes of ethics established by national professional organisations (ACA, 2014; APA, 2017; BACP, 2013; BPS, 2009; Harper, 2006; Pacquiao, 2003). The codes of ethics within psychotherapy and counselling are grounded in a set of widely recognised universal values. Beauchamp and Childress (2012) outline several of these core principles:

- **Beneficence**: Psychotherapists have a duty to promote the well-being of clients by working in their best interests and providing interventions that are both effective and beneficial.
- **Non-maleficence**: Practitioners are obligated to avoid causing harm or exploitation, striving to minimise risks and prevent negative outcomes for clients.
- **Fidelity**: This principle highlights the importance of integrity, loyalty, and trustworthiness, requiring therapists to uphold professional commitments and ethical standards.
- **Autonomy**: Respecting clients' capacity for independent decision-making, therapists are expected to empower individuals to make informed choices regarding their care.
- **Justice**: This value highlights fairness and equality in service provision, ensuring access to care without discrimination or bias.

Together, these principles serve as the foundation for ethical codes in psychotherapy, shaping professional conduct and guiding decision-making. Additional universal values, including beneficence, non-maleficence, fidelity, responsibility, integrity, justice, and respect for human rights and dignity, are formally codified in the Ethical Principles of Psychologists and Code of Conduct (APA, 2017). Another core principle that is often overlooked is self-care. Barnett (2008) argues that self-care is not merely a personal responsibility but also an essential ethical value. This is reflected in Principle A of the *General Principles of the Ethics Code*, which stresses the importance of maintaining self-care to preserve moral integrity and safeguard the well-being of both clients and practitioners. Practitioners who neglect their own well-being risk diminishing their capacity to act competently, compassionately, and responsibly in their professional roles. Without adequate self-care, stress, burnout, and impaired judgement may undermine the practitioner's ability to uphold other ethical principles such as beneficence, non-maleficence, and fidelity. Thus, self-care functions as a foundational value that sustains ethical practice and ensures that professionals remain capable of meeting the needs of those they serve. However, Barnes and Teehan (2022) argue that while ethical codes instruct psychotherapists to avoid exploitative or harmful practices, they provide limited direction on how to address the diverse and individualised treatment needs of clients. Moreover, these universal ethical principles may not always align with the values of developing nations or non-Western indigenous communities. Many of the existing guidelines were developed without fully considering linguistic, cultural, and socioeconomic differences (Harper, 2006; Lovering & Rassool, 2014; Rassool, 2024; Ray, 2010).

The idea of universally applicable ethical norms in the international milieu reflects the aspiration to establish principles that transcend cultural, religious, and social boundaries. Proponents of universalism argue that certain moral values, such as human dignity, justice, and the prohibition of inhumane treatment, are intrinsic to the human condition and therefore valid everywhere (Anabo et al., 2019; Beauchamp & Childress, 2013; Council for International Organizations of Medical Sciences, 2016, Winkler, 2022). This perspective underpins instruments such as the *Universal Declaration of Human Rights* which seeks to articulate standards of freedom, equality, and justice that apply globally. Others advocate for cultural relativism, emphasising the need to account for specific cultural, social, and religious contexts and divergent viewpoints when establishing ethical standards (Eshetu, 2017). For example, Western traditions often emphasise individual autonomy and rights, while many Asian, African, or indigenous traditions prioritise community harmony, collective responsibility, and relational ethics. Similarly, religious traditions offer diverse moral visions:

Christian ethics may centre on concepts of love and forgiveness, and Islāmic ethics on justice and submission to divine will. In Islām, ethical behaviour is firmly grounded in divine guidance, inspiring Muslims to lead moral lives in pursuit of God's favour. This orientation is not simply a matter of individual preference or social convention; rather, it reflects the all-encompassing ethical framework of Islām, which extends to professional and personal behaviour, family relations, societal responsibilities, and even care for the environment. These differences highlight how ethics is context-dependent, shaped by cultural traditions, religious orientations, and social practices.

A middle ground is often pursued through dialogical approach, such as intercultural ethics or Rawls's notion of "overlapping consensus" (1993), which stress respectful engagement, negotiation, and the pursuit of shared values without erasing cultural distinctiveness. Such approaches validate the significance of cultural diversity while simultaneously affirming the importance of collective commitments to human dignity, peace, and justice within global governance. Winkler (2022) highlights the pressing need for interfaith and intercultural perspectives in ethical discourse. From this perspective, universal ethics may be grounded in natural law, interpreted through both secular and religious frameworks, or derived from an intrinsic principle of human existence, namely, human dignity. This ongoing debate illustrates the complexity of reconciling ethical principles across diverse cultural and religious traditions, while highlighting the necessity of approaches that both respect difference and foster shared ethical practice.

1.4 Ethics and Therapeutic Relationship

Ethics in psychotherapy provide the foundation for building effective, respectful, and safe therapeutic relationships. As the cornerstone of psychotherapy, the therapeutic relationship creates the interpersonal space in which assessment, intervention, and healing unfold. From an ethical perspective, the therapeutic relationship is both clinical and moral, requiring therapists to integrate clinical expertise with responsibilities to uphold autonomy, promote well-being, and prevent harm. Contemporary practice is guided by key ethical principles such as autonomy, beneficence, non-maleficence, fidelity, and justice, which are operationalised through obligations such as informed consent, confidentiality, professional competence, and the maintenance of appropriate boundaries (Gutheil & Gabbard, 1993).

Another important aspect of the therapeutic relationship is its inherent asymmetry: therapists possess professional authority, privileged access to sensitive client information, and significant influence over client outcomes. This power imbalance, rooted in the client's vulnerability and the therapist's expertise, empathise the necessity of maintaining clear professional boundaries (Gutheil & Gabbard, 1993; Koch & Cratsley, 2021). It is therefore the therapist's responsibility to establish and safeguard these boundaries in order to ensure ethical, client-centred care (Opland & Torrico, 2024). For example, a therapist working with a client who discloses family conflict might be tempted to intervene directly in the client's relationships. Ethical practice requires the therapist to maintain professional distance, facilitating therapeutic growth and coping strategies without taking sides or becoming involved personal, while ensuring the client feels supported and understood. Ethical boundary theory differentiates between clinically justified, therapeutic boundary crossings and harmful boundary violations, with the latter, particularly sexual or exploitative interaction, representing serious ethical breaches (Gutheil & Gabbard, 1993). To manage these risks, therapists are expected to maintain clear role definitions, document clinical decisions carefully, and seek consultation when needed, ensuring that professional boundaries are consistently upheld (Gutheil & Gabbard, 1993).

Although universal professional codes establish core ethical rule, such as respecting clients, maintaining confidentiality, informed consent and avoiding harm, cultural and religious values add additional layers of meaning and expectation. These religious beliefs and values shape clients' views of what is right or important in therapy and influence how therapists engage with them, and the development of the therapeutic relationship. Contemporary professional ethics increasingly recognises that therapists must practice with cultural humility and competence: clinicians are ethically obliged to understand clients' cultural, spiritual, and moral worlds and to adapt practice accordingly. This approach reframes ethical duties, such as respect for autonomy and confidentiality, so they are exercised in culturally informed ways that enhance trust and therapeutic effectiveness (APA, 2017).

In the context of Islāmic psychotherapy, the development of a strong therapeutic alliance rests on genuine respect for clients' moral, cultural, and religious worldviews, without presuming adherence to particular religious norms or to the therapist's personal values. Ethical engagement is grounded in humility, openness, empathy, and compassionate curiosity rather than moral judgement or corrective intent. This orientation is consistent with the Qur'ânic emphasis on wisdom and ethical sensitivity in human engagement and guidance. As Allāh state:

ٱدْعُ إِلَىٰ سَبِيلِ رَبِّكَ بِٱلْحِكْمَةِ وَٱلْمَوْعِظَةِ.

- *Invite to the way of your Lord with wisdom and good instruction* (An-Naḥl, 16:125, interpretation of the meaning).

This understanding reflects the Qur'ânic intent, refrains from moral instruction or value imposition, and aligns closely with established ethical principles in psychotherapy, particularly respect for autonomy, dignity, and relational care. Within this ethical and cultural framework, therapists are expected to respect religious practices such as prayer and modesty, remain attentive to family-centred models of decision-making, and incorporate spiritual resources when these are meaningful to the client's therapeutic goals. Clinicians working with Muslim clients are therefore encouraged to explore religious beliefs early in the therapeutic process and to collaborate in ways that align clinical interventions with clients' spiritual values, including the use of faith-consistent coping strategies (Attum et al., 2023; Rassool, 2024, 2025).

In clinical practice, ethical work with Muslim clients requires sensitivity to how religious and cultural values shape therapeutic engagement. Particular attention may be needed in managing confidentiality when family members or religious leaders are involved in decision-making, as these figures often play a significant role in clients' lives. Gender-related norms of modesty may also influence the therapeutic relationship, with some clients experiencing greater comfort when working with a therapist of the same gender, especially when discussing sensitive personal or family matters. In such contexts, gender matching can be an important consideration in fostering trust, respect, and therapeutic openness.

Different psychotherapeutic approaches understand the therapeutic relationship in their own ways, and each deal with the ethical challenges it raises according to its particular framework. Table 1.1 presents an outline of the types of therapeutic relationships and key ethical considerations across psychotherapeutic approaches.

Table 1.1 Types of therapeutic relationships and key ethical considerations across psychotherapeutic approaches

Approach	Types of the therapeutic relationship	Key ethical considerations
Psychoanalysis	Hierarchical and interpretive. Therapist holds authority and interprets client material; transference and countertransference shape the relationship	Boundaries, managing power, avoiding exploitation
Cognitive-behavioural therapy (CBT)	Collaborative and structured. Therapist acts as a coach/partner; relationship is goal-oriented and functional	Informed consent, transparency, respect for autonomy
Solution-focused brief therapy	Client-led and empowering. Therapist supports client in identifying solutions; relationship emphasises client autonomy and strengths	Avoiding imposition, ensuring realistic goals.
Narrative therapy	Egalitarian and co-constructive. Therapist and client jointly explore and re-author client's life stories; power is shared	Sharing power, cultural sensitivity, respecting client narrative
Client-centred (humanistic) therapy	Warm, empathetic, and authentic. Therapist offers unconditional positive regard and emotional presence; relationship is non-directive	Maintaining boundaries while fostering genuine connection
Existentialist therapy	Authentic and reflective. Therapist engages deeply with client's search for meaning, freedom, and responsibility; relationship emphasises personal authenticity.	Supporting autonomy, handling existential distress ethically
Family therapy	Systemic and relational. Therapist mediates among multiple family members; relationship is dynamic and context-dependent	Confidentiality, fairness, balancing multiple relationships
Islāmic Psychotherapy	Ethically collaborative and spiritually informed. The therapist respects clients' Islāmic moral and spiritual frameworks while maintaining professional neutrality; the relationship is grounded in *ḥikmah* (wisdom), *raḥmah* (compassion), and mutual trust	Avoiding religious coercion or moral imposition, maintaining role boundaries, respecting autonomy, managing dual roles, cultural and religious sensitivity, and safeguarding client welfare with justice

1.5 The Relationship Between Worldview and Ethics

In the therapeutic relationship, the interpersonal connection between therapist and client fundamentally shapes the process of understanding, growth, and change. At the heart of this connection is the concept of worldview, the set of beliefs, values, assumptions, and philosophical orientations through which therapists and clients interpret human experience. For Muslims, the Islāmic worldview provides a framework that covers essential aspects such as philosophy, values, ethics, emotions, language, culture, and religion. It shapes their way of thinking and offers guidance for engaging with the world in accordance with Islāmic principles, thereby influencing both thought and behaviour. For Muslims this worldview acts as a set of parameters encompassing a wide range of fundamental matters, including philosophy, themes, values, emotions, ethics, language, culture, and religion. Rassool (2024) suggests that it is through this worldview that individuals interpret and interact with the world, grounded in Islāmic principles and perspectives, and influencing believers' thoughts, intentions, and actions. Rassool (2024) delineates that "The Islāmic worldview (*Tasawur or Ru'yah al-Islām li al-Wujud*) or the Qur'ānic worldview is integral to the epistemology, ontology, and axiology of Islāmic psychotherapy, providing a comprehensive framework that shapes the understanding and practice of therapy. The Islāmic worldview is rooted in the Qur'ān, *Sunnah,* and Islāmic civilisation" (p.19).

A person's worldview plays a key role in shaping their ethical beliefs and behaviour. Ethics is not separate from how people understand life, human nature, and the world around them. Different worldview, religious, cultural, or philosophical, provides frameworks that guide what individuals consider right or wrong. As a result, understanding someone's worldview helps explain why they make certain moral choices and how they approach ethical dilemmas. As Sherwood (2003) notes, worldviews serve as faith-based answers to ultimate questions, shaping how individuals perceive and respond to moral dilemmas. Worldviews encompass beliefs about the meaning of life, death, and suffering, which form the basis for values and norms guiding behaviour. These beliefs influence how individuals prioritise and evaluate ethical considerations. Mifsud and Sammut (2023) highlight that worldviews capture symbolic universes, social axioms, and moral foundations, which collectively shape values and ethical frameworks.

Mohamed (2018) explains in the context of Islām, ethical principles are inseparable from the worldview articulated in the Qur'ân, which grounds moral responsibility in divine purpose and accountability. The Islāmic worldview is grounded in the *Tawhîdic* paradigm and encompasses all aspects of life for its followers. It is founded on three core principles: *Tawhîd* (Theism), *khilāfah* (Vicegerency), and '*adālah* (Justice). These principles not only define the Islāmic worldview but also serve as the foundation for the objectives (*Maqasid*) and the guiding framework for human life in this world (Abdullah & Nadvi, 2011). Beyond the *Tawhîdic* dimension, the Islāmic worldview also includes a strong ethical (moral–*akhlāq*) component. This ethical dimension is comprehensive, emphasising principles such as respect for humanity, social justice, equality, inclusivity in human interactions, moral courage to uphold the truth, tolerance of diversity, moral restraint, forgiveness in the face of provocation, disciplined and prudent living, charitable responsibility, respect for life, the use of reason and intellect, accountability for one's actions, and the centrality of justice (*'adl*) in society (Alwee, 2005). The ethical dimension of the Islāmic worldview is further exemplified in the Qur'ânic verse where Allāh state.

سَيْلَّ رَّبِلْٱ نأَ اولُّوَتُ مْكُهَوجُوُ لَبَقِ قِرِشْمَلْٱ بِرِغْمَلْٱوَ نَّكِلَوَ رَّبِلْٱ نْمَ نَمَاءَ لِّلٱبِ مِوْيَلْٱوَ
رِخِلْأَٱ ةِكَئِلَٰمَلْٱوَ بِتَٰكِلْٱوَ نَۧيِّبِنَّلٱوَ ىتَاءَوَ لَامَلْٱ ىٰلَعَ ۦهِبِّحُ ىوِذَ ىٰبَرْقُلْٱ ىٰمَتَيَلْٱوَ
نَيكِسَٰمَلْٱوَ نَبْٱوَ لِيبِسَّلٱ نَيلِئِآسَّلٱوَ ىفِوَ بِاقَرِّلٱ مَاقَأَوَ ةَوٰلَصَّلٱ ىتَاءَوَ ةَوٰكَزَّلٱ
نَوفُومُلْٱوَ
نَيذِلَّٱ كَئِلَٰوْأُ سِأْبَلْٱۗ نَيحِوَ ءِآرَّضَّلٱوَ ءِآسَأْبَلْٱ ىفِ نَيرِبِٰصَّلٱوَۖ اودُهَٰعَ اذَإِ مْهِدِهْعَبِ
نَوقُتَّمُلْٱ مُهُ كَئِلَٰوْأُوَۖ اوقُدَصَ

- *Righteousness is not in turning your faces towards the east or the west. Rather, the righteous are those who believe in Allāh, the Last Day, the angels, the Books, and the prophets; who give charity out of their cherished wealth to relatives, orphans, the poor, "needy" travellers, beggars, and for freeing captives; who establish prayer, pay alms-tax, and keep the pledges they make; and who are patient in times of suffering, adversity, and in "the heat of" battle. It is they who are true "in faith", and it is they who are mindful "of Allāh".* (Al-Baqarah 2:177, interpretation of the meaning).

These core ethical and moral values serve as integrating principles, organising standards of behaviour and values into a coherent and unified system that constitutes the Islāmic worldview. Through this framework, Muslims interpret and engage with the realities of the world. It is also important to recognise that the Islāmic worldview encompasses both an Islāmic epistemological system and an Islāmic methodology (Rassool, 2023).

Therapy is shaped by the interaction between the therapist's and the client's worldviews. Clients bring their own values, cultural assumptions, and beliefs about human nature, which influence their expectations of communication, disclosure, and the therapeutic process. For example, clients from collectivist cultures may emphasise family involvement and shared guidance, while those from individualist cultures may prioritise independence, autonomy, individualism, and personal choice. A therapist's worldview also shapes what they see as meaningful interventions, how they view collaboration, and the importance they place on empathy, trust, and support in fostering change. It further influences their understanding of professional boundaries, authority, autonomy, and ethical responsibilities. An ethical dilemma arises when the therapist's worldview differs from that of the client or when Islāmic values appear to conflict with therapeutic norms, for example, around family roles, decision-making sexuality, or autonomy Overall, worldview serves as the foundation for both clinical judgement and the therapeutic relationship.

1.6 Key Ethical Dilemmas in Integrating Spirituality into Therapy

While integrating spirituality and religion into therapy can be beneficial, it also necessitates careful ethical considerations. Integrating spirituality into therapy presents a range of ethical challenges that can be organised into four broad themes. First, boundaries and dual roles can be blurred when therapists also serve as members of clients' faith communities, consult clergy or faith-leader, or are asked to provide spiritual guidance beyond their scope, making it vital to maintain confidentiality and clear professional limits. Richards and Bergin (1997) highlighted ethical concerns in integrating religion into therapy, particularly dual relationships, where therapists simultaneously act as religious and professional figures. This dual role risks blurring professional boundaries, imposing religious values, violating church-state separation, and practicing outside one's competence. They also warned that such practices could trivialise the sacred.

Second, professional competence is crucial. Therapists should not rely solely on personal faith or spiritual inclination; rather, they must acquire formal clinical training to competently address spiritual concerns. This requires balancing spiritual sensitivity with evidence-based psychological practice, while also acknowledging the methodological and ethical uncertainties inherent in integrating spirituality into therapy. In the context of Islāmic psychotherapy, practitioners should be firmly grounded in psychology through accredited graduate and postgraduate training in counselling, clinical psychology, or psychotherapy. In addition, they should possess adequate foundational preparation in Islāmic studies, including Islāmic theology (*ʿaqīdah*), the Qur'ān and its sciences (including *tafsīr*), Prophetic traditions (*ḥadīth*), Islāmic jurisprudence (*fiqh*) and its legal theory (*uṣūl al-fiqh*), the Prophetic biography (*sīrah*), and Islāmic ethics, to ensure that spiritual interventions are informed, accurate, and ethically responsible. As Gonsiorek (2003) emphasised, personal belief alone does not constitute expertise; developing professional skills helps counter the misconception that only therapists who share a client's faith can provide effective care.

Third, client welfare and safety must remain central, requiring respect for client autonomy, avoidance of imposing personal values, careful consideration of potential spiritual harm, particularly for those with past religious trauma, and obtaining informed consent before introducing spiritual interventions. Finally, cultural and religious sensitivity involves recognising the diversity of spiritual expression, avoiding stereotypes, and guarding against both negative biases (e.g., dismissing religion) and positive biases (e.g., idealising religious clients). Collectively, these themes underline the delicate balance between honouring spirituality and maintaining professional ethics. Simmonds (2004) further noted that integrating spirituality requires tolerance for uncertainty, greater accountability for one's actions, and commitment to spiritual practice for authentic professional growth.

Plante (2007) also highlighted ethical responsibilities in this area, including showing respect for clients' religious and spiritual values without stereotyping,

Table 1.2 Ethical challenges in integrating spirituality into therapy

Theme	Ethical challenges	Key considerations
Professional competence	Competence & scope of practice (Gonsiorek 2003). Evidence-based practice vs. Spiritual practices—responsibility & uncertainty (Simmonds 2004)	Therapists must acquire appropriate skills, avoid overreliance on personal faith, balance spiritual practices with professional standards, and tolerate ambiguity in integration
Boundaries & dual roles	Dual relationships (Richards & Bergin 1997). Confidentiality concerns. End-of-life & existential issues	Risks of blurred roles, role conflict, boundary violations, or sharing sensitive disclosures when consulting clergy; therapists must respect limits of their role
Client welfare & safety	Respecting client autonomy vs. Therapist beliefs. Risk of spiritual harm. Informed consent	Clients' spiritual worldviews must be respected; interventions should not retraumatise or impose therapist's values; informed consent is essential for spiritual practices
Cultural & religious sensitivity	Cultural & religious sensitivity (Gonsiorek 2003). Bias (positive & negative)	Therapists should avoid stereotyping, respect diversity within and across faiths, and remain alert to both positive and negative biases toward spirituality

and taking responsibility for recognising how such beliefs influence their well-being. Therapists must act with integrity, being honest about their skills and limitations, and demonstrate competence by seeking appropriate training in spiritual and religious issues, just as in other areas of practice. Above all, they should prioritise concern for client welfare, particularly when religious beliefs may cause harm to the individual or others. Table 1.2 presents a summary of the ethical challenges in integrating spirituality into therapy.

1.7 Conclusion

Psychotherapy cannot be separated from ethical considerations and the spiritual or religious contexts of human experience. In Islāmic context, this interplay is especially profound, since therapy must align with both professional codes and divine accountability. However, integrating spirituality into psychotherapy presents both opportunities and challenges, requiring therapists to navigate ethical, professional, and cultural complexities carefully. Competence is essential and must be grounded in formal training rather than personal faith, ensuring that therapists can ethically address spiritual concerns while maintaining professional boundaries and avoiding imposition of their own beliefs. Client welfare and safety remain central, including respecting autonomy, preventing spiritual harm, and obtaining informed consent when incorporating religious or spiritual interventions. Barnett and Johnson's (2011) guidelines provide a practical framework for integration, emphasising respectful assessment of clients' spiritual beliefs, evaluating the connection between spirituality and presenting problems, incorporating findings into informed consent, addressing countertransference, consulting with experts or the client's clergy when appropriate, making informed decisions about treatment or referral, and continuously monitoring outcomes. Ultimately, the successful inclusion of spirituality in therapy depends on balancing respect for clients' spiritual worldviews with adherence to professional standards, fostering cultural and religious sensitivity, and cultivating reflective and competent practitioners who can ethically and effectively support the spiritual dimensions of client well-being.

References

Abdullah, M., & Nadvi, M. J. (2011). Understanding the principles of Islāmic worldview. *The Dialogue, 4*(3), 268–289.

Alexander, M., Moreira-Almeida, A., Mosqueiro, B. P., & Bhugra, D. (Eds.). (2021). *Spirituality and mental health across cultures*. Oxford University Press. https://doi.org/10.1093/med/9780198846833.001.0001

Alwee, A. I. (2005, August 27). *Ethical dimension of Islam*. Young AMP's Focus Group Discussion Series No. 1, National University of Singapore. http://thereadinggroup.sg/Articles/Ethical%20Dimension%20of%20Islam.pdf

American Counseling Association. (2014). *Code of ethics*. Author. https://www.counseling.org/knowledge-center/ethics

American Psychological Association. (2017a). *Ethical principles of psychologists and code of conduct* (2002; amended June 1, 2010, and January 1, 2017). https://www.apa.org/ethics/code

American Psychological Association. (2017b). *Multicultural guidelines: An ecological approach to context, identity, and intersectionality*. Author. http://www.apa.org/about/policy/multicultural-guidelines.pdf

Anabo, I. F., Elexpuru-Albizuri, I., & Villardón-Gallego, L. (2019). Revisiting the Belmont Report's ethical principles in internet-mediated research: Perspectives from disciplinary associations in the social sciences. *Ethics Information Technology, 21*, 137–149.

Araullo, A. (2010). Erich Fromm's psycho-spiritual discourse. *Fromm Forum* (English Edition). Tuebingen (Selbstverlag) (pp. 52–56).

Attum, B., Hafiz, S., Malik, A., & Shamoon. Z. (2023, July 3). *Cultural competence in the care of Muslim patients and their families*. In StatPearls. StatPearls Publishing. https://www.ncbi.nlm.nih.gov/books/NBK499933/

Barnett, J. E. (2008). Impaired professionals: Distress, professional impairment, self-care, and psychological wellness. In M. Herson & A. M. Gross (Eds.), *Handbook of clinical psychology (Volume One)* (pp. 857–884). John Wiley & Sons.

Barnett, J. E., & Johnson, W. B. (2011). Integrating spirituality and religion into psychotherapy: Persistent dilemmas, ethical issues, and a proposed decision-making process. *Ethics & Behavior, 21*(2), 147–164.

Barnett, J., & Teehan, D. (2022). Ethics and values in psychotherapy. *Psychotherapy Bulletin, 57*(2), 11–16.

Beauchamp, T. L., & Childress, J. F. (2012). *Principles of biomedical ethics* (7th ed.). Oxford University Press.

Blando, J. A. (2006). Spirituality, religion, and counseling. *Counseling and Human Development, 39*(2), 1–14.

British Association for Counselling & Psychotherapy. (2013). *Ethical framework for good practice in counselling and psychotherapy*. Author.

British Psychological Society. (2009). *Code of ethics and conduct*. Author.

Council for International Organizations of Medical Sciences (CIOMS). (2016). *International ethical guidelines for health-related research involving humans* (4th ed.). CIOMS.

Currier, J. M., Stevens, L. T., Isaak, S. L., Smith, T., & Zlomke, K. (2020). Understanding preferences for addressing spirituality among adults seeking outpatient mental health care. *The Journal of Nervous and Mental Disease, 208*(6), 514–516. https://doi.org/10.1097/NMD.0000000000001164

Ellenberger, H. F. (2018). *The discovery of the unconscious: The history and evolution of dynamic psychiatry*. Basic Books.

Eshetu, Y. (2017). Understanding cultural relativism: A critical appraisal of the theory. *International Journal of Multicultural and Multireligious Understanding, 4*(6), 24–30.

Fromm, E. (1950). *Psychoanalysis & religion*. Yale University Press.

Gonsiorek, J. C., Richards, P. S., Pargament, K. I., & McMinn, M. R. (2009). Ethical challenges and opportunities at the edge: Incorporating spirituality and religion into psychotherapy. *Professional Psychology: Research and Practice, 40*, 385–395.

Gutheil, T. G., & Gabbard, G. O. (1993). The concept of boundaries in clinical practice: Theoretical and risk-management dimensions. *American Journal of Psychiatry, 150*(2), 188–196. https://doi.org/10.1176/ajp.150.2.188

Harper, M. G. (2006). Ethical multiculturalism: An evolutionary concept analysis. *Advances in Nursing Science, 29*(2), 110–124. https://doi.org/10.1097/00012272-200604000-00004

Jung, C. G. (2013). *Psychology and religion*. Yale University Press.

Koch, U., & Cratsley, K. (2021). The history and ethics of the therapeutic relationship. In M. Trachsel, J. J. Messer, & C. L. Müller (Eds.), *The Oxford handbook of psychotherapy ethics* (online ed.). Oxford University Press. https://doi.org/10.1093/oxfordhb/9780198817338.013.90

Lovering, S., & Rassool, G. H. (2014). Ethical dimensions in caring. In G. H. Rassool (Ed.), *Cultural competence in caring for Muslim patients* (pp. 39–51). Palgrave Macmillan.

Mifsud, R., & Sammut, G. (2023). Worldviews and the role of social values that underlie them. *PLoS ONE, 18*(7), Article e0288451. https://doi.org/10.1371/journal.pone.0288451

Opland, C., & Torrico, T. J. (2024, October 6). *Psychotherapy and therapeutic relationship*. In StatPearls. StatPearls Publishing. https://www.ncbi.nlm.nih.gov/books/NBK608012/

Oman, D. (2018). *Why religion and spirituality matter for public health: Evidence, implications, and resources* (1st ed.). Springer.

Oxhandler, H. K., Pargament, K. I., Pearce, M. J., Vieten, C., & Moffat, K. M. (2021). Current mental health clients' attitudes regarding religion and spirituality in treatment: A national survey. *Religions, 12*(6), 371. https://doi.org/10.3390/rel12060371

Oxford Dictionaries. (2024). *Ethics*. Oxford University Press. https://www.oxfordreference.com/search?q=Ethics&searchBtn=Search&isQuickSearch=true

Pacquiao, D. (2003). Cultural competence in ethical decision-making. In M. Andrews, & J. Boyle (Eds.), *Transcultural concepts in nursing care* (4th ed., pp. 503–532). Lippincott Williams & Wilkins.

Pargament, K. I. (2011). *Spiritually integrated psychotherapy: Understanding and addressing the sacred*. Guilford Press.

Plante, T. G. (2016). Principles of incorporating spirituality into professional clinical practice. *Practice Innovations, 1*(4), 276–281. https://doi.org/10.1037/pri0000028

Rassool G. Hussein. (2023). *Islāmic psychology: The basics*. Routledge.

Rassool G. Hussein. (2024). *Exploring the intersection of Islāmic spiritual and psychotherapy: Healing the soul*. Springer.

Rassool, G. H. (2025). *Spiritual integration in Islāmic psychotherapy: Unveiling the therapist's soul*. Routledge.

Rawls, J. (1993). *Political liberalism*. Columbia University Press.
Ray, M. (2010). Transcultural caring ethics. In M. Ray (Ed.), *Transcultural caring dynamics in nursing and health care* (pp. 62–92). F. A. Davis.
Richards, P. S., & Bergin, A. E. (1997). A spiritual strategy for counseling and psychotherapy. *American Psychological Association*. https://doi.org/10.1037/10241-000
Richards, P. S., & Bergin, A. E. (Eds.). (2014). *Handbook of psychotherapy and religious diversity* (2nd ed.). American Psychological Association. https://doi.org/10.1037/14371-000
Sherwood, D. A. (2003). *Chapter 2 The relationship between beliefs and values in social work practice: worldviews make a difference*. https://www.nacsw.org/Download/CSW/Worldviews.pdf?utm_source=chatgpt.com
Smith-MacDonald, L., Norris, J. M., Raffin-Bouchal, S., & Sinclair, S. (2017). Spirituality and mental well-being in combat veterans: A systematic review. *Military Medicine, 182*(11), e1920–e1940. https://doi.org/10.7205/MILMED-D-17-00099
Trachsel, M., Gaab, J., Biller-Andorno, N., Tekin, Ş., & Sadler, J. Z. (Eds.). (2019). *Oxford handbook of psychotherapy ethics* (Online ed.). Oxford University Press. https://doi.org/10.1093/oxfordhb/9780198817338.001.0001
Vieten, C., Oxhandler, H. K., Pearce, M., Fry, N., Tanega, C., & Pargament, K. (2023). Mental health professionals' perspectives on the relevance of religion and spirituality to mental health care. *BMC Psychology, 11*(1), 439. https://doi.org/10.1186/s40359-023-01466-y
Wilber, K. (2000). *Integral psychology: Consciousness, spirit, psychology*. Shambhala Publications.
Winkler, E. A. (2022). Are universal ethics necessary? And possible? A systematic theory of universal ethics and a code for global moral education. *SN Social Science, 2*, 66. https://doi.org/10.1007/s43545-022-00350-7

Chapter 2
Islāmic Psychotherapy and Counselling: An Overview

2.1 Introduction

The twenty-first century has witnessed remarkable evolution in the fields of Islāmic psychology, psychotherapy, and counselling, both as academic disciplines and as practical approaches to mental health. This development is closely linked to the broader Islāmic awakening (*aṣ-Ṣaḥwah al-Islāmiyyah*) or *Tajdīd* (revival), which emerged as a collective response to the historical and post-colonial challenges faced by Muslim communities worldwide and the Islāmisation of Knowledge movement (Rassool, 2025). The Islāmic awakening is a multifaceted phenomenon shaped by colonial legacies, globalisation, socioeconomic inequality, political oppression, and episodes of genocide, as well as by a deep desire to reaffirm and revitalise Islāmic traditions. This revival has sparked a re-envisioning of Islāmic thought and scholarship, driving an intellectual and spiritual renewal aimed at addressing the psychological, emotional, social, and spiritual needs of Muslims in contemporary contexts. Amid these challenges, there has been a growing recognition of the importance of aligning psychological well-being with Islāmic teachings and values. This growing awareness has led to the emergence of Islāmic psychology, psychotherapy, and counselling as distinct fields that contribute to scholarly discourse while offering essential support to Muslims navigating the complexities of mental health. Islāmic psychotherapy and counselling offer structured methods to integrate faith with psychological practice, helping individuals harmonise their spiritual commitments with their psychological and emotional well-being.

The discipline integrates Islāmic principles, teachings, and ethics with established psychological theories and therapeutic interventions, presenting a holistic view of mental health and psycho-spiritual concerns. It highlights the interconnection between body, mind, and soul, emphasising the importance of bringing one's actions, thoughts, and emotions into alignment with Islāmic values. Within

G. H. Rassool, *Ethical Dilemmas in Islāmic Psychotherapy*,
https://doi.org/10.1007/978-3-032-26515-9_2

this framework, individuals are able to confront personal struggles, traumas, and challenges while drawing upon Islāmic spiritual resources for healing and growth. Importantly, practitioners must recognise the diversity within Muslim communities, the heterogeneity of the *Ummah*, the influence of cultural and contextual realities, and the complex interplay of religion, society, and individual experience.

Islāmic counselling [psychotherapy] has been defined as a form of counselling which incorporates spirituality into the therapeutic process and has a faith-based perspective. A more succinct definition is that "Islāmic counselling [psychotherapy] is a form of counselling that incorporates spirituality into the therapeutic process" (Rassool, 2016, p.17). However, since the starting point of Islāmic psychotherapy focuses on the *nafs* or self rather than the psyche (mind), Rassool (2018, 2020) has redefined Islāmic psychotherapy and counselling as the use of interpersonal skills to support the holistic development of the self (*nafs*), intellect (*ʿaql*), body (*jasad*), and heart (*qalb*), grounded in Islāmic spirituality. This expanded definition seeks to encompass the overarching framework of Islāmic psychotherapy and counselling. It adopts a holistic approach by acknowledging the all-encompassing nature of the self and recognising the interconnections between the psychological and metaphysical domains. By acknowledging the holistic nature of the self, this definition encapsulates all dimensions of human nature and emphasises the intricate interplay between psychological and metaphysical elements.

Rassool (2025) has redefined Islāmic psychotherapy as "a therapeutic approach that integrates Islāmic spirituality and evidence-based psychology to promote holistic well-being encompassing mental, emotional, and spiritual health" (p. 28). This definition highlights the dual focus of Islāmic psychotherapy: the integration of Islāmic spirituality with evidence-based psychological principles, with the overarching goal of promoting holistic well-being. It emphasises mental, emotional, and spiritual dimensions, reflecting the comprehensive nature of human experience within an Islāmic framework. Spirituality is recognised as a central component rather than an optional addition, while evidence-based practice ensures clinical credibility. The definition highlights holistic care in alignment with both Islāmic ethical standards and psychological principles. In Islāmic psychotherapy, the therapist's role extends beyond conventional clinical practice, incorporating methods grounded in Islāmic teachings, ethical principles, and healing traditions. By providing a moral and spiritual framework to help clients address feelings of guilt, shame, and the need for forgiveness, the therapist also assumes a guiding role that aligns with Islāmic values. However, this dual responsibility of therapeutic and spiritual guidance can give rise to ethical dilemmas in clinical practice (Rassool, 2016, 2024a, 2024b, 2025).

This chapter offers an overview of Islāmic psychotherapy, exploring its core principles, therapeutic methods, practical considerations, and the ethical dilemmas that may arise in clinical practice. Within the context of this chapter and the book as a whole, the terms counselling and psychotherapy will be used interchangeably. This reflects an understanding of their overlapping and complementary roles in providing mental health support and therapeutic care.

2.2 Contributions of Classical Islāmic Scholars to Mental Health and Psychology

The origins of Islāmic psychotherapy or counselling can be traced back to the early period of Islām, particularly through the life and teachings of the Prophet Muhammad (ﷺ). Beyond being a spiritual leader, the Prophet (ﷺ) served as a guide and source of support for those facing personal and social challenges. His interactions with companions demonstrated deep compassion, empathy, and wisdom, offering counselling, advice (*naṣīḥah*), guidance, and comfort to those in need. For instance, he would provide emotional support by listening attentively, offering practical advice, and helping others navigate difficulties in their lives. One example is found in the hadīth narrated by Abu Ruqayyah Tameem ibn Aus ad-Daari (may Allāh be pleased with him), in which the Prophet Muhammad (ﷺ) said: "Religion is *naṣīḥah*." When asked, "To whom, O Messenger of Allāh ?" he replied: "To Allāh, His Book, His Messenger, the leaders of the Muslims, and their common folk" (Muslim, (a)). This hadīth highlights the importance of offering sincere counsel as an essential aspect of faith, encompassing loyalty to divine guidance and the responsibility to care for others. Similarly, Abu Hurairah (may Allāh be pleased with him) narrated that the Prophet (ﷺ) said: "The rights of a believer over another believer are six," among which is, "if he seeks your advice, you must give it" (Muslim, (b)). These narrations emphasise that *naṣīḥah* entails providing sincere guidance, supporting others in matters of both worldly life and the hereafter, offering protection from harm, encouraging virtuous deeds, discouraging wrongdoing with gentleness, and showing genuine compassion. In addition to the Prophet's example, many classical Islāmic scholars made significant contributions to the understanding of psychological well-being, inner peace, and human development.

The foundations of Islāmic psychotherapy are deeply rooted in the intellectual and spiritual traditions of early Islāmic scholarship. These contributions reflect a holistic understanding of human nature, integrating psychological, ethical, and spiritual dimensions. Classical scholars emphasised the interplay between the mind, body, and soul, laying the groundwork for approaches that resonate with contemporary psychotherapy. Their writings demonstrate an appreciation for human cognition, emotion, and behaviour, alongside the centrality of spiritual and moral guidance in achieving mental and emotional well-being (Rassool, 2019; Rassool & Luqman, 2023a).

Al-Kindi (Abu Yusuf Ya'qub ibn Ishaq al-Kindi) was among the earliest Islāmic polymaths to explore the nature of human consciousness. He examined dreams and their significance in understanding perception and mental states, providing a philosophical and psychological framework that connected inner experiences with external reality (Rassool, 2023b). By recognising the interpretive value of dreams, Al-Kindi contributed to early efforts in comprehending the unconscious processes that influence human behaviour, a concept that modern psychology has further developed through psychoanalytic and cognitive approaches.

Building upon this philosophical foundation, Ibn Sina (Avicenna) made substantial contributions to the understanding of cognition, emotion, and mental health. He emphasised the role of the intellect in acquiring knowledge and understanding the human psyche, while also acknowledging the profound influence of emotions on behaviour and well-being. Ibn Sina's recognition of conditions resembling depression and anxiety, and his advocacy for therapeutic interventions such as music and art, highlights an early integration of mind–body approaches. His exploration of dream interpretation further illustrates an understanding of the psyche's symbolic and experiential dimensions, bridging spiritual insight with empirical observation.

Al-Razi (Abu Bakr Muhammad ibn Zakariya al-Razi) extended this understanding by examining the interconnection between mental and physical health. He classified a wide range of psychological conditions and emphasised the influence of environmental and social factors on mental well-being. Al-Razi's approach to treatment incorporated both pharmacological interventions and psychotherapeutic techniques, reflecting a holistic model that resonates with modern biopsychosocial frameworks. His emphasis on the therapeutic environment and the psychological dimensions of illness underscores the historical awareness of psychosomatic interactions in human health. The integration of ethical, spiritual, and psychological dimensions is particularly evident in the work of Imam Al-Ghazâlî (Abu Hamid Muhammad ibn Muhammad Al- Ghazâlî). Al-Ghazâlî emphasised self-reflection, self-examination, and the purification of the soul (*Tazkiyah al-nafs*) as essential to personal development and mental well-being. His focus on cultivating virtuous character traits ('a*khlaq*) and incorporating practices such as meditation, prayer, and *tafakkur* (contemplation) illustrates a model of psycho-spiritual therapy, where moral and spiritual health are considered inseparable from psychological health. Al-Ghazâlî's work demonstrates that spiritual practices can enhance emotional regulation and resilience, anticipating modern therapeutic techniques that integrate contemplation and reflective practice. Al-Balkhi (Abu Zayd Al-Balkhi), father of cognitive therapy, is recognised for his systematic approach to mental disorders. He classified various conditions and explored the interplay between psychological and physical well-being, including pharmacological treatments and cognitive-behavioural strategies. Al-Balkhi's use of techniques akin to cognitive restructuring and behavioural interventions, alongside relaxation methods, reflects a sophisticated understanding of mental health and prefigures contemporary psychotherapeutic practices such as cognitive-behavioural therapy (Rassool, 2025). By linking cognitive, emotional, and physiological factors, he provided an early example of integrative therapy that balances empirical observation with ethical and spiritual guidance.

Ibn Taymiyyah (Taqī ad-Dīn Ahmad ibn Abd al-Halim al-Harrani) further emphasised the connection between intellect (*'aql*), emotions (*nafs*), and spiritual growth. He highlighted the role of self-examination (*muhasabah*) and introspection in achieving self-awareness and ethical conduct, aligning closely with contemporary psychological concepts of self-regulation and reflective practice. Ibn Taymiyyah also stressed the cultivation of virtuous character traits and avoidance of sinful behaviour as central to mental and emotional well-being, bridging spiritual ethics with practical guidance for personal development. Ibn Qayyim al-Jawziyyah extended this approach by exploring the relationship between the soul, body, and emotional health. He emphasised the cultivation of positive emotions such as gratitude, patience, and love as key contributors to psychological well-being. His holistic approach integrates spiritual, ethical, and emotional dimensions, highlighting the interconnectedness of mental health and spiritual development. By promoting practices that enhance positive affect and resilience, Ibn Qayyim provided a framework for a psycho-spiritual approach that resonates with modern positive psychology (Rassool & Luqman, 2023). Ibn Hazm (Abu Muhammad Ali ibn Ahmad ibn Sa'id ibn Hazm) contributed significantly to the understanding of emotions and the role of relationships in mental health. He explored the nature of love, attachment, and interpersonal bonds, highlighting how emotional connections influence well-being and personal development. His insights into attachment, emotional regulation, and the cultivation of healthy relationships prefigure modern psychotherapy's focus on relational dynamics and social-emotional development.

Ar-Rāghib al-Aṣbahānī addressed self-actualisation, educational psychology, and personality development. He theorised about emotional states and behavioural regulation through worship (*'ibadah*), linking cognitive, emotional, and spiritual development. His work emphasised the role of individual differences, physical and cognitive development, and personality traits in shaping human behaviour, illustrating a sophisticated understanding of developmental and educational psychology within an Islāmic framework (Rassool, 2019). Ibn al-Jawzi extended developmental perspectives by examining cognitive and emotional growth. He highlighted the importance of self-awareness, self-control, and reflection in achieving spiritual and psychological health. He also emphasised the effects of toxic thoughts and harmful emotions on mental well-being, offering strategies for emotional regulation and refinement of the soul. His focus on virtues such as honesty, patience, humility, and gratitude exemplifies a holistic approach to psycho-spiritual development (Rassool, 2016; Rassool & Luqman, 2023). Ibn Rajab al-Hanbali emphasised the purification of the heart and cultivation of positive character traits, integrating spiritual, ethical, emotional, physical, and sexual development. He highlighted repentance (*tawbah*), contentment (*qanāʿah*), and gratitude (*shukr*) as essential for psychological and spiritual health. His writings provide practical guidance for overcoming negative traits through self-introspection, self-discipline, and reliance on God, reflecting a comprehensive model of human development that balances ethical, emotional, and spiritual dimensions. Finally, Ibn Khaldun explored human behaviour and social dynamics, focusing on the concept of *'asabiyyah* (group solidarity) and its impact on social structures. He analysed how the attitudes, behaviours, and mentalities of rulers, leaders, and societies influence historical and social outcomes, effectively laying the foundations for cultural and social psychology. His work demonstrates that individual mental health and societal conditions are interrelated, highlighting the psychological motivations of human behaviour in a sociocultural context (Rassool & Luqman, 2023).

Taken together, these contributions illustrate a comprehensive approach to understanding human psychology within the Islāmic tradition. Classical scholars integrated philosophical inquiry, theological guidance, and empirical observation to develop models of mental health, emotional well-being, and personal development. Their emphasis on self-reflection, ethical conduct, spiritual cultivation, and cognitive-emotional regulation resonates with contemporary psychological theories and therapeutic practices, including mindfulness, cognitive-behavioural therapy, and positive psychology (Rassool, 2016; Rassool & Luqman, 2023). The historical continuity of these ideas has contributed to what Rassool (2019) terms the *"Dodo Bird Revival of Islāmic Counselling,"* reflecting a renewed recognition of the relevance of classical insights for modern psychotherapy. By integrating spiritual, ethical, and psychological dimensions, Islāmic psychotherapy offers a culturally and spiritually sensitive framework that addresses mental, emotional, and spiritual needs. The classical works of Al-Kindi, Ibn Sina, Al-Razi, Al-Ghazâlî, Al-Balkhi, Ibn Taymiyyah, Ibn Qayyim al-Jawziyyah, Ibn Hazm, Ar-Rāghib al-Aṣbahānī, Ibn al-Jawzi, Ibn Rajab al-Hanbali, and Ibn Khaldun remain vital resources for understanding the psycho-spiritual foundations of mental health within an Islāmic context (Rassool & Luqman, 2023; Rassool, 2023a).

2.3 Paradigm of Islāmic Psychotherapy

The Islāmic worldview plays a central role in shaping the therapeutic process, enabling a deeper understanding of the self and fostering a stronger connection with faith. A key principle within this paradigm is the application of evidence-based psychology, which refers to the use of scientific research and empirical findings to inform psychological assessment, diagnosis, and treatment. Knowledge derived from observation, logical reasoning, experimentation, and sense perception is valued, and such methodologies are not to be neglected. By relying on well-established research, psychologists can make informed decisions about effective interventions, assessments, and strategies for addressing diverse mental health issues, ensuring that therapeutic practices are both reliable and effective. However, within an Islāmic framework, the acceptance of scientific evidence is contingent upon its alignment with the criteria of Divine revelation. Rassool (2023b) highlights that Muslim psychologists should place Islāmic ethical considerations above rational and empirical evidence, with the Qur'ān and *Sunnah* serving as the primary sources of knowledge. He further argues that there is no contradiction between divine knowledge and rational-empirical inquiry, as both ultimately originate from God, the Almighty. This principle ensures that psychological practice remains faithful to Islāmic teachings while incorporating empirical insights.

The paradigm of Islāmic psychotherapy is rooted in the epistemology, ontology, and axiology of Islāmic teachings, drawing upon revealed knowledge and reason as sources of understanding, a holistic conception of the human being, and a value system centred on moral responsibility and spiritual well-being. Within this framework, human experience is understood as an interconnected whole encompassing physical, psychological, social, environmental, and spiritual dimensions. While there is no single universally accepted model, common elements include belief in monotheism (*tawḥīd*), reliance on divine revelation, adherence to Islāmic ethics and values, following the Prophet Muhammad (ﷺ) as an exemplar, recognition of the metaphysical nature of the soul, principles of Islāmic anthropology, integration of faith and psychology, cultural competence, and a holistic approach to mental health. Together, these components establish a comprehensive framework that guides Islāmic psychotherapy and features and underline its commitment to holistic well-being in line with Islāmic teachings. Table 2.1 provides a summary of the key elements of the Paradigm of Islāmic psychotherapy.

Table 2.1 Key elements of the paradigm of Islāmic Psychotherapy

Element	Description
Tawḥīd (Monotheism)	Central belief in the Oneness of God, serving as the foundation for spiritual, moral, and psychological well-being
Divine revelation	Guidance from the Qur'ān and *Sunnah* as primary sources of knowledge, shaping therapeutic principles and ethical standards
Prophetic model	Following the life and teachings of Prophet Muhammad (ﷺ) as a role model for counselling, empathy, moral guidance, and psycho-spiritual care
Islāmic ethics and values	Upholding principles such as justice, compassion, honesty, patience, and respect, which form the ethical basis of therapeutic practice
Nature of the self (*nafs, rūḥ, qalb, ʿaql*)	Recognition of the metaphysical and spiritual dimensions of human existence, including the soul, intellect, and heart
Islāmic anthropology	Understanding human nature as created by God, with the purpose of worship and moral responsibility, influencing psychological perspectives
Integration of faith and psychology	Merging psychological knowledge with Islāmic teachings to develop culturally and spiritually relevant therapeutic practices
Evidence-based psychology	Application of empirical research and scientific findings in therapy, while evaluating them against the criteria of Divine revelation
Holistic approach	Addressing the physical, psychological, social, spiritual, and environmental dimensions of health to promote comprehensive well-being
Cultural competence	Sensitivity to cultural, social, and religious contexts when providing therapy within diverse Muslim communities

2.4 Epistemology, Ontology, and Axiology in Islāmic Psychotherapy

Islāmic psychotherapy is grounded in the philosophical foundations of epistemology, ontology, and axiology as articulated within the Islāmic tradition. These three domains provide the intellectual, spiritual, and ethical underpinnings for understanding human nature, psychological distress, and pathways to healing. By embedding these principles into the therapeutic process, Islāmic psychotherapy develops a distinct paradigm in mental health care, one that is holistic, spiritually anchored, and ethically informed, while differentiating itself from conventional therapeutic models.

Epistemology in Islāmic psychotherapy is grounded in the principle of *tawḥīd* (the oneness of God), where revelation from the Qur'ān and *Sunnah* is regarded as the highest and most authoritative source of knowledge. Other sources such as reason (*'aql*), empirical observation, experimentation, and spiritual insight (*ilhām*) are also valued, but only when they remain in alignment with revelation. This ensures that knowledge is not fragmented but unified under divine guidance, shaping both understanding and practice in a way that is deeply rooted in the Islāmic worldview. This approach, often described as *epistemological integration* (Malkawi, 2014), highlights the complementarity between divine knowledge, rational inquiry, and scientific evidence. While revelation takes precedence, empirical science and reason play important roles in interpreting and applying Islāmic teachings within daily life and psychological practice. Ultimately, knowledge in this framework is pursued with the purpose of drawing closer to God, ensuring that therapeutic processes remain spiritually anchored while also benefiting from rational and scientific insights.

Ontology in Islāmic psychotherapy acknowledges the dual nature of human beings, comprising both physical and metaphysical dimensions such as the *nafs* (self), *'aql* (intellect), *rūḥ* (soul), *qalb* (heart), and *al-iḥsās* (emotions). This holistic view highlights the interconnectedness of these elements and stresses that true healing must integrate psychological, physical, social, and spiritual aspects of life. Central to this framework is the concept of *fiṭrah*, the innate human disposition toward truth and morality, which therapy seeks to realign individuals with as a pathway to healing and self-realisation. This ontological foundation also includes belief in the afterlife (*ākhirah*), which shapes how Muslims understand human purpose, suffering, and ultimate accountability. By situating psychological well-being within an eternal framework, Islāmic psychotherapy provides clients with a sense of meaning, direction, and resilience. In this way, ontology ensures that therapy is not only focused on worldly challenges but also aligned with the broader spiritual journey of the soul.

Axiology in Islāmic psychotherapy centres on the role of values, ethics, and virtues in promoting mental and spiritual well-being. Rooted in Qur'ānic teachings and Prophetic traditions, it emphasises values such as justice (*al-'adl*), compassion (*raḥmah*), patience (*aṣ-ṣabr*), gratitude (*ash-shukr*), forgiveness (*al-'afw*), honesty (*aṣ-ṣidq*), hope (*ar-rajā'*), as essential components of psychological health. The process of *tazkiyat al-nafs* (purification of the soul) is especially important, involving conscious self-reflection, moral development, and the cultivation of virtuous character traits. Through this value-based approach, therapy helps individuals align their thoughts, behaviours, and emotions with Islāmic ethics, fostering harmony and resilience. By integrating virtues into daily life, such as gratitude in adversity, forgiveness in conflict, or patience in hardship, clients experience not only psychological relief but also deeper spiritual fulfilment. Axiology thus provides a moral compass for Islāmic psychotherapy, ensuring that therapeutic practice is ethically grounded, spiritually enriching, and oriented towards holistic well-being.

Taken together, epistemology, ontology, and axiology form the philosophical and practical core of Islāmic psychotherapy. Epistemology provides the framework for integrating revelation, reason, and science; ontology situates healing within the holistic nature of human existence and the eternal journey of the soul; and axiology anchors therapeutic practice in values and ethics that cultivate virtue and resilience. Together, these dimensions ensure that Islāmic psychotherapy is not only evidence-informed and rationally coherent but also spiritually grounded, ethically responsible, and fully aligned with the Islāmic worldview.

2.5 Roles of the Islāmic Psychotherapist: Multiple and Dualistic Functions

Islāmic psychotherapy is built upon a holistic framework that incorporates a variety of therapeutic approaches, including Islāmic Integrated Person-Centred Counselling (iPPC), Islāmic Integrated Cognitive Behaviour Therapy (iCBT), Islāmic Integrated Narrative Therapy, Islāmic Solution-Focused Brief Therapy (iFBT), Islāmic Integrated Acceptance and Commitment Therapy (iACT), Islāmic Integrated Schema Therapy (IST), Islāmic Integrated Family Therapy (iFT), Islāmic Integrated Logo Therapy (iLT), and Islāmic Eye Movement Desensitization and Reprocessing (iEMDR). Central to this framework is the integration of spiritual interventions drawn from the Qur'ān, *Sunnah*, and the wider spiritual tradition of Islām. Storytelling and metaphors from sacred texts provide clients with moral guidance and psychological insight, allowing them to reframe personal challenges through the lens of divine wisdom. Contemplative practices, inspired by Qur'ānic injunctions to reflect and remember God, cultivate self-awareness, and strengthen spiritual grounding. Supplication nurtures hope (*rajā'*) and trust in God (*tawakkul*), while guided imagery makes use of spiritual symbols to foster healing and growth. Behavioural activation is reconceptualised in a spiritual context, encouraging engagement in religiously meaningful practices that enhance both mood and life purpose. Where applicable, dream analysis, undertaken by those qualified in its Prophetic dream interpretation, offers further insight into subconscious processes within a spiritually anchored framework. Taken together, these methods infuse therapy with spiritual depth, ensuring that psychological healing is closely intertwined with moral and spiritual development. The overarching goal of Islāmic psychotherapy is to provide mental health care that is both spiritually grounded and culturally focused, maintaining alignment with Islāmic values and principles. Therapists adopt a flexible approach, whether directive, non-directive, integrative, or eclectic, adapting techniques to the unique needs and preferences of clients. Through this adaptability, Islāmic psychotherapy delivers effective, personalised care that supports psychological well-being while simultaneously respecting and strengthening the client's cultural and spiritual identity.

The role of the psychotherapist within an Islāmic framework is inherently multidimensional, extending far beyond the conventional parameters of secular psychotherapy. For a detailed exploration of the roles, competencies, and scope of practice of Islāmic psychotherapists, refer to Rassool (2023b, Chapter 4). Rassool (2023b) proposed a model for the development of competence that outlines four essential domains in which psychotherapists should maintain proficiency throughout their professional careers. These domains include: Islāmic ethics, fundamental competencies, functional competencies, and developmental competencies (p. 84). While Western therapeutic models primarily emphasise psychological assessment, diagnosis, and evidence-based interventions, Islāmic psychotherapy is shaped by a broader worldview in which psychological health is inseparable from spiritual, moral, and social well-being (Rassool, 2024a, 2024b, 2025). The role of the Islāmic psychotherapist is inherently multifaceted, encompassing a combination of generic therapeutic responsibilities common to all psychotherapists and specific roles unique to the integration of Islāmic principles, moral guidance, and spiritual care. Recognising this distinction helps clarify the scope of practice and the ethical responsibilities that accompany dual or multiple roles.

Generic roles refer to the core functions that the Islāmic psychotherapist shares with secular psychotherapists, grounded in universal principles of mental health care: These roles are foundational, ensuring that the psychotherapist meets professional and ethical standards of mental health practice, including maintaining confidentiality, upholding client autonomy, and following evidence-based approaches Specific roles emerge from the integration of Islāmic principles into psychotherapy, reflecting the dual or multiple functions that distinguish Islāmic psychotherapists from their secular counterparts. Specific roles thus extend the therapist's responsibilities beyond the clinical setting, encompassing spiritual mentorship, moral guidance, and community-oriented interventions. While these roles enrich therapy and foster holistic healing, they also create potential ethical dilemmas that require careful navigation, transparency, and collaboration with religious scholars when appropriate (Rassool, 2025). An outline of the generic roles and specific roles of the Islāmic psychotherapist is presented in Table 2.2.

Table 2.2 Generic roles and specific roles of the Islāmic psychotherapist

Category	Roles/functions	Description/examples
Generic roles	Therapeutic alliance	Establishing a trusting, empathetic, and safe environment that encourages client disclosure and emotional exploration
	Assessment and evaluation	Conducting psychological and spiritual assessments, monitoring progress, and adapting interventions to the client's evolving needs
	Clinical interventions	Assessing, diagnosing, and treating psychological distress using evidence-based approaches such as CBT, solution-focused therapy, narrative therapy, humanistic approaches, or integrative psychotherapy
	Psychoeducation	Providing clients with coping strategies, behavioural tools, and education to manage mental health challenges effectively
	Education and professional development	Training and mentoring future professionals by integrating spiritual, ethical, and clinical competencies
	Research and knowledge advancement	Promoting ethically sound, culturally relevant, and spiritually aligned research; developing evidence-based interventions, culturally sensitive assessment tools, and innovative psychotherapy models; disseminating findings to enhance practice and inform policy (Auda, 2021; Rassool, 2024b)
	Advocacy and support	Helping clients navigate social systems, access resources, and address environmental factors impacting mental health
Specific roles	Spiritual interventions	Storytelling from the Qur'ān and hadīth, metaphors, contemplative practices, techniques fostering hope (*rajā'*) and trust in God (*tawakkul*), guided imagery and visualisation, and behavioral activation within a spiritual framework
	Spiritual and moral guidance	Offering *naṣīḥah* (sincere advice) consistent with Qur'ān, Sunnah, and classical scholarship; guiding clients on ethical dilemmas, fostering virtues, and promoting *Shari'ah*-compliant behaviours
	Religious education and integration	Supporting clients in integrating prayer (*ṣalāh*), supplication (*du 'ā'h*), and remembrance of God (*dhikr*) into daily life as therapeutic tools

(continued)

Table 2.2 (continued)

Category	Roles/functions	Description/examples
	Cultural and religious competence	Tailoring interventions to respect and affirm clients' cultural and spiritual identity, ensuring therapy is relevant and effective within an Islāmic worldview
	Community engagement	Promoting family and societal well-being through marital/family counselling, conflict resolution, and psycho-spiritual education, reflecting Islām's communal focus
	Ethical navigation	Mediating conflicts between psychological principles, client autonomy, and religious obligations, especially with behaviours challenging *Shari'ah*, such as substance use, gambling, pornography, or LGBT+ issues (Rassool, 2025)

2.6 Conclusion

Islāmic psychotherapy offers a holistic framework that integrates psychological practice with Islāmic spirituality, ethics, and culture. Rooted in the Qur'ān, *Sunnah*, and the intellectual legacy of classical scholars, it affirms the interconnectedness of mind, body, and soul while addressing the psychological, emotional, and spiritual needs of Muslim clients. The paradigm is shaped by its epistemological, ontological, and axiological foundations, ensuring that knowledge, human nature, and values are understood through an Islāmic lens. By drawing on both empirical psychology and faith-based principles, this approach demonstrates that mental health care can be scientifically sound, culturally sensitive, and spiritually meaningful. The role of the Islāmic psychotherapist is multifaceted, combining the universal responsibilities of psychotherapy with faith-based functions rooted in Islāmic principles. On the one hand, generic roles include establishing a therapeutic alliance, conducting assessment and evaluation, delivering evidence-based clinical interventions, providing psychoeducation, engaging in research and professional development, and advocating for client well-being. These responsibilities ensure adherence to professional standards such as confidentiality, client autonomy, and ethical practice. On the other hand, specific roles arise from the integration of Islāmic teachings, encompassing spiritual interventions such as Qur'ānic storytelling, guided imagery, and practices fostering hope (*rajā'*) and trust in God (*tawakkul*), as well as offering *naṣīḥah* (sincere advice), facilitating religious practices like prayer and dhikr, and addressing moral dilemmas through a

Sharīʿah-informed lens. The dual or multiple roles position the therapist not only as a clinician but also as a moral and spiritual guide, enriching the therapeutic process while simultaneously creating ethical challenges that must be managed with integrity, transparency, and collaboration with religious scholars when appropriate.

References

Auda, J. (2021). *Re-envisioning Islāmic Scholarship: Maqasid methodology as a new approach.* Claritas Books.

Malkawi, F. H. (2014). *Epistemological integration: Essentials of an Islāmic methodology.* The International Institute of Islāmic Thought.

Muslim (a). *Hadīth 7,* 40 Hadīth an-Nawawi. https://sunnah.com/nawawi40:7

Muslim (b). Sahih Muslim 2162b. In-book reference: Book 39, Hadith 6 USC-MSA web (English) reference: Book 26, Hadith 5379. https://sunnah.com/muslim:2162b

Rassool, G. H. (2016). *Islāmic counselling: from theory to practice.* Routledge.

Rassool, G. H. (2018). *Towards the development of a theoretical framework and model of Islāmic Psychotherapy and Counselling: Challenges and opportunities.* Unpublished paper.

Rassool, G. H. (2019). Chapter 22: Islāmic Counselling: The Dodo bird revival. In G. Hussein Rassool (Ed.), *Evil eye, jinn possession and mental health issues from an Islāmic perspective.* Routledge.

Rassool, G. H. (2020). *Towards a redefinition of Islāmic psychotherapy and counselling.* Lecture at Al-Balagh Academy. Islāmic Counselling and Psychology-Level 2. July 2020.

Rassool, G. H. (2023a). *Islāmic psychology the basics.* Routledge.

Rassool, G. H. (2023b). *Islāmic psychology: Human behaviour and experience from an Islāmic perspective.* Routledge.

Rassool G. H. (2024a). *Exploring the intersection of Islāmic spiritual and psychotherapy: Healing the soul.* Springer.

Rassool, G. H. (2024b). *Integrated research methodologies in Islāmic psychology* (1st ed.). Focus Series on Islāmic Psychology & Psychotherapy: Routledge.

Rassool, G. H. (2025). *Islāmic counselling & psychotherapy* (2nd ed.). Routledge.

Rassool, G. H., & Luqman, M. (2023). *Foundations of Islāmic psychology.* Routledge.

Chapter 3
Foundations and Psychoethics of Islāmic Psychotherapy and Counselling

3.1 Introduction

Ethics, a branch of philosophy, concerns itself with moral issues and judgements. It is defined as "the moral principles that govern a person's behaviour or the conducting of an activity" (Oxford University Press, 2024). In essence, ethics involves a set of behavioural rules based on notions of what is morally "right" or "wrong" and "good" or "bad," as guided by established ethical core standards. Ethical codes have thus been formulated to define professional standards, clarify expectations, and safeguard clients from potential harm. Universal ethics refers to a set of moral principles that underpin professional ethical conduct. The most widely recognised principles include justice, non-maleficence, beneficence, autonomy, and truthfulness.

While these frameworks are secular and universally oriented, they emphasise broad moral values such as beneficence, respect, and integrity. Yet, because they are not based on a divinely revealed moral system, they may lack a deeper spiritual or moral grounding. Historically, many therapists have relied on ethical perspectives shaped by Judaeo-Christian traditions, which, although influential, do not fully capture the moral and spiritual dimensions that are central to the worldview of Muslims. Consequently, Western ethical codes may overlook crucial faith-based and moral considerations essential to an Islāmic understanding of human behaviour and ethical responsibility. When working with Muslim clients, it is therefore necessary for practitioners to incorporate the Islāmic ethical framework, which is rooted in divine revelation and emphasises spiritual accountability before Allāh. Islāmic ethics extend beyond professional duties to promote holistic well-being, guided by the Qur'ān, the *Sunnah*, and centuries of Islāmic scholarship. This chapter examines the distinctions between universal ethical codes and Islāmic ethical principles in psychotherapy, exploring their foundational values, guiding principles, and the implications for culturally and spiritually sensitive practice.

G. H. Rassool, *Ethical Dilemmas in Islāmic Psychotherapy*,
https://doi.org/10.1007/978-3-032-26515-9_3

3.2 Universal Ethical Codes of Conduct

Professional organisation, such as the British Psychological Society (BPS) and the American Psychological Association (APA), has developed comprehensive ethical frameworks that guide psychologists in their professional conduct, research, and clinical practice. The BPS Code of Ethics and Conduct (2021) is structured around four core principles: Respect, Competence, Responsibility, and Integrity. These principles provide a foundation for ethical decision-making and reflect the Society's commitment to promoting dignity, fairness, and professional accountability. The BPS code emphasises the importance of cultural sensitivity, ongoing professional development, and responsible use of psychological knowledge. It applies to all members working in diverse contexts, including research, education, counselling, and organisational psychology. Similarly, the APA Ethical Principles of Psychologists and Code of Conduct (most recently revised in 2017) outlines five general principles: Beneficence and Non-maleficence, Fidelity and Responsibility, Integrity, Justice, and Respect for People's Rights and Dignity. The APA code serves as both a set of aspirational goals and enforceable standards for ethical practice. It addresses key areas such as confidentiality, informed consent, competence, multiple relationships, and research ethics. Together, the BPS and APA codes reflect a shared commitment to protecting clients and participants, ensuring professional integrity, and promoting ethical, evidence-based psychological practice within their respective regions and beyond.

The Universal Declaration of Ethical Principles for Psychologists was developed and approved in 2008 by the International Union of Psychological Science (IUPsyS) and the International Association of Applied Psychology (IAAP) (Ad Hoc Joint Committee, 2008). The Declaration outlines four key principles:

- Respect for the Dignity of Persons and Peoples
- Competent Caring for the Well-being of Persons and Peoples
- Integrity
- Professional and Scientific Responsibilities to Society

Although these frameworks are secular and universally oriented, they do emphasise fundamental moral and ethical values such as beneficence, respect, competence, and integrity. These universal ethical principles serve as important guidelines for professional conduct and decision-making. However, their practical application can present challenges in diverse cultural contexts (Oppong, 2019). While they offer a general framework for addressing ethical dilemmas, the interpretation and implementation of these principles often depends on the particular cultural, social, and contexts in which they are implemented.

This variability highlights that ethical practice is not entirely universal in effect; rather, it requires sensitivity to cultural norms, societal expectations, and contextual factors to ensure that ethical guidelines are meaningful and appropriately applied. In addition, because they are not based on a divinely revealed moral and ethical system, they may lack a deeper spiritual or moral grounding.

Consequently, Western ethical codes may overlook crucial faith-based and moral considerations essential to an Islāmic understanding of human behaviour and ethical responsibility.

3.3 Foundations of Islāmic Ethics in Psychotherapy

Islāmic bioethics is a branch of ethics that examines moral and ethical issues in the context of Islāmic principles and values, particularly in relation to medical and biological research and practices. Also known in Arabic as *al-akhlaq al-tibbiyyah* (الأخلاق الطبية), Islāmic bioethics provides guidance on ethical matters concerning human life (Shomali, 2008). Similarly, Islāmic psychoethics refers to "the Islāmic ethical principles and guidelines that govern the practice of psychotherapy" (Rassool, 2025, p.52). It involves integrating Islāmic beliefs in a manner consistent with Islāmic teachings, offering therapists a framework to deliver culturally sensitive and morally sound psychological interventions.

In the Islāmic tradition, the Qur'ān and *Sunnah* serve as primary sources for guidance on the intricate relationship between medicine and ethics. The development of Prophetic medicine (*Tibb al-Nabawi*) and the contributions of scholars such as Ibn al-Qayyim and Al-Dhahabi have been instrumental in shaping ethical discourse around medical care. Central to Islāmic theology is the belief that God is the ultimate healer, possessing the power to both cause and cure illness. Therefore, placing trust in God as the ultimate Healer is considered essential, acknowledging His role as the originator and sustainer of health. Simultaneously, Islāmic scholars stress the importance of seeking medical treatment as an expression of reliance on God (*tawakkul*), reflecting a balance between divine trust and proactive human action. Islāmic ethics (*'akhlaq*) are also further informed by secondary sources such as *Ijma* (scholarly consensus), *Qiyas* (analogical reasoning), and *Ijtihad* (independent reasoning). Ethical practice in Islām extends beyond professional obligations to encompass spiritual and moral dimensions, linking human actions to accountability before Allāh (*taqwa*, or God-consciousness).

Throughout history, ethical principles within the Islāmic tradition have been applied in ways that demonstrate a strong commitment to moral values in medical practice and research. From the early days of the Islāmic state to contemporary times, scholars have contributed to the understanding and implementation of ethical considerations grounded in Islāmic teachings, fostering an ongoing dialogue between medicine, ethics, and religious principles. Ethical guidelines and oversight mechanisms were established to govern the conduct of physicians, even during the lifetime of the Messenger of Allāh (ﷺ) (WHO, 2005). During the era of the Islāmic Caliphate, regulatory measures such as inspection and oversight (*hisbah*) were implemented to ensure physicians conducted themselves properly and were held accountable for their practices. Islāmic legal scholars emphasised that individuals practising in any professional field must possess the requisite expertise in their respective disciplines. These measures aimed to regulate the practice of medicine and maintain high ethical standards within Islāmic society. The Messenger of Allāh (ﷺ) is reported to have said, "Anyone who practises medicine when he is not known as a practitioner will be held responsible" (Abū Dāwūd), highlighting the principle of accountability in professional practice.

In Islāmic ethics, individuals providing medical or psychotherapeutic services must hold appropriate credentials and recognition as qualified practitioners to safeguard the welfare and safety of clients. This principle emphasises the necessity for Islāmic psychotherapists to possess specialised knowledge, skills, and training to deliver competent care, in alignment with broader Islāmic ethical values of responsibility and accountability. Upholding professional competence is considered essential, reflecting the Islāmic ethos of performing duties with excellence (*ihsān*) across personal, professional, and social domains. This commitment ensures that clients receive effective therapeutic interventions from qualified professionals who adhere to ethical standards, thereby protecting their well-being and maintaining Islāmic moral values.

Islāmic psychoethics is a discipline concerned with the mental, emotional, and spiritual well-being of individuals, placing a strong emphasis on the ethical practice of psychological care, mental health interventions, and therapeutic relationships (Rassool, 2025). Unlike secular psychotherapies, Islāmic psychoethics not only addresses ethical issues commonly encountered in psychotherapy such as professional competence, boundaries and dual relationships, confidentiality, informed consent, respect for clients' autonomy, maintaining privacy, avoiding exploitation, appropriate handling of cultural and religious differences, the acceptance of gifts, managing conflicts of interest, and dealing with transference and countertransference, but also engages with broader moral and existential questions related to life, death, illness, suffering, meaning, and the use of spiritual interventions in therapy. Islāmic psychoethics draws on the *Maqāṣid al-Sharīʿah* (higher objectives of Islāmic law), which aims to preserve and fulfil five primary objectives, also known as the "five essentials" or "higher goals":

- Preservation of religion (*hifz al-din*): this objective involves protecting and preserving the principles, teachings, and practices of the Islāmic faith, including monotheism, devotion to Allāh, and religious rituals.
- Preservation of life (*hifz al-nafs*): Islāmic law places significant importance on preserving human life, prohibiting actions that cause harm, violence, or endangerment.
- Preservation of intellect (*hifz al-aql*): *Shariah* recognises and encourages the importance of rationality, intellect, and knowledge, promoting intellectual development and critical thinking.
- Preservation of lineage/progeny (*hifz al-nasl*): Islāmic law aims to preserve and strengthen family and societal structures, promoting marriage, protecting family rights, and ensuring the continuity of lineage and future generations.
- Preservation of property (*hifz al-mal*): *Shar'iah* ensures the protection of property rights, advocating for economic justice and equitable distribution of wealth within society while prohibiting theft, fraud, and exploitation.

These objectives highlight the holistic approach of Islāmic law toward promoting individual and societal well-being, emphasising principles of justice, compassion, and human dignity. The *Qawāʿid al-Fiqhiyyah* (or *ʿilm al-qawāʿid al-fiqhiyyah*) (Al-Hisni, 1997; Elgariani, 2012), commonly referred to as legal maxims, serve as a guiding framework for addressing complex legal issues and adapting Islāmic law to contemporary circumstances. These objectives reflect the holistic approach of Islāmic law (*Sharīʿah*) in promoting both individual and societal well-being, emphasising key principles such as justice (*ʿadl*), compassion (*ihsān*), and human dignity (*karāmah*). Central to this framework are the core values of Islāmic ethics, including *tawhîd* (Unity of God), which recognises that ethical behaviour stems from submission to the will of Allāh; *ʿadl* (Justice), ensuring fairness and balance in all interactions; *ihsān* (Excellence and compassion), striving for moral and professional excellence with empathy; *hurmah* (Sanctity of life and dignity), safeguarding human dignity as a divine trust; and *amānah* (Trust and accountability), maintaining confidentiality and integrity as sacred obligations. Together, the values, objectives and legal maxims of Islāmic ethics offer a comprehensive, principled approach that guides behaviour, protects human dignity, and promotes societal welfare in alignment with divine guidance.

3.4 Principles of Psychoethics

There are a number of principles of Islāmic ethics, and among the key principles of Islāmic psychoethics is *tawhîd* (Unity of God) which is the foundational principle. Figure 3.1 shows the core principles of Islāmic psychoethics. *Tawhîd* refers to the oneness of God, the doctrine of God's absolute unity upon which all of Islām is founded (Rassool, 2023). Every act of behaviour or ritual, whether internal or external, holds no true meaning or value if this principle is in any way compromised, emphasising that all ethical behaviour originates from submission to the will of Allāh. *Tawhîd* serves as the spiritual and moral cornerstone, guiding all human actions within the framework of divine accountability. In practical terms, it reminds individuals that ethical conduct is not merely a social or professional requirement but a spiritual obligation. By recognising Allāh as the ultimate authority, individuals are encouraged to align their intentions, decisions, and actions with divine guidance, ensuring that moral and ethical principles are observed consistently in all areas of life.

The second principle of Islāmic psychoethics highlights "the inherent honour and dignity of all human beings" (WHO, 2005, p.1). Islāmic teachings strongly emphasise that every individual, regardless of race, gender, or social status, possesses intrinsic worth granted by Allāh. As stated in the Qur'ān,

وَلَقَدْ كَرَّمْنَا بَنِى

- *And indeed, We have honoured the Children of Adam.* (Al-'Isrā' 17:70, interpretation of the meaning).

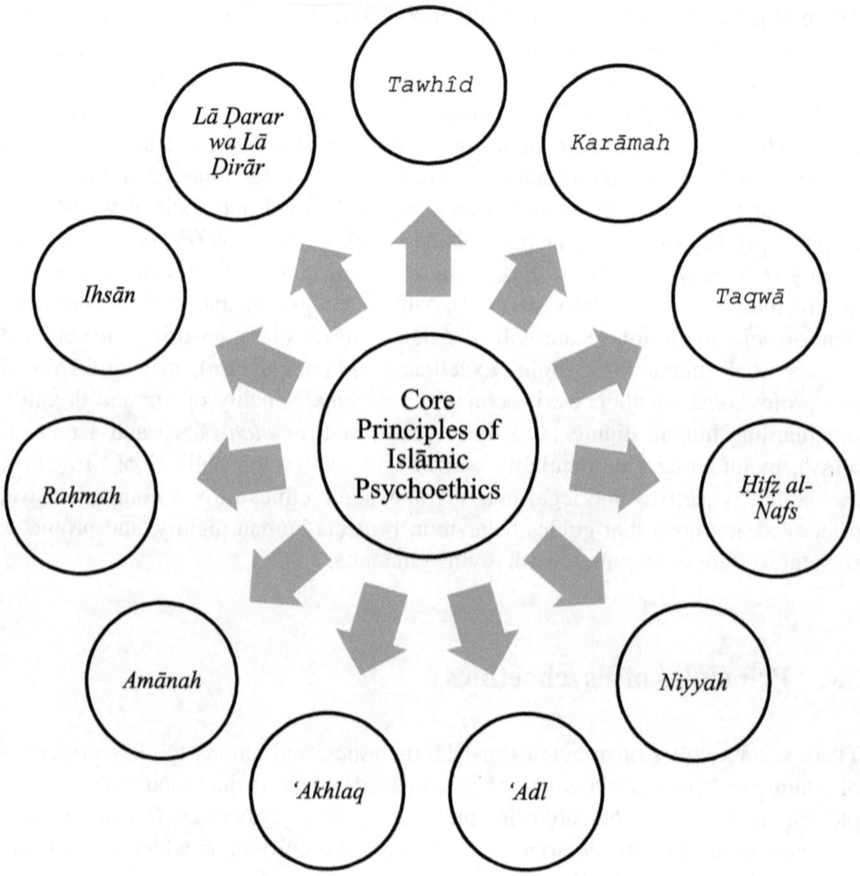

Fig. 3.1 Core Principles of Islāmic Psychoethics

In this verse, Allāh declares that He has honoured the children of Adam, granting them dignity by creating them in the most excellent and perfect form (Ibn Kathir, 2000). This foundational principle requires individuals to uphold the dignity, privacy, and confidentiality of others, particularly in fields such as health care, education, and counselling. Practically, this means that professionals, including psychologists and medical practitioners, are responsible for protecting individuals' autonomy and rights, promoting informed decision-making, and maintaining respect in all interactions. Honouring an individual, from an Islāmic ethical perspective, involves safeguarding their overall health and well-being while respecting their personality, privacy, and confidentiality. It also affirms their right to access complete psychological or medical information and to make independent decisions concerning their health within the framework of Islāmic values. This principle emphasises patient-centred care, ensuring that dignity, autonomy, and individual rights are consistently upheld in professional practice.

Taqwā (God-consciousness), the third principle, complements *tawhîd* by emphasising awareness of accountability before Allāh in every action. Allāh says in the Qur'ân:

إِنَّ أَكْرَمَكُمْ عِندَ ٱللَّهِ أَتْقَىٰكُمْ.

- *...Indeed, the most noble of you in the sight of Allāh is the most righteous of you.* (Al-Ḥujurāt 49:13, interpretation of the meaning).

The verse affirms that genuine honour and distinction are attained only through t*aqwā* (piety, righteousness, and moral consciousness) rather than through social standing, wealth, or lineage. Within ethical and professional settings, this principle encourages respect, justice, and equality, reminding individuals to treat others with fairness and dignity regardless of their status or background. *Taqwā* cultivates a continuous awareness of moral responsibility, guiding individuals to act ethically even in the absence of external supervision. It nurtures an inner sense of accountability before God, which becomes the foundation for integrity and upright conduct. For professionals, *taqwā* functions as an internal moral compass, ensuring that every decision and action aligns with divine values and ethical standards. It safeguards against the influence of societal pressures or personal gain, promoting sincerity, honesty, and consistency in fulfilling one's duties with a consciousness of God's presence and ultimate judgement.

The fourth principle is that every human being has the right to live and to the maintenance of life. In Islām, the concept of lifesaving encompasses more than physical preservation; it includes psychological, spiritual, and social aspects (WHO, 2005). Islām strongly emphasises the holistic nature of human existence, recognising the deep interconnection between the body, mind, and spirit. The Qur'ān (5:32) declares:

وَمَنْ أَحْيَاهَا فَكَأَنَّمَا أَحْيَا ٱلنَّاسَ.

- *And whoever saves one life, it is as if he had saved all of mankind.* (Al-Mā'idah 5:32, interpretation of the meaning).

This verse highlights the profound moral value Islām places on the sanctity and preservation of life. Consequently, every human being has the inherent right to live and to have their life protected and sustained. In Islāmic ethics, the act of saving a life goes beyond mere physical preservation; it also includes nurturing psychological stability, spiritual growth, and social well-being (WHO, 2005). The teachings of Islām advocate for a holistic approach to health and emphasise the creation of a just society that upholds human dignity and promotes the overall quality of life for all individuals. For therapists and healthcare professionals, this principle requires considering the broader implications of their intervention, supporting not only the physical health of individuals but also their mental, emotional, and spiritual welfare, thereby safeguarding life in its fullest and most meaningful sense.

Niyyah (intention), the fifth principle, lies at the heart of Islāmic psychoethics, serving as the foundation for determining the moral value of any action. Alqamah bin Waqqas al Laithi said that he heard `Umar bin al-Khattab (may Allāh be pleased with him), addressing the people, and he said: I heard the Messenger of Allāh (ﷺ) say: "Action is but by intention and each person will have but that which he intended…" (Ahmad). In Islām, deeds are not judged solely by their outward form but by the sincerity and purity of the intention behind them. A person's actions gain ethical significance only when they are motivated by a genuine desire to seek Allāh's pleasure and to do what is right. This principle teaches that even outwardly similar actions can differ greatly in moral worth depending on the intention driving them. Acts performed with selfish motives, negligence, or a desire for recognition lose their ethical value, while those undertaken with sincerity, humility, and righteousness are elevated in the sight of God. *Niyyah* therefore becomes the measure of spiritual authenticity and ethical integrity, ensuring that actions reflect true devotion and moral consciousness rather than superficial compliance. In professional and practical settings, *niyyah* encourages individual, such as therapists or counsellors, to approach their work with honesty, compassion, and a sincere commitment to serve others. It transforms routine duties into acts of worship when performed with the right intention. By grounding professional practice in sincerity and purpose, this principle promotes a culture of ethical excellence where service, empathy, and accountability are prioritised over personal gain or mere procedural fulfilment. Ultimately, it reminds professionals that genuine ethical conduct begins within the heart and manifests through sincere and purposeful action.

Equity/Justice (*ʿadl*), the sixth principle, is central to Islāmic psychoethics, mandating fairness, balance, and impartiality in all aspects of life. This principle encompasses legal, social, and interpersonal justice, ensuring that individuals receive their rightful dues and are treated equitably. Muslims consider justice in its general context to be one of the most obligatory and necessary obligations, since Allāh commanded it in His sayings (Al-Jaza'iry, 2001):

إِنَّ ٱللَّهَ يَأْمُرُ بِٱلْعَدْلِ وَٱلْإِحْسَٰنِ وَإِيتَآئِ ذِى ٱلْقُرْبَىٰ وَيَنْهَىٰ عَنِ ٱلْفَحْشَآءِ وَٱلْمُنكَرِ
وَٱلْبَغْىِ ۚ.

- *Indeed, Allāh orders justice and good conduct and giving to relatives and forbids immorality and bad conduct and oppression.*(An-Naĥl 16:90, interpretation of the meaning).

إِنَّ ٱللَّهَ يُحِبُّ ٱلْمُقْسِطِينَ.

- *Indeed, Allāh loves those who act justly.*(Al-Hujurāt 49:9, interpretation of the meaning).

قُلْ أَمَرَ رَبِّى بِٱلْقِسْطِ.

- *Say, [O Muhammad], "My Lord has ordered justice."* (Al-'A'rāf 7:29, interpretation of the meaning)

In Islām, God's teachings strongly emphasise the principle of equity, calling upon individuals to uphold fairness and justice in every aspect of life. Throughout the Qur'ān, believers are repeatedly commanded to act just, whether in giving truthful testimony, delivering fair judgements, promoting reconciliation, or safeguarding the rights of the oppressed. Verses such as "*And when you testify, be just*" (Qur'ān 6:152), "*When you judge between people, judge with justice*" (Qur'ān 4:58), "*Then make peace between them with justice and act equitably*" (Qur'ān 49:9), and "*Concerning the oppressed among children, maintain justice for orphans*" (Qur'ān 4:127) serve as powerful reminders of this divine command. These teachings collectively highlight that justice is not limited to legal or social matters but is a comprehensive moral obligation that permeates all human interactions. Upholding equity reflects one's obedience to God and ensures the preservation of harmony, dignity, and moral integrity within society. The Islāmic concept of equity (*'adl*) extends far beyond legal or social justice; it is a core ethical principle that shapes moral behaviour, professional integrity, and interpersonal relations. Within psychoethics, the principle of equity provides a profound framework for ensuring fairness, compassion, and respect in therapeutic and clinical practice. It requires practitioners to treat every individual with equal dignity and consideration, recognising the inherent worth of each person as part of the divine creation, regardless of their background, beliefs, or circumstances.

In the context of psychotherapy, equity guides professionals to provide balanced and unbiased care, ensuring that every client receives equal access to treatment and support. This means avoiding favouritism, prejudice, or discrimination based on race, gender, religion, socioeconomic status, or mental health condition. Upholding equity also means acknowledging and addressing systemic inequalities that may affect a client's mental well-being, such as social injustice, marginalisation, or stigma, and working toward empowerment and inclusion. From an Islāmic ethical standpoint, practicing equity in psychotherapy is both a moral duty and an act of worship. It reflects obedience to God's command to act justly and compassionately toward others. A therapist guided by equity recognises that fairness in care is not merely a professional standard but a spiritual responsibility, where each decision and intervention should aim to promote holistic well-being, mental, emotional, social, and spiritual. Equity prohibits any form of discrimination based on gender, race, religion, political affiliation, social status, or any other factor. This aligns closely with the World Health Organization's vision of "*Health for all*" (WHO, 2005, p. 2), reflecting Islām's deep commitment to universal human welfare, compassion, and justice in service delivery. In this sense, equity becomes a central pillar of psychoethics, integrating faith-based morality with professional ethics to ensure that healing is pursued with justice, empathy, and integrity.

'Akhlaq (Virtue and morality), seventh principle, forms the ethical foundation of psychoethics, guiding psychologists and mental health professionals to cultivate personal and professional virtues. In practice, *'akhlaq* encourages the development of qualities such as honesty, empathy, patience, humility, and respect for human dignity. These virtues are essential in establishing trustful and therapeutic relationships with clients, fostering an environment where individuals feel safe, understood, and valued. By embedding *'akhlaq* into their professional conduct, practitioners ensure that their interventions are not merely technical but are also morally grounded, promoting holistic well-being for clients.

Amānah (Trust and accountability), eighth principle, complements *'akhlaq* by emphasising the duty to act responsibly and uphold the trust placed in professionals. In Islāmic psychotherapy and health care, *amānah* entails maintaining client confidentiality, respecting commitments, delivering services competently, and safeguarding the rights and welfare of those under care. It reinforces the ethical imperative that practitioners are accountable not only to their clients but also to the broader moral and social framework dictated by Islāmic teachings. Qur'ān 4:58 (Surah al-Nisā') explicitly highlights the importance of fulfilling trusts and judging with justice, which serves as a critical guideline for ethical decision-making in professional contexts. Together, *'akhlaq* and *amānah* establish a comprehensive framework for psychoethical practice, linking personal virtue with professional responsibility. By adhering to these principles, mental health professionals are guided to make ethical choices that balance technical competence with moral integrity, protect client rights, and promote justice and fairness in all interactions. They form a foundation for reflective practice, where the moral character of the practitioner and their accountability to others ensure that therapeutic interventions are both effective and ethically sound, in alignment with Islāmic ethical teachings.

Raḥmah, ninth principle, often translated as compassion and mercy, emphasises the therapist's duty to act with genuine empathy, care, and concern for the client's holistic well-being. In the context of Islāmic psychotherapy, *raḥmah* extends beyond simple empathy or professional courtesy; it involves an active, morally guided effort to understand clients' experiences, alleviate suffering, and support their psychological, emotional, and spiritual growth. This principle is deeply rooted in Islāmic teachings, where compassion is considered a moral obligation and a reflection of God's mercy toward His creation. Jarir ibn 'Abdullah reported that the Messenger of Allah (ﷺ), may Allah bless him and grant him peace, said, "Whoever is denied compassion is denied good" (Al-Adab Al-Mufrad). In practice, *raḥmah* requires the therapist to cultivate patience, kindness, and ethical sensitivity in every interaction, ensuring that interventions do not cause harm and are attuned to the client's needs, vulnerabilities, and cultural-religious context. It also involves recognising the interconnectedness of psychological and spiritual health, integrating guidance that promotes mental well-being while aligning with the client's moral and spiritual values. Overall, *raḥmah* elevates the ethical practice of psychotherapy from technical competence to morally and spiritually guided care. It reminds therapists that their role is not only to address symptoms or facilitate behavioural change but also to nurture the client's holistic well-being, promoting healing, resilience, and alignment with ethical and spiritual values.

The tenth principle in Islāmic psychoethics emphasises the pursuit of excellence (*ihsān*/proficiency), reflecting a commitment to consistently perform at the highest level in all aspects of life. This aspiration is deeply valued in Islām and is regarded as a divine injunction:

إِنَّ ٱللَّهَ يَأۡمُرُ بِٱلۡعَدۡلِ وَٱلۡإِحۡسَٰنِ.

- *Indeed, Allāh orders justice and to have ihsan (perfection)* (An Naĥl 16:90, interpretation of the meaning).

The Prophet Muhammad (ﷺ) further reinforces this principle in the hadīth narrated by Shaddad bin Aws (may Allāh be pleased with him), stating: "Verily Allāh has prescribed *ihsān* (proficiency, perfection) in all things" (Muslim). This hadīth highlights the Islāmic principle of performing every action with excellence and compassion, even in tasks that might seem routine or mundane. *Ihsān* in Islām is not limited to technical skill or competence; it encompasses performing every action with moral consciousness, compassion, and mindfulness of God's accountability (*taqwā*). Within the context of Islāmic psychoethics, Ihsān serves as a guiding principle for mental health practitioners, encouraging them to approach therapy with not only professional competence but also moral and spiritual excellence. For Islāmic psychotherapists, *ihsān* implies that interventions should be delivered with sensitivity, empathy, and attention to the holistic well-being of clients, addressing not only psychological concerns but also emotional, social, and spiritual dimensions. Ethical practice under this principle requires therapists to be meticulous, ensuring that every therapeutic action maximises benefit and minimises potential harm (aligned with the principle of non-maleficence). Moreover, Ihsān motivates therapists to cultivate virtue and good character (*'akhlaq*) in their interactions, demonstrating generosity, patience, and compassion toward clients, especially those experiencing significant emotional distress or societal disadvantage. It encourages therapists to engage in continuous self-improvement, professional development, and reflective practice, striving for mastery in both clinical skills and ethical discernment. Finally, the principle of *Ihsān* in Islāmic psychoethics integrates spiritual accountability, professional excellence, and compassionate service, ensuring that mental health care is delivered not merely as a technical task, but as a morally and spiritually conscious practice aimed at holistic human well-being.

The eleventh principle of Islāmic psychoethics, founded on the concept of no harm / non-maleficence, is derived from the Prophetic hadīth narrated by Abū Sa 'īd al-Khudrī (may Allāh be pleased with him), in which the Messenger of Allāh (ﷺ) said: "There should be neither harming (*ḍarar*) nor reciprocating harm (*ḍirār*)" (Ibn Mājah). This profound teaching forms the basis of one of the five major legal maxims (*al-Qawā'id al-Fiqhiyyah*) in Islāmic jurisprudence: *"Al-Ḍarar yuzāl,"* "Harm must be eliminated." It establishes that any form of harm, physical, psychological, spiritual, social, or economic, must be prevented, mitigated, or removed whenever possible. This maxim serves as a universal ethical compass across diverse fields, including health care, psychology, and Islāmic psychotherapy, guiding decision-making toward the preservation of well-being and justice. In the context of Islāmic psychoethics, this principle highlights a therapist's profound moral and spiritual duty to ensure that psychological interventions, counselling approaches, and therapeutic advice do not cause harm, whether physical, emotional, or spiritual, to clients. It demands that practitioners uphold confidentiality, maintain professional competence, and avoid any form of coercion, exploitation, or manipulation. Beyond professional conduct, it extends to promoting compassion, fairness, and self-restraint in all interpersonal and societal dealings. Significantly, the Islāmic conception of non-maleficence is not confined to the mere avoidance of harm but is deeply anchored in the higher objectives of *Sharī'ah* (*Maqāṣid al-Sharī'ah*) and within this framework, preventing harm becomes an active moral responsibility, to remove harm where it exists, prevent it before it arises, and safeguard the collective welfare (*maṣlaḥah*) of the community. Table 3.1 outlines the key core principles of Islāmic psychoethics.

Table 3.1 Key core principles of Islāmic psychoethics

Value/principle	Description
Tawhîd (Unity of God)	Ethical conduct is derived from submission to Allāh. All decisions and actions in therapy are spiritually accountable
Inherent honour and dignity (*karāmah*)	Every person has intrinsic worth, deserving respect, privacy, and autonomy in mental and emotional care
Taqwā (God-consciousness)	Awareness of accountability before Allāh ensures integrity and ethical conduct beyond external oversight
Right to life / Preservation of life (*Ḥifẓ al-Nafs*)	Psychological interventions must preserve life and promote holistic well-bein, mental, spiritual, and physical
Niyyah (Intention)	Moral value is attached to sincere intentions behind therapeutic actions
*'Adl (*Equity / Justice)	Justice, fairness, and non-discrimination guide therapeutic practice and societal well-being
'Akhlaq (Virtue, Morality, Good character)	Therapists are expected to uphold ethical character, empathy, and moral excellence in all actions
Amanah (Trust and accountability)	Confidentiality, professional responsibility, and ethical integrity are considered sacred obligations
Raḥmah (Compassion & mercy)	Acting with mercy, empathy, and genuine concern for clients' emotional, psychological, and spiritual well-being
Ihsān (Excellence & compassion)	Striving for proficiency and excellence in interventions, with compassion towards the vulnerable
Lā Ḍarar wa Lā Ḍirār (No Harm / Non-maleficence)	Therapists must avoid causing harm, both directly and indirectly, prioritising client and community welfare

3.5 Universal Ethics and Islāmic Psychoethics: Congruence and Incongruence

Universal ethics consists of broadly shared moral principles, such as justice, beneficence, non-maleficence, autonomy, fidelity, and truthfulness, that aim to protect human dignity and promote individual and societal well-being. In psychology, these principles are formalised through professional codes such as those of the APA and BPS, which emphasise competence, integrity, responsibility, respect, and accountability in addressing ethical challenges. Islamic psychoethics complements these frameworks through a spiritually grounded approach rooted in the Qur'ān, Sunnah, and Islamic jurisprudence, emphasising moral accountability through *tawḥīd* and *taqwā*. By integrating values such as right intention (*niyyah*), moral character (*akhlāq*), excellence (*iḥsān*), compassion (*raḥmah*), justice (*'adl*), trust (*amānah*), and the prevention of harm (*lā ḍarar wa lā ḍirār*), Islamic psychoethics aligns with universal ethical standards while adding a dimension of spiritual responsibility, thereby supporting holistic and ethically sound psychological care. The points of congruence between universal ethics, including APA and BPS codes, and Islāmic psychoethics reflect shared commitments to fundamental principles that ensure ethical, responsible, and client-centred practice.

Justice and equity: Both frameworks emphasise fairness, impartiality, and the non-discriminatory treatment of clients. In APA and BPS ethics, justice involves equitable access to services, avoiding biases based on race, gender, religion, or socioeconomic status, and upholding professional responsibility to treat all clients fairly. Similarly, Islāmic psychoethics emphasises *ʿadl* (justice), ensuring that all clients are treated with respect and dignity, and that interventions consider not only individual welfare but also broader societal equity. Therapists in both systems are called to maintain fairness, ensuring ethical standards are upheld across all client interactions.

Non-maleficence and beneficence: Avoiding harm and promoting well-being are core to both ethical systems. APA and BPS highlight the duty to prevent physical, psychological, or social harm while fostering clients' growth and welfare. Islāmic psychoethics similarly emphasises *lā ḍarar wa lā ḍirār* (no harm) and *raḥmah* (compassion) but extends this principle to include spiritual and communal well-being. Therapists are encouraged not only to prevent harm but also to actively promote holistic wellness, integrating psychological, emotional, social, and spiritual dimensions of care.

Confidentiality and respect for autonomy: Maintaining client confidentiality and obtaining informed consent are central in both universal and Islāmic frameworks. APA and BPS codes prioritise client privacy, ensuring information is protected and clients' autonomous choices are respected. Islāmic psychoethics similarly values confidentiality as a sacred trust (*amānah*) and respects autonomy but situates it within a moral and spiritual framework. Decisions are made collaboratively with clients, while aligning with ethical and spiritual responsibilities, ensuring that client choices do not contravene moral or religious obligations.

Truthfulness and integrity: Honesty and transparency are essential to building trust in therapeutic relationships. APA and BPS ethics emphasise the importance of truthfulness in professional conduct, accurate representation of qualifications, and integrity in client interactions. Islāmic psychoethics similarly stresses *sidq* (truthfulness) and moral integrity, viewing honesty as both a professional and spiritual duty. Upholding truth fosters accountability, strengthens trust, and promotes ethical consistency, aligning both secular and spiritual dimensions of practice.

The points of incongruence between universal ethics, as represented by APA and BPS codes, and Islāmic psychoethics stem primarily from differences in foundational orientation, conceptions of the self, and the role of spiritual accountability.

Source of moral authority: Universal ethics is secular, deriving authority from professional consensus, legal frameworks, and rational reasoning. Ethical principles are human-centred and socially negotiated to ensure fairness, accountability, and protection of clients. By contrast, Islāmic psychoethics is theocentric; moral authority originates from divine guidance found in the Qur'ân, *Sunnah*, and Islāmic jurisprudence. Ethical conduct is considered an act of worship (*ibadah*) and is linked to accountability in the afterlife, adding a spiritual dimension absent in secular frameworks.

Concept of the self and human nature: Western ethical frameworks view individuals as primarily autonomous, rational agents capable of making independent decisions. In contrast, Islāmic psychoethics views humans as a spiritual-psychological unity comprising *nafs* (self), *'aql* (intellect), *rūh* (spirit), and *qalb* (heart). Therapy is thus not only about supporting personal choice or autonomy but also about guiding clients toward moral and spiritual alignment with divine principles. This reflects a collectivistic and spiritually embedded orientation, emphasising communal well-being and alignment with God's will, in contrast to the individualistic orientation common in secular ethics.

Purpose of psychotherapy: In universal ethics, the primary goal of therapy is psychological well-being, autonomy, and adaptive functioning. Islāmic psychoethics broadens this objective to include spiritual purification (*tazkiyat al-nafs*), moral growth, and *dhikr* (remembrance of God) as integral components of healing. Psychological interventions are therefore intertwined with spiritual development and ethical refinement, rather than focusing solely on symptom reduction or functional adaptation.

Autonomy and authority: APA and BPS ethics prioritise client autonomy, often preferring non-directive approaches where therapists facilitate self-determined decision-making. In Islāmic psychoethics, autonomy is balanced with *Shari'ah* principles, ensuring that clients' decisions do not violate moral or religious obligations. Therapists may offer guidance consistent with faith-based ethics, emphasising moral responsibility and alignment with divine commands. This introduces a framework of guided autonomy, where ethical and spiritual considerations inform decision-making.

Spiritual accountability: A distinct divergence lies in the role of spiritual accountability. Universal ethics emphasises responsibility to clients, the profession, and society, but Islāmic psychoethics adds accountability to God as a central determinant of ethical behaviour. This spiritual dimension reinforces moral vigilance and consistent ethical conduct, encouraging practitioners to integrate both professional competence and spiritual mindfulness in their work.

In summary, despite differences in philosophical and spiritual foundations, both universal ethics (APA/BPS) and Islāmic psychoethics align on essential principles such as fairness, protection from harm, respect for clients' rights, and the promotion of trust and moral integrity within therapeutic practice. These shared values offer a robust ethical framework for psychologists working with clients from diverse cultural and religious backgrounds. Overall, while both systems uphold core commitments to justice, beneficence, and human dignity, universal ethics is secular, individualistic, and grounded in rational reasoning, whereas Islāmic psychoethics is theocentric, collectivistic, and spiritually oriented. Key divergences arise from differences in sources of moral authority, understanding of human nature, therapeutic goals, and the integration of client autonomy with divine guidance. Table 3.2 summarises the points of congruence and incongruence between universal ethics and Islāmic psychoethics.

Table 3.2 Comparison of universal ethics and Islāmic psychoethics: Points of congruence and incongruence

Ethical Domain / Principle	Points of Congruence	Points of Incongruence
Source of moral authority	Both provide structured ethical guidance and accountability for professional practice	Universal ethics is secular, grounded in professional consensus, legal frameworks, and rational reasoning; Islāmic psychoethics is theocentric, rooted in the Qur'ān, Sunnah, and *sharīʿah*, with accountability to god and the hereafter (*tawḥīd*)
Human dignity (*karāmah*)	Both uphold respect for human dignity, rights, privacy, confidentiality, and fairness in treatment	Islāmic psychoethics frames dignity as a divine trust and moral obligation, while universal ethics frames it primarily as a human right
Justice and equity (*ʿadl*)	Both emphasise fairness, non-discrimination, impartiality, and ethical treatment of clients	Islāmic psychoethics extends justice to include spiritual, societal, and communal responsibilities, whereas universal ethics focuses mainly on individual and legal fairness
Non-maleficence & beneficence	Both prioritise avoiding harm and promoting client well-being	Islāmic psychoethics includes spiritual and communal well-being, while universal ethics focuses primarily on physical, psychological, and social dimensions
Confidentiality & trust (amānah)	Both stress confidentiality, professional responsibility, and trust in the therapeutic relationship	In Islāmic psychoethics, trust is also a moral and spiritual obligation before god, not solely a professional duty
Autonomy and decision-making	Both recognise client participation and informed consent in therapeutic decisions	Universal ethics prioritises individual autonomy; Islāmic psychoethics balances autonomy with moral guidance and *Sharīʿah*-informed values
Truthfulness & integrity (*ṣidq*)	Both require honesty, transparency, and integrity to maintain professional trust and accountability	In Islāmic psychoethics, truthfulness is also an act of worship with spiritual accountability, beyond professional expectations

(continued)

Table 3.2 (continued)

Ethical Domain / Principle	Points of Congruence	Points of Incongruence
Intention (*niyyah*)	Both value ethical conduct and responsible practice	Islāmic psychoethics explicitly emphasises sincerity of intention behind therapeutic actions, while universal ethics focuses on observable professional behaviour
Virtue & moral character (*akhlāq*)	Both emphasise ethical conduct, respect, empathy, and responsibility	Islāmic psychoethics places greater emphasis on personal moral and spiritual virtues as integral to therapeutic practice
Professional excellence (*iḥsān*)	Both promote competence, quality care, and ongoing professional development	Islāmic psychoethics integrates spiritual and moral excellence alongside technical competence
Concept of the self & human nature	Both aim to support holistic well-being and psychological functioning	Universal ethics views humans primarily as autonomous, rational agents; Islāmic psychoethics views humans as integrated spiritual–psychological beings (*nafs, qalb, ʿaql, rūḥ*) within a communal context
Purpose of psychotherapy	Both seek to alleviate distress and enhance functioning and well-being	Islāmic psychoethics integrates spiritual purification (*tazkiyat al-nafs*), moral growth, and remembrance of god (*dhikr*) as core aspects of healing
Spiritual accountability (*taqwā*)	Not explicitly addressed in universal ethics	Unique to Islāmic psychoethics: ethical practice is guided by god-consciousness and accountability beyond external regulation

3.6 Conclusion

Ethical codes serve to establish professional standards, outline expected conduct, and safeguard clients from potential harm in psychotherapy and counselling. Historically, in diverse settings, therapists operating within moral frameworks influenced by the Judaeo-Christian tradition have provided services to Muslim clients. When engaging with Muslim clients, it is essential for therapists to have a comprehensive understanding of Islāmic practices and psychoethical principles to prevent or reduce ethical conflicts. Additionally, recognising and respecting the multiple perspectives on ethical decision-making is crucial to avoid misunderstandings and ensure culturally and spiritually sensitive care. Universal ethics and Islāmic psychoethics share many core values, including justice, non-maleficence, beneficence, fidelity, and respect for human dignity. Both frameworks seek to prevent harm, promote well-being, and uphold ethical treatment in therapy. However, they diverge in foundational grounding, spiritual accountability, and the integration of divine purpose and moral intention. While universal ethics is secular and human-centred, Islāmic psychoethics is theocentric, linking professional conduct to God-consciousness, spiritual growth, and adherence to Shariah principles. In multicultural and multi-faith clinical settings, these frameworks can complement each other, allowing therapists to respect universal professional standards while addressing clients' spiritual and ethical needs.

References

Abū Dāwūd. *Sunan Abi Dawud 4586*. In-book reference: Book 41, Hādīth 93 English translation: Book 40, Hādīth 4569. Hasan (Al-Albani). https://sunnah.com/abudawud:4586

Ad Hoc Joint Committee. (2008). *Universal declaration of ethical principles for psychologists*. Retrieved from http://www.am.org/iupsys/ethics/univdecl2008.htm

Ahmad. Musnad Ahmad 300. In-book reference: Book 2, Hadith 207. Sahih (Darussalam Bukhari and Muslim (1907) (Darussalam.). https://sunnah.com/ahmad:300

Al-Adab Al-Mufrad. *Al-Adab Al-Mufrad 463*. In-book reference: Book 26, Hadith 2. English translation: Book 26, Hadith 463. https://sunnah.com/adab:463

Al-Hisni, Taqi al-Din.N. (1997) *Kitab al-Qawa'id*. Maktabat al-Rushd.

Al-Jaza'iry, A. B. J. (2001). Justice and equity. In *Minhaj al Muslim*. Darussalam. https://www.islaam.net/main/display.php?id=1280&category=76

American Psychological Association. (2017). *Ethical principles of psychologists and code of conduct*. APA. https://www.apa.org

British Psychological Society. (2021). *Code of ethics and conduct*. BPS. https://www.bps.org.uk

Elgariani, F. S. (2012). *Al-Qawā'id al-Fiqhiyyah (Islāmic legal maxims): Concept, functions, history, classifications and application to contemporary medical issues* (Doctoral thesis, University of Exeter). University of Exeter Repository. https://ore.exeter.ac.uk/repository/bitstream/handle/10036/4001/ElgarianiF.pdf

Ibn Kathir. (2000). *Tafsir ibn Kathir* (Trans. J. Abualrub, N. Khitab, H. Khitab, A. Walker, M. Al-Jibali, & S. Ayoub). Darussalam Publishers and Distributors.

Ibn Majah. *Forty Hadith of an-Nawawi. Hadith 32, 40*. Hadith an-Nawawi. A hasan hadīth. https://sunnah.com/nawawi40:32

Muslim. *An Nawawi Forty Hadīth. Hadīth 17, 40*. Hadith an-Nawawi. https://sunnah.com/nawawi40:17

Oppong, S. (2019). When the ethical is unethical and the unethical is ethical: Cultural relativism in ethical decision-making. *Polish Psychological Bulletin, 50*(1), 18–28.

Oxford University Press. (2024). *Ethics*. In Oxford reference. https://www.oxfordreference.com/search?q=Ethics&searchBtn=Search&isQuickSearch=true

Rassool, G. Hussein. (2023). *Islāmic psychology: The basics*. Routledge.

Rassool, G. Hussein. (2025). *Islāmic counselling & psychotherapy* (2nd ed.). Routledge.

World Health Organization. (2005). *Islāmic code of medical and health ethics* (EM/RC52/7). WHO Regional Committee for the Eastern Mediterranean. http://applications.emro.who.int/docs/EM_RC52_7_en.pdf

Chapter 4
Ethical Dilemmas in Islāmic Psychotherapy and Counselling

4.1 Introduction

Psychotherapy inherently involves ethical responsibility, as practitioners must balance ethical decision-making with the goal of promoting clients' psychological well-being and while supporting the mental health. Ethical dilemmas are an inherent part of psychotherapy and mental health practice, arising whenever practitioners encounter conflicts between professional guidelines, client needs, personal beliefs and values, and situational complexities. Managing these dilemmas requires careful judgement, critical reflection, and strict adherence to a robust ethical framework, such as those provided by professional bodies like the American Psychological Association (APA), the British Psychological Society (BPS) or the International Association of Muslim Psychologists (IAMP). Psychologists and therapists must weigh multiple factors, including the well-being of the client, the potential impact on third parties, legal obligations, and the maintenance of trust and confidentiality. Cultural, spiritual, and ethical considerations further complicate decision-making in mental health practice. Ethical dilemmas often emerge when cultural norms, religious beliefs, or family expectations intersect with standard psychological practices. For instance, issues such as consent, confidentiality, autonomy, conflicting values, divergent worldviews, dual relationships, and therapeutic boundaries may take on additional layers of complexity in culturally diverse contexts, requiring therapists to integrate culturally competent approaches with professional ethical standards. Lindsay and Colley (1995) examined ethical dilemmas experienced by members of the British Psychological Society. Their findings identified two primary categories of ethical challenges. The first encompassed traditional professional issues, such as breaches or concerns related to confidentiality. The second involved tensions between psychologists' preferred professional practices and the limitations or demands set by their employing organisations, including institutional policies within the National Health Service.

G. H. Rassool, *Ethical Dilemmas in Islāmic Psychotherapy*,
https://doi.org/10.1007/978-3-032-26515-9_4

In the context of Islāmic psychotherapy, integrating spirituality into the therapeutic process can significantly enhance healing and personal growth; however, it also introduces unique ethical dilemmas that are seldom encountered in secular or conventional approaches. These challenges often emerge at the intersection of professional responsibilities, cultural norms, gender dynamics, and faith-based interventions, requiring therapists to strike a careful balance between psychological professionalism and religious-cultural sensitivity. Such ethical considerations are inherently complex, demanding that practitioners skilfully align psychological principles with the moral, spiritual, and ethical framework of Islām. Influential factors such as family dynamics, gender roles, dual or multiple relationships, notions of autonomy and individuality, and the observance of religious duties profoundly shape therapeutic interactions and client expectations. Common ethical tensions arise when maintaining confidentiality within contexts that emphasise family involvement, addressing psychological concerns that may seem at odds with religious values, or navigating multiple relationships within tightly connected communities. Knapp et al. (2015) suggested that such challenges arise within ethical grey areas, where solutions are not immediately clear and cannot be reduced to simple right–wrong distinctions. In these situations, no single law, regulation, court ruling, or provision of the APA Ethics Code can prescribe an exact course of action for psychologists.

This chapter explores the ethical dilemmas commonly encountered in both mainstream psychotherapy and Islāmic psychotherapy, highlighting the similarities, distinctions, and underlying principles that guide ethical decision-making within each framework. By examining both perspectives, this chapter aims to illuminate how ethical challenges manifest across different paradigms of care, secular, and faith based.

4.2 Domains of Ethical Tension in Psychotherapy

Ethical dilemmas are a fundamental aspect of psychotherapeutic practice, arising when professional principles conflict, legal and ethical obligations diverge, or cultural and spiritual values intersect with clinical care. Hegde (2019) describes an ethical dilemma in psychotherapy as a situation in which any choice between alternatives requires compromising one or more ethical principles. These dilemmas stem from competing moral values, making it challenging to determine the most ethically appropriate course of action. Knapp et al. (2017) observe that such situations can be particularly stressful for psychologists, who aim to act ethically but may encounter circumstances where professional ethical codes provides limited or ambiguous guidance. This brief review explores key domains of ethical tension in psychotherapy.

4.3 Confidentiality in Psychotherapy: Ethical Dilemmas and Complexities

Confidentiality is widely regarded as a cornerstone of ethical practice in psychotherapy, forming the foundation of trust that allows clients to share sensitive, personal, and often distressing information openly. This assurance of privacy is essential for authentic engagement and meaningful therapeutic work (Camadan et al., 2021; Lindsay & Clarkson, 1999; Pope & Vetter, 1992; Şensoy & İkiz, 2023; Sivis-Cetinkaya, 2015). The APA Ethics Code explicitly permits breaches of confidentiality in cases where there is a serious risk of harm to the client or others (American Psychological Association, 2017). Similarly, mandatory reporting laws require therapists to disclose suspected child abuse or neglect, even when such disclosure may undermine client trust or the therapeutic relationship (Remley & Herlihy, 2020). Despite its centrality, confidentiality is rarely absolute. Therapists often encounter ethically ambiguous situation, so-called gray areas, where competing duties must be carefully weighed, and the appropriate course of action is not immediately obvious.

A common ethical tension arises when a client presents a risk of harm, such as suicidal ideation, homicidal intent, or behaviours that could seriously injure another person. In such cases, breaching confidentiality is ethically justified to prevent harm, reflecting the principles of non-maleficence and beneficence, while still attempting to respect client autonomy under conditions of uncertainty (Hedge, 2019). For example, if a client expresses detailed plans to harm themselves or another individual, a therapist must weigh the ethical and legal duty to intervene, potentially contacting emergency services or family members, against the client's expectation of privacy.

Child protection mandates introduce additional complexities. Therapists are legally and ethically required to report suspected abuse, even if the client requests confidentiality. For instance, if a minor discloses sexual or physical abuse, therapists must navigate reporting procedures while maintaining a supportive therapeutic stance to protect the child's psychological safety and minimise trauma (Lindsay & Clarkson, 1999). Confidentiality may also be challenged by court orders or legal demands. Therapists may be compelled to release records under subpoena, creating a tension between legal obligations and the ethical responsibility to safeguard client information (Behnke, 2004). In such cases, therapists must balance compliance with the law while limiting disclosures to only the necessary information to protect client privacy. Group therapy settings add further ethical complexity. Unlike individual therapy, therapists cannot fully control how participants share or protect sensitive information. Maintaining confidentiality in a group requires establishing clear rules, educating members about the limits of privacy, screening participants, and actively monitoring disclosures. For example, if a group member shares information about another client outside the session, the therapist must address the breach, reinforce boundaries, and restore a safe therapeutic environment (Corey et al., 2014, 2018).

Cultural and contextual factors can further complicate confidentiality. Western individualistic notions of privacy may conflict with family-centred or collectivist values in non-Western contexts, where family involvement in decision-making or access to client information is expected. Therapists must navigate these cultural pressures, clarifying boundaries, negotiating consent, and helping clients understand the limits of confidentiality while respecting cultural norms (Fisher, 2013). For example, in some communities, a parent may expect full disclosure of an adolescent's therapy sessions. A culturally competent therapist would carefully explain confidentiality limits and, when appropriate, engage in joint sessions to respect family involvement without violating ethical obligations.

In sum, confidentiality is not simply a procedural requirement; it is a core ethical commitment that supports the therapeutic alliance and promotes client trust, safety, and well-being. Ethical dilemmas arise whenever confidentiality intersects with competing responsibilities: protecting clients from harm, complying with legal mandates, respecting client autonomy, and negotiating cultural expectations. Addressing these dilemmas requires thoughtful judgement, adherence to professional and legal standards, and sensitivity to cultural, contextual, and individual factors. Therapists must carefully weigh principles such as non-maleficence, beneficence, and client autonomy, often making decisions under conditions of uncertainty or emotional stress (Hedge, 2019). By navigating these challenges ethically, therapists can maintain client trust while fulfilling their dual responsibilities to the client, society, and the law.

In Islāmic psychoethics, confidentiality is not only a professional obligation but also a moral and spiritual responsibility. Decisions to breach confidentiality, such as when a client poses imminent danger to themselves or others, are guided by moral accountability to Allāh (*taqwā*), ensuring that actions serve both client safety and spiritual responsibility. This perspective emphasises the importance of intention (*niyyah*), where the therapist's inner motivation and ethical reasoning are as crucial as the external action. Unlike secular frameworks, which focus primarily on legal compliance and professional standards, Islāmic psychoethics integrates spiritual accountability, encouraging therapists to consider both worldly and divine consequences in decision-making. When it comes to child protection and mandatory reporting, Islāmic psychoethics similarly mandates disclosure in cases of abuse or neglect. However, this obligation is framed as a fulfilment of *amānah,* a trust or moral duty, and societal responsibility under *Shari'ah*, balancing the protection of the vulnerable with compassion (*raḥmah*) and moral integrity. While universal ethics prioritises the safety and rights of the child, the Islāmic perspective explicitly incorporates divine accountability, guiding therapists to act in accordance with both ethical principles and spiritual law.

In situations involving court orders or legal demands, therapists in Islāmic frameworks must still comply with legal requirements, but ethical reflection is guided by principles of justice (*'adl*) and God-consciousness. This dual accountability ensures that any breach of confidentiality is minimised and morally justified, reinforcing the therapist's responsibility to uphold trust and integrity in both

professional and spiritual dimensions. Similarly, in group therapy settings, Islāmic psychoethics emphasises the cultivation of moral virtues among participants.
وَلْتَكُن مِّنكُمْ أُمَّةٌ يَدْعُونَ إِلَى الْخَيْرِ وَيَأْمُرُونَ بِالْمَعْرُوفِ وَيَنْهَوْنَ عَنِ الْمُنكَرِ
وَأُولَـٰئِكَ هُمُ الْمُفْلِحُونَ.

- *And let there be [arising] from you a nation inviting to [all that is] good, enjoining what is right and forbidding what is wrong, and those will be the successful.* (Ali-'Imran 3:104, interpretation of the meaning).

Beyond procedural compliance, therapists encourage compassion (*raḥmah*), personal responsibility, and ethical behaviour within the group, reinforcing both interpersonal ethics and spiritual development. Cultural and contextual factors are also carefully considered within Islāmic psychoethics. Therapists are encouraged to balance client privacy with communal or family expectations, guided by *Shari'ah* principles and cultural respect. This approach contrasts with universal ethics, which prioritises individual autonomy; Islāmic psychoethics explicitly integrates collective and spiritual considerations, ensuring that therapeutic decisions respect both social and religious norms. Finally, the broader ethical framework of Islāmic psychoethics encompasses truthfulness (*ṣidq*), moral integrity, and structured reflection. Ethical conduct is viewed as an act of worship, with therapists accountable not only to clients and professional standards but also to Allāh. This integration of professional and spiritual responsibility provides a structured framework for navigating complex ethical dilemmas, offering guidance that is both morally and spiritually grounded. By incorporating these principles, Islāmic psychoethics ensures that therapy is delivered with ethical rigour, compassion, and holistic consideration for the client's psychological, social, and spiritual well-being. Table 4.1 outlines the key confidentiality dilemmas in psychotherapy: Universal ethics vs. Islāmic psychoethics.

4.4 Dual Relationships and Boundary Issues

Dual relationships and boundary concerns represent central ethical considerations in psychotherapy. In mainstream practice, they are framed through professional codes such as the APA Ethics Code, whereas in Islāmic psychotherapy, they are contextualised through Qur'ânic principles such as *amānah* (trust), *maslaha* (public interest), and the moral obligation to avoid harm. Both frameworks emphasise protecting the therapeutic alliance, though they differ in how boundaries are conceptualised and justified.

From a mainstream psychotherapy perspective, dual relationships occur when a therapist assumes more than one role with a client, such as friend, teacher, employer, or business partner (APA, 2017). These overlapping roles can introduce significant risks, including exploitation, impaired clinical judgement, conflicts of interest, and potential harm to the client. Not all dual relationships are inherently unethical; for example, attending a client's graduation may be considered a

Table 4.1 Key confidentiality dilemmas in psychotherapy: Universal ethics vs. Islāmic psychoethics

Confidentiality dilemmas	Universal / Professional ethics	Islāmic psychoethics	Key differences/ considerations
Risk of harm	Breach of confidentiality is justified if the client poses imminent danger to self or others, in line with non-maleficence and beneficence (APA, 2017; Hedge, 2019)	Breach is also ethically justified, but guided by moral accountability to Allāh (*taqwā*), ensuring decisions serve both client safety and spiritual responsibility	Islāmic perspective adds spiritual accountability and intention (*niyyah*) to professional decision-making
Child protection / mandatory reporting	Therapists must report suspected abuse or neglect, even against client wishes, prioritising legal and ethical protection of the child (Lindsay & Clarkson, 1999)	Reporting remains mandatory, but framed as fulfilling *amānah* (trust) and societal duty under *Shari'ah*, balancing protection of the child with compassion (*raḥmah*) and moral integrity	Both emphasise protection of the vulnerable, but Islāmic psychoethics integrates divine accountability and moral guidance
Court orders / legal demands	Records may be released under subpoena; therapists should limit disclosure to what is necessary to comply with law (Behnke, 2004)	Similar compliance is required, but decisions are guided by ethical reflection (*'adl*) and God-consciousness, ensuring minimal breach of trust while maintaining moral integrity	Islāmic psychoethics adds spiritual consideration and ethical deliberation beyond legal obligations
Group therapy & shared spaces	Confidentiality is challenging; requires clear rules, informed consent, participant education, and ongoing monitoring (Corey et al., 2014, 2018)	Same procedural strategies apply; additionally, fostering *raḥmah* (compassion) and moral responsibility among participants reinforces ethical and spiritual trust	Islāmic perspective emphasises ethical virtues and moral cultivation among participants, not only procedural compliance
Cultural & contextual conflicts	Western ethics prioritises individual autonomy and privacy; therapists must navigate family expectations while protecting client confidentiality (Fisher, 2013)	Balances client privacy with communal or family values, guided by *Shari'ah* principles, cultural sensitivity, and spiritual accountability	Islāmic psychoethics explicitly integrates collective and spiritual considerations, whereas universal ethics focuses on individual rights

(continued)

Table 4.1 (continued)

Confidentiality dilemmas	Universal / Professional ethics	Islāmic psychoethics	Key differences/ considerations
Truthfulness & integrity	Therapists must be honest and transparent about limits of confidentiality to build trust (APA, 2017)	Truthfulness (*ṣidq*) is also an act of worship; ethical conduct includes both professional and spiritual integrity	Spiritual dimension reinforces moral vigilance alongside professional honesty
Ethical gray areas	No clear legal or code-based answer; therapists rely on ethical judgment, balancing competing duties (Hedge, 2019)	Ethical reflection is guided by professional standards and spiritual principles, including *taqwā*, *niyyah*, and *ʿadl*	Islāmic psychoethics adds a structured framework for moral reflection and accountability to Allāh

benign boundary crossing, whereas sexual or exploitative relationships are strictly prohibited (Barnett & Johnson, 2015). Ethical codes stress transparency, informed consent, and consultation when boundary dilemmas arise, and research shows that blurred boundaries can erode trust and increase malpractice risk (BACP, 2018; Zur, 2016). Therapists are encouraged to carefully evaluate potential risks and benefits, engage in reflective practice, and, when necessary, refer clients to another qualified professional to maintain treatment efficacy.

In Islāmic psychotherapy, ethical guidance regarding dual relationships is rooted in *amānah* (trustworthiness), *ihsān* (excellence in conduct), and *maslaha* (public interest). The therapeutic relationship is viewed as a sacred trust (*amānah*) in which the client entrusts their emotional vulnerability and well-being to the therapist, making the preservation of clear boundaries a moral and spiritual obligation. Acting with *iḥsān* requires the therapist to uphold the highest standard of ethical conduct by anticipating potential harm, avoiding role confusion, and prioritising the client's needs and interests over personal or social considerations. At the same time, the principle of *maṣlaḥah* emphasises the promotion of benefit and the prevention of harm, guiding ethical decision-making by assessing whether a dual relationship risks exploitation, compromised objectivity, or psychological harm. Together, these principles frame dual relationships not merely as professional boundary issues but as matters of moral accountability and spiritual responsibility in Islāmic psychotherapy.

In Muslim-majority or closely-knit communities, therapists may naturally occupy overlapping roles, such as being a religious advisor, family acquaintance, or community member. These contexts require heightened vigilance to avoid exploitation or harm. Boundary issues are framed not only professionally but also spiritually: maintaining confidentiality and clear boundaries fulfils divine trust (*amānah*) and protects human dignity (*karāmah*). Islāmic ethics further emphasises *niyyah* (intention) and accountability before Allāh, alongside adherence to professional standards. Practically, therapists are advised to consult both professional codes and qualified religious scholars when navigating complex dual relationships, ensuring that interventions are culturally and spiritually congruent (Barnett & Johnson, 2015; Zur, 2016).

In both frameworks, the management of dual relationships involves careful assessment, reflective practice, and ongoing supervision. While mainstream ethics prioritises minimising harm and maintaining objectivity, Islāmic psychoethics adds a dimension of moral and spiritual accountability. Therapists are encouraged to conduct themselves with *taqwā*, ethical vigilance, and *ihsān*, ensuring that the therapeutic relationship is maintained with integrity, compassion, and holistic consideration for the client's psychological, social, and spiritual well-being.

4.5 Professional Competence and Scope of Practice

Professional competence is a foundational principle in ethical psychotherapy, ensuring that clients receive safe, effective, and culturally appropriate care. In mainstream psychotherapy, competence requires that practitioners operate within the boundaries of their education, supervised experience, and credentials, while continually expanding knowledge through continuing education, supervision, and consultation (American Counseling Association, 2014; American Psychological Association, 2017). Cultural and contextual competence is equally critical; therapists must be responsive to clients' cultural, religious, and community norms, as practicing beyond one's cultural understanding can increase the risk of harm, misdiagnosis, or ineffective interventions (Pope & Vasquez, 2019; Welfel, 2016). Maintaining competence is an ongoing responsibility, necessitating reflective practice, mentorship, and professional development, particularly in areas such as trauma-informed care, multicultural counselling, and emerging modalities like teletherapy (Barnett & Johnson, 2015; Sue et al., 2019).

The scope of practice in mainstream frameworks is legally and professionally defined, encompassing licensure regulations, contractual obligations, institutional policies, and clearly delineated role boundaries. Therapists should avoid role drift, such as providing medical, financial, or legal advice, and instead coordinate with other professionals while safeguarding client interests through informed consent (Pope et al., 2021; Remley & Herlihy, 2020). Ethical practice also requires careful risk management, including clear documentation, timely referrals, and transparency when a case exceeds the therapist's competence (Corey et al., 2014).

In Islāmic psychotherapy, competence is framed as both a professional and spiritual responsibility. Ethical foundations include *amānah* (trustworthiness) and *ihsān* (excellence in conduct), reflecting Qur'ânic directives to render trusts faithfully and judge with justice (Qur'ân 4:58; 16:90).

إِنَّ ٱللَّهَ يَأْمُرُكُمْ أَن تُؤَدُّوا ٱلْأَمَانَاتِ إِلَىٰ أَهْلِهَا وَإِذَا حَكَمْتُم بَيْنَ ٱلنَّاسِ أَن
تَحْكُمُوا بِٱلْعَدْلِ ۚ

- *Indeed, Allāh commands you to render trusts to whom they are due and when you judge between people to judge with justice*. (An-Nisā' 4:58, interpretation of the meaning).

نِاسَحْلِإلاَو لِدْعَلْابِ رُمُأْيَ الله نَّإِ

- *Indeed, Allah orders justice and good conduct…* (al-Naĥl 16:90, interpretation of the meaning)

These verses establish *amānah* and *ihsān* as core ethical obligations that shape both personal character and social order in Islām. The verse in Qur'ān 4:58 frames trust and justice as divine commands governing responsibility, authority, and decision-making, emphasising that rights must be fulfilled and judgements rendered independently. The verse in Qur'ān 16:90 expands this moral vision by pairing justice with good conduct. Therapists bear dual accountability: adherence to professional standards and moral responsibility before Allāh. Competence requires both professional training and informed integration of Islāmic perspectives where appropriate, ensuring interventions are culturally and spiritually sensitive without overstepping religious authority if one is not a scholar.

It is narrated by 'Amr b. Suh'aib: On his father's authority, said that his grandfather reported the Messenger of Allah (ﷺ) said: "Anyone who practices medicine when he is not known as a practitioner will be held responsible" (Abū Dāwūd). This hadīth emphasises the fundamental Islāmic principle of accountability and professional competence in health care and related helping professions. Ethical responsibility is not limited to good intentions alone; rather, it requires demonstrable expertise, recognised competence, and adherence to appropriate standards of practice. Just as physicians in Islāmic history were expected to practise within their competence and avoid harm, Islāmic psychotherapists are likewise obligated to work within their professional scope, seek appropriate supervision, and prioritise client well-being. Oversight, ethical regulation, and accountability mechanisms remain essential, particularly given the sensitive integration of psychological care with spiritual guidance.

From an Islāmic ethical perspective, all professional actions are bound by *Sharī 'ah*, meaning that behaviour is directly accountable to divine guidance. Professionalism therefore extends beyond legal compliance or organisational norms to encompass moral and spiritual responsibility. Sharī 'ah-based competence is similarly defined by three core characteristics: *kafā'ah, himmat al- 'amal*, and *amānah* (Ghozali et al., (2019); Rukiah, 2015;. In Islāmic psychotherapy, competence encompasses not only mastery of evidence-based psychological theories and clinical interventions but also a deep understanding of Islāmic psychology, psychotherapy, and foundational Islāmic studies. This combination ensures that practitioners can deliver ethically sound, culturally congruent, and spiritually informed care. *Kafā'ah*, having the requisite skills, expertise, and qualification, guides practitioners to know when they are capable of practicing independently and when they remain in an apprentice stage requiring supervision and further training. *Himmat al- 'amal* reflects the diligence, motivation, and sustained effort necessary to maintain high standards, while amānah emphasises trustworthiness, accountability, and faithful fulfilment of professional and spiritual responsibilities. Together, these principles form a holistic framework for professional competence, blending technical skill, ethical integrity, and spiritual accountability. Applied to clinical practice, they ensure that Islāmic psychotherapists act as responsible, capable, and morally conscientious professionals, honouring both the dignity of clients (*karāmah*) and the trust (*amānah*) placed in them by Allāh and society.

These ethical principles directly inform contemporary Islāmic psychology and psychotherapy. Practitioners bear a moral responsibility to ensure competence, ethical integrity, and accountability in clinical work. Just as physicians in early Islāmic society were required to demonstrate recognised expertise and adhere to ethical standards, Islāmic psychotherapists are obligated to obtain appropriate training, work within their scope of competence, and actively avoid causing harm (*lā ḍarar wa lā ḍirār*). Continuous supervision, consultation, and ethical oversight are crucial safeguards, particularly given the integration of psychological care with spiritual and religious dimensions.

Overall, professional competence in both mainstream and Islāmic psychotherapy is not a fixed achievement but an ongoing process. It encompasses technical skills, cultural-spiritual sensitivity, reflective practice, and moral accountability. By integrating these elements, therapists can deliver ethically sound, effective, and holistic care that respects clients' psychological, social, and spiritual needs while maintaining adherence to professional and Islāmic ethical standards (Barnett & Johnson, 2015; Bhargava & Sriram, 2016; Camadan et al., 2021; Şensoy & İkiz, 2023).

4.6 Informed Consent

Informed consent is a fundamental ethical obligation rooted in client autonomy and human rights (United Nations, 1948). It ensures that clients understand the purpose, methods, risks, benefits, and limitations of therapy before services begin. Ethical dilemmas often arise when therapists must balance autonomy with beneficence; for example, providing full disclosure about possible trauma processing may overwhelm a vulnerable client with severe anxiety or PTSD, potentially discouraging them from engaging in therapy (Beauchamp & Childress, 2019). Ensuring comprehension is critical, particularly when working with minors, vulnerable populations, or clients with cognitive or developmental impairments. For instance, a therapist working with a child with autism spectrum disorder may need to simplify consent language, use visual aids, or engage caregivers in the process to facilitate voluntary and informed decision-making (Heerman, 2015; Petrini, 2011).

Informed consent is not a single event but an ongoing process. Therapists must revisit consent whenever treatment goals, methods, or circumstances change, ensuring clients remain informed and engaged throughout the therapeutic relationship (West, 2002). For example, if a therapy plan shifts from individual cognitive-behavioural therapy to a group-based intervention, clients should be informed about new confidentiality considerations and group dynamics. Documentation of consent is necessary for both legal and ethical accountability, while culturally sensitive approaches are required in diverse settings to respect client values, norms, and expectations (Sue et al., 2007). The rise of telehealth has further complicated consent, introducing issues related to privacy, data security, and digital boundaries; for instance, clients may need to be informed about the limits of confidentiality when using video platforms or encrypted messaging (Knapp & VandeCreek, 2012).

Within Islāmic psychotherapy, informed consent is framed through *amānah* (trust) and *niyyah* (intention). Therapists hold moral accountability before Allāh, emphasising transparency and honesty in the therapeutic relationship. Dilemmas may arise when disclosure risks shame, harm, or social repercussions in family or communal contexts; for example, a young Muslim woman disclosing familial abuse may face community backlash, requiring careful ethical and culturally sensitive guidance. Consent must also consider *maṣlaḥah* (public interest), meaning that disclosure may be ethically required if withholding information could result in harm to family, community, or client. Role clarity is essential, as Muslim clients may perceive therapists as religious guides. Consent must clearly delineate the boundaries between psychological care and spiritual guidance, avoiding conflation of the two roles. Language and cultural accessibility are critical, ensuring that consent aligns with Islāmic values while remaining clinically relevant, for instance, providing consent forms or explanations in the ethnic language (if appropriate) for clients who prefer those languages, while explaining therapeutic processes in a culturally familiar context.

Both mainstream and Islāmic psychotherapy emphasise that informed consent safeguards client dignity, autonomy, and well-being. Mainstream practice focuses on legal accountability and individual rights, whereas Islāmic psychotherapy situates consent within a broader moral, spiritual, and communal framework. The central ethical challenge is balancing full disclosure with sensitivity, ensuring that clients are informed while preserving trust, promoting welfare, and respecting cultural and religious norms.

4.7 Professional and Interpersonal Practice Dilemmas

Ethical challenges in psychotherapy also extend to professional and interpersonal interactions, including colleague behaviour, supervision, sexual conduct, and academic responsibilities. Lindsay and Clarkson (1999) found that approximately 9% of reported dilemmas related to colleague conduct, including perceived incompetence, unprofessional remarks, or disputes over referrals and fees. Sexual misconduct, comprising 8% of dilemmas, involved inappropriate relationships, consent issues, or awareness of unethical behaviour by colleagues. Academic and training dilemmas, accounting for 6%, often arose in supervision, assessing competence, or balancing loyalty to institutions with client protection. Competence-related concerns (6%) included assigning cases beyond expertise or addressing impaired colleagues.

Managing these dilemmas requires adherence to professional codes, consultation, and reflective practice. Therapists must prioritise client welfare, maintain integrity, and navigate complex professional relationships while upholding ethical standards. Failure to do so can compromise client safety, damage professional credibility, and undermine the ethical climate of the therapeutic community.

4.8 Cultural Competence and Value Conflicts

Cultural competence is a central aspect of ethical psychotherapy, guiding therapists to respect and adapt to clients' cultural backgrounds, values, and worldviews. In mainstream psychotherapy, the APA Ethics Code emphasises cultural competence as a core component of professional competence, requiring therapists to be aware of their own biases, adapt communication styles, and integrate culturally relevant interventions (American Psychological Association, 2017; Sue & Sue, 2016). Ethical dilemmas can arise when therapists' personal values clash with those of clients, such as differing attitudes toward family roles, sexuality, or spirituality. In these situations, ethical practice demands avoiding the imposition of personal beliefs while addressing harmful or maladaptive values, often through supervision, consultation, or referral when conflicts cannot be reconciled (Corey et al., 2014; Fisher, 2013). For example, a therapist working with a client from a collectivist background may need to modify individual-focused interventions to accommodate family expectations without compromising treatment goals.

In Islāmic psychotherapy, cultural competence is framed through *adab* (proper conduct) and *ihsān* (excellence), emphasising respect for Islāmic values such as modesty, family hierarchy, and spiritual practices. Therapists integrate Qur'ânic concepts and Prophetic traditions where appropriate, tailoring therapy to align with communal identity and collective welfare priorities. Value conflicts can emerge when Western therapeutic norms, such as prioritising individual choice, clash with Islāmic principles that emphasise *maslahah* (public interest) and *taqwā* (God-consciousness). Resolution of such conflicts often involves *shura* (consultation) and balancing professional ethics with religious guidance, ensuring that therapists maintain role clarity when clients expect both psychological support and religious counsel. For instance, a therapist may need to navigate a situation where a client seeks advice on marital decisions: the therapist provides psychological guidance while deferring religious rulings to a qualified scholar, thus preserving ethical and spiritual boundaries.

Across both frameworks, cultural competence requires therapists to cultivate self-awareness, humility, and reflective practice, recognising systemic and cultural power dynamics while prioritising the client's perspective. In mainstream practice, this may involve adapting interventions to accommodate collectivist or minority cultural norms, while in Islāmic psychotherapy, it additionally entails respecting spiritual values, religious practices, and communal obligations without compromising clinical integrity. By integrating these principles, therapists can ethically and effectively navigate value conflicts and provide culturally congruent care that honours client dignity, promotes trust, and fosters holistic well-being (Sue et al., 2019).

4.9 Operational Ethics in Therapeutic Practice

Johnson (2025) defined Operational ethics as "the practice of embedding moral responsibility and social accountability directly into the heart of how your organization operates." That is, running "clean, fair, and accountable" operation. Operational ethics in psychotherapy can be defined as the practical application of ethical principles in day-to-day clinical practice, encompassing procedural, relational, and administrative actions. This ensures client safety, maintains professional accountability, and upholds the integrity of the therapeutic process. This is not the "what" of ethics but also the "how" of putting them into practice. In mainstream psychotherapy, operational ethics is expressed through practices such as informed consent and confidentiality, ensuring that clients understand the purpose, methods, risks, benefits, and limitations of therapy while documenting these processes for accountability. Competence and scope of practice require therapists to work within the limits of their training, certification, licence to practice, accreditation, seeking supervision or making referrals when confronted with cases that exceed their expertise.

Boundary management is another critical aspect, with therapists expected to maintain professional distance, set clear limits on dual relationships, and monitor any potential boundary crossings to prevent harm. Cultural competence operationalises ethical responsibility in day-to-day interactions by adapting interventions to clients' cultural, spiritual, and social contexts. Administrative practices, such as contract, managing termination and continuity of care, record-keeping, and financial transparency, are integral components of operational ethics. Abrupt endings, incomplete or overly detailed documentation, and ambiguous financial arrangements can compromise client safety and trust, requiring therapists to communicate clearly, maintain accurate records, and establish fair, transparent policies.

In Islāmic psychotherapy, operational ethics integrates these professional and procedural standards with Qur'ânic guidance and Prophetic principles. Practice is framed as fulfilling *amānah* (trust), which requires honesty, transparency, and safeguarding client dignity at every stage of therapy. Therapists are accountable not only to professional standards but also spiritually, maintaining integrity in their decision-making and interactions. Decisions are guided by *maslaha* (public interest), balancing individual confidentiality with the welfare of the client, family, and community. This ensures that interventions do not inadvertently cause harm and promote collective well-being, in accordance with the *Maqāṣid al-Sharī 'ah,* the higher objectives of Islāmic law. For instance, preserving *ḥifẓ al-nafs* (protection of life) may justify limited disclosure if a client poses imminent danger to themselves or others, while safeguarding *ḥifẓ al- ʻaql* (intellect) can involve psychoeducation and psychotherapy to support sound decision-making. Preserving *ḥifẓ al-dīn* (faith), *ḥifẓ al-nasl* (family/lineage), and *ḥifẓ al-māl* (wealth/property) further guides ethical choices, ensuring therapy aligns with moral, spiritual, and social imperatives. Clear role delineation is crucial, as therapists must differentiate between psychological guidance and religious authority to prevent conflating spiritual and clinical responsibilities. Cultural congruence is emphasised through respect for Islāmic values such as modesty, family hierarchy, and spiritual practices, operationalised via culturally resonant language, metaphors, and interventions. Administrative aspects, such as termination, documentation, and fee management, are equally important and are guided by *taqwā* (God-consciousness), reinforcing accountability not only to professional standards but also to Allāh.

In both mainstream and Islāmic psychotherapy, operational ethics is vital for protecting clients, maintaining trust, and upholding the integrity of the therapeutic process. While mainstream approaches primarily focus on procedural, legal, and professional accountability, Islāmic operational ethics situates these responsibilities within a broader moral, spiritual, and communal framework. This integration ensures that all clinical and administrative decisions respect client welfare, adhere to professional standards, and fulfil divine trust, promoting ethically sound, effective, and culturally sensitive care in every aspect of practice.

4.10 Ethical Dilemmas in Islāmic Psychotherapy

The integration of spirituality into psychotherapy offers profound opportunities for healing, meaning-making, and identity formation. However, it also introduces complex ethical dilemmas, particularly around boundaries, competence, and value imposition. Therapists, particularly Muslim practitioners, encounter unique ethical challenges that stem from the intersection of professional psychological ethic, largely shaped by Western norms, and Islāmic cultural, moral, and religious values. Islāmic psychotherapists often experience ethical and moral conflicts when their personal faith-based values diverge from the Western ethical standards that guide the therapeutic process. Ethical dilemmas commonly arise in areas such as confidentiality, informed consent, dual relationships, competence, cultural and value conflicts, and the integration of spiritual practices. Dasti et al., (2019) emphasise that Muslim therapists often have to navigate unique ethical situations that arise from the intersection of religion, culture, and psychology. The absence of clear guidance in Western ethical codes creates additional challenges, requiring practitioners to rely on both professional judgement and religious principles to make sound decisions (p. 252).

Western ethical frameworks often emphasise individualism, personal autonomy, self-expression, and value neutrality, expecting therapists to suspend personal judgements and maintain a secular approach in all client interactions. In contrast, Islāmic values prioritise community well-being, collective responsibility, self-discipline, and spiritual development, placing strong emphasis on moral accountability, family integrity, and adherence to religious precepts. This divergence can create complex dilemmas, particularly when clients seek assistance with issues that contradict Islāmic teaching such as abortion, assisted suicide, premarital relationships, homosexuality, gambling, or addiction (Rassool, 2016, 2025). Matters involving divorce, sexuality, or religious obsession can also pose ethical uncertainty. In such instances, Islāmic psychotherapists must navigate the tension between maintaining professional integrity and remaining faithful to their religious and moral convictions These value-based tensions frequently compel clinicians to make difficult ethical decisions, including whether, according to Elzamzamy and Keshavarzi (2019) to "(a) accept or decline working with a particular client, (b) refer the client to another therapist, (c) disclose their own personal values, or (d) manage or set aside their own beliefs during therapy" (p. 43).

In Islāmic psychotherapy, therapists often take on multiple roles beyond their clinical duties, including spiritual guide, companion, or advisor through practices like *da'wah* (the Islāmic duty of inviting others to religious understanding) and *nasīhah* (offering sincere advice). These overlapping roles can create ethical challenges as professional, spiritual, and social identities intersect with client expectations. Dual and multiple relationships are common in close-knit communities, such as shared mosques, family ties, or community leadership. Such overlaps can blur boundaries, create conflicts of interest, and introduce power imbalances. These situations may also bias clinical judgement. Careful boundary management and transparent communication are therefore essential to maintain ethical practice.

Conflicts between personal faith-based values and professional ethical codes are another significant challenge. Situations involving premarital sexual activity, abortion, homosexuality, substance use, or gambling may place Islāmic therapists in tension between respecting client autonomy, adhering to Western-informed ethical guidelines, and remaining faithful to their religious convictions. Gender dynamics, modesty, and physical contact further complicate therapy, as cultural and religious norms may influence acceptable interactions between male and female therapists and clients. Therapists must ensure that therapeutic interventions respect client comfort and religious principles while maintaining clinical effectiveness. Similarly, addressing issues related to sexuality, spiritual interventions, and informed consent requires clarity about the purpose, boundaries, and potential impacts of interventions to prevent harm and uphold client autonomy. Working with vulnerable populations such as minors, women in conservative households, or clients with mental health challenges adds additional layers of ethical complexity. Therapists must balance the protection of client welfare with respect for communal or familial expectations, ensuring that ethical standards guide decision-making in culturally sensitive ways.

Other considerations include navigating gift-giving, using technology in therapy, and ensuring professional competence and proficiency in both Islāmic teachings and psychological practice. Providing services beyond one's expertise or issuing religious guidance without proper qualification poses ethical risks. Competence in Islāmic psychotherapy is a moral and spiritual obligation, encompassing *kafā'ah* (skills and expertise), *himmat al- 'amal* (work ethic), and *amānah* (trust and accountability). Therapists are encouraged to pursue supervision, ongoing training, and consultation with qualified scholars when integrating Islāmic teachings. These factors are essential to maintain ethical integrity, protect client welfare, and provide culturally congruent care in Islāmic psychotherapy. These ethical dilemmas will be examined in subsequent chapters in the book. Table 4.2 summarises the key ethical dilemmas in Islāmic psychotherapy.

Ethical dilemmas in Islāmic psychotherapy arise from the intersection of professional obligations, cultural norms, and religious values. Therapists must integrate professional competence, moral accountability, and *Shari 'ah* principles to navigate challenges related to confidentiality, informed consent, dual relationships, competence, value conflicts, and spiritual integration. Structured consultation, ongoing supervision, and reflective practice are essential for ethically sound, culturally sensitive, and spiritually aligned care, promoting client well-being while honouring both professional standards and divine trust.

4.11 Conclusion

Ethical dilemmas in psychotherapy, whether in secular or Islāmic context, represent the intersection of moral values, professional standards, and human complexity. Both traditions emphasise the protection of client welfare, the necessity of professional integrity, and the maintenance of trust within the therapeutic relationship. However, Islāmic psychotherapy introduces additional layers of moral responsibility derived from divine guidance and spiritual accountability. Whereas Western frameworks prioritise individual autonomy and value neutrality, Islāmic ethics situate therapy within a broader moral vision that seeks to harmonise psychological healing with spiritual growth and community well-being. The integration of faith within therapeutic practice calls for heightened ethical awareness, particularly regarding boundaries, confidentiality, gender relations, and the therapist's multiple roles as clinician, advisor, and spiritual companion. Navigating these dimensions demands both professional competence and deep understanding of Islāmic moral philosophy. Ultimately, ethical practice in Islāmic psychotherapy is not solely about adhering to professional codes but about embodying a moral and spiritual ethos rooted in *taqwā* (God-consciousness) and *amānah* (trust).

Table 4.2 Summary of key ethical dilemmas in Islāmic psychotherapy

Ethical Domain	Core Issue / Dilemma	Key Considerations	Ethical Response / Guiding Principle
Value conflicts	Clash between western ethical standards and islāmic moral values	Autonomy vs. communal welfare; secular neutrality vs. spiritual accountability	Balance professional ethics with Islāmic moral reasoning and context-sensitive practice
Dual & multiple roles	Therapist as counselor, spiritual guide, or advisor	Overlapping social/religious ties; blurred roles	Clarify roles, maintain transparency, and seek supervision
Boundaries	Difficulty maintaining professional distance	Client familiarity through mosque or family networks	Establish clear boundaries; discuss limits early in therapy
Gender & modesty	Gender norms influence therapeutic interaction	Restrictions on touch, seating, and privacy	Respect modesty while ensuring professional conduct and client comfort
Sexuality & moral issues	Working with clients on issues like premarital sex or homosexuality	Conflict between therapist's faith and client autonomy	Uphold a non-judgmental stance; refer when neutrality is compromised
Informed consent	Ensuring comprehension within collectivist or religious contexts	Family involvement; cultural communication styles	Use culturally appropriate language and review consent regularly
Spiritual & religious interventions	Integrating faith-based elements into therapy	Risk of overstepping therapeutic boundaries	Gain informed consent; ensure interventions are ethical and clinically appropriate
Confidentiality	Balancing privacy with communal responsibility	Family expectations; *Shari 'ah*-based exceptions	Protect confidentiality unless disclosure prevents serious harm or benefits the public
Professional competence	Limited training integrating psychology and Islāmic ethics	Lack of standardised Islāmic psychotherapy frameworks	Pursue dual training, ongoing supervision, and professional development
Technology in therapy	Online therapy poses privacy and gender interaction issues	Cultural and digital boundaries	Use secure platforms and respect Islāmic norms in virtual spaces
Gift-giving	Cultural expression of gratitude vs. ethical risk	Reciprocity norms may create obligation	Accept symbolic gifts only; maintain objectivity
Financial ethics	Fair fees vs. accessibility of care	Potential exploitation or inequality	Maintain transparency, fairness, and compassion
Record Keeping	Balancing thoroughness and confidentiality	Sensitive or communal information	Keep secure, minimal, and factual documentation

(continued)

Table 4.2 (continued)

Ethical Domain	Core Issue / Dilemma	Key Considerations	Ethical Response / Guiding Principle
Vulnerable populations	Working with clients with restricted autonomy (e.g., minors, women)	Family pressure, power imbalance	Prioritise client welfare and informed participation
Termination & continuity	Managing dependency or lifelong mentorship expectations	Cultural views of ongoing guidance	Plan termination carefully; provide referrals when needed

References

Abū Dāwūd. *Sunan Abi Dāwūd 4586.* In-book reference: Book 41, Hadith 93. English translation: Book 40, Hadith 4569. Hasan (Al-Albani). https://sunnah.com/abudawud:4586

American Counseling Association. (2014). *ACA code of ethics.* https://www.counseling.org/resources/aca-code-of-ethics.pdf

American Psychological Association. (2017). *Ethical principles of psychologists and code of conduct.* https://www.apa.org/ethics/code

Barnett, J. E., & Johnson, W. B. (2015). *Ethics desk reference for counselors* (2nd ed.). American Counseling Association. https://doi.org/10.1002/9781119221555

Beauchamp, T. L., & Childress, J. F. (2019). *Principles of biomedical ethics* (8th ed.). Oxford University Press.

Behnke, S. H. (2004). Ethics rounds-disclosures of confidential information under the new APA Ethics Code: A process for deciding when, and how. *Monitor on Psychology, 35*(8), 78.

Bhargava, S., & Sriram, S. (2016). Counsellor characteristics and the counselling experience. In S. Sriram (Ed.), *Counselling in India* (pp. 23–42). Springer. https://doi.org/10.1007/978-981-10-0584-8_2

BACP (2018). Ethical Framework for the Counselling Professions. British Association for Counselling and Psychotherapy. https://www.bacp.co.uk/media/3103/bacp-ethical-framework-for-the-counselling-professions-2018.pdf

Camadan, F., Topsakal, C., & Sadıkoğlu, İ. (2021). An examination of the ethical dilemmas of school counsellors: Opinions and solution recommendations. *Journal of Psychologists and Counsellors in Schools, 31*(1), 76–93. https://doi.org/10.1017/jgc.2020.16. (Original work published 2021).

Corey, G., Corey, M. S., & Callanan, P. (2014). *Issues and ethics in the helping professions* (9th ed.). Cengage Learning.

Corey, M. S., Corey, G., & Corey, C. (2018). *Groups: Process and practice* (10th ed.). Cengage Learning.

Dasti, R., Farhan, R., Naqvi, T. F., Sitwat, A., & Bokharey, I. Z. (2020). Ethical and moral dilemmas in psychotherapy: Applying a religiously sensitive framework to therapy. In A. Bagasra, & M. Mackinem (Eds.), *Working with Muslim clients in the helping professions* (pp. 242–258). Information Science Reference/IGI Global. https://doi.org/10.4018/978-1-7998-0018-7.ch013

Elzamzamy, K., & Keshavarzi, H. (2019). Navigating ethical dilemmas in mental health practice between professional ethics and Islāmic values. *The Journal of Islāmic Faith and Practice,* 2(2), 40–71. https://journals.indianapolis.iu.edu/index.php/JIFP/article/view/23274

Fisher, C. B. (2013). *Decoding the ethics code: A practical guide for psychologists* (3rd ed.). Sage Publications.

Ghozali, M., Syamsuri, Daniar, Purwana, A. E., & Cahyanti, L. D. (2019). *Professionalism concept of work ethic in Islāmic perspective.* In Proceedings of the International

Conference on Business, Law, and Pedagogy (ICBLP 2019). EAI. https://doi.org/10.4108/eai.13-2-2019.2286200

Heerman, W. J., White, R. O., & Barkin, S. L. (2015). Advancing informed consent for vulnerable populations. *Pediatrics, 135*(3), e562–e564. https://doi.org/10.1542/peds.2014-3041

Hegde, S. (2019, January 30). What is an ethical dilemma? *ScienceABC.* https://www.scienceabc.com/social-science/what-is-an-ethical-dilemma-definition-examples-real-life.html

Johnson, T. (2025, January 12). *Operational ethics: The future of operational excellence.* LinkedIn. https://www.linkedin.com/pulse/operational-ethics-missing-metric-define-future-charles-xdule/

Knapp, S. J., Gottlieb, M. C., & Handelsman, M. M. (2015). Ethical dilemmas in psychotherapy: Positive approaches to decision making. *American Psychological Association.* https://doi.org/10.1037/14338-000

Knapp, S., Gottlieb, M. C., & Handelsman, M. M. (2017). Enhancing professionalism through self-reflection.*Professional Psychology: Research and Practice, 48*(3), 167–174. https://doi.org/10.1037/pro0000135

Knapp, S., & VandeCreek, L. (2012). *Practical ethics for psychologists: A positive approach.* American Psychological Association.

Lindsay, G., & Colley, A. (1999). Ethical dilemmas of psychotherapists. *The Psychologist, 12*(4), 200–206.

Lindsay, G., & Clarkson, P. (1999). Ethical dilemmas of psychotherapists. *The Psychologist, 12*(4), 182–185.

Petrini, C. (2011). Informed consent from cognitively impaired persons: Ethical and legal considerations. *Annali Dell'istituto Superiore di Sanità, 47*(4), 353–362. https://doi.org/10.4415/Ann_11_04_06

Pope, K. S., & Vetter, V. A. (1992). Ethical dilemmas encountered by members of the American Psychological Association: A national survey. *American Psychologist, 47*(3), 397–411. https://doi.org/10.1037/0003-066X.47.3.397

Pope, K. S., & Vasquez, M. J. T. (2019). *Ethics in psychotherapy and counseling: A practical guide* (5th ed.). JohnWiley & Son.

Pope, K. S., Vasquez, M. J. T., Chavez-Dueñas, N. Y., & Adames, H. Y. (2021). *Ethics in psychotherapy and counseling: A practical guide* (6th ed.). Wiley.

Rassool, G. H. (2016). *Islāmic Counselling. An Introduction to Theory and Practice.* Routledge.

Rassool, G. H. (2025). Islāmic Counselling & Psychotherapy. An Introduction to Theory and Practice (2nded.). Routledge.

Remley, T. P., & Herlihy, B. (2020). *Ethical, legal, and professional issues in counseling* (6th ed.). Pearson.

Rukiah, R. (2015). Strategy of Sharia human resource development facing global market. *At-Tijaroh: Journal of Management Science and Islāmic Business, 1*(2), 105–121.

Şensoy, G., & İkiz, F. E. (2023). Ethical dilemmas of school counsellors: A vignette study. *Journal of Psychologists and Counsellors in Schools, 33*(1), 102–115. https://doi.org/10.1017/jgc.2022.1. (Original work published 2023).

Sivis-Cetinkaya, R. (2015). Ethical dilemmas of Turkish counsellors: A critical incidents study. *British Journal of Guidance & Counselling, 43*(4), 476–491. https://doi.org/10.1080/03069885.2015.1051994

Sue, D. W., Capodilupo, C. M., Torino, G. C., Bucceri, J. M., Holder, A. M. B., Nadal, K. L., & Esquilin, M. (2007). Racial microaggressions in everyday life: Implications for clinical practice. *American Psychologist, 62*(4), 271–286. https://doi.org/10.1037/0003-066X.62.4.271

Sue, D. W., & Sue, D. (2016). Counseling the culturally diverse: theory and practice. 7th edition. John Wiley & Sons.

Sue, D. W., Sue, D., Neville, H. A., & Smith, L. (2019). *Counseling the culturally diverse: Theory and practice* (8th ed.). John Wiley & Sons.

United Nations. (1948). *Universal Declaration of Human Rights.* https://www.un.org/en/about-us/universal-declaration-of-human-rights

Welfel, E. R. (2016). *Ethics in counseling and psychotherapy: Standards, research, and emerging issues* (6th ed.). Cengage Learning.
West, W. (2002). Some ethical dilemmas in counselling and counselling research. *British Journal of Guidance & Counselling, 30*(3), 261–268. https://doi.org/10.1080/0306988021000002308
Zur, O. (Ed.). (2016). *Multiple relationships in psychotherapy and counseling: Unavoidable, common, and mandatory dual relations in therapy* (1st ed.). Routledge.

Chapter 5
Therapist, Companion, or Shaykh? The Ethical Challenges of Multiple Roles

5.1 Introduction

Professional boundaries and dual or multiple overlapping relationships pose ongoing ethical challenges across healthcare disciplines, particularly in psychotherapy. The role of the Islāmic psychotherapist is inherently multifaceted, integrating both the conventional responsibilities of a psychotherapist and the distinctive duties derived from Islāmic ethical and spiritual frameworks. According to Crowden (2014), "A dual or multiple overlapping relationship is present when a psychotherapist simultaneously is in two, or more, different roles in their relationship with the person (or persons) who has (or have) come to them seeking help" (p.11). This chapter uses the more commonly used term "dual relationship" to refer to both dual and multiple relationships. Beyond providing standard psychological assessment, planning of care, and intervention, the Islāmic psychotherapist also serves as a facilitator of moral and spiritual growth, aligning therapeutic goals with the client's faith-based values. Recognising this dual nature is crucial for understanding the scope of practice and the ethical boundaries that define Islāmic psychotherapy. On the one hand, the therapist functions within the professional codes of psychology, maintaining confidentiality, objectivity, and evidence-based practice. On the other, they embody the role of a spiritual guide who supports the client's relationship with Allāh, offering counsel that fosters both psychological well-being and spiritual alignment.

In the context of Islāmic psychotherapy, the establishment of proper professional boundaries refers to the clear definition and consistent maintenance of professional codes of ethics, and Islāmic ethical and moral behaviours within the therapeutic relationship. Such boundaries serve to safeguard both the client and the therapist by ensuring that the relationship remains within limits that promote trust, respect, and psychological safety, while also upholding the therapist's accountability before Allāh. This approach integrates professional ethical

G. H. Rassool, *Ethical Dilemmas in Islāmic Psychotherapy*,
https://doi.org/10.1007/978-3-032-26515-9_5

standards with Islāmic moral principles such as *amānah* (trust), *adab* (proper conduct), and *ihsān* (excellence). Maintaining these boundaries is essential for facilitating effective, spiritually congruent care and preventing potential harm or role confusion within the therapeutic alliance (Crowden, 2008). These dual or multiple frameworks require sensitivity to potential role conflicts, ensuring that spiritual guidance complements rather than replaces clinical care. In essence, the Islāmic psychotherapist bridges two domains, the scientific understanding of the human psyche and the spiritual wisdom of Islāmic tradition, creating a holistic model of care that addresses the mind, body, and soul. This approach positions the therapist not only as a mental health professional but also as a moral companion, helping clients achieve emotional healing while nurturing their faith and ethical consciousness. The focus of this chapter is to explore the ethical challenges associated with the multiple roles undertaken by Islāmic psychotherapists and counsellors. It also examines the complexities of navigating dual relationships and maintaining professional boundaries, particularly within close-knit Muslim communities, where overlapping social and religious roles are often unavoidable.

5.2 Boundary Violations and Boundary Crossings

In the ethics of psychotherapy, it is important to distinguish between boundary violations and boundary crossings, as the two are not synonymous and differ significantly in intent, impact, and ethical evaluation. Boundary violations are actions by a therapist that are unethical, exploitative, or harmful to the client. They typically involve a misuse of professional authority or a departure from standards of integrity and decency, resulting in a breach of trust and disruption of the therapeutic frame. Such violations often manifest as exploitative dual relationship, most commonly of a sexual or financial nature, and represent serious ethical misconduct that may also constitute legal offences (Gabbard & Lester, 1995; Gutheil & Gabbard, 1993; Williams, 1997). Examples include pursuing personal gain through professional relationships, engaging in sexual or financial exploitation, or manipulating a client's emotional dependence for non-therapeutic purposes. These behaviours fundamentally compromise the client's welfare and the integrity of psychotherapy and are therefore regarded as unequivocally unethical and professionally impermissible (Crowden, 2008; Quadrio, 2004).

Boundary crossings in Islāmic psychotherapy differ from boundary violations in that they may occur without exploitation and are not necessarily unethical. A boundary crossing refers to any deviation from the strictest professional role (Gutheil & Gabbard, 1998; Knapp & Slattery, 2004), including departures from traditional "office-only," "no self-disclosure," or rigid risk management practices (Lazarus & Zur, 2002). Examples of ethical boundary crossings may include therapist self-disclosure, giving or receiving culturally appropriate small gifts or *Eid* [Muslim festival] greeting cards, nonsexual touch, incidental meetings outside the office, or occasional home visits. However, they may, in some contexts, serve a legitimate therapeutic or cultural purpose, such as attending a client's important community event, offering a supportive gesture, or engaging in culturally appropriate interpersonal warmth, provided such actions are done with clinical judgement, transparency, and the client's best interests in mind (Zur, 2016). Some encounters, such as unplanned meetings in public, may occur spontaneously and are managed with caution and ethical awareness, ensuring they do not compromise professional integrity or violate Islāmic ethical standards. The ethical acceptability of boundary crossings depends on context, intent, and the potential for misunderstanding or harm. When carefully managed, they can strengthen rapport and therapeutic alliance, but when unmonitored or repeated, they risk escalating into boundary violations. Thus, both boundary violations and boundary crossings must be evaluated through the dual lenses of professional ethics and *Shari 'ah*-based moral accountability. Table 5.1 presents a comparison of boundary crossings and boundary violations in western and Islāmic psychotherapy ethics.

5.3 Therapist, Companion, or Shaykh? Navigating Ethical Dilemmas

The practice of Islāmic psychotherapy presents a unique intersection between clinical psychology and spiritual care. While this integration offers a culturally congruent and holistic framework for healing, it also introduces a number of ethical complexities stemming primarily from the multiple roles. These are bound by professional ethics and a faith-oriented guide grounded in Islāmic values. The integration of spiritual elements into clinical practice invariably introduces diverse ethical challenges, compelling practitioners to critically examine the implications of multiple role relationships (Crowden, 2008). The complexity becomes particularly evident when mental health professionals navigate the intricate intersection of therapeutic practice and spiritual guidance within culturally specific contexts, requiring a careful balance between respecting clients' spiritual values and maintaining professional boundaries, especially in settings where traditional spiritual authorities hold significant influence (Tunç & Ekşi, 2025). Ultimately, navigating multiple roles in Islāmic psychotherapy requires balancing the communal and religious expectations of the client with professional ethics, ensuring that dual relationships or roles enhance therapeutic outcomes without compromising confidentiality, objectivity, or the client's trust.

5.3.1 Therapeutic Modalities

Different psychotherapeutic approaches conceptualise boundaries and professional relationships in distinct ways, a consideration that is especially relevant for Islāmic

Table 5.1 Comparison of boundary crossings and boundary violations in western and Islāmic psychotherapy ethics

Aspect	Western Psychotherapy Ethics	Islāmic Psychotherapy Ethics
Definition of boundary crossing	A deliberate and limited deviation from conventional professional conduct undertaken to enhance therapeutic effectiveness (Gutheil & Gabbard, 1998; Lazarus & Zur, 2002)	A contextually justified action taken by the therapist to promote *maslahah* (benefit) and *ihsan* (excellence) in care, provided it does not contradict *Shari 'ah* or professional ethics
Definition of boundary violation	An unethical or exploitative act that misuses professional power and harms the client (Gabbard & Lester, 1995; Quadrio, 2004)	An act that breaches *amanah* (trust) or leads to *zulm* (harm or injustice), exploiting the client's vulnerability or violating *Shari 'ah* principles
Ethical justification for boundary crossing	May be justified when intended to promote therapeutic benefit, provided it remains transparent, consensual, and within ethical guidelines	Permissible when motivated by *ikhlas* (sincere intention), ensures *maslahah*, and does not compromise *hurmah* (sanctity) or *akhlaq* (moral integrity)
Examples of ethical boundary crossings	Therapist self-disclosure, culturally appropriate small gifts, incidental encounters, nonsexual touch, and home visit	Expressing empathy through culturally and religiously appropriate means—such as verbal reassurance, *du 'a*, or community-based engagement—while maintaining modesty and professional decorum
Indicators of boundary violation	Sexual or financial exploitation, manipulation, or dual relationships for personal gain	Any action that violates *Shari 'ah*, compromises the therapist's integrity, causes psychological or spiritual harm, or breaches *amanah*
Moral foundation	Grounded in the ethical principles of beneficence, nonmaleficence, autonomy, and justice	Grounded in *Maqasid al-Shari 'ah* (preservation of life, intellect, dignity, and faith), *ihsan*, *ikhlas*, and *amanah*

psychotherapists who frequently operate within overlapping religious, cultural, and community networks. The therapeutic modality adopted by a practitioner plays a crucial role in determining how boundaries are understood, how professional distance is maintained, and whether dual or multiple relationships may be ethically permissible. As such, ethical decision-making around boundaries cannot be separated from theoretical orientation.

Humanistic and relational approaches, including person-centred and Gestalt therapies, place the therapeutic relationship itself at the core of change. These modalities emphasise authenticity, empathy, presence, and relational depth. Within this framework, carefully considered and non-exploitative dual relationships, such as attending a community event or acknowledging shared social space, may be viewed as potentially therapeutic when they strengthen trust and rapport. Jourard (1971) argued that appropriate therapist openness and relational authenticity can enhance therapeutic effectiveness, supporting the view that not all dual relationships are inherently unethical. Similarly, behavioural, cognitive-behavioural, family systems, and culturally responsive approaches generally evaluate dual relationships pragmatically rather than prohibiting them outright. Williams (1997) observed that behavioural theory does not inherently preclude social interaction with clients, provided it does not undermine treatment goals or lead to harm. Lazarus and Zur (2002) further contend that nonsexual, non-exploitative dual relationships may be ethically acceptable if they are likely to benefit the client or, at minimum, do not compromise professional judgement.

In contrast, psychoanalytic and psychodynamic traditions adopt a markedly different stance on boundaries. These approaches prioritise therapist neutrality, anonymity, and emotional distance to facilitate transference and unconscious processes. From this perspective, any form of dual relationship is typically discouraged, as it risks contaminating the analytic frame, interfering with transference dynamics, and undermining the therapeutic process (Epstein & Simon, 1990; Simon, 1991).

For Islāmic psychotherapists, these theoretical differences have heightened ethical implications. Practitioners often share religious spaces, communal ties, or cultural identities with clients, making strict boundary separation difficult to maintain. Consequently, ethical boundary management requires careful consideration of therapeutic orientation, community realities, power dynamics, and the principles of *amānah* (trust), *lā ḍarar* (non-harm), and *ihsān* (ethical excellence). Rather than applying rigid rules, therapists must engage in reflective practice, consultation, and supervision to determine whether boundary crossings are clinically justified, culturally appropriate, and ethically sound. Table 5.2 presents the therapeutic orientations and ethical perspectives on boundaries and dual relationships.

5.3.2 The Therapeutic Alliance

The therapeutic alliance, that is, the bond of trust, collaboration, and mutual understanding between therapist and client, is a critical factor in determining whether a dual relationship can be managed ethically and effectively. For an Islāmic psychotherapist, who may occupy multiple roles in a client's life, this factor becomes even more significant. A strong and stable alliance, built on clear communication, respect, and professional integrity, allows the therapist and client to negotiate boundaries transparently, even in contexts where religious or community roles overlap. For example, short-term counselling or sessions primarily focused on education may present fewer risks in navigating dual relationships than long-term therapy that addresses deep emotional or transference-based issues (Zur,

Table 5.2 Therapeutic orientations and ethical perspectives on boundaries and dual relationships

Therapeutic Approach	View of Boundaries	Stance on Dual Relationships	Ethical Rationale
Humanistic / Relational (e.g., Person-Centred, Gestalt)	Flexible, relationally grounded	Limited, non-exploitative dual relationships may be acceptable	Emphasises authenticity, empathy, and the therapeutic relationship as the agent of change (Jourard, 1971)
Behavioural	Pragmatic and outcome-focused	Not inherently opposed if no harm occurs	Theory does not preclude social contact if treatment goals are preserved (Williams, 1997)
Cognitive-Behavioural (CBT)	Structured but adaptable	Conditional acceptance based on benefit vs. harm	Focuses on effectiveness, transparency, and client welfare
Family Systems Therapy	Contextual and relational	Often unavoidable and sometimes necessary	Considers interconnected relationships and social systems
Culturally Sensitive / Multicultural Approaches	Contextually flexible	Dual roles may be ethically managed	Acknowledges communal norms and cultural realities (Lazarus & Zur, 2002)
Psychoanalytic / Psychodynamic	Strict, formal, and consistent	Generally prohibited	Protects neutrality, transference, and analytic boundaries (Epstein & Simon, 1990; Simon, 1991)
Islāmic Psychotherapy (Integrative)	Principled yet context-aware	Managed cautiously through consultation	Guided by *amānah*, *lā ḍarar*, *ihsān*, and community realities

2007, p. 40). When therapy has concluded successfully and both parties maintain a clear understanding of their former professional roles, limited post-therapy interactions such as attending a client's wedding, mosque event, or community gathering may be ethically acceptable.

In Islāmic communities, where the therapist may also serve as a religious advisor, community leader, social worker, or educator, such dual interactions can strengthen trust and cultural congruence, provided boundaries are openly discussed and expectations clearly established. Conversely, if the therapeutic alliance is fragile or still developing, dual relationships may introduce significant risks. Clients dealing with trauma, attachment difficulties, or high dependence may misinterpret the therapist's intentions, particularly if the therapist also holds a religious or community authority role. In such cases, even well-intentioned dual interactions could compromise therapeutic progress or create ethical dilemmas. Maintaining clear, consistent professional boundaries, within the Islāmic teachings' context, is therefore essential to safeguard the therapeutic process and prevent role confusion or exploitation.

In summary, the quality and stability of the therapeutic alliance largely determine whether a dual relationship can be ethically and safely managed. For Islāmic psychotherapists, this requires balancing professional responsibilities with religious, cultural, and community expectations, ensuring that multiple roles do not compromise client welfare, confidentiality, or therapeutic integrity.

5.3.3 Professional Boundaries in Islāmic Psychotherapy

In Islāmic psychotherapy, as in all therapeutic contexts, professional boundaries are essential for ensuring the safety, integrity, and effectiveness of the therapeutic relationship. Boundaries protect both the client and the therapist from ethical breaches, emotional enmeshment, and role confusion.

In Islāmic psychotherapy, the therapist may assume multiple interrelated roles, such as: Therapist/counsellor (*mushir*): providing psychological guidance grounded in both evidence-based techniques and Islāmic principles; Spiritual mentor (*murabbi/murshid*), nurturing the client's spiritual development and connection to Allāh; Moral educator (*mu'allim*), offering insights into Islāmic values, virtues, and ethics; Compassionate listener (*sāmi '*), embodying empathy (*rahmah*) and non-judgmental presence; and Community member (*ummati*), recognising the interconnectedness between individual well-being and communal health. Because of these overlapping roles, boundary management becomes both more complex and more crucial.

One of the foremost challenges is role fluidity or role dilution. Clients may not always distinguish between the therapist's professional and spiritual capacities, viewing them simultaneously as a counsellor, mentor, and religious guide. This can lead clients to seek not only psychological support but also religious or personal advice, blurring the lines between therapeutic guidance and spiritual mentorship. In conventional psychotherapy, therapists typically avoid giving direct advice, focusing instead on facilitating clients' self-exploration and insight. In contrast, an Islāmic psychotherapist may take on a more enabling role, which can include offering guidance or advice, especially when it aligns with the client's cultural, spiritual, or moral framework. Contemporary research suggests that advice-giving can be ethically appropriate if it respects the client's autonomy, considers cultural norms, and is delivered in a collaborative, supportive way (Duan et al., 2018). This approach allows the therapist to include spiritual guidance and practical help without taking away the client's control over their decisions.

In Islāmic psychotherapy, the act of seeking and giving advice (*nasīhah*) is not merely an incidental element of the therapeutic process; it is an essential component rooted in the Islāmic tradition. Unlike many Western models of psychotherapy, which often emphasise neutrality and client-led discovery, Islāmic psychotherapy recognises that offering guidance is part and parcel of the therapist's role. However, on the authority of Tameem ibn Aus ad-Daree (may Allāh be pleased with him): The Prophet (ﷺ) said, "The *deen* (religion) is *nasīhah* (advice, sincerity).” We said, “To whom?” He (ﷺ) said, “To Allāh, His Book, His Messenger, and to the leaders of the Muslims and their common folk” (Muslim). The Arabic word نَّصِيحَةُ (*naṣīḥah*) is often translated as “advice” but in this context carries the deeper meaning of sincerity, genuine counsel, and goodwill. The hadīth teaches that the essence of the religion is sincerity/advice directed toward five dimensions including the common people of the Muslims (brotherhood, community welfare). In clinical terms for an Islāmic psychotherapist, this ḥadīth highlights the importance of providing sincere advice that prioritises the client’s well-being and ensures that any counsel aligns with both therapeutic goals and Islāmic values, supporting the client holistically, spiritually, emotionally, and psychologically.

However, while advice and guidance are central to Islāmic psychotherapy, they must be provided within clear professional and ethical boundaries. Within Islām, sincere advice (*naṣīḥah*) is grounded in compassion, empathy, and a genuine desire for others’ well-being, as articulated by scholars such as Ibn Rajab. It involves wishing for others what one wishes for oneself, avoiding harm, and prioritising collective welfare over personal interest. *Naṣīḥah* further encompasses moral responsibility, respect, and solidarity within the community. Ultimately, sincere advice reflects a commitment to achieving benefit and goodness for others with integrity and sincerity. The therapist’s role is not to dictate or impose personal opinions, but to facilitate understanding through the lens of Islāmic principles and psychological insight. This requires discernment: knowing when to provide direct guidance and when to encourage self-reflection. The therapist must remain aware that their position carries spiritual and moral authority, and thus advice should always be grounded in authentic knowledge, humility, and a genuine desire for the client’s spiritual and emotional growth. In this sense, offering guidance in Islāmic psychotherapy is both a therapeutic intervention and an act of worship, a form of *amānah* (trust) that must be exercised responsibly. It reflects the delicate balance between being a professional therapist and a moral guide, ensuring that clients are supported in both their psychological healing and their journey toward spiritual well-being.

One significant challenge in Islāmic psychotherapy is managing dual relationships, particularly in smaller or close-knit Muslim communities where therapists and clients often share overlapping social, religious, or familial networks. Clients and therapists may attend the same mosque, participate in the same study circles (*halaqāt*), or have mutual acquaintances. In addition, therapists may engage with clients through community leadership roles, such as involvement in schools, charities, or social committees. For Islāmic psychotherapists who also serve as *imāms* or religious leaders within their community, encounters with clients in both therapeutic and communal settings, such as Friday prayers, religious classes, or community events, are often unavoidable. While these interactions can strengthen trust and rapport, they also risk blurring professional boundaries and compromising confidentiality. Maintaining transparency and obtaining informed consent are therefore critical to prevent role confusion and preserve ethical practice. This is particularly important when providing marital or family therapy while also serving as a religious advisor; the therapist must clearly distinguish between therapeutic guidance and religious counsel to avoid overstepping boundaries or exerting undue influence.

The interconnectedness of community roles can make full anonymity and professional distance difficult to maintain. While overlapping roles may enhance cultural understanding and client comfort, therapists must remain vigilant in safeguarding confidentiality, ensuring that information shared in therapy is not influenced by community interactions or their position of religious authority. Careful attention to boundaries allows therapists to steer dual roles effectively while maintaining both professional objectivity and ethical integrity. From an Islāmic perspective, therapists must uphold *amānah* (trustworthiness) and *sitr* (concealment of others' faults), ensuring that information shared in therapy remains confidential regardless of communal overlap. Ethical awareness and self-discipline are therefore essential to preserve the sanctity of the therapeutic relationship.

5.3.4 Integrating Clients' Spiritual and Religious Dimensions

One of the central challenges within Islāmic psychotherapy involves maintaining appropriate professional boundaries while integrating clients' spiritual and religious dimensions into the therapeutic process. This intersection between psychological care and Islāmic spiritual well-being presents complex ethical and practical dilemmas that require cultural sensitivity, theological literacy, and professional judgement. When psycho-spiritual issues emerge in therapy, such as questions of faith, divine will, or moral struggle, these boundaries can easily blur, demanding careful reflection grounded in both Islāmic principles and clinical ethics. For many Muslim clients, faith is not merely a personal belief system but a comprehensive framework shaping their worldview, identity, and daily conduct. Their spiritual practices such as prayer (*salat*), supplication (*du'ā'h*), remembrance (*dhikr*), and reliance on God (*tawakkul*), often serve as sources of comfort, meaning, and resilience in times of distress. In this context, Islāmic psychotherapists who skilfully integrate Islāmic concepts and therapeutic interventions can strengthen clients' emotional well-being, enhance therapeutic rapport, and foster a sense of spiritual alignment. However, practitioners must map a delicate balance: while drawing upon Islāmic values to support healing, they must avoid imposing personal interpretations of faith or neglecting the client's unique spiritual experience. Overstepping into religious instruction risks compromising therapeutic neutrality, whereas dismissing the spiritual dimension undermines the holistic nature of Islāmic psychotherapy. Ethical frameworks within Islāmic psychotherapy emphasise respect for client autonomy (*ikhtiyar*) and recognition of human diversity as part of divine creation. Islāmic psychotherapists are called to uphold *adab* (professional and moral conduct) by creating safe, non-judgemental spaces where clients can express their religious concerns authentically. By maintaining this balance, Islāmic psychotherapists adhere to both their professional obligations and the spiritual values that form the foundation of the therapeutic encounter.

Another potential dilemma stems from the tension between *da 'wah* (preaching) and the ethical obligation to respect client autonomy. While encouraging spiritual growth may be aligned with Islāmic values, therapists must ensure that such guidance does not become prescriptive or coercive. Similarly, the blurred distinction between therapeutic counselling and religious guidance (*irshād and nasīhah*) can complicate the therapeutic relationship, as clients may perceive the therapist not only as a clinician but also as a moral or spiritual authority. This dual perception raises further concerns about the risk of imposing personal religious beliefs or interpretations on clients, which could inadvertently influence their therapeutic choices or self-perception. The dual role of therapist and religious guide thus presents ongoing ethical challenges, especially when attempting to integrate *tazkiyah* (purification of the self) and *shifā'* (healing) into psychotherapeutic frameworks in a way that is both spiritually authentic and clinically sound.

To manage this challenge, Islāmic psychotherapists must be guided by several foundational principles. Foremost among these is the principle of informed consent, which requires that clients clearly understand how their spiritual and religious beliefs will be incorporated into the therapeutic process. As part of the therapeutic contract, it is essential for both therapist and client to discuss the extent to which spiritual and religious matters will be addressed. Moreover, Muslim clients often expect Islāmic psychotherapists to approach their concerns through an Islāmic lens, offering interventions that integrate psychological insight with spiritual guidance. Before examining the spiritual dimensions of treatment, practitioners should initiate thoughtful discussions about the client's beliefs and the significance these hold in their daily life and coping processes. By engaging in active listening and posing open-ended questions, therapists can demonstrate respect for the client's values and preferences while gaining a deeper understanding of their worldview. For instance, therapists might initiate discussions about clients' spiritual needs early in the therapeutic process, allowing clients to express their wishes regarding the role of spirituality in sessions. By doing so, therapists respect their clients' autonomy while also ensuring that the therapeutic focus remains client centred. Additionally, utilising referral networks with spiritual leaders or *imām,* and community support systems can provide clients with the additional resources they may need without placing the burden solely on the therapist. This collaborative approach not only upholds ethical standards but also allows practitioners to tailor interventions that are both clinically effective and spiritually congruent.

Finally, it is important to recognise that addressing clients' spiritual and religious needs is not a one-size-fits-all undertaking. Each client brings a unique set of beliefs, experiences, and expectations that shape their engagement with spirituality. In addition, Muslims constitute a heterogeneous rather than a homogeneous group, meaning they represent a vast diversity of cultures, traditions, theological interpretations, and personal experiences. Although united by core beliefs such as the oneness of God (*tawḥīd*) and the Prophetic model of Muhammad (ﷺ), Muslims differ significantly in how they understand, express, and integrate their faith into daily life. These variations are shaped by multiple factors including ethnicity, geography, language, education, sectarian affiliation (such as Sunni, Shia, or Sufi traditions), and levels of religiosity. In the context of Islāmic psychotherapy, acknowledging this diversity is essential. Therapists must avoid assuming a single "Muslim perspective" or applying one-size-fits-all religious interventions. Instead, they should approach each client as a unique individual whose spiritual beliefs and practices are influenced by personal, cultural, and contextual factors.

5.3.5 Issue of Power, Authority, and Gender Dynamics

The issue of power and authority is particularly pronounced in Islāmic psychotherapy. Because the therapeutic model is often grounded in Islāmic teachings, clients may perceive the therapist not only as a psychologist or mental health professional but also a spiritual authority. This perception can instil the therapist with considerable influence over the client's beliefs, behaviours, and moral decisions. These overlapping roles can blur the boundaries between spiritual, communal, and therapeutic functions, making it essential to manage power dynamics with heightened ethical awareness. If not managed carefully, this can lead to overreliance, role confusion, or unintentional coercion, particularly if the client feels religiously obligated to follow the therapist's guidance. While this dynamic can enhance the therapist's capacity to guide clients toward holistic well-being, it also carries the risk of spiritual authoritarianism, where the therapist's opinions may unintentionally be treated as religious rulings (*fatāwā*). Islāmic ethics therefore call for *tawāḍu* ' (humility) and *ikhlāṣ* (sincerity) on the therapist's part, ensuring that guidance is given with wisdom (*ḥikmah*), compassion (*raḥmah*), and an awareness of one's limits. The therapist must recognise that ultimate guidance (*hidāyah*) comes from Allāh alone, not from their personal authority.

Islām does not categorically prohibit cross-gender therapy; however, it requires that such interactions strictly adhere to Islāmic principles of modesty (*ḥayā'*), *adab* (proper conduct), and *taqwā* (God-consciousness) in all interactions between men and women and professionalism. Within the context of Islāmic psychotherapy, these values serve as guiding principles for maintaining professionalism and moral integrity rather than as strict prohibitions against therapeutic engagement between genders. In situations where a same-gender therapist is unavailable or when therapeutic necessity arises, engagement between male and female clients and therapists may be permissible within the limits defined by Islāmic ethics. Despite the permissibility of cross-gender therapy, most scholars and Islāmic psychotherapists recommend same-gender pairings whenever feasible. This aligns more comfortably with the Islāmic ethos of modesty and minimises potential boundary challenges.

Same-gender therapy tends to allow both therapist and client to engage more freely without concern about crossing interpersonal limits or cultural sensitivities. Same-gender therapeutic relationships often enable both the therapist and the client to engage more openly, without the added concern of crossing interpersonal boundaries or navigating cultural sensitivities. Working with a therapist of the same gender can also enhance the client's sense of comfort, safety, and mutual understanding, as shared social and cultural experiences may facilitate greater empathy and trust. This dynamic often makes it easier for clients to discuss sensitive or personal issues, such as trauma, sexuality, or body image, in a more relaxed and secure therapeutic environment. There is evidence indicating that therapeutic outcomes may be influenced by the gender pairing of the client and therapist. A large-scale study conducted in Germany observed a trend suggesting that same-gender client–therapist dyads tended to achieve slightly better outcome, including greater symptom reduction and improved quality of life within psychodynamic therapy, particularly among female client–therapist pairs (Schmalbach et al., 2022).

Islāmic legal maxims (*Qawāʿid al Fiqhiyyah*) act as guiding principles that help scholars and practitioners apply Islāmic law consistently, logically, and in a way that aligns with both textual sources and overarching ethical objectives. The relevant (Islāmic legal maxim) in the context of cross-gender therapy is:

تارَوظْحَملا حُيبِتُ تارَورُضَّلا

- Necessities permit the prohibited. (*al-ḍarūrāt tubīḥ al-maḥẓūrāt*)

This principle means that when a person faces a genuine necessity (*ḍarūrah*), certain actions that would normally be prohibited (*maḥẓūrāt*) become temporarily permissible, but only to the extent required to remove the necessity. The limitation is expressed in a related maxim:

اهَرِدَقَبِ رُدَّقَتُ ةرَورُضَّلا

- Necessity is to be assessed according to its extent. (*al-ḍarūrah tuqaddaru bi-qadarihā*)

In other words, the permission granted under necessity is not absolute; it must remain strictly limited to what is required to address the specific need. Within the framework of Islāmic psychotherapy, this aligns with the general jurisprudential maxim that necessity permits the prohibited to the extent of the necessity. Accordingly, when a same-gender therapist is unavailable, or when a client feels greater comfort and trust with a particular therapist due to expertise or therapeutic rapport, cross-gender therapy may be deemed permissible. However, such permission is conditional and must be accompanied by strict adherence to ethical and professional safeguards. These include maintaining modesty and professionalism in all communication and behaviour, ensuring that interactions remain respectful and free from inappropriate familiarity. Seclusion should be avoided, with sessions ideally conducted in professional environments that safeguard privacy without complete isolation, such as offices with visible entryways or virtual sessions conducted with appropriate decorum. Boundaries in communication must also be upheld, meaning contact outside of therapy (through social media, texting, or informal exchanges) should remain minimal and strictly professional. Furthermore, self-awareness on the part of both therapist and client is crucial; if emotional transference, attraction, or boundary tension arises, supervision or consultation should be sought promptly.

5.3.6 Therapist's Self-Awareness, Motives, and Competence

Therapists must continuously reflect on their intentions, emotional responses, and capacity to remain objective when considering dual relationships or multiple relationships. Self-awareness is essential to ensure that any interaction with a client, inside or outside therapy, serves the client's best interests rather than the therapist's personal needs or desires. Professionals must regularly examine their own beliefs and biases to ensure they do not unintentionally project these onto clients. Engaging in clinical supervision or peer consultation can provide valuable insights and feedback, serving as a safeguard against potential ethical dilemmas. Reflective practices, including journaling or meditation, can also contribute to greater self-awareness, allowing professionals to evaluate their motivations when addressing spiritual matters. For example, if a therapist is contemplating attending a client's wedding, they must carefully evaluate their motivation: is it truly client-centred, aimed at supporting the client's well-being and social connection, or self-serving, fulfilling personal curiosity or social gain? Such reflection helps prevent conflicts of interest, protects professional boundaries, and ensures that dual relationships do not compromise therapeutic integrity.

The therapist's personal, cultural, and professional factors play a significant role in determining whether to engage in dual relationships, and this is particularly relevant for Islāmic psychotherapists, who often navigate multiple overlapping roles within their clients' religious and community contexts. Therapists who are more communal or embedded in collectivist cultures, common in many Muslim communities, may be more open to dual relationships, such as interacting with clients in mosque activities, community events, or family gatherings, as these interactions can strengthen trust, cultural understanding, and therapeutic rapport. In contrast, therapists from more individualistic or privacy-focused backgrounds may find such dual roles challenging or ethically complex (Lazarus & Zur, 2002). Additionally, the therapist's professional training and orientation shape how these dual relationships are approached. Islāmic psychotherapists trained in integrated Islāmic-oriented frameworks may view overlapping roles, such as serving simultaneously as a religious advisor, educator, or therapist, as potentially beneficial if they support client well-being and are ethically managed. Conversely, those trained in analytic or risk-averse approaches may be more cautious and strive to maintain strict separation between therapeutic and community or religious roles

(Williams, 1997; Zur, 2005). By combining self-awareness, reflection on motives, cultural sensitivity, and professional competence, therapists can navigate dual relationships in a way that safeguards client welfare while respecting cultural and community contexts.

5.4 Maintaining Boundaries Within the Islāmic Framework

In Islāmic psychotherapy, maintaining professional boundaries is both an ethical necessity and a reflection of spiritual accountability. The therapist must ensure that the therapeutic relationship remains effective, respectful, and aligned with Islāmic teachings.

Each therapeutic session should begin with a sincere intention (*niyyah*) to serve the client for the sake of Allāh. This spiritual grounding ensures that the therapist's actions are motivated by genuine care and service rather than personal gain, recognition, or emotional attachment. By focusing therapy on *khidmah* (service) and ethical responsibility, the therapist strengthens both professional integrity and spiritual awareness. Upholding proper Islāmic manners (*adab*) is essential in every therapeutic interaction. This includes demonstrating respect, honesty, confidentiality, and modesty in speech, manner, and behaviour. For example, the therapist avoids judgemental language, listens attentively, and treats the client's personal disclosures with the utmost discretion. Maintaining *adab* ensures that therapy not only meets professional standards but also embodies Islāmic moral values.

At the outset of therapy, the therapist should clearly define their roles. While the integration of Islāmic values may be part of the therapeutic process, the therapist is not a religious scholar (*ʿālim*) issuing *fatāwā* (religious rulings or legal opinions in Islām). Clarifying this distinction helps prevent role confusion, manages client expectations, and safeguards the therapeutic relationship from being perceived as religious instruction or moral judgement. Islāmic norms regarding modesty and gender interaction (*ḥayā'*) must be observed to maintain ethical and comfortable therapy. This includes dressing modestly, using appropriate language, and establishing professional physical and verbal boundaries, particularly in cross-gender sessions. Gender sensitivity helps foster trust while respecting both Islāmic teachings and the client's comfort. Therapists should maintain clear limits regarding contact outside scheduled sessions, including digital communication. Unrestricted availability may lead to over-dependence, emotional blurring, or boundary violations. Clear policies on session times, messaging, and emergency contact reinforce professional limits while allowing the client to receive structured and focused support. Regular clinical supervision and consultation with qualified supervisors or Islāmic scholars help ensure that therapeutic practice remains ethically and religiously sound. These external perspectives allow the therapist to reflect on potential biases, ethical dilemmas, or spiritual complexities that may arise, supporting ongoing professional development and accountability.

By adhering to these principles, an Islāmic psychotherapist ensures that therapy remains a space of ethical integrity, spiritual awareness, and professional competence, protecting both the client and the therapist while integrating Islāmic values into psychological care. A summary of maintaining boundaries within the Islāmic framework is outlined in Table 5.3.

Table 5.3 Maintaining professional boundaries within the Islāmic psychotherapy framework

Ethical principle/domain	Description	Practical application in Islāmic Psychotherapy
Intention (*Niyyah*)	Therapy as an act of service and spiritual accountability	Begin sessions with sincere intention to serve the client for the sake of Allāh (khidmah), avoiding personal gain or emotional dependency
Proper Conduct (*Adab*)	Moral and professional comportment	Demonstrate respect, humility, honesty, confidentiality, and non-judgmental listening in all interactions
Role clarity	Distinction between therapist and religious authority	Clearly define the therapist's role as a clinician, not a mufti or religious scholar issuing fatāwā
Boundary management	Prevention of role confusion and exploitation	Set clear limits on dual relationships, community interactions, and post-therapy contact
Modesty & gender sensitivity (Ḥayā')	Ethical conduct in cross-gender interactions	Maintain professional dress, language, seating arrangements, and appropriate physical boundaries
Digital & contact boundaries	Managing accessibility and availability	Establish clear policies for messaging, social media, emergency contact, and session scheduling
Confidentiality (Amānah & Sitr)	Protection of client trust and privacy	Safeguard client disclosures regardless of communal overlap, except where serious harm necessitates disclosure
Supervision & consultation	Ethical and spiritual accountability	Seek regular supervision and consult qualified scholars for complex ethical or religious matters
Self-awareness & reflection	Monitoring motives and biases	Engage in reflective practice to ensure actions remain client-centered and ethically sound
Professional competence	Clinical and religious proficiency	Maintain training in evidence-based psychology and foundational Islāmic knowledge, with ongoing development

(continued)

Table 5.3 (continued)

Ethical principle/domain	Description	Practical application in Islāmic Psychotherapy
Boundary Principle	Islāmic Concept	Practical Application in Therapy
Niyyah (Intention)	Sincere intention to serve Allah	Begin each session with the aim of helping the client for Allah's sake, avoiding personal gain or attachment
Adab (Professional Etiquette)	Respect, honesty, modesty, confidentiality	Listen attentively, maintain respectful communication, protect client information, demonstrate ethical conduct
Clear Role Definition	Maintaining professional and religious boundaries	Clarify at the start that the therapist is not a religious scholar issuing fatwas, but a professional integrating Islāmic values
Supervision and Consultation	Accountability and self-reflection	Seek guidance from supervisors or Islāmic scholars to handle ethical dilemmas and maintain professional and religious alignment
Gender Sensitivity	Ḥayā' (modesty) and proper conduct between genders	Observe modest dress, respectful communication, and professional limits, especially in cross-gender therapy
Boundaries of Availability	Preservation of professionalism	Set clear limits on session times and digital contact to prevent over-dependence or boundary violations

5.5 A Summary of Ethical Challenges in Multiple Roles of an Islāmic Psychotherapist

In Islāmic psychotherapy, therapists frequently manage the complex interplay between professional, psychological, and spiritual responsibilities, which gives rise to a range of ethical dilemmas. One key challenge involves maintaining professional boundaries while addressing clients' spiritual needs. Clients may seek guidance that spans both psychological support and religious counsel, placing the therapist in a position where the lines between therapeutic counselling, spiritual mentorship, and religious instruction (*irshād* and *nasīhah*) can become blurred. This overlap increases the risk of inadvertently imposing personal beliefs or appearing as a religious authority, particularly when the therapist is perceived as an imām or community leader. Another ethical consideration arises from the therapist's dual role in promoting psychological well-being (*shifā'*) and spiritual purification (*tazkiyah*). Integrating these elements requires careful judgement to ensure that religious practices such as prayer, supplication, or other devotional acts complement rather than conflict with psychological treatment methods. The therapist must also be sensitive to client autonomy, avoiding a tension between the impulse to engage in *da 'wah* (preaching) and the ethical requirement to respect the client's personal beliefs, values, and decision-making.

In smaller or closely connected communities, additional dilemmas emerge from multiple overlapping relationships. Therapists may encounter clients in social, familial, or religious settings, or provide guidance in both community and therapeutic contexts. While such familiarity can strengthen trust, it also complicates confidentiality, anonymity, and professional objectivity. The therapist must therefore navigate these dual relationships carefully, establishing transparency and informed consent to prevent role confusion or undue influence. Finally, therapists often face the challenge of being approached for both psychological and spiritual support, which can heighten the risk of overstepping professional boundaries. Balancing these responsibilities requires constant ethical reflection, self-awareness, and adherence to Islāmic principles of modesty, integrity, and respect for the client's dignity. Collectively, these dilemmas illustrate the nuanced and multifaceted nature of ethical practice in Islāmic psychotherapy, where psychological, spiritual, and communal considerations intersect.

5.6 Clinical Vignette: Boundary and Dual-Role Dilemma in Islāmic Psychotherapy

Dr. Amina is an Islāmic psychotherapist working in a close-knit Muslim community. One of her clients, Fatima, a 28-year-old woman experiencing anxiety related to marital conflict, attends the same mosque as Dr. Amina. After several sessions, Fatima invites Dr. Amina to attend a women's Qur'ânic study circle where Fatima is a regular participant. Fatima explains that seeing her therapist in the community would help her feel supported and less isolated. Dr. Amina recognises that accepting the invitation may strengthen rapport and affirm communal belonging, values highly regarded in Islāmic contexts. However, she is also concerned that attending the gathering could blur professional boundaries, compromise confidentiality, or create expectations of informal advice outside therapy sessions. Additionally, other community members may infer a therapeutic relationship, potentially violating Fatima's privacy. Dr. Amina reflects on her ethical obligations through both professional guidelines and Islāmic principles of *amānah* (trust) and *ihsān* (excellence in conduct). After consultation with a supervisor, she discusses the issue openly with Fatima, explaining the potential risks and boundaries involved. Together, they agree that Dr. Amina will not attend the gathering but will explore alternative ways to strengthen Fatima's social support within therapy, while maintaining clear professional limits.

Ethical Issues Illustrated.

- Dual and multiple relationships in close-knit communities
- Balancing relational closeness with professional boundaries
- Protecting confidentiality and client dignity
- Integrating cultural sensitivity without compromising ethical standards
- Applying Islāmic ethical principles alongside professional ethics

This vignette demonstrates how boundary dilemmas in Islāmic psychotherapy require reflective judgement, consultation (shūrā), transparency, and role clarity, ensuring that care remains ethically sound, culturally congruent, and spiritually accountable.

Reflective questions aligned with each ethical issue, designed to prompt ethical reasoning and self-awareness in Islāmic psychotherapy practice:

- How might my existing social, religious, or community relationship with this client influence my clinical judgement and therapeutic neutrality?
- At what point does familiarity risk compromising my role as a therapist entrusted with *amānah*, and would referral better protect the client's best interests?
- How can I demonstrate *raḥmah* (compassion) and cultural competence without creating emotional dependence, role confusion, or boundary erosion?
- Are my current actions strengthening the therapeutic alliance, or are they blurring professional limits in ways that could cause harm?
- Am I safeguarding the client's privacy and dignity as a sacred trust, and under what conditions, if an, would disclosure be justified by *maṣlaḥah* (public interest) or harm prevention?
- If disclosure becomes necessary, how can I minimise harm and preserve the client's dignity to the greatest extent possible?
- Where is the line between ethical cultural accommodation and compromising professional or moral standards, particularly in relation to power imbalances or harmful norms?
- How can *shūrā (*consultation), clinical supervision, or ethical review support sound decision-making in this situation?
- How do *taqwā* (God-consciousness) and professional accountability jointly guide my actions, and could I ethically justify this decision both to my profession and before Allāh?

5.7 Conclusion

Steering professional boundaries while attending to clients' spiritual and religious needs requires a precise balance of ethical rigour and cultural competence. Within Islāmic psychotherapy, this balance is further complicated by the intersection of clinical practice with religious meaning-making. Dual relationships, multiple roles, gender dynamics, and therapeutic power differentials therefore necessitate heightened self-awareness, transparent communication, and strict adherence to both psychological and Islāmic ethical frameworks. The ethical landscape of Islāmic psychotherapy is shaped by the need to reconcile clinical professionalism with spiritual authenticity. As the roles of the Islāmic psychotherapist increasingly encompass the functions of Therapist, Companion, and, for some clients, a quasi-*Shaykh*-like figure, these overlapping positions create inherent risks for role confusion and boundary diffusion. Rather than eliminating these roles, which are deeply embedded in Muslim cultural and spiritual expectation, practitioners must manage them with clear role definitions, structured boundaries, and regular supervision. Such measures help prevent unethical forms of dependency while preserving the spiritual resonance that many clients seek.

Ultimately, ethical Islāmic psychotherapy requires integrating scientific competence with Islāmic moral virtues. Boundaries must be upheld not only as professional safeguards but also as expressions of *taqwā* (God-consciousness) and accountability before Allāh. Practitioners are called to embody *tawāḍu'* (humility) and *ikhlāṣ* (sincerity), offering guidance with *ḥikmah* (wisdom) and *raḥmah* (compassion), while recognising that definitive guidance (*hidāyah*) rests with Allāh alone. This ethical posture allows the psychotherapist to inhabit multiple roles responsibly while maintaining therapeutic integrity.

References

Crowden, A. (2008). Professional boundaries and the ethics of dual and multiple overlapping relationships in psychotherapy. *Monash Bioethics Review, 27*(1–2), 10–27. https://doi.org/10.1007/BF03351302

Duan, C., Knox, S., & Hill, C.E. (2018). Advice Giving in Psychotherapy. In E.L. MacGeorge & L.M. Van Swol (Eds.), *The Oxford Handbook of Advice* (online). Oxford Handbook Online. https://doi.org/10.1093/oxfordhb/9780190630188.013.11.

Epstein, R. S., & Simon, R. I. (1990). The exploitation index: An early warning indicator of boundary violations in psychotherapy. *Bulletin of the Menninger Clinic, 54*(5), 450–465.

Gabbard, G. O., & Lester, E. P. (1995). *Boundaries and boundary violations in psychoanalysis*. Basic Books.

Gutheil, T. G., & Gabbard, G. O. (1993). The concept of boundaries in clinical practice: Theoretical and risk-management dimensions. *American Journal of Psychiatry, 150*(2), 188–196. https://doi.org/10.1176/ajp.150.2.188

Gutheil, T. G., & Gabbard, G. O. (1998). Misuses and misunderstandings of boundary theory in clinical andregulatory settings. *The American journal of psychiatry, 155*(3), 409–414. https://doi.org/10.1176/ajp.155.3.409

Ibn Rajab. *Jaami' al-'Uloom wa'l-Hukam* (p. 80), cited in Islām Q&A. (2018).*Etiquette of giving advice*. https://Islāmqa.info/en/answers/225160/ etiquette-of-giving-advice

Jourard, S. M. (1971). *The transparent self.* Van Nostrand Reinhold.

Knapp, S. J., & Slattery, J. M. (2004). Professional boundaries in nontraditional settings. *Professional Psychology: Research and Practice, 35*(5), 553–558. https://doi.org/10.1037/0735-7028.35.5.553

Lazarus, A. A., & Zur, O. (2002). *Dual relationships and psychotherapy.* Springer Publishing Company.

Muslim. *Forty Hadith of an-Nawawi*. Hadith 7, 40 Hadith an-Nawawi. https://sunnah.com/nawawi40:7

Quadrio, C. (2004). Boundary violations in psychotherapy. *Psychotherapy in Australia, 10*(3), 28–33.

Simon, R. I. (1991). Psychological injury caused by boundary violation: Precursors to therapist-patient sex. *Psychiatric Annals, 21*(10), 614–619.

Schmalbach, I., Albani, C., Petrowski, K., & Brähler, E. (2022). Client-therapist dyads and therapy outcome: Does sex matching matters? A cross-sectional study. *BMC Psychology*, *10*(1), 52. https://doi.org/10.1186/s40359-022-00761-4

Tunç, M., & Ekşi, H. (2025). Sacred tensions: How mental health professionals navigate spirituality, ethics, and professional identity. *Pastoral Psychology*. https://doi.org/10.1007/s11089-025-01244-0

Williams, M. H. (1997). Boundary violations: Do some contended standards of care fail to encompass commonplace procedures of humanistic, behavioral, and eclectic psychotherapies? *Psychotherapy, 34*(3), 238–249.

Zur, O. (2005). Dumbing down of psychology: Manufactured consent about the depravity of dual relationships in therapy. In R. H. Wright & N. A. Cummings (Eds.), *Destructive trends in mental health: The well-intentioned road to harm* (pp. 253–282). Brunner-Routledge.

Zur, O. (2007). *Boundaries in psychotherapy: Ethical and clinical explorations.* American Psychological Association.

Zur, O. (Ed.). (2016). *Multiple relationships in psychotherapy and counseling: Unavoidable, common, andmandatory dual relations in therapy* (1st ed.). Routledge.

Chapter 6
Confidentiality and Informed Consent: Ethical Practices in the Islāmic Therapeutic Context

Saima Khan

6.1 Introduction

Mental health care involves the careful handling of deeply personal thoughts, emotions, and life experiences. Across cultures and belief systems, ethical practice in psychotherapy is grounded in the protection of human dignity, personal autonomy, and trust between the therapist and the client. These ethical foundations become especially significant when therapeutic work intersects with strong religious, cultural, and familial values (Ernstmeyer & Christman, 2025). Confidentiality and informed consent are central to developing a safe and trusting therapeutic alliance. In psychotherapy, clients often disclose highly sensitive personal information, including trauma, family conflict, and internal distress, that can be deeply stigmatised in their cultural or religious communities. Maintaining confidentiality encourages clients to speak openly, supports emotional processing, and fosters psychological healing (American Psychological Association, 2017).

For many Muslim clients, additional layers of vulnerability can accompany therapeutic engagement. Stigma surrounding mental health, honour-based cultural norms, and expectations of familial loyalty may heighten fear of disclosure. In some communities, mental health struggles are interpreted as moral weakness, spiritual deficit, or social shame, leading clients to withhold information unless they are assured of privacy (Chamsi-Pasha & Albar, 2016). In collectivist societies, personal identity is often closely intertwined with family reputation, communal belonging, and moral expectations. As a result, breaches of confidentiality, real or perceived, can carry consequences that extend beyond the individual to the

Dr. Saima Khan (Bath Spa University Academic Centre Ras Al Khaimah, Ras Al Khaimah, United Arab Emirates) is the sole author of this chapter. Editorial review and substantive editing were conducted by Professor Dr. G.Hussein Rassool.

G. H. Rassool, *Ethical Dilemmas in Islāmic Psychotherapy*,
https://doi.org/10.1007/978-3-032-26515-9_6

family and community at large. This amplifies the ethical responsibility of Islāmic psychotherapists and mental health professionals to ensure that confidentiality is clearly explained, consistently upheld, and culturally understood, particularly when working with Muslim clients whose social realities may intensify the risks of disclosure (Chu, 2024).

In parallel, therapists operating within Muslim contexts may encounter complex expectations regarding transparency, moral accountability, and family involvement. Requests for information from parents, spouses, or religious authorities may be framed as acts of care, guidance, or religious duty. Without a clear ethical framework, clinicians may experience tension between respecting client autonomy and responding to culturally embedded expectations of collective responsibility. These dynamics highlight the need for an approach to confidentiality and informed consent that is both clinically sound and ethically grounded in Islāmic moral reasoning (Muhsin, 2021). Informed consent, therefore, assumes particular importance in Islāmic therapeutic settings. Beyond procedural consent, it requires ongoing dialogue, clarity about boundaries, and sensitivity to power differentials shaped by age, gender, religious authority, and family hierarchy. When informed consent is inadequately addressed, clients may feel coerced, misunderstood, or spiritually conflicted, undermining both therapeutic outcomes and ethical integrity (Packer, 2011).

Islāmic teachings strongly emphasise human dignity (*karāmah al-insān*) and the preservation of honour. The Qur'ân warns against intrusion into others' privacy and the dissemination of private matters (Al-Ḥujurāt, 49:12). Similarly, the Prophet Muhammad () taught that when someone confides in another and then turns away, the information entrusted is a trust (*amānah*) that must be protected (Abū Dāwūd). These Islāmic foundations contextualise modern ethical standards, making confidentiality not only a professional requirement but also a spiritual imperative.

This chapter examines the Islāmic foundations of confidentiality, modern psychotherapeutic standards, informed consent from both clinical and Islāmic ethical perspectives, common dilemmas in Muslim contexts, and practical integrative frameworks. Case vignettes and guidance for therapist self-awareness are included to illustrate ethical complexities in culturally sensitive practice.

6.2 Islāmic Foundations of Confidentiality

6.2.1 Qur'ânic Foundations

The Qur'ân places a high value on preserving human dignity and avoiding intrusion or harmful disclosure. In Surah Al-Ḥujurāt, Allāh explicitly instructs believers to refrain from spying or backbiting:

لَاوَ ۖ مٌثۡإِ نِّظَّلٱ ضَعۡبَ نَّإِ نِّظَّلٱ نَمِّ ارًيِثَكَ أوُبِنَتَجۡٱ أوُنَمَاءَ نَيذِلَّٱ اهَيُّأَٰٓيَ
أوُقَّتَّٱوَ ۚ هُومُتُهۡرِكَفَ اتًيۡمَ هِيخِأَ مَحۡلَ لَكُأۡيَ نأَ مۡكُدُحَأَ بُّحِيُأَ ۚ اضًعۡبَ مكُضُعۡبَّ بتَغۡيَ لَاوَ أوُسَّسَجَتَ
مٌيحِرَّ بٌاوَّتَ للَّهَٱ نَّإِ ۚ للَّهَٱ

- *O you who have believed, avoid much [negative] assumption. Indeed, some assumption is sin. And do not spy or backbite each other. Would one of you like to eat the flesh of his brother when dead? You would detest it. And fear Allāh; indeed, Allāh is Accepting of repentance and Merciful.* (Al-Ḥujurāt, 49:12, interpretation of the meaning).

This verse situates confidentiality within broader ethical imperatives of respect, privacy, and communal harmony. It emphasises that uncovering or revealing what others would dislike, especially without consent, is morally condemned. Elsewhere, Allāh commands the fulfilment of trusts:

تِنَٰمَلۡأَٱ اودُّؤَتُ نأَ مۡكُرُمُأۡيَ للَّهَٱ نَّإِ

- *Indeed, Allāh commands you to render trusts to whom they are due…*

(An-Nisā' 4:58, interpretation of the meaning).

This verse forms a foundational principle for confidentiality as trust (*amānah*), including in therapeutic contexts, where clients place their vulnerabilities in the care of professionals.

6.2.2 Prophetic (Sunnah) Foundations

The Prophetic tradition reinforces the sanctity of trust and discretion. Jabir bin Abdullah narrated that the Messenger of Allāh () said: "When a man narrates a narration, then he looks around, then it is a trust" (Tirmidhī). This hadīth directly parallels the therapist's duty to protect disclosures shared in confidence. When clients speak privately within therapy, the ethical duty to keep that information secure aligns with fulfilling a trust ordained by divine guidance. The Prophet () also warned against divulging others' faults and emphasised guarding personal matters. Across numerous authentic narrations preserved in the Ṣaḥīḥ collection, most notably Ṣaḥīḥ Bukhārī and Ṣaḥīḥ Muslim, the betrayal of trusts, including personal confidences and matters affecting one's reputation, is identified as a sign of moral deficiency. Within the Islāmic ethical tradition, the principle remains consistent: disclosing private information without genuine necessity is strongly condemned (Salahi, 2001).

6.2.3 Classical Islāmic Ethical Thought

Islāmic moral philosophy emphasises *satr*, "concealing faults" as an ethical virtue. Concealing another's shortcomings promotes social cohesion and protects individuals from ridicule or harm. In Islāmic jurisprudence and ethics, private sins or struggles are distinguished from public harms; only matters that pose immediate danger to others may justify disclosure. Classical scholars articulate that confidentiality preserves honour (*karāmah*) and community stability (Shaykh Haytham Tamim, 2025). For example, a person's reputation and dignity are considered inviolable (*hurmah*), and exposing private matters without necessity is ethically prohibited. This aligns with therapeutic confidentiality: revealing a client's inner life without consent risks psychological harm, stigmatisation, and fracture of trust (Shaykh Haytham Tamim, 2025).

6.2.4 *Maqāṣid Al-Sharīʿah Perspective*

The objectives of Islāmic law (*Maqāṣid al-Sharīʿah*) include the protection of five essentials: faith, life, intellect, lineage, and property. Protection of honour and personal dignity is part of safeguarding the self and intellect. Confidentiality in mental health care directly supports these objectives by ensuring that private psychological content, which often pertains to thoughts, feelings, and vulnerabilities, is not improperly disclosed, thereby preventing harm to clients and their families (Padela, 2022). Confidentiality is not secrecy for secrecy's sake; rather, it is a preventive ethical responsibility. It assures clients that their personal information will not be misused or exposed, thus preserving psychological safety and social dignity. This aligns Islāmic ethics with modern psychotherapy standards, both prioritising safeguarding individuals from harm and betrayal of trust (Muhsin, 2021).

6.3 Confidentiality in Modern Psychotherapy

6.3.1 *Ethical Codes*

In mainstream psychotherapy, confidentiality is a core ethical mandate. The American Psychological Association (APA), Standard 4.0, outlines that psychologists must safeguard confidential information obtained through any medium and must take precautions to protect such information (APA, 2017). Confidentiality extends to all identifiable client data, including session content, assessments, and written records. Professional codes also require that psychologists inform clients at the start of therapeutic services about the nature and limits of confidentiality, ensuring informed engagement (APA, 2017). Similar principles are upheld in the British Psychological Society (BPS) standards and other allied ethical frameworks, emphasising that confidentiality should only be breached under ethically justified and legally mandated circumstances (BPS, 2021).

6.3.2 Legal and Ethical Limits of Confidentiality

Although confidentiality is vital, it is not absolute. Modern ethical standards recognise exceptions in cases where withholding information would cause significant harm:

- Risk of harm to self or others: Therapists may be ethically required to disclose confidential information to prevent imminent danger (McConville, 2013).
- Abuse and safeguarding obligations: Reporting requirements may compel disclosure to protect children, elders, or vulnerable individuals (Darby & Weinstock, 2018).
- Court-mandated disclosure: Legal orders may necessitate the release of information if certain criteria are met (McConville, 2013).

Such exceptions are designed to balance client privacy with broader ethical duties to prevent harm. Therapists are expected to clarify these limits during the informed consent discussion (Darby & Weinstock, 2018).

Importance for Marginalised and High-Risk Clients

For clients who face stigma or discrimination, strict protection of confidentiality is paramount. Marginalised individuals may be reluctant to seek help if disclosure could lead to social or legal repercussions. Ethical practice requires clinicians to be sensitive to these risks, clearly communicate confidentiality boundaries, and support clients in navigating consent and disclosure choices in culturally respectful ways (Baik, 2022).

6.4 Informed Consent: Islāmic and Clinical Perspectives

6.4.1 Clinical Foundation

Informed consent is a foundational principle in psychotherapy, reflecting respect for client autonomy, transparency, and ethical practice (APA, 2017, Standard 3.10). It involves communicating the nature, goals, risks, benefits, and alternatives of therapy in language the client can understand, enabling clients to make informed choices about participation. Clinically, informed consent is not simply a signed form; it is an ongoing process, revisited as treatment progresses or as new interventions are proposed (Gerke et al., 2022).

Key elements of informed consent include:

- Disclosure: Clients must be provided with sufficient information regarding therapeutic approaches, confidentiality limits, risks, and expected outcomes.
- Comprehension: Clients should understand the information, with clinicians assessing comprehension through dialogue, feedback, or teach-back methods.
- Voluntariness: Consent must be given freely, without coercion or undue influence from family, authority figures, or social pressure.
- Capacity: Clinicians must assess whether the client has the mental capacity to make decisions. For minors or dependent individuals, additional ethical safeguards are required (Eberle et al., 2021).

Informed consent protects clients from coercion, enhances engagement, and ensures that therapy respects individual autonomy and dignity. In multicultural contexts, clear communication of confidentiality and consent fosters trust and prevents misunderstandings that could compromise therapeutic outcomes (Eberle et al., 2021).

6.4.2 *Islāmic Ethical Parallels*

Islāmic ethics offers parallel principles that align closely with modern clinical informed consent.

a) *Ikhtiyār* (Free moral choice): Humans are endowed with free will, accountable for their actions before Allāh. Allāh state in the Qur'ân:

لَآ إِكۡرَاهَ فِي ٱلدِّينِۖ قَد تَّبَيَّنَ ٱلرُّشۡدُ مِنَ ٱلۡغَيِّۚ

- *There shall be no compulsion in [acceptance of] the religion. The right course has become clear from error.* (Al-Baqarah, 2:256, interpretation of the meaning).

This verse highlights that guidance must be chosen freely, emphasising non-coercion, a principle directly translatable to therapeutic consent. Clients must engage voluntarily in therapy, with their choices respected.

b) *Niyyah* (Intention): Islāmic ethics places strong emphasis on the moral significance of intention. Engagement in therapy should therefore be grounded in informed and sincere *niyyah*, ensuring that the client's understanding and participation are aligned with both ethical responsibility and spiritual accountability. Prophetic teachings highlight that actions are judged by intentions. Umar bin Al Khattab (may Allāh be pleased with him) reported the Apostle of Allāh () as saying "Actions are to be judged only by intentions…" (Abū Dāwūd). This reinforces that consent involves conscious and deliberate choice.
c) Accountability before Allāh: Every decision carries spiritual responsibility. Ethical disclosure, truthful explanation, and honouring client autonomy reflect

moral duties beyond secular ethics. Therapists, therefore, act as guardians of trust, ensuring clients' informed choices are respected (Packer, 2011).

d) Prophetic model of non-coercive guidance: The Prophet () consistently employed gradual and compassionate counsel, allowing individuals to embrace change voluntarily. Therapy, approached as a form of guidance rather than compulsion, is consistent with this ethical model, especially when supporting clients navigating familial or cultural pressures.

By integrating *ikhtiyār* and *niyyah* with psychologically informed consent, therapists ensure that clients' rights, autonomy, and moral agency are protected, while enforcing the spiritual dimensions of ethical practice (Packer, 2011).

6.5 Power, Authority, and Consent in the Therapeutic Relationship

Therapeutic relationships, by their very nature, involve an unequal distribution of power and authority between the clinician and the client. This asymmetry arises not only from differences in professional knowledge and therapeutic expertise but also from clients' expectations of guidance, trust, and moral judgement. In secular psychotherapy research, power imbalance has been explicitly identified as a central ethical dimension of the therapeutic encounter because it influences client autonomy, self-determination, and willingness to disclose sensitive personal information. Acknowledging and ethically managing this imbalance is critical to upholding both confidentiality and informed consent across cultural and religious contexts, a point that becomes particularly salient in Muslim therapeutic settings (Boyd, 1996).

6.6 Therapeutic Power Dynamics: Clinical Insights

In the clinical literature, power is recognised as an inherent feature of the therapist-client relationship. Therapists are invested with professional authority and are expected to offer expertise, structure, and direction, while clients often approach therapy from a position of vulnerability or uncertainty. This differential can unintentionally lead clients to defer to clinicians, even when they lack a full understanding of therapeutic processes or consent implications. The findings from a research study indicate that if therapists are unaware of these dynamics, the imbalance may compromise the client's autonomy and interfere with meaningful participation in treatment planning and decision-making (van Mens-Verhulst, 1991). Moreover, implicit power disparities may be reinforced by societal inequalities such as gender, socioeconomic status, education, and culture. When these intersect with therapist authority, they can inadvertently suppress client agency, reducing consent to a superficial assent rather than a genuinely informed choice. A therapeutic ethics review emphasises that clinicians must remain aware of how power is enacted and perceived within therapeutic settings to avoid unintended coercion and to foster genuinely collaborative relationships (Boyd, 1996).

6.7 Cultural and Religious Dimensions of Power in Muslim Contexts

In collectivist and religiously oriented societies, such as many Muslim communities, power asymmetries are further shaped by cultural norms around authority, respect, and social hierarchy. Respect for elders, deference to professionals, and communal decision-making are often deeply embedded in interpersonal relations. In therapy, these cultural frames can influence clients' perceptions of the therapist's role, sometimes conflating professional authority with moral or spiritual authority (Stingl & Bernd Hanewald, 2025). Islāmic medical ethics research highlights that in Muslim contexts, the relational dynamics of care are deeply influenced by norms of respect, social cohesion, and religious values (Chamsi-Pasha, & Albar, 2016). Clients may interpret confidentiality and consent through a lens shaped by familial obligations and community expectations, rather than individual autonomy alone. In some cases, clients may agree to treatment or disclose information not solely based on personal understanding but in deference to the perceived authority of the clinician as an expert or advisor (Chamsi-Pasha & Albar, 2016). This interaction between cultural norms and therapeutic power underlines the necessity of a culturally responsive ethical approach where therapists attend to how power is experienced by Muslim clients. Therapists must not assume that verbal consent alone reflects genuine comprehension and voluntariness; instead, they should engage in iterative consent processes, checking for understanding and encouraging clients to express reservations without fear of judgement or disapproval (Stingl & Bernd Hanewald, 2025).

6.8 Power, Authority, and Islāmic Ethical Principles

Islāmic ethical thought has long engaged with questions of authority, autonomy, and moral responsibility, domains that intersect directly with contemporary concerns about power in psychotherapy. At its core, Islāmic ethics emphasises that moral agency (*ikhtiyār*) is a divine trust; humans are responsible for their choices and actions before Allāh, and no individual, regardless of status, should wield authority in a way that undermines another's moral agency. In this sense, the principle of free moral choice in Islām parallels the ethical requirement for voluntary and informed consent in clinical practice (Fazal, 2025).

Clinical respect for autonomy is not antithetical to Islām; rather, Islāmic bioethics reframes autonomy within a broader framework of relational obligations and spiritual accountability. Scholars note that informed consent should not be reduced to procedural formality; it must embody genuine understanding and voluntary acceptance, consistent with religious norms that prohibit coercion and encourage moral agency (*ikhtiyār*). This framing aligns with broader Islāmic bioethical writings emphasising patient dignity and the importance of respecting individual decision-making capacity within a morally accountable framework (Rathor et al., 2011). Furthermore, Islāmic medical ethical scholarship underlines that those therapeutic relationships, like all human relationships, must be grounded in *adab* (ethical conduct) and *ihsan* (excellence in moral action). Early Islāmic texts on ethical medical conduct, such as *Adab al-Tabib* [Isḥāq ibn ʿAlī al-Ruhāwī], elaborate on the physician's duty to maintain confidentiality, act with integrity, and avoid imposing authority in a manner that harms the patient's dignity or autonomy. These historical frameworks dovetail with modern concerns about the ethical use of power in therapy and the imperatives of informed consent and confidentiality (Fazal, 2025).

6.9 Practical Ethical Implications for Therapy

In light of the intersections of power, culture, and religion, therapists working with Muslim clients should employ approaches that minimise coercive influence and strengthen informed consent. Specific ethical strategies include:

- Iterative consent processes: Consent should be revisited regularly, not assumed once at intake, especially when discussing sensitive topics, changes in treatment plans, or limits of confidentiality. This protects against assent that is motivated by deference rather than understanding, a risk amplified in cultures of authority (AIMS, 2025).
- Explicit discussion of roles: Therapists should clarify that their role is not reflective of spiritual authority or moral judgement but is grounded in professional support for psychological well-being. This reduces the likelihood that clients feel morally obliged to comply rather than choose freely (Rothman & Coyle, 2018).
- Cultural and religious sensitivity: Clinicians should be familiar with relevant Islāmic ethical values regarding autonomy, trust, and dignity. This enables explanations of confidentiality and consent in language that honours the client's moral worldview, reducing perceived power distance (AIMS, 2025).
- Encouraging active participation: Therapists should routinely invite clients to ask questions, express disagreement, and articulate their preferences in ways that affirm agency rather than compliance (AIMS, 2025).
- Supervision and reflection: Clinicians must engage in regular supervision and self-reflection to recognise how their own cultural assumptions, professional authority, and interpersonal style may inadvertently exercise power over clients (Rothman & Coyle, 2018).

6.10 Integrating Power Awareness into Ethical Frameworks

Ethical frameworks that integrate power dynamics do not reject therapist authority; instead, they emphasise its responsible use in ways that promote client agency, dignity, and moral responsibility. Modern psychotherapy ethics recognises that balanced power dynamics contribute to trust, rapport, and client empowerment, essential conditions for effective therapeutic work (van Mens-Verhulst, 1991). In Muslim therapeutic contexts, this integration involves harmonising professional ethical standards with Islāmic ethical values that affirm human dignity, moral agency, and the responsibility of both parties to uphold trust *(amānah)*. By addressing power explicitly, therapists can create environments where confidentiality and consent are genuinely meaningful, not merely formal requirements, but lived ethical commitments that reflect both clinical excellence and Islāmic moral coherence (Rathor et al., 2011).

6.11 Ethical Dilemmas in a Muslim Context

Therapists working with Muslim clients may encounter specific dilemmas arising from cultural and religious norms:

6.11.1 Family Involvement vs. Client Autonomy

In collectivist Muslim societies, families often assume decision-making authority, sometimes overriding individual preference. A client may wish to explore sensitive issues (e.g., marital conflict, trauma, gender identity) in therapy, while family members demand disclosure. This creates tension between respecting client autonomy and accommodating legitimate family concerns (Fazal, 2025). Clinical strategies include:

- Negotiating boundaries for disclosure.
- Explaining confidentiality and its limits.
- Facilitating family involvement only when consented to by the client.

From an Islāmic perspective, the Qur'ân (Surah Al-Ḥujurāt 49:12) and Prophetic teachings caution against violating privacy. While family guidance is valued, ethical breaches that harm the client or violate amānah are impermissible (Muhsin, 2021).

6.11.2 Pressure to Disclose to Relatives or Religious Authorities

Religious or community leaders may request client information, believing it serves spiritual or moral guidance. Therapists must weigh the duty of confidentiality against communal expectations (Fazal, 2025).

- Clinical principle: Protect client privacy, educate stakeholders about therapy ethics, and document consent if disclosure occurs (Ricou et al., 2023).
- Islāmic principle: *Amānah* and *satr* forbid exposing private matters unless necessary to prevent harm (Abū Dawūd, Ibn Majah).
- Ethical implication: Private disclosures are morally binding and must not be shared without valid justification. *Satr*, that is concealing others' faults and private matters. It was narrated that Abu Hurairah that the Messenger of Allāh () said "whoever conceals (the faults of) a Muslim, Allāh will conceal him (his faults) in this world and the Day of Resurrection…" (Ibn Majah).

6.11.3 Community-Based Therapy Settings

Group or community-based interventions may inadvertently expose participants' identities or struggles. Therapists should establish confidentiality agreements, orient participants to privacy rules, and monitor adherence.

- Clinical guidance: Pre-session consent, anonymisation, and careful facilitation (Ricou et al., 2023).
- Islāmic guidance: Maintaining honour and dignity (*karāmah*) remains paramount; public shaming or involuntary disclosure violates ethical and spiritual mandates (Muhsin, 2021).

6.11.4 Confidentiality with Minors and Dependents

Working with children or dependent adults adds complexity. Parents or guardians may demand access to session content. Clinicians must balance:

- Child's or dependent's autonomy.
- Guardian rights and responsibilities.
- Legal requirements and ethical standards (Fazal, 2025).

Islāmically, protecting the dignity and well-being of minors aligns with *ḥifẓ al-nafs* and *ḥifẓ al- 'aql* (protection of life and intellect). Disclosures must prioritise harm prevention while safeguarding trust (Muhsin, 2021).

Table 6.1 Integration of core psychotherapy ethics with Islāmic ethical principles

Clinical Principles	Islāmic Values	Applications
Confidentiality	*Amānah* (Trust)	Protect client disclosures; uphold trust
Informed Consent	*Ikhtiyār* (Free Will / Choice)	Respect client autonomy; ensure voluntary participation
Transparency	*Ṣidq* (Truthfulness)	Honest communication; clarify therapy goals, risks, and limits
Harm Prevention	*Lā Ḍarar wa lā Ḍirār* (No harm nor reciprocating harm)	Ethical disclosure only when necessary to prevent greater harm

6.12 Integrative Ethical Framework

An integrated approach that aligns clinical ethics with Islāmic moral principles to guide decision-making is presented in Table 6.1.

This table illustrates the alignment between foundational ethical principles in psychotherapy and corresponding Islāmic moral values. Concepts such as *amānah* (trust), *ikhtiyār* (free will), *ṣidq* (truthfulness), and the legal-ethical maxim *lā ḍarar wa lā ḍirār* (no harm nor reciprocating harm) provide a coherent moral framework that complements contemporary clinical ethics. Together, they emphasise respect for client autonomy, the safeguarding of confidentiality, honesty in therapeutic relationships, and the ethical obligation to prevent harm. This integrated approach highlights how Islāmic ethical teachings can meaningfully inform and reinforce professional standards in mental health practice.

Clinical Application:

- Therapists use the framework to navigate complex scenarios: family pressure, cultural obligations, community expectations, and legal mandates.
- It provides a decision-making hierarchy: protect trust (*amānah*), respect autonomy (*ikhtiyār*), ensure honesty (*ṣidq*), and prevent harm (*la ḍarar*) (Ricou et al., 2023).

Islāmic Ethical Alignment:

- Qur'ân and Sunnah provide foundational principles for these decisions.
- Ethical frameworks such as *Maqāṣid al-Sharīʻah* reinforce the protection of dignity, life, intellect, and social welfare (Malik, 2020).

6.13 Case Vignettes

Ethical principles such as confidentiality and informed consent acquire their full significance when examined through real-world clinical failures and ethical dilemmas. While theoretical discussions establish normative standards, documented cases demonstrate the profound psychological, social, and moral consequences that arise when trust is violated or ethically strained. In Muslim contexts, where stigma, honour, and communal identity often intensify the impact of disclosure, the repercussions of ethical failure can be particularly severe (AIMS, 2025). The following real cases illustrate how breaches of confidentiality and ethically justified disclosures have occurred in practice, and how these situations can be evaluated through both professional clinical ethics and Islāmic moral principles.

6.13.1 Case 1: The Vastaamo Psychotherapy Data Breach (Finland)

What Happened: Between 2018 and 2020, Vastaamo, one of Finland's largest private psychotherapy providers, experienced a massive cybersecurity breach that resulted in the theft of confidential psychotherapy records belonging to approximately 33,000 clients. The compromised data included names, personal identification numbers, contact information, diagnostic details, and, most critically, detailed psychotherapy session notes documenting trauma histories, abuse experiences, and intimate psychological struggles (Tanner, 2024). After gaining access to the database, the perpetrator attempted to extort the clinic. When this effort failed, the hacker began contacting patients directly, sending emails demanding payment in cryptocurrency in exchange for withholding publication of their therapy notes. When many clients refused or were unable to pay, portions of the stolen therapy data were released online. Victims described the experience as profoundly distressing, with many reporting panic, shame, re-traumatisation, and fear of social exposure. Some individuals required additional mental health support as a direct result of the breach. The perpetrator was eventually identified, prosecuted, and sentenced to imprisonment for aggravated extortion and data breach offenses. However, for many victims, the psychological and reputational harm was irreversible (Tanner, 2024).

Clinical Ethical Perspective

From a clinical ethics standpoint, the Vastaamo breach represents a systemic failure to uphold the most fundamental ethical obligation in psychotherapy: the protection of confidentiality. Professional ethical codes emphasise that psychotherapy records require the highest level of protection due to their sensitivity. Although the breach occurred through cyber intrusion rather than direct clinician misconduct, the ethical responsibility of institutions to ensure secure storage and access controls remains paramount (Ricou et al., 2023). The consequences of this failure were not merely administrative or legal; they directly undermined the therapeutic process. Psychotherapy depends on the assumption that disclosures will remain private. Once that assumption collapses, clients may withdraw from treatment, withhold information, or avoid seeking help altogether. The breach thus damaged not only individual clients but also public trust in mental health services.

Islāmic Ethical Perspective

From an Islāmic ethical perspective, this case constitutes a serious violation of *amānah* (trust). Clients entrusted their most vulnerable experiences to therapists under an implicit moral contract of protection. The Qur'ân commands believers to fulfil trusts faithfully (An-Nisā' 4:58), and the Prophet Muhammad () explicitly taught that private speech entrusted to another is an *amānah* that must not be betrayed (Abū Dāwūd). The public exposure of therapy records violates the Islāmic obligation of *satr*, concealing the private struggles of others, and directly undermines *karāmahal-insān* (human dignity). In Islāmic moral reasoning, exposing what a person would be humiliated by is considered a grave ethical wrong, regardless of whether the exposure occurs intentionally or through negligence. Particularly in honour-based cultures, such exposure may result in social isolation, marital consequences, or familial conflict, magnifying harm beyond the individual (Malik, 2020). Ethical Implication: This case illustrates that confidentiality in psychotherapy is not merely a professional duty but a moral and spiritual trust. Failure to safeguard it constitutes ethical betrayal (*khiyānah*), even in the absence of malicious intent.

6.13.2 Case 2: Digital Therapy Records Exposure—Confidant Health (United States)

What Happened: In 2021, a security researcher discovered that Confidant Health, a U.S.-based digital mental health platform, had left a large database publicly accessible without authentication. The exposed data included more than 120,000 files containing therapy intake forms, clinical notes, and personal health information, as well as over 1.7 million activity logs detailing user engagement with mental health services. Although there was no confirmed evidence that the data were actively exploited, the exposure remained accessible for a period of time, placing clients at risk of identity exposure and confidentiality violations. The incident was publicly reported by Wired, prompting widespread concern about privacy practices in tele-mental health services (Newman, 2021).

Clinical Ethical Perspective

This case highlights the ethical challenges associated with the rapid expansion of digital and tele-mental health platforms. Ethical guidelines clearly state that confidentiality obligations apply equally to electronic records and digital communication. Failure to secure databases, even unintentionally, constitutes an ethical lapse with potential clinical consequences. Clients who engage in digital therapy often assume that technological safeguards are in place. When such safeguards fail, trust is eroded, and clients may become reluctant to disclose sensitive information. This is particularly problematic for marginalised populations who already face stigma and fear of surveillance (Ricou et al., 2023).

Islāmic Ethical Perspective and Implication

Islāmic psychoethics does not differentiate between physical and digital breaches of trust. Information entrusted through any medium remains an *amānah*. Negligent exposure of confidential data contradicts Qur'ânic commands to protect entrusted responsibilities (An-Nisā' 4:58) and violates the Prophetic emphasis on guarding private matters. Moreover, Islāmic moral reasoning emphasises prevention of harm (*la ḍarar*). Ethical responsibility includes taking reasonable preventive measures to avoid foreseeable harm. Failure to implement basic security protections, therefore, represents a breach of moral accountability, even in the absence of malicious intent (Malik, 2020). As psychotherapy increasingly relies on digital platforms, ethical accountability expands to include technological competence and preventive safeguards as integral components of confidentiality.

6.13.3 *Case 3: Tarasoff V. Regents of the University of California (United States)*

What Happened: The landmark legal case Tarasoff v. Regents of the University of California (1976) arose when a university student disclosed to his therapist a credible intention to kill a specific individual. The therapist notified campus police, who briefly detained the client but released him. The intended victim was not warned and was later killed. The California Supreme Court ruled that mental health professionals have a duty to take reasonable steps to protect identifiable individuals when a client poses a serious and imminent threat, even if doing so requires breaching confidentiality (Laves, 1979).

Clinical and Islāmic Ethical Perspective

This case established that confidentiality in psychotherapy is not absolute. Ethical and legal standards recognise that preventing imminent harm to others may ethically justify limited disclosure. However, such disclosure must be carefully constrained, proportionate, and clearly documented. The Tarasoff ruling continues to shape ethical decision-making in clinical practice worldwide (Ricou et al., 2023).

Islāmic ethics similarly prioritise the preservation of life (*ḥifẓ al-nafs*). The Prophetic principle "*lā ḍarar wa lā ḍirār*" (no harm and no reciprocating harm) provides moral justification for breaching confidentiality when it is necessary to prevent serious harm. In this framework, disclosure is not a betrayal of trust but a morally justified intervention aimed at preventing greater injustice (Malik, 2020). Both Islāmic ethics and clinical standards converge in affirming that confidentiality may be ethically breached only under conditions of clear, serious harm, never for convenience, social pressure, or moral policing.

6.13.4 Case 4-Confidentiality and Familial Pressure in a Collectivist Context

Dwairy (2006) documents a clinical case involving a young Muslim woman in a Middle Eastern context who presented with depressive symptoms, emotional withdrawal, and somatic complaints. Her distress was closely linked to sustained familial pressure to enter an arranged marriage she did not emotionally accept. While the family framed their involvement as religiously and culturally appropriate, the client experienced the pressure as psychologically overwhelming and reported feelings of entrapment, guilt, and fear of social rupture. As therapy progressed, family members approached the therapist directly, requesting information about the client's disclosures and emotional state. They justified their request on moral and religious grounds, asserting that family authority and collective welfare entitled them to insight into the therapeutic process. This placed the therapist at the intersection of professional confidentiality, cultural expectations, and perceived religious obligation (Dwairy, 2006).

The therapist explicitly refused to disclose confidential information, grounding this decision in professional ethical standards while carefully refraining from confidentiality not as defiance of family values, but as a protective measure essential for psychological healing. Importantly, the therapist avoided adversarial framing, instead emphasising respect for the family's concern while maintaining clear ethical boundaries (Dwairy, 2006). Therapeutic work focused on emotional regulation, expression of ambivalence, and strengthening the client's internal coping resources rather than directing behavioural outcomes related to marriage. Over time, the client's depressive symptoms reduced, and she reported improved emotional clarity and self-efficacy, even though the external family conflict remained unresolved (Dwairy, 2006).

Dwairy highlights this case as illustrative of how confidentiality, often perceived as culturally "Western," can be ethically and clinically justified within Muslim contexts when framed as *amānah* (trust) and protection from harm. The case demonstrates that maintaining confidentiality does not undermine communal values; rather, it can preserve relational stability by preventing premature confrontation and psychological collapse.

6.14 Synthesis and Relevance for Muslim Therapeutic Contexts

These real-world cases demonstrate that breaches of confidentiality, whether through negligence, technological failure, or ethically mandated disclosure, carry profound psychological and moral consequences. In Muslim contexts, where social stigma and honour norms intensify the impact of disclosure, the ethical responsibility to safeguard trust becomes even more critical. Islāmic ethics and professional psychotherapy converge in their emphasis on confidentiality as a sacred trust, informed consent as moral agency, and disclosure only as a last resort to prevent serious harm. Together, these cases reinforce the necessity of culturally sensitive, ethically vigilant practice that protects both psychological well-being and spiritual dignity (AIMS, 2025).

6.15 Therapist Self-Awareness and Boundaries

Ethical practice in Muslim contexts requires therapists to cultivate self-awareness and establish professional boundaries.

1. **Avoiding Moral Surveillance**
   - The therapists must avoid assuming a moral policing role (AIMS, 2025).
   - The clinical focus is on supporting client growth and autonomy, rather than enforcing cultural, religious, or familial norms (Ricou et al., 2023).
   - Self-reflection, supervision, and adherence to ethical codes help prevent boundary violations (Corey, Corey, & Callanan, 2019).
2. **Recognising Cultural Guilt Responses**
   - Many Muslim clients internalise guilt related to perceived religious or social failure (AIMS, 2025).
   - Therapists should differentiate between pathological guilt and culturally normative religious reflection (Corey, Corey, & Callanan, 2019).
   - Providing psychoeducation and normalising experiences within an Islāmic ethical framework reduces distress and reinforces trust (Ricou et al., 2023).
3. Ethical Documentation and Digital Confidentiality
   - Accurate record-keeping is essential, but it must also safeguard confidentiality.
   - Electronic health records should have restricted access, password protection, and secure storage (AIMS, 2025).
   - Clinicians should avoid sharing identifiable client information via unsecured channels (Corey, Corey, & Callanan, 2019).
   - Islāmic ethical alignment: documentation should honour *amānah*, ensuring entrusted information is neither exposed nor misused (AIMS, 2025).

6.16 Conclusion

Confidentiality and informed consent occupy a central position in ethical psychotherapy, serving as safeguards for trust, dignity, and client autonomy. Within the Islāmic ethical framework, these principles are not external professional impositions but are intrinsically tied to foundational moral values such as *amānah* (trust), *karāmah al-insān* (human dignity), and moral accountability before Allāh. Qur'ânic injunctions against intrusion and the Prophetic emphasis on safeguarding entrusted speech establish confidentiality as a spiritual responsibility, while Islāmic concepts of *ikhtiyār* (free moral choice) and *niyyah* (intentionality) reinforce the ethical necessity of informed, voluntary consent.

In Muslim cultural contexts, Islāmic psychotherapists often navigate complex dynamics involving family involvement, communal expectations, and religious authority. This chapter demonstrates that ethical practice requires neither uncritical accommodation of cultural norms nor rigid application of secular standards, but rather an integrative approach grounded in both Islāmic moral reasoning and professional clinical ethics. By aligning confidentiality with *amānah*, informed consent with *ikhtiyā*r, transparency with *ṣidq*, and ethical disclosure with the principle of *la ḍarar* (no harm), therapists can respond to ethical dilemmas with clarity and integrity. Ultimately, confidentiality and informed consent function not only as clinical safeguards but as acts of ethical worship, reinforcing trust, protecting the vulnerable, and ensuring that psychotherapy within Islāmic contexts remains both professionally sound and spiritually coherent.

References

Abū Dāwūd. *Sunan Abi Dāwūd 2201*. In-book reference: Book 13, Hadith 27. English translation: Book 12, Hadith 2195. Sahih (Al-Albani).https://sunnah.com/abudawud:2201

AIMS. (2025). *Ethical Standards*. Aimsonline.org. https://www.aimsonline.org/ethical-standards \

American Psychological Association. (2017). *Ethical principles of psychologists and code of conduct*. American Psychological Association. https://www.apa.org/ethics/code/ethics-code-2017.pdf

Baik, S. W. (2022). Therapists owe marginalized clients more than empathy. *Asparagus Magazine*. https://www.asparagusmagazine.com/articles/therapists-owe-solidarity-to-marginalized-clients-who-face-racism-oppression-and-violence

BPS. (2021). *Code of ethics and conduct*. Explore.bps.org.uk; British Psychological Society. https://explore.bps.org.uk/content/report-guideline/bpsrep.2021.inf94

Boyd, K. K. (1996). Power imbalances and therapy. *Focus (San Francisco, Calif.), 11*(9), 1–4. https://pubmed.ncbi.nlm.nih.gov/11363821/

Chamsi-Pasha, H., & Albar, M. (2016). Doctor-patient relationship. Islāmic perspective. *Saudi Medical Journal, 37*(2), 121–126. https://doi.org/10.15537/smj.2016.2.13602

Chu, T. (2024). *The impact of individualism and collectivism on psychotherapy: Is therapy in North America individualistic? Exploring the infusion of collectivism into therapy practices (Master's capstone)*. National University System. https://repository.nusystem.org/server/api/core/bitstreams/82b399f3-3633-4b09-a600-1c1bd52741b5/content

Corey, G., Corey, M. S., & Callanan, P. (2019). *Issues and ethics in the helping professions* (10th ed.). Cengage Learning. https://faculty.cengage.com/works/9780357670552

Darby, W. C., & Weinstock, R. (2018). The limits of confidentiality: Informed consent and psychotherapy. *Focus, 16*(4), 395–401. https://doi.org/10.1176/appi.focus.20180020

Dwairy, M. (2006). *Counseling and psychotherapy with Arabs and Muslims: A culturally sensitive approach.* Arab Psychological Services. http://arabpsynet.com/Books/Dwairy.B1.pdf

Eberle, K., grosse Holtforth, M., Inderbinen, M., Gaab, J., Nestoriuc, Y., & Trachsel, M. (2021). Informed consent in psychotherapy: A survey on attitudes among psychotherapists in Switzerland. *BMC Medical Ethics, 22*(1). https://doi.org/10.1186/s12910-021-00718-z

Ernstmeyer, K., & Christman, E. (2025, November). *Legal and ethical considerations in mental health care.* Nih.gov; Chippewa Valley Technical College. https://www.ncbi.nlm.nih.gov/books/NBK616992/

Fazal, I. (2025, August 30). Islāmic Medical Ethics: A legacy of compassionate care. *Journal of the British Islāmic Medical Association.* https://jbima.com/article/Islāmic-medical-ethics-a-legacy-of-compassionate-care/

Gerke, L., Meyrose, A., & Nestoriuc, Y. (2022). Informed consent for psychotherapy: Ethical illusion or clinical reality? A survey about psychotherapists' attitudes and practices in Germany. *Clinical Psychology & Psychotherapy, 30(*1). https://doi.org/10.1002/cpp.2790

Ibn Majah. *Sunan Ibn Majah 225*: Introduction, Hadith 0. English translation: Vol. 1, Book 1, Hadith 225. Sahih (Darussalam). https://sunnah.com/ibnmajah:225

Laves, R. (1979). Tarasoff Vs The Regents of The University of California et al—The Mental Health Worker as Expert in the Prediction of Violent Behavior. *Office of Justice Programs.* www.ojp.gov. https://www.ojp.gov/ncjrs/virtual-library/abstracts/tarasoff-vs-regents-university-california-et-al-mental-health

Malik, R. (2020, January 14). Islāmic ethics and psychology. *Research Center for Islāmic Legislation and Ethics* (CILE). https://www.cilecenter.org/research-publications/op-ed/Islāmic-ethics-and-psychology

McConville, T. (2013). The ethics of confidentiality and its limits. *Counselling in Scotland,* Autumn 2013. COSCA. https://www.cosca.org.uk/application/files/1115/2119/7619/The_Ethics_of_Confidentiality__its_Limiits_CIS_Autumn_201311-10-17.pdf

Muhsin, S. M. (2021). Medical confidentiality ethics: The genesis of an Islāmic Juristic perspective. *Journal of Religion and Health, 61*(4), 1–14. https://doi.org/10.1007/s10943-021-01313-7

Newman, L. H. (2021). *Therapy records were exposed in an unsecured database.* Wired. https://www.wired.com/story/confidant-health-therapy-records-database-exposure/

Padela, A. (2022). Maqāṣidī models for an "Islāmic" medical ethics: Problem-solving or confusing at the bedside? *American Journal of Islam and Society, 39*(1–2), 72–114. https://doi.org/10.35632/ajis.v39i1-2.3069

Packer, S. (2011). Informed consent with a focus on Islāmic views. *The Journal of IMA, 43*(3), 215–218. https://doi.org/10.5915/43-3-9040

Rathor, M. Y., Abdul Rani, M. F., Shah Bin Mohamad Shah, A., Bin Leman, W. I., Akter, S. F. U., & Bin Omar, A. M. (2011). The principle of autonomy as related to personal decision making concerning health and research from an 'Islāmic viewpoint'. *Journal of the Islāmic Medical Association of North America, 43*(1). https://doi.org/10.5915/43-1-6396

Ricou, M., Neto, D. D., Silva, A. N., & Marina, S. (2023). Ethical principles in psychotherapy within a broad psychological and medical deontological framework: An international comparison. *Quaderns de Psicologia, 25*(2), e1867. researchportal.ulisboa.pt

Rothman, A., & Coyle, A. (2018). Toward a framework for Islāmic psychology and psychotherapy: An Islāmic Model of the soul. *Journal of Religion and Health, 57*(5), 1731–1744. https://doi.org/10.1007/s10943-018-0651-x

Salahi, A. (2001). Guidance from the Prophet: Keeping people's faults secret. *Arab News.* https://www.arabnews.com/node/215762

Shaykh Haytham Tamim. (2025, April 24). Major Principles of Islam: Conceal the faults of others—Utrujj. *Utrujj.* https://www.utrujj.org/major-principles-of-islam-conceal-the-faults-of-others/

Stingl, M., & Hanewald, B. (2025). Culturally sensitive psychotherapy—Technique or attitude? *Frontiers in Psychology, 16.* https://doi.org/10.3389/fpsyg.2025.1599855

Tanner, J. (2024, April 30). A Finnish hacker was imprisoned for accessing thousands of psychotherapy records and demanding ransoms. *AP News.* https://apnews.com/article/finland-court-hacking-ransom-psychotherapy-center-b03183e5ca66a768d743f7e84b368829

Tirmidhī. *Jami` at- Tirmidhī 1959.* In-book reference: Book 27, Hadith 65. English translation: Vol. 4, Book 1, Hadith 1959. Hasan (Darussalam). https://sunnah.com/tirmidhi:1959

Van Mens-Verhulst, J. (1991). Perspective of power in therapeutic relationships. *American Journal of Psychotherapy, 45*(2), 198–210. https://doi.org/10.1176/appi.psychotherapy.1991.45.2.198

Chapter 7
Balancing Autonomy, Individual Rights, and Community Values in Islāmic Psychotherapy

Saima Khan

7.1 Introduction

Human psychological experience does not develop in isolation. Thoughts, emotions, values, and behaviours are shaped through continuous interaction with family systems, cultural norms, moral frameworks, and social expectations. Across societies, individuals learn who they are and how they ought to live through relationships with others, while simultaneously negotiating personal desires, internal conflicts, and aspirations for self-determination (Sadownik, 2023). Mental health concerns often emerge precisely at the intersection of these forces, where personal needs encounter relational obligations and moral expectations. Psychotherapy, as a space for reflection and healing, is therefore inevitably influenced by broader ethical questions concerning the self, responsibility, and belonging (Vyskocilová & Prasko, 2013). Modern psychological practice has largely evolved within sociocultural contexts that prioritise individualism. As a result, core ethical principles such as autonomy, self-determination, privacy, and individual rights occupy a central position in clinical theory and practice (Markus & Kitayama, 1991). Psychological well-being is frequently conceptualised as the individual's ability to make independent choices, establish personal boundaries, and pursue self-defined goals. While this framework has proven effective in many contexts, it does not always seamlessly translate across cultures in which identity is relationally embedded and moral life is understood as a collective endeavour (Sue & Sue, 2016). In such settings, distress is often not experienced solely as an internal psychological phenomenon but as a rupture in relational harmony, moral coherence, or social belonging (Dwairy, 2006).

Dr. Saima Khan (Bath Spa University Academic Centre Ras Al Khaimah, Ras Al Khaimah, United Arab Emirates) is the sole author of this chapter. Editorial review and substantive editing were conducted by Professor Dr. G.Hussein Rassool.

G. H. Rassool, *Ethical Dilemmas in Islāmic Psychotherapy*,
https://doi.org/10.1007/978-3-032-26515-9_7

Islāmic societies and Muslim communities, whether in majority or minority contexts, commonly reflect collectivist orientations in which family, community, and moral accountability play a significant role in shaping individual identity (Dwairy, 2006). Within these contexts, personal choices are frequently understood to carry relational and communal consequences. Decisions regarding marriage, education, career, religious practice, and lifestyle are rarely viewed as purely individual matters but are instead situated within networks of obligation, care, and moral responsibility. Consequently, psychological distress may arise not only from intrapsychic conflict but from tensions between personal autonomy, perceived religious duties, and communal expectations. Islāmic moral thought provides a comprehensive ethical framework that addresses these tensions by affirming both individual agency and collective responsibility. The Qur'ân consistently acknowledges human choice and accountability while situating moral life within a broader social and spiritual order (Al-Kahf 18:29; Al-Baqarah 2:256). Individuals are recognised as morally responsible agents endowed with intellect and volition, yet they are simultaneously described as members of families and communities bound by ethical duties toward others. Concepts such as *amānah* (trust), *'adl* (justice), *raḥmah* (mercy), and *maṣlaḥah* (public interest) reflect an ethical vision in which personal conduct and communal well-being are deeply interconnected (Kamali, 2008).

Within the context of psychotherapy, this ethical worldview raises important clinical questions.

- How can therapists respect client autonomy while remaining sensitive to family and community values that are central to the client's identity?
- How should individual rights such as confidentiality and informed consent be upheld in collectivist environments where shared decision-making is normative?
- What ethical stance should therapists adopt when clients' choices conflict with religious teachings or communal expectations?

These questions are not merely theoretical; they arise regularly in clinical practice and require thoughtful, principled responses (APA, 2017). Islāmic psychotherapy has emerged as a growing field seeking to integrate established psychological knowledge with Islāmic ethical and spiritual principles. Rather than offering a separate or alternative psychology, Islāmic psychotherapy seeks to contextualise therapeutic practice within an Islāmic worldview, integrating psychological methods with spiritual, moral, and cultural values grounded in the Qur'ân and *Sunnah* (Rassool, 2025). This integration does not reject contemporary clinical ethics but engages them critically, recognising both their strengths and their limitations when applied across diverse cultural settings. Central to this endeavour is the need to balance autonomy, individual rights, and community values in a manner that preserves psychological safety, ethical integrity, and cultural relevance.

Autonomy, within this framework, cannot be understood solely as unrestricted individual freedom. From an Islāmic perspective, autonomy is meaningful when exercised with awareness of moral accountability and relational impact (Kamali,

2008). At the same time, Islāmic ethics strongly affirms human dignity and rejects coercion, compulsion, and unjust control over personal conscience (Al-Baqarah 2:256; Al-Isrā' 17:70). Similarly, individual rights such as privacy, confidentiality, and protection from harm are deeply rooted in Islāmic legal and moral traditions, often articulated through the language of trust and inviolability. These principles closely parallel professional psychological ethics, providing a strong foundation for ethical therapeutic practice (APA, 2017). Community values, however, introduce complexity. While communal responsibility is central to Islāmic moral life, it can become ethically problematic when invoked to justify intrusion, shame, or psychological harm. In therapeutic settings, uncritical prioritisation of community norms risks silencing individual suffering and transforming therapy into a tool of social regulation (Dwairy, 2006). Islāmic psychotherapy must therefore navigate a delicate ethical terrain, honour the importance of family and community while resist practices that undermine individual dignity or mental health.

Balancing these dimensions requires more than cultural sensitivity; it demands ethical clarity and humility. Therapists must be able to distinguish between supporting a client's moral reflection and imposing moral outcomes, between acknowledging communal values and enforcing conformity, and between respecting religious teachings and maintaining professional boundaries (Sue & Sue, 2016). This balance is particularly challenging for Muslim therapists who may share the client's faith and experience internal moral tensions when professional obligations appear to conflict with personal beliefs. The ethical task of Islāmic psychotherapy, therefore, is not to resolve these tensions by privileging one domain over another but to hold them in constructive dialogue. Such an approach recognises that psychological well-being, moral integrity, and relational harmony are not mutually exclusive goals. Instead, they can be pursued together through ethically grounded, reflective, and client-centred practice (Vyskocilová & Prasko, 2013).

This chapter examines the ethical challenge of balancing autonomy, individual rights, and community values within Islāmic psychotherapy. It explores how these principles are conceptualised within contemporary clinical ethics and Islāmic moral thought, highlighting areas of convergence and tension. The chapter analyses common ethical dilemmas encountered in therapeutic practice, proposes a balanced Islāmic therapeutic model, and outlines integrative frameworks and strategies for ethical clinical work. Through documented case reflections and discussion of therapist positionality, the chapter aims to offer a nuanced, ethically grounded approach to psychotherapy that is responsive to both professional standards and Islāmic ethical commitments.

7.2 Autonomy

Autonomy is a foundational concept in ethical thinking about persons and agency, referring broadly to an individual's capacity to self-govern, the ability to deliberate, make choices, and act in accordance with one's own reasons and values

(Motloba, 2018). In general ethical theory, autonomy is rooted in the idea that persons are moral agents with intrinsic worth, capable of exercising judgement and shaping the course of their lives. This conceptualisation appears in philosophical discussions of moral agency and human dignity, where autonomy is not merely freedom from external constraint but the capacity for reflective self-determination, a capability that sustains moral responsibility and personal integrity. In research ethics, for example, "respect for persons" encompasses the right to exercise autonomy and protects vulnerable individuals who may have diminished capacity to do so (Motloba, 2018).

In contemporary clinical psychology, this ethical commitment to autonomy translates into practices such as informed consent, collaborative treatment planning, transparency about therapeutic options, and shared decision-making (APA, 2017). Clients are viewed as active partners whose choices should guide the therapeutic process rather than as passive recipients of expert direction. This emphasis reflects empirical findings showing that when clients perceive their choices as genuinely self-endorsed rather than imposed, they engage more deeply in therapy and achieve more durable change (Güleç, 2024). Central to these practices is the avoidance of coercion, manipulation, or undue influence that might compromise the authenticity of client choices. In the context of mental health care, honouring autonomy also means recognising the impact of cognitive, emotional, and relational factors on decision-making capacity, requiring clinicians to support clients' understanding without overriding their preferences (Ryan et al., 2021).

Islāmic ethical thought affirms human agency as moral trust (*amānah*) entrusted by God, embedding human choice within a framework of dignity, accountability, and ethical responsibility. Human beings are recognised as capable of meaningful choice (*ikhtiyār*), yet this capacity is never morally neutral. Rather, autonomy acquires its ethical significance through conscious awareness of moral consequence, spiritual purpose, and responsibility toward both God and society (Kamali, 2008). The Qur'ân explicitly acknowledges the reality of choice and moral responsibility, stating:

وَقُلِ ٱلْحَقُّ مِن رَّبِّكُمْ ۖ فَمَن شَآءَ فَلْيُؤْمِن وَمَن شَآءَ فَلْيَكْفُرْ ۚ

- *And say, 'The truth is from your Lord, so whoever wills—let him believe; and whoever wills—let him disbelieve.'*"(Al-Kahf 18:29, interpretation of the meaning).

At the same time, it establishes the foundational principle of non-coercion in matters of faith:

لَآ إِكْرَاهَ فِى ٱلدِّينِ ۖ

- *There is no compulsion in religion* (Al-Baqarah, 2:256, interpretation of the meaning).

Together, these verses emphasise choice, accountability, and dignity in belief and ethical decision-making. They also affirm voluntary moral agency while rejecting forced belief or imposed conscience. Within this framework, autonomy is neither denied nor absolutised Thinkers such as Imām al-Ghazālī emphasised that human choice attains moral legitimacy only when exercised with awareness of spiritual accountability and ethical restraint (Al-Ghazālī, 1964; Griffel, 2009). Unrestricted freedom, detached from moral purpose, was understood as a potential source of psychological imbalance and spiritual harm rather than human flourishing. Consequently, Islāmic jurisprudence conceptualises agency not as an unconditional entitlement but as a trust for which individuals are answerable, particularly in relation to the social and moral consequences of their actions. As Kamali (2008) notes, personal freedom in Islāmic ethics is always situated within a broader concern for justice, social harmony, and collective well-being.

This ethical orientation distinguishes Islāmic conceptions of autonomy from secular models that prioritise individual freedom abstracted from moral, spiritual, or communal reference points. Islāmic scholars have cautioned that such atomistic understandings may be insufficient in contexts where identity, values, and ethical reasoning are deeply intertwined with faith and communal belonging (Sachedina, 2009). Within Islāmic moral reasoning, autonomous choice therefore involves more than cognitive capacity or personal preference; it entails ethical deliberation that integrates spiritual commitments, relational obligations, and concern for the welfare of others. In therapeutic contexts, this understanding allows clinicians to honour client self-determination while remaining attuned to the internal moral conflicts, spiritual values, and communal responsibilities that shape decision-making. Autonomy, from this perspective, emerges not as unrestricted self-assertion but as responsible freedom, a dynamic balance between self-governance and moral responsiveness (Motloba, 2018). It remains ethically essential for respecting personhood, clinically empowering for meaningful engagement in therapy, and spiritually grounded as an expression of accountability aligned with higher ethical purposes.

7.3 Individual Rights

Individual rights refer to the fundamental entitlements that persons possess by virtue of their inherent human dignity. Within general ethical theory and human rights discourse, these rights include the right to dignity, privacy, bodily integrity, freedom from harm, informed consent, and equitable treatment (Beauchamp & Childress, 2019). Their moral authority rests on universal principles of justice and respect for persons, functioning as essential safeguards against exploitation, coercion, discrimination, and abuse of power. Rights-based frameworks do not merely protect individual autonomy; they secure the basic conditions required for psychological safety, social participation, and human flourishing (Longley, 2021). A rights-based ethical stance functions as a protective counterbalance, ensuring that individuals are not compelled to sacrifice personal dignity or psychological safety in the name of social harmony or communal expectation. Respect for individual rights thus enables therapists to support clients' well-being while navigating complex relational and cultural dynamics with ethical clarity (Kemp, 2023).

Islāmic ethical and legal traditions similarly affirm the sanctity of individual right (*ḥuqūq al-ʿibād*) as integral to moral life. The Qur'ân explicitly grounds human rights in divine honour, declaring:

مَدَاءَ ىَنِبَ انَمْرَّكَ دْقَلَوَ

- *We have certainly honoured the children of Adam* (Al-Isra, 17:70, interpretation of the meaning).

Classical Islāmic jurisprudence elaborates a robust framework of personal rights, including the right to privacy, bodily integrity, protection from harm, and the safeguarding of reputation. These rights are regarded as morally inviolable except in cases of compelling ethical necessity, emphasising the seriousness with which personal dignity is protected in Islāmic law (Kamali, 2008). Modern Islāmic human rights instruments, such as the Cairo Declaration on Human Rights in Islām, further articulate principles of dignity, equality, justice, and social welfare within an Islāmic moral framework, emphasising that individual rights and communal well-being are mutually reinforcing rather than oppositional (Organization of Islāmic Cooperation, 1990). Taken together, individual rights emerge as a shared ethical commitment across moral philosophy, clinical practice, and Islāmic ethics. They function as essential conditions for dignified personhood, foundational protections within psychotherapy, and divinely rooted moral obligations that safeguard both personal integrity and social justice. In therapeutic settings, this convergence provides a powerful ethical basis for respecting client autonomy, preserving confidentiality, and protecting psychological safety while remaining sensitive to cultural and religious contexts.

7.4 Community and Collective Responsibility

While autonomy and individual rights foreground personal agency and protection, ethical understanding of human life also recognises that individuals are fundamentally relational beings, shaped by families, cultures, institutions, and communities. General ethical theory and social-ecological perspectives emphasise that psychological well-being is embedded within broader social structures, and that identity, distress, and coping cannot be fully understood apart from the relational environments in which individuals are situated. From this standpoint, ethical responsibility extends beyond the individual to encompass collective conditions that support or undermine human flourishing (Minuchin, 1974). Contemporary psychological science increasingly reflects this relational orientation.

Ecological and system-based models conceptualise individuals as embedded within multiple, interacting layers of influence, including family systems, community networks, cultural norms, and societal values. Bronfenbrenner's ecological systems theory (1995), for example, highlights how psychological development and well-being are shaped by ongoing interactions between the individual and their social environment, while family systems theory underlines that individual symptoms often reflect broader relational patterns rather than isolated intrapsychic dysfunctions. Therapeutic effectiveness, therefore, frequently depends on attending to the interpersonal, cultural, and socioeconomic contexts that contribute to both vulnerability and resilience. Interventions that neglect these dimensions risk being culturally incongruent, clinically ineffective, or ethically insensitive (Guy-Evans, 2025).

In clinical practice, this relational awareness requires therapists to engage sensitively with the social worlds their clients inhabit. Understanding family dynamics, communal expectations, and cultural values allows clinicians to support clients in navigating tensions between personal needs and collective obligations without undermining individual dignity or agency. In multicultural and collectivist contexts, including many Muslim-majority societies, identity is often defined relationally, with family loyalty, communal reputation, and social harmony holding significant psychological importance. Research findings indicate that disregarding these factors may lead to reduced engagement, premature termination of therapy, or experiences of cultural invalidation (Anderson, Bautista & Hope, 2019). Ethical practice, therefore, involves recognising how community expectations shape distress and decision-making, while ensuring that therapy does not become a vehicle for enforcing conformity or suppressing individual well-being (Sue et al., 2009).

Islāmic moral philosophy places collective responsibility at the centre of ethical life, framing moral conduct as a shared obligation rather than a purely individual concern. The Qur'ân repeatedly situates ethical behaviour within a communal horizon, commanding justice, excellence, and care for others while prohibiting wrongdoing and harm:

إِنَّ ٱللَّهَ يَأْمُرُ بِٱلْعَدْلِ وَٱلْإِحْسَٰنِ وَإِيتَآئِ ذِى ٱلْقُرْبَىٰ وَيَنْهَىٰ عَنِ ٱلْفَحْشَآءِ
وَٱلْمُنكَرِ وَٱلْبَغْىِ ۚ

- *Indeed, Allāh commands justice, excellence, and giving to relatives, and He forbids immorality, wrongdoing, and oppression* (An-Nahl 16:90, interpretation of the meaning).

The concept of *ummah* (community) reflects this orientation, portraying believers as a morally accountable collective entrusted with promoting good and preventing harm:

كُنتُمْ خَيْرَ أُمَّةٍ أُخْرِجَتْ لِلنَّاسِ تَأْمُرُونَ بِٱلْمَعْرُوفِ وَتَنْهَوْنَ عَنِ ٱلْمُنكَرِ

- *You are the best nation produced [as an example] for mankind. You enjoin what is right and forbid what is wrong.* (Al-Imran, 3:110, interpretation of the meaning).

Abū al-Aʿlā al-Mawdūdī(n.d.) explains that An-Nahl (16:90) lays down a comprehensive moral code by commanding justice, kindness, and care for relatives while forbidding immorality, injustice, and oppression, thereby forming the ethical foundation of a just and harmonious society. In Āli-ʿImrān (3:110), Aʿlā al-Mawdūdī clarifies that the Muslim community is called the best community not by birth or race, but by fulfilling its responsibility to promote good, prevent wrongdoing, and remain firm in faith in Allāh; neglect of these duties results in the loss of this moral leadership, as seen in the failure of most of the People of the Book to uphold true obedience. Classic Islāmic jurisprudence further articulates this communal ethic through the principle of *maṣlaḥah* (public interest), which seeks to preserve essential human and social values, including life, intellect, lineage, property, and faith, at both individual and societal levels. Jurists such as Al-Shāṭibī (n.d.) stressed that moral judgement should take into account the wider social impact of individual behaviour, highlighting that personal actions are closely tied to the well-being of the community as a whole. Importantly, this emphasis on communal responsibility does not translate into coercive moral surveillance or the erosion of personal boundaries. Islāmic ethics instead stresses moral persuasion, wisdom (*ḥikmah*), compassion, and restraint (Islāmqa, 2001).

Community values and relational obligations must be acknowledged as meaningful dimensions of clients' lived experience, yet they should never be imposed or used to override individual dignity, autonomy, or psychological safety (Islamqa, 2001). Therapeutic engagement focuses on how communal expectations influence distress, identity conflict, and coping, rather than on enforcing moral conformity. By adopting this relational ethical stance, therapists can validate the emotional significance of belonging while supporting clients in navigating personal boundaries, internal moral tensions, and complex social roles with clarity, compassion, and ethical integrity (Sue et al., 2009).

7.5 Point of Tension and Ethical Dilemmas

Ethical tensions in Islāmic psychotherapy most frequently emerge at the intersection of autonomy, individual rights, and communal responsibility. These tensions are not incidental but structurally embedded within therapeutic work involving Muslim clients, particularly in collectivist cultural contexts where moral, familial, and religious obligations are deeply intertwined. Unlike Western clinical settings, where autonomy is often treated as a self-evident ethical priority, Muslim clients may experience autonomy as morally ambiguous, relationally risky, or spiritually fraught.

7.5.1 Autonomy Versus Familial Authority

One of the most persistent ethical dilemmas arises when client autonomy conflicts with family authority, particularly in decisions related to marriage, career paths, religious observance, or living arrangements. In many Muslim societies, family involvement is not merely cultural but morally valourised, often framed through religious language emphasising obedience, respect, and social cohesion (Dwairy, 2006). Clients who experience distress in these contexts may struggle with guilt, fear of social rupture, and internalised moral conflict. From a clinical ethics perspective, privileging family demands over client well-being violates the principles of autonomy, beneficence, and non-maleficence (APA, 2017). Yet rigid application of individualistic ethics risks alienating clients and undermining therapeutic alliance. Therapists must therefore navigate a narrow ethical path: supporting client agency without dismissing the relational realities that shape the client's moral world (Sue & Sue, 2016).

Islāmic ethics offers a nuanced framework for this tension. While honouring parents (*birr al-wālidayn*) is a core moral obligation, it is not unconditional. The Qur'ân explicitly limits obedience when harm or moral violation is involved:

وَإِن جَاهَدَاكَ عَلَىٰٓ أَن تُشْرِكَ بِى مَا لَيْسَ لَكَ بِهِۦ عِلْمٌ فَلَا تُطِعْهُمَا ۖ وَصَاحِبْهُمَا فِى
ٱلدُّنْيَا مَعْرُوفًا ۖ

- *But if they strive to make you associate with Me that of which you have no knowledge, do not obey them; yet accompany them in [this] world with kindness.* (Luqman, 31:15, interpretation of the meaning).

This verse establishes a critical ethical distinction between moral agency and relational conduct. Clients are not required to surrender conscience or psychological safety in the name of obedience, yet they are encouraged to maintain kindness and respect. In therapy, this principle supports boundary-setting that is neither adversarial nor submissive, allowing clients to assert agency while preserving relational dignity.

7.5.2 *Moral Disagreement and Therapist Neutrality*

A further ethical dilemma arises when therapists experience moral or theological disagreement with client choices. Muslim therapists, in particular, may struggle internally when client decisions conflict with religious teachings, raising concerns about complicity or moral compromise (Malik, 2020). Clinical ethics emphasises non-imposition of values, yet neutrality does not imply moral indifference. Islāmic ethics guides the principle of *niyyah* (intention). 'Umar bin Al Khattab (may Allāh be pleased with him) reported the Apostle of Allāh (ﷺ) as saying "Actions are to be judged only by intentions"(Abū Dāwūd (b)). Therapeutic work grounded in compassion, sincerity, and harm reduction remains ethically valid even amid moral disagreement. Empathy does not require theological endorsement. Indeed, Islāmic tradition recognises restraint, patience, and avoidance of harm as moral virtues. Supporting psychological well-being without directing moral outcomes is therefore not ethical abdication but ethical discipline (Malik, 2020).

7.5.3 *Empirical Evidence of Ethical Strain*

Qualitative research consistently documents the emotional and ethical strain experienced by Muslim therapists navigating these tensions. Therapists frequently report experiencing fear of moral transgression, uncertainty about professional boundaries, and heightened risk of burnout. Jackson (2019) notes that therapists' uncertainty often appears as anxiety about unintentionally crossing ethical boundaries, which can weaken their confidence in clinical decision-making. This perspective resonates with Jameton's (1984) seminal work on moral distress, which describes the psychological tension that occurs when professionals feel unable to act in accordance with their ethical principles. Building on this, Litz and Kerig (2019) introduced the concept of moral injury, highlighting the significant impact that perceived ethical violations can have on therapists' well-being. These ethical pressures are further intensified by the risk of burnout, a multifaceted syndrome involving emotional exhaustion, depersonalisation, and diminished feelings of personal accomplishment (Maslach & Leiter, 2016). The findings of research in nursing ethics indicate that unresolved moral distress directly contributes to burnout and emotional fatigue (Oh & Gastmans, 2015), emphasising the critical role of supervision, ethics education, and self-care strategies in reducing these risks within psychotherapy practice. These factors highlight significant occupational hazards for therapists and the ethical need for better support systems, such as improved supervision and clearer guidelines for navigating complex ethical dilemmas, to ensure both clinician well-being and client safety.

7.6 Balanced Islāmic Therapeutic Model

The ethical tensions outlined above necessitate a therapeutic model capable of holding autonomy, individual rights, and community values in dynamic balance rather than hierarchical opposition. Islāmic psychotherapy requires a framework that neither collapses into moral relativism nor functions as a mechanism of religious or social enforcement. A balanced Islāmic therapeutic model rests on three interdependent ethical pillars:

a. Professional clinical ethics
b. Islāmic moral principles
c. Contextual-relational awareness

These domains are not discrete but mutually informing. Professional ethics provide the foundational safeguards of autonomy, beneficence, non-maleficence, justice, and fidelity (APA, 2017). Islāmic moral principles, particularly *raḥmah* (mercy), *ʿadl* (justice), *niyyah* (sincerity), and *iḥsān* (ethical excellence), infuse practice with moral depth without displacing professional standards (Al-Ghazālī, 2005). Awareness of context allows practitioners to respond effectively to family, community, and sociocultural influences on a client's distress. Within this model, autonomy is respected but not absolutised. Clients are supported in making informed choices while exploring relational, emotional, and moral consequences. This aligns with the Qur'ânic affirmation of agency:

وَقُلِ ٱلْحَقُّ مِن رَّبِّكُمْ ۖ فَمَن شَآءَ فَلْيُؤْمِن وَمَن شَآءَ فَلْيَكْفُرْ ۚ

- *The truth is from your Lord; whoever wills—let them believe, and whoever wills—let them disbelieve.* (Al-Kahf, 18:29)

Crucially, the model distinguishes support from endorsement. Therapists provide validation, containment, and empathy without assuming responsibility for moral approval. This principle reflects the ethical distinction between extending empathy and compassion toward individuals while maintaining critical evaluation of their actions. For example, one can care for, support, and respect a person without condoning harmful or unethical behaviour. The model also explicitly rejects the instrumentalisation of therapy for communal control. While community values are acknowledged, they are not permitted to override psychological safety or client dignity. Qur'ânic warnings against publicising faults support this ethical restraint.

7.7 Integrative Practice Framework

Islāmic psychotherapy benefits from a framework grounded in the Qur'ânic principle of ethical moderation and balance:

اطِسَوَ ةًمَّأُ مْكُانَلْعَجَ كَلِذَكَوَ

- *And thus, We have made you a median [i.e. Just] community* (*ummatan wasatan*) (Al-Baqarah, 2:143, interpretation of the meaning)

The phrase "*ummatan wasatan,*" often translated as "a just, balanced, or moderate community," emphasises equilibrium in beliefs, behaviour, and social conduct. In a therapeutic context, the principle of balance and moderation can guide clinicians to help clients develop emotional regulation, ethical decision-making, and integration of spiritual values into daily life. Just as the *ummah* is called to be a model of fairness and moderation, individuals can cultivate inner balance while navigating challenges, ethical dilemmas, and relational dynamics. Table 7.1 shows the integration of Islāmic ethical principles in psychotherapy practice

Table 7.1 Integration of Islamic ethical principles in psychotherapy practice

Ethical Domains	Islāmic Ethical Principles	Clinical Application in Psychotherapy
Autonomy	*Ikhtiyār* (Moral agency and choice)	Supports client-led decision-making, informed consent, and respect for personal boundaries without coercion.
Compassion	*Raḥmah* (Mercy and care)	Establishes emotional safety, empathic attunement, and non-judgmental therapeutic presence.
Justice	*'Adl* (Fairness and equity)	Ensures equitable treatment, protects clients from harm, stigma, or misuse of therapeutic power.
Welfare	*Maṣlaḥah* (Best interest and harm prevention)	Prioritises psychological well-being, harm reduction, and long-term therapeutic benefit.
Moderation	*Wasatiyyah* (Balance and ethical restraint)	Guides clinicians in balancing individual rights, relational obligations, and cultural-religious contexts

This integrative model affirms autonomy without endorsing moral isolation and recognises community values without permitting coercion. By holding professional ethics and Islāmic moral principles in dynamic balance, it offers a clinically grounded and ethically coherent framework for therapeutic practice within Muslim contexts.

7.8 Case Reflections

The following case reflection are drawn from established clinical and empirical literature on psychotherapy with Muslim clients. It is presented to illustrate how ethical tensions around confidentiality and community responsibility manifest in real clinical settings, and how an integrative Islāmic ethical framework can be applied in practice. Identifying details are omitted, and the cases are analytically summarised in line with the original authors' reports.

7.8.1 Case 1-Autonomy, Religious Conflict, and Non-directive Care

Rothman and Coyle (2018) present a documented clinical vignette involving a practicing Muslim adult client who sought psychotherapy for persistent anxiety, guilt, and identity conflict linked to perceived tensions between personal aspirations and religious expectations. The client reported intrusive self-criticism, fear of spiritual failure, and chronic rumination over whether pursuing personal goals constituted moral deviation. Psychological distress was exacerbated by concerns that therapy itself might undermine religious commitment or signal weak faith. The therapist adopted a non-directive, autonomy-supportive stance grounded in ethical psychotherapy and Islāmic moral sensitivity. Rather than offering prescriptive religious interpretations or attempting to resolve theological uncertainty, the therapist focused on emotional regulation, meaning-making, and exploration of the client's lived religious experience. Islāmic concepts were introduced only when initiated by the client and were used to facilitate reflection rather than dictate moral outcomes. The therapist explicitly avoided assuming the role of religious authority, thereby preserving professional boundaries and safeguarding client agency.

Over the course of therapy, the client demonstrated significant reductions in anxiety and self-reproach, despite the persistence of unresolved religious ambiguity. Improvement was associated with increased psychological flexibility, enhanced self-compassion, and the normalisation of moral struggle as part of spiritual development. Rothman and Coyle emphasise that therapeutic progress occurred not through resolving religious doctrine but through validating internal conflict and supporting autonomous moral reflection (Rothman & Coyle, 2018).

This case provides strong empirical support for autonomy-affirming, non-coercive psychotherapy within Islāmic contexts. It illustrates how professional ethics, respect for autonomy, non-maleficence, and role clarity can be coherently integrated with Islāmic ethical principles such as *raḥmah* (compassion), *ikhtiyār* (moral agency), and avoidance of coercion. The case challenges assumptions that psychological healing requires theological resolution and demonstrates that honouring faith does not necessitate moral prescription. Instead, ethical Islāmic psychotherapy protects dignity and agency while allowing religious meaning to emerge organically.

7.9 Conclusion

Ethical practice in Islāmic psychotherapy requires the integration of professional clinical ethics with Islāmic moral principles and contextual relational awareness. Autonomy, individual rights, and communal responsibility are not mutually exclusive but interdependent dimensions of ethically grounded care. The chapter has demonstrated that therapists can uphold client self-determination while remaining sensitive to moral, familial, and communal frameworks, mitigating tensions between personal agency and collective obligations. Case reflections illustrate that ethical clarity and compassionate engagement, when informed by Islāmic concepts such as *amānah, raḥmah,* and *niyyah*, can enhance therapeutic efficacy without compromising spiritual or relational values. The integrative model proposed emphasises *wasatiyyah*, advocating balance, moderation, and ethical restraint as central to culturally responsive practice. By operationalising ethical principles through value-sensitive alliance-building, narrative approaches, emotion regulation, and boundary work, clinicians can support clients' psychological well-being, moral reflection, and social harmony simultaneously. Ultimately, Islāmic psychotherapy is not merely a culturally adapted modality but a robust ethical framework that reconciles professional obligations with spiritual and communal dimensions of human life. This approach fosters therapeutic environments where dignity, agency, and relational integrity coexist, providing a coherent, ethically principled pathway for the care of Muslim clients navigating complex moral and psychosocial landscapes.

References

Abū Dāwūd. Sunan Abi Dāwūd 2201. In-book reference: Book 13, Hadith 27. English translation: Book 12, Hadith 2195. Sahih (Al-Albani). https://sunnah.com/abudawud:2201

Al-Ghazālī, A. H. (1964). *The criterion of action (Mīzān al-ʿamal)* (M. A. Quasem, Trans.). University of Malaya Press.

Al-Shāṭibī, Abū Isḥāq (n.d.). *Al-Muwāfaqāt fī Uṣūl al-Sharīʿah*. Dār al-Maʿrifah.

American Psychological Association. (2017). *Ethical principles of psychologists and code of conduct*. https://www.apa.org/ethics/code

Anderson, K. N., Bautista, C. L., & Hope, D. A. (2019). Therapeutic alliance, cultural competence and minority status in premature termination of psychotherapy. *The American Journal of Orthopsychiatry, 89*(1), 104–114. https://doi.org/10.1037/ort0000342

Banerjee, S., Mareena, S., & Wesley. (2023). *Boundary constructions in psychotherapeutic relationships. International Journal of Psychology and Counseling, 11*(1), 1–12. https://doi.org/10.25215/1101.028

Beauchamp, T. L., & Childress, J. F. (2019). *Principles of biomedical ethics* (8th ed.). Oxford University Press. https://global.oup.com/academic/product/principles-of-biomedical-ethics-9780190640873

Bronfenbrenner, U. (1995). Developmental Ecology through Space and Time: A Future Perspective. In P. Moen, G. H. Elder, & K. Lüscher (Eds.), *Examining Lives in Context: Perspectives on the Ecology of Human Development* (pp. 619–647). American Psychological Association.

Bukhārī and Muslim. *Mishkat al-Masabih 56.* In-book reference: Book 1, Hadith 50. Muttafaqun 'alayh (Zubair `Aliza'i). https://sunnah.com/mishkat:56

Dwairy, M. (2006). *Counseling and psychotherapy with Arabs and Muslims: A culturally sensitive approach.* Arab Psychological Services. http://arabpsynet.com/Books/Dwairy.B1.pdf

Griffel, F. (2009). *Al-Ghazālī's philosophical theology.* Oxford University Press.

Güleç, S. (2024). The Application of Self-Determination Theory in Psychological Counseling Process. *İçtimaiyat(Türk Eğitim Sisteminde Değişimler ve Yeni Eğilimler),* 201-212. https://doi.org/10.33709/ictimaiyat.1541995

Guy-Evans, O. (2025). Bronfenbrenner's ecological systems theory. *Simply Psychology.* https://www.simplypsychology.org/Bronfenbrenner.html

Islamqa. (2001). Islamqa.info. https://islamqa.info/en/answers/11403/enjoining-what-is-good-and-forbidding-what-is-evil

Jackson, M. M. (2019). The wisdom of therapist uncertainty. *Psychotherapy.net.* https://www.psychotherapy.net

Jameton, A. (1984). *Nursing practice: The ethical issues.* Prentice-Hall.

Kamali, M. H. (2008). *Sharī'ah law: An introduction.* Oneworld Publications. https://oneworld-publications.com/work/shariah-law/

Kemp, R. (2023). Human rights and the ethics of clinical psychology. *Clinical Psychology Forum, 1*(368), 68–69. https://doi.org/10.53841/bpscpf.2023.1.368.68

Litz, B. T., & Kerig, P. K. (2019). Introduction to the special issue on moral injury: Conceptual challenges, methodological issues, and clinical applications. *Journal of Traumatic Stress, 32*(3), 341–349. https://doi.org/10.1002/jts.22405

Longley, R. (2021, May 27). What are individual rights? Definition and examples. *ThoughtCo.* https://www.thoughtco.com/individual-rights-definition-and-examples-5115456

Maslach, C., & Leiter, M. P. (2016). Burnout: A multidimensional perspective. In C. L. Cooper & P. L. Perrewé (Eds.), *The Routledge companion to wellbeing at work* (pp. 37–49). Routledge.

Maududi, Abul A'la (n.d.). *Tafhim al-Qur'an, commentary on Qur'an.* Islamic Publications,

Markus, H. R., & Kitayama, S. (1991). Culture and the self: Implications for cognition, emotion, and motivation. *Psychological Review, 98*(2), 224–253. https://doi.org/10.1037/0033-295X.98.2.224

Malik, R. (2020, June 14). Islāmic ethics and psychology. *Research Center for Islāmic Legislation and Ethics.* https://www.cilecenter.org/research-publications/op-ed/Islāmic-ethics-and-psychology

Motloba, P. D. (2018). Understanding of the principle of autonomy (Part 1). *South African Dental Journal, 73*(6), 418–420. https://doi.org/10.17159/2519-0105/2018/v73no5a7

Minuchin, S. (1974). *Families and family therapy.* Harvard University Press. https://www.hup.harvard.edu/catalog.php?isbn=9780674292369

Oh, Y., & Gastmans, C. (2015). Moral distress experienced by nurses: A quantitative literature review. *Nursing Ethics, 22*(1), 15–31. https://doi.org/10.1177/0969733013502803

Organization of Islāmic Cooperation. (1990). *Cairo Declaration on Human Rights in Islam.* https://elearning.icrc.org/detention/en/story_content/external_files/Human%20Rights%20in%20Islam%20(1990).pdf

Rassool, G. Hussein. (2025). *Islamic counselling and psychotherapy: Theory, practice, and contemporary applications* (2nd. ed.). Routledge.

Rothman, A., & Coyle, A. (2018). Toward a framework for Islāmic psychology and psychotherapy: An Islāmic model of the soul. *Journal of Religion and Health, 57,* 1731–1744. https://pmc.ncbi.nlm.nih.gov/articles/PMC6132620/

Ryan, R., Lynch, M., Vansteenkiste, M., & Deci, E. (2021). Motivation and autonomy in counseling, psychotherapy, and behavior change: A look at theory and practice. APA. https://www.apa.org/education-career/ce/motivation-autonomy.pdf

Sachedina, A. (2009). *Islāmic biomedical ethics: Principles and application.* Oxford University Press. https://global.oup.com/academic/product/Islāmic-biomedical-ethics-9780195378504

Sadownik, A. (2023, August 25). *Bronfenbrenner: Ecology of human development in ecology of collaboration.* ResearchGate. https://www.researchgate.net/publication/373383997_Bronfenbrenner_Ecology_of_Human_Development_in_Ecology

Sue, S., Zane, N., Nagayama Hall, G. C., & Berger, L. K. (2009). The case for cultural competency in psychotherapeutic interventions. *Annual Review of Psychology, 60*(1), 525–548. https://doi.org/10.1146/annurev.psych.60.110707.163651

Sue, D. W., & Sue, D. (2016). *Counseling the culturally diverse: Theory and practice* (7th ed.). Wiley. https://doi.org/10.22302/iribb.jur.mp.v82i1.260

Tirmidhī. *Jami` at- Tirmidhī 1425.* Book 17, Hadith 4. English translation: Vol. 3, Book 15, Hadith 1425. Sahih (Darussalam).https://sunnah.com/tirmidhi:1425

Vyskocilová, J., & Prasko, J. (2013). Ethical reflection and psychotherapy. Neuro Endocrinology Letters, 34(7), 590–600. https://www.researchgate.net/publication/260369633_Ethical_reflection_and_psychotherapy

Chapter 8
Navigating Faith, Ethics, and Care: Islāmic Psychotherapy with LGBTQ+ Clients

Saima Khan

8.1 Introduction

Islāmic psychotherapist, regardless of their personal beliefs, is ethically required to offer respectful, non-judgemental, and caring support to all clients, even when a client's identity or lifestyle differs significantly from their own values or worldview (APA, 2017). For Islāmic therapists, counsellors, and mental health professional, this responsibility can become particularly complex when working with LGBTQ+ clients, as Islāmic teachings traditionally prohibit same-sex relations and do not affirm non-binary gender identities. This tension between professional ethics and personal or religious convictions presents a unique challenge that requires careful navigation (Jaspal, 2012). At the heart of this challenge lies the need for balance between religious authenticity and therapeutic empathy, between upholding Islāmic moral values and respecting the psychological well-being and dignity of the client. Islāmic therapists and counsellors may struggle with internal conflicts, unclear boundaries, or fear of enabling actions they believe are religiously impermissible. At the same time, LGBTQ+ clients who identify as Muslim often carry deep emotional burdens, including guilt, shame, spiritual confusion, and rejection. It is within this delicate space, between faith and identity, healing and belief, that the therapeutic relationship must be carefully and compassionately navigated (Jaspal, 2012).

This chapter approaches the issue from an Islāmic perspective, asking how Muslim therapists can remain faithful to their religious commitments while also fulfilling their ethical duty to support and care for LGBTQ+ clients. It considers the guidance of the Qur'ān and *Sunnah* in navigating such situations and raises three central questions:

Dr. Saima Khan (Bath Spa University Academic Centre Ras Al Khaimah, Ras Al Khaimah, United Arab Emirates) is the sole author of this chapter. Editorial review and substantive editing were conducted by Professor Dr. G.Hussein Rassool.

G. H. Rassool, *Ethical Dilemmas in Islāmic Psychotherapy*,
https://doi.org/10.1007/978-3-032-26515-9_8

- Where do the boundaries lie for practitioners of faith? How can they provide effective psychological support without compromising their religious values?
- And what frameworks can help them balance professional integrity with spiritual fidelity?

To address these questions, the chapter will examine foundational Islāmic teachings on sexuality and gender; outline the ethical responsibilities of therapists; propose culturally and theologically grounded therapeutic strategies; and recommend training pathways for Islāmic therapists, counsellors and mental health professionals. The aim is not to resolve theological debates, but rather to offer a ethically informed and faith-sensitive framework for practice that supports conscientious engagement with LGBTQ+ clients.

8.2 Theological Foundations: Islāmic Views on Gender and Sexuality

8.2.1 Background

For Islāmic therapists, counsellors and mental health professionals. the intersection of religious belief and modern understandings of gender and sexuality can present profound ethical and theological dilemmas. To navigate this terrain responsibly, it is imperative first to understand what the Islāmic tradition teaches on these subjects. This section outlines the primary scriptural sources, Qur'ân and *hadīth,* along with classical juristic interpretations and some emerging scholarly reflections, particularly regarding same-sex attraction and non-binary gender identities (Al-Krenawi & Graham, 2009).

8.2.2 Qur'ânic Perspectives on Gender and Sexuality

The Qur'ān provides the foundational framework for Islāmic perspectives on human sexuality and gender relations, establishing principles that are later elaborated upon through the *Sunnah*, *hadīth*, and the scholarly tradition of *fiqh* (jurisprudence). These sources together shape a moral and legal discourse that informs Muslim understandings of sexual ethics, family structures, and social conduct For Islāmic therapists, counsellors, and mental health professionals, engaging with these foundational teachings is essential for navigating the ethical and theological dimensions of practice, particularly when addressing sensitive issues related to sexuality and identity.

A central tenet in Islāmic thought is the concept of creation in pairs, which classical scholarship has traditionally interpreted as establishing a binary framework of male and female. Within this framework, Islāmic law and theology consistently uphold the principle that God created only these two genders, forming the basis for normative understandings of gender and sexual ethics. The Yaqeen Institute for Islāmic Research (2022) notes that, within *Shari'ah*, biological sex and modern notions of "psychological gender" are not distinguished. People are generally expected to identify and express themselves according to their biological sex, with deviations considered exceptional and analogous to contemporary understandings of gender dysphoria. The Qur'ān conveys the Islāmic paradigm of gender and sexuality in multiple passages including:

اهيأي سانلا اوقتا مكبر يذلا مكقلخ نم سفن ةدحاو قلخو اهنم اهجوز ثبو امهنم
لاجر اريثك ءاسنو ۚ.

- *O mankind, fear your Lord, who created you from one soul and created from it its mate and dispersed from both of them many men and women…*"(An-Nisa, 4:1, interpretation of the meaning).

.اهجوز اهنم لعج مث ةدحو سفن نم مكقلخ

- *He created you from one soul. Then He made from it its mate,…* (Az-Zumar, 39:6, interpretation of the meaning).

.وَمَا خَلَقَ ٱلذَّكَرَ وَٱلْأُنثَىٰٓ

- *And [by] He who created the male and the female* (Al-Layl, 92:3, interpretation of the meaning).

.وَأَنَّهُۥ خَلَقَ ٱلزَّوْجَيْنِ ٱلذَّكَرَ وَٱلْأُنثَىٰ

- *And that He created the two mates: the male and the female.* (An Najm, 53:45. interpretation of the meaning).

.وَ مِن كُلِّ شَيْءٍ خَلَقْنَا زَوْجَيْنِ لَعَلَّكُمْ تَذَكَّرُونَ

- *And of all things We created two mates[counterparts]; perhaps you will remember.* (Adh-Dhariyat, 51:49, interpretation of the meaning)

وَلَيْسَ ٱلذَّكَرُ كَٱلْأُنثَىٰ ۖ

- *And the male is not like the female.* (Ali-'Imran, 3:36, interpretation of the meaning).

ۚ ةمحرو ةدوم مكنيب لعجو اهيلإ اونكستل اجوزأ مكسفنأ نم مكل قلخ نأ ۦهتايآ نمو
.نوركفتي موقل تايآل كلذ يف نإ

- *And among His signs is that He created for you spouses from among yourselves that you may find tranquility in them; and He placed between you affection and mercy. Indeed, in that are signs for a people who give thought.* (Ar-Rum, 30:21. interpretation of the meaning).

These verses recognise two genders and affirm the duality of creation and have been foundational for the traditional Islāmic understanding of gender and marriage. They highlight both the unity of human origin and the complementarity of male and female as partners within the divine order. Within the Qur'ānic framework, human sexuality is primarily situated in the context of heterosexual marital relations, serving not only the procreative purpose of sustaining humanity but also spiritual and ethical purposes, such as fostering companionship, tranquillity, and moral responsibility. For Islāmic therapists, these foundational teachings frame discussions of gender and sexuality within an ethic of balance, responsibility, and mutual respect, while also raising questions about how to navigate contemporary challenges in practice.

8.2.3 The Story of Lot (Lūṭ)

The preaching of Prophet Lot (Lūṭ) (ملاسلا هيلع) and what happened between Him and His People, Allāh tells us that His Prophet Lot (ملاسلا هيلع), denounced his people for their evil deed and their immoral actions in having intercourse with males, a deed which none of the sons of Adam had ever committed before them. When confronted by Prophet Lot (ملاسلا هيلع), the people responded with defiance and mockery. Instead of reflecting on their actions, they challenged him to bring down God's punishment if his message were true. This reaction illustrates both the gravity of their sins and their obstinate rejection of prophetic guidance, themes that recur across the Qur'ānic accounts of their destruction.

The Qur'ān explicitly addresses same-sex relations in the narrative of Prophet Lut (ملاسلا هيلع) in at least nine different chapters (*sūrats*) of the Qur'ān (Al-A'rāf (7:80–84); Hūd (11:77–83); Al-Hijri (15:57–77); Al-Anbiyā' (21:74–75); Al-Shu'arā' (26:160–175); Al-Naml (27:54–58); Al-'Ankabūt (29:28–35); Al-Ṣāffāt (37:133–138); and Al-Qamar (54:33–39), across more than seventy-five verses (*ayahs*). The Qur'ān identifies the central sin of the people of Lot as engaging in sexual relations with men, that is, "*approaching men with desire* (*shahwah*) *instead of women*," and presents this behaviour as the main reason for God's condemnation of them. Allāh say in the Qur'ān:

وَلُوطًا إِذْ قَالَ لِقَوْمِهِۦٓ أَتَأْتُونَ ٱلْفَـٰحِشَةَ مَا سَبَقَكُم بِهَا مِنْ أَحَدٍ مِّنَ ٱلْعَـٰلَمِينَ.

إِنَّكُمْ لَتَأْتُونَ ٱلرِّجَالَ شَهْوَةً مِّن دُونِ ٱلنِّسَآءِ ۚ بَلْ أَنتُمْ قَوْمٌ مُّسْرِفُونَ.

- *And [We had sent] Lot when he said to his people, "Do you commit such immorality as no one has preceded you with from among the worlds?[[i.e., people]. Indeed, you approach men with desire, instead of women. Rather, you are a transgressing people.* ('A'rāf 7:80–81, interpretation of the meaning).

While a few passages (e.g., Al-'Ankabūt, 29:29) briefly allude to additional misdeeds, the Qur'ān consistently highlights their primary transgression as 'approaching males with desire (shahwah) instead of women

أَئِنَّكُمْ لَتَأْتُونَ ٱلرِّجَالَ وَتَقْطَعُونَ ٱلسَّبِيلَ وَتَأْتُونَ فِى نَادِيكُمُ ٱلْمُنكَرَ ۖ.

- *Indeed, you approach men and obstruct the road and commit in your meetings [every] evil.* (Al-'Ankabūt, 29:29, interpretation of the meaning).

According to the exegesis of Ibn ʿAbbās (n.d.), the people of Lot were guilty of multiple forms of corruption. Their most prominent sin was sexual relations between men, a practice explicitly condemned in the Qur'ān. They were also accused of "cutting the road," which commentators understood both literally, through acts of robbery and intimidation of traveller, and figuratively, as disrupting the continuation of progeny by abandoning natural relations between men and women. Furthermore, they engaged in public indecencies during their gatherings, with reports suggesting that they practiced numerous forms of shameless behaviour collectively. Some modern orientalist scholars and activists contend that the sin of the people of Lūṭ was not solely related to consensual same-sex relationships, but rather to coercion, violence, and the violation of hospitality norms (Kugle, 2010). Although this interpretation has gained some traction within feminist Qur'ânic interpretation, progressive or reformist interpretation of the Qur'ân and progressive Muslim circles, it remains highly contested and does not reflect the position of mainstream Islāmic creed and scholarship.

8.2.4 Hadīth Literature on Gender and Sexuality

The *hadīth* corpus, comprising the recorded sayings and actions of the Prophet Muhammad (ﷺ), plays a pivotal role in shaping Islāmic perspectives on gender and sexuality. Hadīth literature addresses both gender and sexuality by outlining complementary roles for men and women, setting norms for modesty and social interaction, and offering guidance on family and communal life. On sexuality, it prescribes ethical principles for marital intimacy, emphasising mutual consent and satisfaction, while prohibiting practices viewed as harmful or disruptive, including extramarital relations, sexual violence, and same-sex relations. Some hadīth also addresses sexual violence, coercion, and harmful practices, forming the basis for juridical rulings in the classical legal schools (*madhāhib*).

The *hadīth* corpus reveals a nuanced treatment of gender-nonconforming individuals, particularly the *mukhannathun* (effeminate men). The Prophet (ﷺ) initially allowed such individuals to be among women until a situation arose that indicated a breach of social decorum. It is narrated by Ibn `Abbas (may Allāh be pleased with him) that the Prophet (ﷺ) cursed effeminate men (those men who are in the similitude (assume the manners of women) and those women who assume the manners of men, and he said, "Turn them out of your houses." The Prophet (ﷺ) turned out such-and-such man, and `Umar turned out such-and-such woman (Bukhārī).

Islāmic legal literature contains extensive discussions on *khunthā* (intersex individuals), prescribing methods for determining legal gender according to predominant physiological traits. This demonstrates that Islāmic tradition has historically recognised the complexity of gender variation, while still upholding normative boundaries. It is narrated by Ibn 'Abbas (may Allāh be pleased with him) that the Prophet (ﷺ) cursed women who imitate men and men who imitate women (Abū Dāwūd (a)). Classical jurists, including Imām an-Nawawī and Ibn Qudāmah, drew a clear distinction between natural, innate characteristics and intentional acts of imitating the opposite gender. They condemned cross-dressing or gender imitation when it was undertaken to deceive others, disrupt social norms, or blur established gender boundaries. However, when gender ambiguity arose from innate physiological traits (*khilqah*), such as in cases of intersex individuals, it was not considered morally blameworthy. Instead, jurists approached these cases with a degree of legal and ethical nuance, seeking to determine appropriate social and legal classifications without attributing sin to what was understood as a natural condition (Uddin, 2017).

Jabir (may Allāh be pleased with him) reported God's Messenger (ﷺ) as saying, "The thing I fear most for my people is what Lot's people did" (Tirmidhî & Ibn Majah). This *hadīth* conveys the Prophet's (ﷺ) deep concern regarding the moral and social transgressions exemplified by the people of Lūṭ, traditionally understood to include sexual immorality and other violations of societal norms. The narration is reported in Tirmidhî & Ibn Majah, but its authenticity has not been fully verified, according to al-Albānī, meaning it requires caution in legal or theological application. The statement is often cited in classical jurisprudence and ethical discussions as a general warning against acts seen as destructive to communal morality.

8.2.5 Classical Jurisprudence: Consensus and Exceptions

Islāmic jurists have generally reached a consensus (*ijma'*) on the prohibition of same-sex acts, grounding their rulings in both Qur'ânic injunctions and hadīth. All four Sunni schools, *Hanafi, Maliki, Shafi 'i*, and *Hanbali*, agree that male–male anal intercourse is *haram* (forbidden), though they differ in the specific punishments prescribed (Maravia, 2022). At the same time, Islāmic jurisprudence has historically taken a more nuanced approach to gender ambiguity, particularly regarding intersex individuals (*khunthā*). Classical *fiqh* authorities, including al-Mawardi and Ibn Qudāmah, provide guidelines for determining legal gender based on physiological characteristics and functional roles. These rulings illustrate that Islāmic law has historically recognised and accommodated complexities in gender classification under certain circumstances (Uddin, 2017). For instance, Imān An-Nawawī addressed the case of *khunthā mushki,* an intersex individual whose predominant gender could not be readily determined, and recommended that legal rulings on matters such as prayer positions, inheritance, and marriage be deferred until clearer signs emerged. This approach demonstrates both an acknowledgement of biological complexity and a juristic emphasis on careful and compassionate adjudication (Uddin, 2017).

8.2.6 *Contemporary Reflections: Between Tradition and New Understandings*

In the contemporary era, Muslim scholars and practitioners are navigating how emerging understandings of gender identity and sexual orientation intersect with Islāmic ethical frameworks. While the majority of scholars continue to uphold traditional prohibitions against same-sex sexual behaviour, an increasing number advocate for pastoral, rather than punitive, approaches (Maravia, 2022). For example, Shaykh Yasir Qadhi emphasises that Muslim therapists should "uphold orthodoxy without cruelty," promoting methods that preserve scriptural integrity while respecting the dignity of individuals experiencing same-sex attraction (Qadhi, 2009).

Shaykh Yasir Qadhi's advice reflects a balance between maintaining traditional Islāmic teachings (*orthodoxy*) and treating individuals with compassion (*without cruelty*). In the context of therapy or pastoral care for Muslims experiencing same-sex attraction, he is advocating that professionals should have a balanced approach that upholds Islāmic principles while treating individuals with dignity, emphasising compassionate guidance and supportive care without shaming or coercion. In short, Qadhi emphasises that adherence to Islāmic teachings does not require harshness or harm; religious guidance and ethical care can coexist with empathy, compassion and respect.

Progressive or reformist scholars such as Scott Siraj al-Haqq Kugle and Dr. Amina Wadud have initiated a re-examination of traditional Islāmic views on gender and sexuality, advocating for interpretations that align with principles of justice, dignity, and individual conscience (Safi, 2017). Kugle (2010) argues the Qur'ān does not inherently condemn same-sex relationship and suggests that traditional interpretations have been influenced by patriarchal cultural norms rather than the core ethical teachings of Islām. His work challenges the prevailing view that homosexuality is incompatible with Islāmic teachings, advocating instead for an inclusive understanding that affirms the dignity of LGBTQ+Muslims. Dr. Amina Wadud (2006), a leading feminist scholar, emphasises the importance of contextual and gender-sensitive interpretations of the Qur'ān. Wadud advocates for a hermeneutical approach that considers the Qur'ān's overarching principles of justice and equality, suggesting that traditional interpretations often reflect patriarchal biases rather than the text's original intent. While progressive, liberal and feminist scholars have pushed for a re-examination of traditional prohibitions on same-sex acts and gender roles, their approaches are not without criticism. Critics argue that these interpretations often rely heavily on contextual or metaphorical readings of Qur'ānic texts, which may depart from classical hermeneutical principles that have guided Islāmic law for centuries. Some contend that prioritising contemporary ethical frameworks such as sexual autonomy or gender equality, risks imposing modern Western values onto the Islāmic tradition, potentially undermining the authority of established jurisprudence (*fiqh*). Besides, traditional scholars caution that these progressive readings may selectively interpret or downplay texts that explicitly address sexual ethics, creating tensions between reformist ideals and scriptural fidelity.

It is important to note that the Fiqh Council (Qadhi, 2022), representing the consensus of mainstream Islāmic scholarly bodies, holds that deliberately attempting to change one's biological sex or gender is impermissible. This prohibition includes the use of hormone therapy, surgical procedures, or any combination of these methods. From an Islāmic legal perspective, all intentional efforts to transition from one sex or gender to another are considered forbidden. The only exception occasionally recognised concerns individuals with intersex conditions, where medical intervention may be used to adjust physical characteristics to more closely correspond with the sex to which the person is determined to belong. Such decisions are made in consultation with qualified medical professionals and are viewed not as altering one's sex, but as clarifying biological status.

8.3 Ethical Considerations and Challenges

Islāmic therapists and counsellors working with LGBTQ+clients operate within a complex ethical landscape, balancing the demands of Islāmic teachings with professional responsibilities in psychotherapy. While Islāmic values and jurisprudence often establish clear boundaries regarding same-sex relationships and gender nonconformity, therapeutic and professional ethics emphasise respect for individual autonomy, emotional well-being, and non-judgemental support. Navigating the intersection of faith and professional care thus poses significant ethical challenges (Mahmood & Ssekamanya, 2020).

There are several ethical challenges faced by Islāmic therapists and counsellors when working with LGBTQ+clients:

Unconditional acceptance vs. religious doctrines: Islām upholds the sacred worth of every human being but prohibits same-sex sexual activity and does not recognise gender identities outside the male–female binary; this can create internal tension for Muslim therapists trained in models that promote unconditional positive regard, including acceptance of all identities and expressions (Malik, 2020). Unconditional acceptance here is about respecting the person's humanity and struggles, listening actively, and being empathetic, while still upholding your professional and value-based standards. Rather than moral affirmation of behaviour, therapists can offer unconditional acceptance of the person, validating their emotional struggles and humanity while maintaining the integrity of Islāmic values (Malik, 2020). The Qur'ânic model of respectful disagreement, as seen in the example of Prophet Abraham (Ibrahim) (عليه السلام), who disagreed with his people's practices yet still addressed them kindly (Ash-Shu 'ara, 26:69–104), offers a prophetic precedent for such therapeutic balance.

Empathy without endorsement: Therapists are not required, either professionally or religiously, to agree with every client's perspective. They are, however, obligated to offer empathy, care, and being nonjudgment (Malik, 2020). The Prophet Muhammad (ﷺ) demonstrated this by always separating sin from the sinner and responding with gentleness: It was narrated from Abu Hurairah (may Allāh be pleased with him) that the Messenger of Allah (ﷺ) said: "Allah is Gentle and loves gentleness, and He grants reward for it that He does not grant for harshness" (Ibn Majah). By adopting a posture of empathy without endorsement, Islāmic therapists and counsellors can support clients' mental health journeys without feeling they are compromising their religious commitments. This nuanced approach allows for healing and integrity to coexist.

Confidentiality and trust: LGBTQ+ clients, especially within conservative Muslim communities, may fear being "outed" to family, religious authorities, or peers. Confidentiality is, therefore, not just an ethical standard but a psychological lifeline (Saha et al., 2019).s Islām elevates this trust (*amānah*) as sacred. It is narrated by Jabir ibn Abdullah (may Allāh be pleased with him) that the Messenger of Allah (ﷺ) said "When a man tells something and then departs, it is a trust" (Abū Dāwūd (b)). Disclosure should only occur when legally required (e.g., imminent harm), and always with transparency and sensitivity.

8.4 Professional Ethical Obligation

Therapists are bound by internationally recognised ethical frameworks such as those from the American Psychological Association, British Association for Counselling and Psychotherapy, and local licensing boards. These standards emphasise confidentiality; non-maleficence and beneficence; autonomy and self-determination; fidelity and professional integrity.

With regard to confidentiality, therapists have an ethical duty to protect clients' personal disclosure, an especially critical concern for LGBTQ+ Muslim clients who may fear judgement or ostracism from family and community if their identities are revealed (American Psychological Association, 2019). Emotional and spiritual struggles commonly experienced by LGBTQ+ individuals, including shame, anxiety, and isolation, must be acknowledged and addressed with empathy and care (Bass & Nagy, 2023). Therapists are also expected to support clients in exploring their identities and making personal decisions free from coercion, even when those decisions diverge from the therapist's own beliefs (British Psychological Society, 2017). Furthermore, practitioners must uphold professional integrity by refraining from imposing their personal or religious convictions on clients (American Psychological Association, 2017). These professional standards provide a universal ethical foundation. For Muslim clinicians, however, they are further enriched and guided by theological principles rooted in Islāmic scripture and jurisprudence. Islāmic ethics provides complementary values that parallel professional guidelines, including *niyyah* (sincere intention), *raḥmah* (compassion), *ʿadl* (justice), and *iḥsān* (excellence in conduct) (See Chap. 3).

8.5 Proposed Therapeutic Framework for Islāmic Therapists Working with LGBTQ+ Clients

Islāmic therapists and counsellors often encounter a profound ethical crossroad when working with LGBTQ+ individuals: the imperative to offer inclusive, non-judgemental care alongside a personal commitment to uphold Islāmic beliefs. Rather than viewing these realms as mutually exclusive, this part proposes a faith-integrated therapeutic framework that allows Muslim clinicians to engage ethically, empathically, and effectively with LGBTQ+ clients while remaining anchored in Islāmic values (Jaspal, 2012). This model is grounded in principles of cultural humility, spiritual compassion, and psychological safety. It aims to empower clients to explore their identity within the context of their faith while supporting therapists in upholding both professional integrity and their own religious conscience.

Culturally and spiritually informed engagement: The therapeutic relationship must begin with an intentional exploration of the client's cultural, familial, and religious context. A thorough intake process should go beyond standard demographic questions to invite an open and respectful dialogue about the client's relationship with Islām, their experience of navigating faith-based stigma, and their internalised beliefs about gender and sexuality. This allows the therapist to attune to the specific nuance of the client's spiritual and emotional landscape. Importantly, therapists should remain curious but non-intrusive, allowing the client to define the role of faith or spirituality in their healing process and avoiding assumptions about religious identity or practice. This process of culturally informed inquiry establishes psychological safety and conveys deep respect for the client's intersectional experience (Maravia, 2022).

Facilitating theological meaning-making and creative reinterpretation: Islāmic therapists are not expected to offer religious rulings. However, they can create space for clients to engage with their theological questions through guided reflection and narrative inquiry. Many LGBTQ+ Muslim clients wrestle with internalised guilt or fear due to traditional interpretations of sacred texts. Using techniques from Islāmic integrated narrative therapy (Rassool, 2026), therapists can gently support clients in exploring their own meaning-making process around Qur'ânic teachings, metaphor, and religious narratives. Clients may, for example, reinterpret verses through metaphors of divine mercy, resilience, or personal struggle *(jihad al-nafs)*, allowing faith to become a source of strength rather than shame. This therapeutic stance encourages clients to reclaim their spiritual agency without pressuring them toward any particular theological stance (Bass & Nagy, 2023).

Affirmative language and emotional validation: A key component of this framework is the use of affirmative therapeutic language, not to endorse a specific behaviour, but to validate the client's lived reality, emotional suffering, and resilience. For many LGBTQ+ Muslims, invisibility and erasure within both religious and queer spaces compound their psychological distress. Therapists can disrupt this pattern by acknowledging the complexity of their identity and affirming their right to dignity, safety, and emotional support. Validation here does not mean theological endorsement; rather, it involves attuning to the pain of isolation, the courage it takes to exist authentically, and the emotional toll of navigating conflicting identities. This approach fosters trust and strengthens the therapeutic alliance (Safi, 2003).

Identity exploration through faith-informed modalities: Many LGBTQ+ Muslim clients experience fractured self-understanding due to perceived incompatibility between their sexual or gender identity and their religious values. Therapists can offer structured identity exploration exercises, journaling prompts, guided visualisation, or expressive art therapy, tailored to the client's cultural and spiritual orientation. For example, a client might be asked to visualise their future self in a spiritually fulfilling and emotionally authentic life, or to write a letter from their compassionate, faith-anchored self to the part of them that feels rejected or ashamed. Such tools allow clients to express internal conflicts in a creative, non-confrontational manner and explore possibilities of integration rather than exclusion. These exercises are especially powerful when anchored in Islāmic concepts such as *niyyah* (intention), *fitrah* (natural disposition), and *rahmah* (divine mercy), allowing the therapeutic process to resonate with both psychological and spiritual meaning (Yaqeen Institute, 2022).

Therapist integrity, ethical self-awareness, and referral boundaries: For Islāmic therapists, this work demands not only clinical skill but also ongoing ethical self-awareness. Therapists must regularly assess their emotional responses, theological boundaries, and capacity to maintain neutrality. This self-monitoring is critical to ensure that personal convictions do not obstruct the client's psychological safety or growth situations where the therapist feels unable to provide affirming care, despite supervision and reflection, referral becomes a moral and professional necessity. Such referrals should be handled with warmth and dignity, framing the transition as an act of care rather than rejection. This protects the client's well-being and upholds the therapist's integrity (Caldwell, 2011). A summary of the therapeutic strategies for Islāmic therapists working with LGBTQ+ clients is presented in Table 8.1.

Collectively, these strategies provide a therapeutic framework that is not only ethically responsible but also clinically effective and spiritually attuned. By integrating professional psychological standards with values rooted in Islāmic ethics, this model equips Muslim therapists to address the unique challenges faced by LGBTQ+ clients. It allows clinicians to uphold fidelity to their faith while simultaneously fostering a safe, compassionate, and affirming therapeutic environment. In doing so, therapists can accompany clients through complex struggles of identity, spirituality, and belonging with both integrity and deep empathy, ensuring that care remains holistic and dignified.

Table 8.1 Therapeutic strategies for Islāmic therapists working with LGBTQ+ clients: An ethically and spiritually grounded framework

Domain	Key practices	Purpose/Outcome	References
Culturally and spiritually informed engagement	Begin with exploration of client's cultural, familial, and religious context; invite open dialogue about Islām, stigma, and beliefs around gender/sexuality; remain curious but non-intrusive	Establish psychological safety and respect for intersectional experiences	Maravia (2022)
Facilitating theological meaning-making & creative reinterpretation	Use Islāmic integrated narrative therapy to help clients reflect on Qur'ānic teachings; reframe texts through mercy, resilience, or *jihad al-nafs*; avoid giving religious rulings	Allow faith to serve as a source of strength instead of shame; support spiritual agency	Bass and Nagy (2023) Rassool (2026)
Affirmative language & emotional validation	Employ affirming but non-prescriptive language; validate lived reality, suffering, and resilience; acknowledge invisibility within religious and queer spaces	Reduce isolation, foster trust, strengthen therapeutic alliance without theological endorsement	Safi (2003)
Identity exploration through faith-informed modalities	Use journaling, guided visualisation, or expressive arts; integrate Islāmic concepts like *niyyah* (intention), *fitrah* (natural disposition), *rahmah* (divine mercy)	Encourage integration of religious and sexual/gender identity; promote creative, non-confrontational self-exploration	Yaqeen Institute (2022)
Therapist integrity, ethical self-awareness & referral boundaries	Maintain self-awareness of emotions and theological limits; ensure neutrality; refer when affirming care cannot be provided, framing it as care not rejection	Protect client's well-being, uphold therapist integrity, ensure ethical practice	Caldwell (2018)

8.6 Case Studies Insights

Islāmic therapists working with LGBTQ+clients often operate in ethically and emotionally charged terrain, balancing their professional duty of care with religious convictions that may not affirm same-sex behaviour or non-binary gender identities. This section presents key studies, interviews, and therapeutic insights that illuminate how therapists manage these dilemmas respectfully and ethically (Dasti et al., 2019). The findings of a qualitative study (Mahmood & Ssekamanya, 2020) show that many Muslim counsellors experienced significant ethical tensions when working with LGBTQ+clients. Much of this internal conflict stemmed from the challenge of reconciling professional obligations to affirm and support clients with personal religious convictions that regard homosexuality as sinful. One counsellor described the inner turmoil.

> *The therapist is also under conflict due to his own personal views on the subject and feels strongly about the emancipation of such individuals, but is reluctant to offer any therapeutic solution that may further jeopardize the client's familial relationships.*

These therapists navigated ethical tension by adopting a stance of empathetic neutrality, clearly distinguishing compassion for the individual from any normative position on behaviour, and, where necessary, engaging in reflective supervision to determine the appropriateness of referral (Mahmood & Ssekamanya, 2020). One significant empirical study examined how Muslim therapists in Malaysia reconcile religious convictions with the ethical imperative to support LGBTQ+clients. Using grounded theory, the study conducted in-depth interviews with six Muslim therapists. The findings revealed three primary value conflicts:

Therapists working with LGBTQ+Muslim clients experienced conflicting goals, as their professional aim to help clients reduce or discontinue same-sex behaviour sometimes clashed with clients' desire for affirmation or practical relationship support. They also navigated conflicting roles, feeling torn between their responsibilities as licensed professionals and their commitments as practicing Muslims. For example, Madam Karimah described the challenge of "needing to give *da'wah* gently" while maintaining therapeutic neutrality. Additionally, therapists occasionally encountered conflicting interests, admitting that personal curiosity about LGBTQ+experiences sometimes risked interfering with professional boundaries. The self-awareness and realignment show that ethical care prevailed despite personal interest, revealing the emotional complexity therapists endure when religious and professional selves collide (Mahmood & Abdallah, 2020).

To manage these challenges, therapists employed several strategies. They sought supervision that aligned with both professional and religious standards, engaged in self-directed study of Western LGBTQ+counselling models with appropriate cultural adaptations, and prioritised religious values whenever moral conflicts arose. Through these approaches, therapists aimed to maintain ethical and culturally sensitive care while honouring both professional and religious commitments. While some actions, such as advising clients that their sexuality was sinful, may contradict affirmative ethics in Western standards, the study reflects the lived challenges Muslim professionals face when Islāmic ethics intersect with modern psychological practice (Mahmood & Abdallah, 2020).

Langroudi and Skinta (2019) proposed an integrative clinical model applying Acceptance and Commitment Therapy (ACT) and Compassion-Focused Therapy (CFT) to Muslim clients from gender and sexual minority backgrounds in diaspora contexts. Their study presented a composite case of a Syrian asylum seeker in the United States experiencing significant internalised shame and religious distress. The Muslim therapist focused on alleviating psychological suffering through ACT-based interventions, including guided mindfulness exercises centred on bodily awareness, self-compassion practices addressing early experiences of vulnerability, and the use of culturally resonant Islāmic metaphors to support compassionate self-reflection. Importantly, the therapeutic work was framed as harm reduction and psychological care, and avoided theological judgement. The therapist acknowledged Islāmic shame-based culture while helping the client reclaim a holistic self-image. Such models offer Islāmic therapist and counsellors non-pathologising, culturally responsive strategies that uphold both ethical integrity and therapeutic empathy (Langroudi & Skinta, 2019).

In another documented clinical case (Langroudi & Skinta, 2019), a Muslim gay asylum seeker named Osama received therapy in the US after fleeing religious persecution. His ACT (Acceptance and Commitment Therapy) therapist used mindfulness and values-based reflection rooted in Islāmic metaphor. In one powerful session, the therapist asked, "*Shall we invite the self-compassionate voice into your life like the blissful sound of Adhan*?", bridging his faith with healing (Langroudi & Skinta, 2019). This approach allowed Osama to connect spiritual values with therapeutic recovery, without asking him to disavow either his religious identity or his sexual orientation. The therapist was not Muslim, but the case illustrates the potential of culturally and spiritually attuned methods that Muslim therapists can adapt (Langroudi & Skinta, 2019). Imām Muhsin Hendricks, while not a clinician, plays a counselling role through the Al-Fitrah Foundation in South Africa. He provides pastoral support to LGBTQ+Muslims, highlighting that "support does not always require agreement." His approach models how religious integrity can coexist with unconditional compassion (Rahim, 2025). A Canadian clinical therapist, cited in Jaspal (2014), discussed the use of celibacy counselling with a gay Muslim client who wished to remain religious. The therapist focused on emotional validation and self-worth while helping the client cope with tension between faith and desire without coercing change (Jaspal, 2014). This approach represents an acceptable form of pastoral support for an individual seeking to uphold their religious commitments without affirming prohibited actions or introducing coercion.

These diverse cases and clinical reflections highlight that while tensions between theology and therapeutic ethics are real, Muslim therapists across contexts are finding thoughtful, compassionate, and culturally congruent ways to support LGBTQ+clients, honouring faith and psychological well-being in the therapeutic space.

8.7 Clinical Reflections

Working in a multicultural and religiously diverse context, as an Islāmic therapist, my therapeutic encounters with LGBTQ+clients have often taken place within layered cultural, religious, and emotional landscapes. I have encountered clients whose lived realities resist easy categorisation, where identity, spirituality, and psychological pain intersect in deeply personal and often silent ways. The following clinical reflections are drawn from my own therapeutic practice. They are presented to illustrate how an ethically grounded, faith-sensitive approach can provide meaningful support to LGBTQ+clients without theological compromise. These cases exemplify my sustained effort to uphold the therapeutic space, one rooted in empathy, discretion, and spiritual humility, while honouring both professional and Islāmic commitments.

8.7.1 Case Study 1: "Jared—Faith, Fear, and Silence"

Background

Jared, a 26-year-old Filipino male living in Dubai, presented with chronic anxiety, social isolation, and difficulty sustaining focus at work. Raised in a conservative Catholic household, he carried a profound sense of spiritual guilt related to his sexual orientation. Jared disclosed in therapy that he identified as gay but lived in constant fear of judgement from his church, community, and himself. Residing in a Muslim-majority context, he felt compelled to conceal his identity, which intensified his isolation and emotional distress. He expressed fears of both divine condemnation and social rejection, noting that therapy was the first space where he had ever revealed his orientation.

Therapeutic Approach

The therapist adopted a person-centred approach, emphasising unconditional positive regard, emotional safety, confidentiality, and nonjudgement. This framework allowed Jared to explore his identity and internal struggles without fear of rejection. His emotional pain was acknowledged without pathologising his orientation. To honour his cultural and spiritual context, the therapist incorporated elements of both Christian and Islāmic ethical traditions, highlighting compassion, introspection, and self-respect, as guiding principles in the therapeutic space. The therapeutic process focused on identifying and dismantling internalised shame, addressing existential fears, and differentiating Jared's sense of identity from sin-based frameworks. Rather than affirming or rejecting his sexual orientation, therapy concentrated on strengthening emotional resilience, fostering cognitive restructuring, and supporting Jared's engagement with spirituality in ways that felt personally meaningful. His internal conflict was reframed as part of his broader emotional and spiritual development, rather than as evidence of personal failure.

Outcome

Over the course of therapy, Jared's symptoms of anxiety significantly diminished. He developed a private spiritual practice rooted in gratitude, reflection, and self-compassion, drawing from both Christian and Islāmic ethical values. Although he chose to remain private about his orientation, Jared reported greater emotional clarity, inner peace, and self-acceptance. His progress was defined not by external disclosure but by his growing capacity to embrace himself as a human being worthy of dignity, presence, and care. While theological resolution was not achieved, Jared attained a sense of inner coherence that supported his ongoing emotional and spiritual well-being.

8.7.2 Case Study 2: "Ismail—Shame and Suppression"

Background

Ismail, a 30-year-old Filipino expat, came to therapy with symptoms of depression, irritability, and sleep disturbance. A few sessions into therapy, he disclosed that he had been grappling with same-sex attraction since adolescence, an experience he had long perceived as a religious failing. Raised in a devout Muslim household and currently married to a woman residing in the Philippines, Ismail described a constant internal war between his values and desires, accompanied by intense guilt and confusion.

Therapeutic Approach

With deep respect for his cultural values and emotional struggles, the therapist provided an empathetic and values-based space. Working within an integrative therapeutic model, the intervention drew upon cognitive-behavioural therapy (CBT), motivational interviewing, and Islāmic psychotherapy. Rather than prescribing decisions regarding marriage or sexual orientation, therapy emphasised creating a safe environment where Ismail could explore his emotional world with honesty. The sessions addressed cognitive distortions related to sin, guilt, and divine punishment. Core Islāmic concepts such as *ikhlāṣ* (sincerity), *tawbah* (repentance), and the understanding that human struggle does not negate spiritual worth were integrated. Ismail was encouraged to reflect on how he might embody emotional integrity, even in the absence of moral certainty.

Outcome

Over the course of ten sessions, Ismail showed marked improvements in sleep quality, emotional regulation, and mood stability. He chose to remain in his marriage and made a conscious effort to engage with his wife more authentically. He also began journaling his inner struggles as an act of self-compassion and spiritual accountability. While therapy did not resolve the underlying tension between identity and faith, it provided Ismail with the tools to hold this tension more gently, reducing self-blame and fostering greater emotional clarity.

8.7.3 Case Study 3: "Amina—Torn Between Two Worlds"

Background
Amina, a 22-year-old Moroccan university student in the United Arab Emirates, presented with symptoms of depression, self-harm, and emotional numbness. In our initial sessions, she disclosed that she identified as bisexual and felt suffocated under her family's strict cultural expectations. She feared being disowned if discovered and struggled with reconciling her faith, values, and identity.

Therapeutic Approach
Amina's therapy was grounded in trauma-informed care, narrative therapy, and Islāmic psychotherapy. The therapist emphasised from the outset that the purpose of therapy was not to change who she was, but to provide a safe and supportive space where she could understand and manage her pain. The focus of the sessions was on cultivating self-compassion, restructuring her relationship with religious guilt, and reclaiming agency over her life decisions. As part of the process, the therapist introduced Islāmic spiritual practices such as *tafakkur* (deep reflection) and journaling, which served as tools for healing and grounding. Cultural sensitivity remained central to the therapeutic work, with explicit attention given to Amina's fears of rejection and the impact of social expectations. The therapist held space for her struggles within a morally reflective framework, approaching her dilemma not as a theological problem to be resolved but as an emotional journey to be navigated.

Outcome
Amina made significant progress over time, reporting a reduction in depressive symptoms and self-harming behaviour. She re-engaged with her academic pursuits and began rebuilding her social life. While she chose not to come out to her family, she developed a more integrated sense of self, one that allowed her to hold her faith and identity in compassionate tension. Therapy helped her prioritise psychological safety and self-understanding, rather than rushing toward disclosure or resolution.

8.7.4 Reflections

These cases highlight the profound ethical and clinical complexity that emerges when working at the intersection of faith, culture, and personal identity. They demonstrate that therapeutic progress does not depend on reaching a theological resolution, but rather on cultivating a space where clients can experience healing, dignity, and self-acceptance. When therapists approach such work with humility, curiosity, and cultural literacy, the therapeutic space becomes one that honours both the sacred and the psychological without contradiction. Faith is neither dismissed nor imposed upon; instead, it is engaged as a living dimension of the client's experience that can be drawn upon for strength, reflection, and growth. These experiences reaffirm the understanding that healing is not about forcing resolution of identity conflicts, but about restoring a client's sense of worth and humanity. Within this process, values such as mercy, presence, and intention become essential. They allow therapy to serve as a bridge, connecting spiritual frameworks with psychological care, and enabling clients to hold their struggles with greater gentleness and coherence.

Ultimately, these cases illustrate that therapy can support clients in carrying tensions that may never fully resolve, while still fostering resilience, clarity, and peace. In doing so, therapy respects the integrity of both faith and identity, affirming that true healing lies in the restoration of dignity and the capacity to live with compassion toward oneself.

8.8 Training and Professional Development

Islāmic psychotherapists and counsellors should develop informed empathy by learning about the spectrum of sexual orientations and gender identities within Muslim communities. Training must address the psychological effects of stigma, concealment, and faith-based rejection, as well as intersectional pressures from family and culture. Trauma-informed approaches are essential to support clients experiencing identity suppression and marginalisation, with the ultimate goal of fostering a non-judgemental clinical stance. Islāmic psychotherapists and counsellors need a foundational understanding of Islāmic teachings on sexuality and gender to support clients facing theological guilt or confusion. This includes knowledge of Qur'ânic verses, *hadīths*, and juristic positions, awareness of diverse scholarly interpretations, and the ability to facilitate client-led reflection without imposing beliefs. Such literacy enables therapists to hold space for both faith and identity in a balanced, non-intrusive way.

Islāmic psychotherapists and counsellors should be trained to navigate ethical dilemmas that arise when personal beliefs intersect with client needs. This involves applying professional ethical codes alongside Islāmic moral principles, engaging in case-based learning around value conflicts and boundaries, and using reflective tools such as supervision, peer consultation, and journaling. Strengthening ethical agility enables therapists to make principled decisions that protect both client care and spiritual integrity. Islāmic psychotherapists and counsellors need training to communicate with compassion, cultural humility, and sensitivity. This involves affirming clients' emotional experiences while respecting religious boundaries, using inclusive and attuned verbal and non-verbal communication, and addressing identity–faith tensions without avoidance or invalidation. Such communication fosters trust and creates a safe space for clients to share vulnerable or spiritually conflicted aspects of themselves. Islāmic psychotherapists and counsellors should have access to structured support systems to manage the internal tensions that arise in faith-integrated work. This includes faith-informed clinical supervision, peer dialogue groups for shared learning, and reflective spaces to explore emotional reactions, value conflicts, and unconscious bias. These supports enhance clinical humility, ethical consistency, and reduce the risk of client harm.

Islāmic psychotherapists and counsellors must cultivate faith-aligned self-care practices to sustain both professional and spiritual well-being. This includes integrating worship, *du 'a'h*, Islāmic contemplation, or *dhikr* into daily practice, setting boundaries to prevent burnout, and reconnecting with Islāmic principles such as *rahmah* (mercy), *niyyah* (intent), and *ihsān* (excellence in conduct). Such grounding allows therapists to maintain presence, patience, and purposeful engagement in their therapeutic role. Table 8.2 presents the core training domains for Islāmic psychotherapists working with LGBTQ+ clients

Table 8.2 Core training domains for Islāmic psychotherapists working with LGBTQ+ clients

Core area	Focus	Key components	Intended outcome
Understanding LGBTQ+ identities in Islāmic and cultural contexts	Educating therapists on the spectrum of sexual orientations and gender identities within Muslim communities	Psychological impact of stigma, concealment, and faith-based rejection Intersectional pressures (family, culture,community) Trauma-informed responses to identity suppression and marginalisation	Develop a non-judgmental, empathic stance rooted in informed understanding rather than ideology
Religious sensitivity and theological literacy	Building therapists' ability to meaningfully engage with faith-related struggles	Knowledge of Qur'ânic verses, *hadīth*, and classical juristic views on sexuality and gender Awareness of diverse interpretations (traditional, reformist, pastoral) Skills for facilitating client-led reflection without imposing beliefs	Enable therapists to hold space for both faith and identity without undermining either
Ethical decision-making in faith-integrated practice	Training in resolving ethical dilemmas where personal belief and client care intersect	Applying professional ethical codes (APA, BACP) alongside Islāmic moral principles Case-based learning on value conflicts, boundaries, and referrals Use of reflective tools (supervision, journaling, peer consultation)	Strengthen ethical agility to make principled decisions while safeguarding client welfare and spiritual integrity

(continued)

Table 8.2 (continued)

Core area	Focus	Key components	Intended outcome
Culturally competent and affirmative communication	Enhancing communication that balances compassion with cultural and religious sensitivity	Language that validates emotional experience while respecting religious frameworks Nonverbal attunement and shame-awareness Dialogues that acknowledge both identity and faith without avoidance or invalidation	Build trust and psychological safety, enabling deeper disclosure and healing
Supervision, peer support, and reflective practice	Providing structured support systems for therapists	Access to faith-informed supervision for LGBTQ+ cases Peer dialogue groups for shared learning and guidance Reflective spaces for exploring emotional reactions, bias, or value conflicts	Foster humility, consistency, and accountability, while reducing risk of harm to clients
Self-care grounded in spiritual practice	Sustaining therapist well-being through spiritually aligned practices	Incorporating worship, du 'ah, contemplation, or *dhikr* into daily rhythm Setting boundaries to prevent burnout and moral fatigue Reconnecting with principles of *rahmah* (mercy), *niyyah* (intent), and *iḥsān* (excellence)	Promote therapist resilience, presence, and purpose in clinical practice

8.9 Conclusion

In conclusion, working and supporting LGBTQ+ clients as an Islāmic psychotherapists and counsellors requires more than clinical competence; it calls for spiritual clarity, ethical courage, and theological humility. This chapter has illustrated that it is entirely possible to walk this fine line with dignity but to remain rooted in Islāmic values while providing LGBTQ+ individuals with care that is empathetic, non-judgemental, and ethically sound. Rather than denying religious conviction or abandoning professional duty, Islāmic psychotherapists and counsellors are encouraged to engage reflectively with both. They can hold space for client narratives without affirming behaviours that contradict their faith, and yet offer the safety, validation, and trust essential to psychological healing. Through intentional therapeutic boundaries, narrative exploration, compassionate language, and ethically conscious referrals, therapists can honour their faith while preventing harm. The experiences shared throughout this chapter reveal that the solution is not a theological compromise but ethical integrity anchored in Islām's own moral teachings of mercy, justice, and intention. In doing so, Islāmic therapists serve not only as clinicians but as witnesses to a model of care where faith and professionalism enrich each other. This chapter ultimately affirms that even in the face of theological complexity, the heart of therapy remains the same: to accompany the other, with presence, respect, and unwavering compassion.

References

Abū Dāwūd (a) *Sunan Abi Dawud 4097*. In-book reference: Book 34, Hadith 78 English translation: Book 33, Hadith 408. Sahih (Al-Albani). https://sunnah.com/abudawud:4097

Abū Dāwūd (b). Sunan Abi Dawud 4868. In-book reference: Book 43, Hadith 96English translation: Book 42, Hadith 4850. Hasan (Al-Albani). https://sunnah.com/abudawud:4868

American Psychological Association. (2017). *Ethical principles of psychologists and code of conduct* (2002, amended June 1, 2010, and January 1, 2017). https://www.apa.org/ethics/code

American Psychological Association. (2019, October 19). *Protecting your privacy: Understanding confidentiality*. https://www.apa.org/topics/psychotherapy/confidentiality

Al-Krenawi, A., & Graham, J. R. (2009). *Islāmic counseling: An introduction to theory and practice*. Routledge.

Bass, B., & Nagy, H. (2023, November 13). Cultural competence in the care of LGBTQ patients. In *StatPearls*. StatPearls Publishing. https://www.ncbi.nlm.nih.gov/books/NBK563176/

British Psychological Society. (2017). *Practice guidelines* (3rd ed.). https://cms.bps.org.uk/sites/default/files/2022-06/BPS%20Practice%20Guidelines%20%28Third%20Edition%29.pdf

Bukhārī. *Sahih al- Bukhārī 5886*. In-book reference: Book 77, Hadith 103 USC-MSA web (English) reference: Vol. 7, Book 72, Hadith 774. https://sunnah.com/bukhari:5886

Caldwell, B. (2018, September 5). Can a religious therapist refuse to treat gay and lesbian clients? *Psychotherapy Notes*. https://www.psychotherapynotes.com/can-a-religious-therapist-refuse-to-treat-gay-and-lesbian-clients/

Dasti, R., Farhan, R., Tehreem Fatima Naqvi, Sitwat, A., & Iram Zehra Bokharey. (2019). Ethical and moral dilemmas in psychotherapy. In *Advances in Religious and Cultural Studies (ARCS) Book Series* (pp. 242–258). https://doi.org/10.4018/978-1-7998-0018-7.ch013

Ibn 'Abbâs (n.d.) *Tanwîr al-Miqbâs min Tafsîr Ibn 'Abbâs*. Tafsir Surah Ankabut ayah 29. https://surahquran.com/tafsir-english.php?sora=29&aya=29

Ibn Majah. *Sunan Ibn Majah 3688*. In-book reference: Book 33, Hadith 32. English translation: Vol. 5, Book 33, Hadith 3688. Sahih (Darussalam). https://sunnah.com/ibnmajah:3688

Jaspal, R. (2012). The construction and management of homosexuality and Muslim identity: A qualitative study of British Pakistani Muslims. *Journal of Homosexuality, 59*(5), 715–735. https://doi.org/10.1080/00918369.2012.694750

Jaspal, R. (2014). *British Muslim gay men: Identity and cultural conflict* (Doctoral dissertation, De Montfort University). DORA De Montfort Open Research Archive. https://www.dora.dmu.ac.uk/handle/2086/9897

Kugle, S. S. a.-H. (2010). *Homosexuality in Islam: Critical reflection on gay, lesbian, and transgender Muslims*. Oneworld.

Langroudi, J. F., & Skinta, M. D. (2019). Working with gender and sexual minorities in the context of Islāmic culture: A queer Muslim behavioural approach. *The Cognitive Behaviour Therapist, 12*, Article e34. https://doi.org/10.1017/S1754470X19000161

Mahmood, A., & Abdallah, S. (2020). Value conflicts in counseling Muslim LGBT clients: Muslim counsellors' experiences. *International Seminar on Guidance and Counseling (ISGC).* https://www.researchgate.net/publication/343763516_Value_Conflicts_in_Counseling_Muslim_LGBT_Clients_Muslim_Counsellors'_Experiences

Mahmood, S. R. S., & Ssekamanya, S. (2020, August 14). Value conflicts in counseling Muslim LGBT clients: Muslim counsellors' experiences. In *Proceedings of the 2nd International Seminar on Guidance and Counseling 2019 (ISGC 2019)* (pp. 143–149). Atlantis Press. https://doi.org/10.2991/assehr.k.200814.032

Malik, R. (2020). Islāmic ethics and psychology [Op-ed]. *Research Center for Islāmic Legislation and Ethics.* https://www.cilecenter.org/research-publications/op-ed/Islāmic-ethics-and-psychology

Maravia, U. (2022, August 1). Pursuing Tas'heeh al-jince (gender-affirming surgery) for the khuntha (intersex person) who experiences gender dysphoria: From the viewpoint of Islāmic Fiqh and bioethics. *Journal of the British Islāmic Medical Association.* https://www.jbima.com/article/pursuing-tasheeh-al-jince-gender-affirming-surgery-for-the-khuntha-intersex-person-who-experiences-gender-dysphoria-from-the-viewpoint-of-Islāmic-fiqh-and-bioethics/

Qadhi, D. Y. (2009, April 13). Dealing with homosexual urges: Yasir Qadhi to Muslim student. *MuslimMatters.org.* https://muslimmatters.org/2009/04/13/dealing-with-homosexual-urges/

Rahim. (2025, February 15). A tribute to Muhsin Hendricks: A life of courage, compassion, and friendship. *Medium.* https://medium.com/@rahimthawer/a-tribute-to-muhsin-hendricks-a-life-of-courage-compassion-and-friendship-13ba9104cfa5

Rassool, G. Hussein. (2026). *Islāmic integrated narrative therapy* (Ist). Routledge.

Safi, O. (2003). *Progressive Muslims: On justice, gender, and pluralism.* Oneworld Publications. https://www.researchgate.net/profile/Omid-Safi/publication/320474752_Progressive_Muslims_On_Justice_Gender_and_Pluralism/links/59e7a5e7458515c3630f9f27/Progressive-Muslims-On-Justice-and-Pluralism.pdf

Saha, K., Kim, S. C., Reddy, M. D., & De Choudhury, M. (2019). The language of LGBTQ+ minority stress experiences on social media.*Proceedings of the ACM on Human-Computer Interaction, 3*(CSCW), 1–22. https://doi.org/10.1145/3361108

Tirmidhî & Ibn Majah. *Mishkat al-Masabih 3577.* In-book reference: Book 17, Hadith 23. https://sunnah.com/mishkat:3577

Uddin, M. (2017). Inheritance of hermaphrodite (khuntha) under Muslim law: An overview. *Beijing Law Review, 8*(2), 226–237. https://doi.org/10.4236/blr.2017.82013

Wadud, A. (2006). *Inside the gender jihad: Women's reform in Islam.* Oneworld.

Yaqeen Institute for Islāmic Research. (2022, October 7). *Islam and the LGBT question: Reframing the narrative.* https://yaqeeninstitute.org/read/paper/islam-and-the-lgbt-question-reframing-the-narrative

Chapter 9
Ethical Considerations in Islāmic Psychotherapy with Vulnerable Clients

9.1 Introduction

The practice of psychotherapy with vulnerable populations presents a complex ethical landscape even within conventional clinical settings. Vulnerable populations include individuals experiencing trauma, abuse, social marginalisation, disability, spiritual distress, or crises of faith (Fisher, 2016). The concept of intersectionality, as articulated by Crenshaw (1989), provides a crucial lens for understanding the complex ways in which social identities overlap to shape individual experiences of privilege and marginalisation and for understanding the complex needs of vulnerable clients in psychotherapy. In this context, intersectionality refers to the interconnected and overlapping nature of social categories, such as gender, ethnicity, socioeconomic status, and religious identity, which together create unique experiences of privilege and marginalisation (Crenshaw, 1989). This is particularly relevant for psychotherapy, as clients rarely experience these identities in isolation; rather, their overlapping nature can profoundly influence psychological well-being, coping strategies, and access to care.

By incorporating religious identity alongside more commonly recognised social categories, the intersectionality framework becomes particularly relevant for Muslim clients, who may face unique challenges such as microaggressions, social exclusion, prejudice, discrimination, and Islāmophobia, often compounded by the visibility of their religious identity (Rassool, 2025). These intersectional and social pressures rarely occur in isolation; instead, they interact with gender, socioeconomic status, ethnicity, and other identity markers, producing complex layers of vulnerability that can profoundly affect psychological well-being, coping mechanisms, and access to mental health services. Research findings indicate that these intersecting social and identity factors, both directly and indirectly, shape the health presentations of vulnerable populations (Harari & Lee, 2021; Turan et al., 2019). For example, a Muslim refugee mother with young children, fleeing a civil

G. H. Rassool, *Ethical Dilemmas in Islāmic Psychotherapy*,
https://doi.org/10.1007/978-3-032-26515-9_9

war, may face compounded stress from forced displacement, Islāmophobia, discrimination, prejudice, caregiving responsibilities, and limited access to health care and social support. The intersection of her refugee status, religious identity, gender, and parental role profoundly shapes her mental health needs and calls for therapeutic approaches that are trauma-informed, culturally sensitive, and attentive to both her psychological and practical challenges.

In Islāmic psychotherapy, recognising these intersecting vulnerabilities is essential for ethical and effective practice. Therapists must understand that clients' experiences of oppression can shape not only their psychological symptoms but also their spiritual, cultural, and social needs. The complexity of providing care increases when psychotherapy is delivered within an Islāmic framework, as clinicians must navigate the interplay of professional standards, religious values, cultural expectations, and spiritual sensitivities. Vulnerable clients often face multiple, overlapping forms of disadvantage that influence their mental health, coping strategies, and overall well-being. By acknowledging these layered realities, therapists can offer care that is culturally sensitive, spiritually attuned, and ethically responsible, addressing the whole person, the interconnectedness of the mind, body, and soul, while respecting their Islāmic values and social context.

This chapter examines the ethical principles guiding Islāmic psychotherapy with vulnerable clients, including survivors of abuse and marginalised Muslim populations. It integrates insights from contemporary psychological research and Islāmic scholarship to inform culturally and spiritually sensitive therapeutic practice. The chapter aims to highlight the ethical responsibilities involved in supporting these communities.

9.2 Understanding Vulnerability and Ethics

The term vulnerability originates from the Latin word for "wound," reflecting the underlying concept of increased risk or the likelihood that an individual may experience illness or harm over a given period (Aday, 1994; Vélez Agosto & Almario-Zgheib, 2024). This concept is closely linked to psychology and psychiatry, as both disciplines engage with the psychic "wounds" (*vulnus*) inherent in the human experience (Montero Orphanopoulos, 2025). Understanding vulnerability in this dual sense, both as a potential for harm and as a marker of psychological susceptibility, provides a foundation for ethically and culturally sensitive care, particularly when working with populations facing complex social, economic, and spiritual challenges.

The World Health Organization (2022) defines vulnerability as "The conditions determined by physical, social, economic, and environmental factors or processes which increase the susceptibility of an individual, a community, assets, or systems to the impacts of hazards" (p. xlviii). In conventional psychology, the American Psychological Association (APA) defines vulnerability succinctly as "the susceptibility to develop a condition, disorder, or disease when exposed to specific agents or circumstances" (American Psychological Association, 2017). However, Montero Orphanopoulos (2025) argues that this definition does not fully capture the breadth of perspectives and recent advances in research on vulnerability within psychopathology. Accordingly, Montero Orphanopoulos (2025) develops an operational definition that incorporates contributions from psychology. "Key dimensions such as predisposition, endogenous factors, latent potential, neutrality, positioning, ethics, openness, horizon, subjectivity, intersubjectivity, exposure, limits, boundaries, attachment, bonding, insufficiency, dependence, emotions, identity, otherness, meaning, process, learning, and interdependence all inform a more comprehensive understanding of vulnerability, one that extends far beyond the notion of the *vulnus* to which an individual is exposed" (p. 33). In psychotherapy research, vulnerability is widely understood as a dynamic predisposition shaped by biological factors, early attachment experiences, cognitive patterns, and sociocultural context (Barlow, 2002; Brewin, 2011). Vulnerability is not solely a risk factor; within therapy it also functions as a mechanism of therapeutic change, as emotional openness, authentic expression, and willingness to engage with painful experiences are associated with stronger therapeutic alliances and improved outcomes (Auerbach, 2007; Gilbert, 2010).

Vulnerability is a foundational concept in both psychological and Islāmic understandings of the human behaviour. In Islāmic psychology, vulnerability refers to an individual's heightened susceptibility to emotional, psychological, or social harm due to factors such as trauma, poverty, disability, displacement, or discrimination. In Islāmic thought, vulnerability is also inherent to the human experience, rooted in the recognition of human dependence on Allāh, the limits of human capacity, and the fluctuating nature of the *nafs* (self). Among Muslim clients, experiences of vulnerability often take on additional layers shaped by their spiritual, cultural, and social environments. For some, psychological distress is intensified by spiritual crises, such as persistent *waswās* (intrusive spiritual doubts), feelings of religious inadequacy, or the belief that emotional suffering reflects personal weakness in *īmān*. Others may struggle with the misinterpretation of religious texts, having internalised punitive or fear-based theological messages that exacerbate guilt, shame, and self-criticism. Vulnerability may also stem from trauma related to religious or cultural abuse, including coercive spiritual authority, misuse of scripture, or community-imposed expectations that restrict autonomy and silence emotional pain. In certain contexts, patriarchal social structures further compound vulnerability by limiting women's agency, constraining help-seeking behaviours, and reinforcing harmful power dynamics within families or communities. For Muslims living as minorities, the psychological burden is intensified by minority stress, Islamophobia, racial discrimination, and societal marginalisation, all of which have been shown to negatively affect mental health (Amer & Hovey, 2012; Rassool, 2025).

Modern clinical ethics emphasises the protection of vulnerable clients through key principles: autonomy, beneficence, non-maleficence, justice, and fidelity (Beauchamp & Childress, 2019). In the context of abuse survivors, autonomy requires therapists to respect and support the survivor's ability to make informed decisions about their care, ensuring they are never coerced or pressured. Beneficence entails actively promoting the survivor's well-being, offering interventions that foster healing, empowerment, and safety. Non-maleficence highlights the imperative to avoid any actions, intentional or unintentional, that could re-traumatise, shame, or further harm the survivor. Justice calls for equitable treatment, advocating for survivors' rights and addressing systemic barriers such as stigma or lack of access to culturally competent services. Finally, fidelity emphasises trustworthiness and the maintenance of professional integrity, ensuring that therapists respect confidentiality, commitments, and the ethical obligations inherent in the therapeutic relationship. Together, these principles provide a structured ethical framework that aligns with both professional and Islāmic commitments to compassion (*raḥmah*) and justice (*'adl*) when working with survivors of abuse.

9.3 Understanding Survivors of Abuse in Muslim Communities

Survivors of abuse, whether intimate partner violence (IPV), child abuse, spiritual or religious coercion, or other forms of interpersonal harm, often present with complex, multilayered trauma that affects emotional, psychological, physical, and sometimes spiritual dimensions of their lives. Within Muslim communities, these experiences are further shaped by cultural norms, family structures, gender expectations, and socio-religious meaning-making. While abuse occurs across all societies, including among Muslims (Istratii & Ali, 2023), the therapeutic context becomes uniquely sensitive when cultural pressures and interpretations of religious teachings influence how survivors understand their experiences and how others respond to them. A central challenge frequently documented in psychological research is stigma. Stigma is consistently identified as one of the most significant barriers preventing Muslim survivors from seeking help. In many cultural settings, discussing abuse, particularly sexual or intimate partner violence, is considered taboo, and survivors may fear backlash, gossip, or blame. This leads to what Hassouneh and Culley (2008) describe as "cultural silencing mechanisms," which suppress disclosure and deepen isolation. Muslim survivors may face added pressure to preserve family harmony, uphold modesty, and avoid bringing shame (*'ayb*) to their families or communities. These dynamics intensify trauma, increase internalised self-blame, and delay help-seeking.

Scholars focusing on therapeutic practice within Muslim communities have highlighted the need for culturally and religiously informed responses. Khalida Haque, in *Islāmically Integrated Psychotherapy and Domestic Abuse*, argues that domestic abuse is often minimised or misunderstood in Muslim contexts. She calls for an integrative therapeutic framework that draws on Qur'ânic and Prophetic teachings alongside contemporary psychological methods to ensure culturally relevant and ethically safe care (Haque, 2026). This aligns with findings from a recent global meta-ethnography, which shows that Muslim women's experiences of domestic violence are deeply interwoven with both cultural identity and religious life. Religion may be weaponised by perpetrators, yet for survivors it can also serve as a source of resilience and meaning (Sharifnia et al., 2025). Beyond cultural pressures, survivors often face practical barriers. Many Muslim women fear judgement, social ostracisation, or accusations of being responsible for the abuse. Limited awareness of support services and concerns about breaking family unity further inhibit disclosure (Afrouz et al., 2020). The findings from psychological research demonstrate that stigma and negative social responses significantly shape survivors' emotional and cognitive processing during recovery. Kennedy and Prock (2018) show that such responses increase vulnerability to further victimisation and restrict access to supportive services. In some contexts, as Batool and Abtahi (2017) poignantly note, survivors may become "social outcasts whose social-self bleeds in the jaws of stigma."

Empirical research findings further illustrate how violence and stigma interact to worsen mental health outcomes. Budhwani and Hearld (2017) found that internalised stigma, particularly constant vigilance against judgement, was strongly associated with depression among Muslim women in the United States. Experiences of physical or sexual abuse amplified the risk of depressive symptoms, showing how violence and stigma together intensify psychological distress. For Muslim survivors in Western settings, structural barriers such as language obstacles, poverty, social marginalisation, and limited access to culturally sensitive services add yet another layer of difficulty (Ali & Ahmed, 2023). International research strengthens this understanding. Studies from Pakistan, including regions such as Gilgit Baltistan and Rawalpindi/Islamabad, consistently show strong links between IPV or domestic violence and elevated levels of depression, anxiety, PTSD, and reduced overall quality of life (Malik et al., 2020). Broader trauma research in Pakistan likewise reveals high rates of PTSD, anxiety, and depression among individuals exposed to violence, with domestic abuse being a major contributing factor (Ishtiaq et al., 2025). In the United States, Oyewuwo et al. (2024) report that Muslim survivors of IPV experience significantly higher levels of stress, anxiety, depression, and PTSD compared to non-survivors, demonstrating the compounded psychological burden placed on this population. Further evidence from Iran confirms the pervasive impact of IPV. Abdoli-Najmi and Mirghafourvand (2024) found that a majority of postpartum women had experienced at least one form of IPV, with sexual coercion particularly prevalent. Survivors showed significantly higher levels of depression and anxiety and markedly reduced maternal functioning. Socioeconomic adversity, such as unemployment and low income, further exacerbated psychological distress.

Across these diverse studies, a consistent picture emerges: survivors within Muslim communities face multilayered challenges shaped by trauma, cultural pressures, stigma, religious narratives, and structural inequality. Effective therapeutic practice requires a deep understanding of these intersecting factors, a commitment to cultural and ethical competence, and an awareness of how systemic barriers influence survivors' lives and mental health. Therapists must therefore approach their work with both clinical sensitivity and cultural humility, ensuring that survivors are supported in ways that validate their experiences, honour their dignity, and promote holistic healing.

9.4 Understanding Refugees and Marginalised Muslim Communities

Muslim refugees and displaced communities constitute one of the largest segments of the global refugee population. While they share many challenges with other refugee populations, research findings indicate that Muslim refugees often face compounded layers of trauma, discrimination, and cultural misunderstanding that uniquely shape their mental health outcomes. Exposure to war, forced displacement, political repression, sexual violence, torture, and the loss of home and family frequently results in complex trauma profiles (Fazel et al., 2005; Hassan et al., 2016; Silove et al., 2017). For many Muslim communities, from Syria, Afghanistan, Somalia, Palestine, Iraq, Yemen, and the Rohingya of Myanmar, traumas are often collective and tied to religious or ethnic identity. Studies among Rohingya refugees demonstrate that identity-targeted violence is associated with higher symptom severity and more chronic post-traumatic stress disorder (PTSD) compared to non-targeted trauma (Tay et al., 2019). Thus, distress among Muslim refugees often arises not only from individual events but also from structural violence, prolonged persecution, and threats to communal existence.

Post-migration stressors further compound these mental health difficulties. The findings from psychological research consistently show that discrimination, legal insecurity, poverty, and acculturative stress exacerbate symptoms of PTSD, depression, and anxiety among displaced populations (Miller & Rasmussen, 2017; Porter & Haslam, 2005). For Muslim refugees, these stressors frequently intersect with religious identity, with visible Muslims, particularly women who wear *hijab*, reporting higher levels of Islamophobia, social exclusion, and stereotyping in host countries such as North America, Europe, Australia, and the UK (Abu-Ras & Abu-Bader, 2009). Such persistent discrimination functions as an ongoing stressor, sometimes described as "daily trauma," compounding pre-existing psychological wounds. Additionally, refugees often experience misunderstanding or lack of cultural sensitivity within service systems regarding modesty norms, gender interactions, prayer practices, halal dietary requirements, and extended family structures (Yako & Biswas, 2014). When these aspects of identity are unacknowledged, refugees may experience a loss of dignity and belonging, further contributing to anxiety, depression, and social withdrawal.

The intersection of gender, culture, and displacement places Muslim refugee women at particular risk. The finding from research studies shows that women face additional barriers such as language difficulties, financial dependence, trauma from war or displacement, and distrust of authorities, which limit engagement with formal services (Guruge et al., 2009). Social and cultural pressures, including fear of dishonour, community judgement, or being perceived as religiously weak, exacerbate stigma and discourage help-seeking (Afrouz et al., 2020; Aloud & Rathur, 2009). Refugee women may also experience "intersectional trauma," arising from the convergence of migration-related stress, racism, gendered expectations, socioeconomic hardship, and marginalisation (Abu-Ras, 2007; Cole, 2009). Exposure to war, displacement, family separation, and ongoing instability can increase vulnerability to abuse within households or refugee camps, and prolonged stress, economic strain, and limited social support, intersecting with patriarchal structures, heighten risks for intimate partner violence (Hassan et al., 2016).

Structural marginalisation further shapes mental health outcomes for Muslim refugees. Poverty, unemployment, limited access to services, and systemic discrimination restrict opportunities for housing, health care, and employment (Zempi & Chakraborti, 2014). Undocumented migrants and asylum seekers face ongoing legal uncertainty, detention trauma, and fear of deportation, all of which exacerbate anxiety, depression, and social withdrawal (Carlsson et al., 2018). These structural factors combine with social stigma and cultural pressures, creating barriers that prevent survivors from seeking support for psychological distress or domestic violence. Cultural and religious stigma, often linked to fear of shame (*'ayb*) or community gossip, frequently suppress disclosure and impede recovery (Hassouneh & Culley, 2008; Padela & Curlin, 2013). Survivors may also distrust authorities due to prior experiences of corruption, persecution, or fear of child removal, further discouraging help-seeking (Rees & Pease, 2007). Moreover, many mental health and domestic violence services lack cultural competence, religious sensitivity, or trained interpreters, making access to support challenging (Abu-Ras & Abu-Bader, 2008).

Despite these considerable challenges, refugee and marginalised Muslim communities demonstrate significant resilience. Research consistently highlights the critical role of social and family support in fostering resilience among refugee populations. The findings of research studies show that refugee children's post-resettlement adjustment is strengthened by a sense of belonging and stable relationships within family and community networks (Marley & Mauki, 2019); social support, including familial and community ties, as a key component of resilience (Steel et al., 2009); maintaining connections with family and community (a "promotion factor") that enhances coping and adaptation (Fazel & Betancourt, 2018); family relationships (Khawaja et al., 2008). Theoretical and empirical literature also highlights the importance of family functioning for mental health outcomes, linking supportive familial environments to lower risks of depression, anxiety, and post-traumatic stress among both children and adults (Bronstein & Montgomery, 2011). Community resilience helps migrant communities manage stress and adapt to challenges, reducing the risks of acculturation stress and preparing them for future adversities. Economic resources, social capital, communication, and shared beliefs all strengthen resilience. Policies and structural support from host countries further facilitate migrants' adjustment, integration, and recovery from stressors (Olcese et al., 2023). Many survivors actively engage in meaning-making and rebuilding their lives after displacement, reflecting collective resilience and the capacity to recover even under extreme adversity.

Psychological research findings consistently highlight that religion is a powerful protective factor for Muslim refugees. Studies of Syrian, Afghan, and Bosnian displaced Muslims demonstrate that Islāmic spiritual practice, such as prayer, Qur'ânic recitation, communal worship, and reliance on God (*tawakkul*), function as emotional regulators and systems of meaning-making that buffer against overwhelming distress (Ai et al., 2003; Ishtiaq et al., 2020). Religious coping has been shown to correlate with lower levels of depression and enhanced resilience among survivors of war, torture, and displacement. For many, faith anchors personal identity, provides moral consistency in unstable environments, and restores a sense of purpose after profound loss, underscoring that religion is central, rather than peripheral, to psychological healing for Muslim refugees. While Islāmic practices support resilience and meaning-making (Aflakseir & Coleman, 2009), some survivors experience spiritual struggles when perpetrators manipulate religious teachings. Abusers may invoke religious duty, obedience, or prescribed gender roles to justify harm or enforce silence, causing survivors to experience increased guilt, confusion, and internal conflict (Abu-Ras, 2007). This form of spiritual abuse is particularly damaging because it distorts sacred teachings and undermines the survivor's spiritual and psychological well-being.

In summary, evidence shows that Muslim refugees and marginalised communities face layered trauma from pre-migration violence, post-migration hardships, discrimination, and cultural stigma, leading to high rates of PTSD, depression, anxiety, and somatic distress. Access to support is often limited by structural barriers and stigma. Refugee women are particularly vulnerable to intimate partner violence and sexual coercion. Despite these challenges, resilience is fostered through strong family networks, community support, faith, and cultural identity. Religious and spiritual practices serve as key coping mechanisms, though misuse of religion can create additional vulnerability. Effective therapeutic care must be trauma-informed, culturally sensitive, and structurally aware. Clinicians should address systemic inequalities, honour spiritual coping, and support survivors in reclaiming dignity and stability.

9.5 Ethical Considerations in Supporting Vulnerable Muslim Populations

Providing therapy for "Vulnerable Muslim Populations," encompassing survivors of domestic and intimate partner violence, as well as refugee and marginalised Muslim community, necessitates an approach that integrates professional psychological knowledge with the moral and ethical guidance of Islāmic principles.

Central to this work is *raḥmah* (compassion), understood not merely as an emotion but as a moral orientation. Allāh say in the Qur'ân.

وَرَحْمَتِى وَسِعَتْ كُلَّ شَىْءٍ ۚ.

- *My mercy encompasses all things.* (Al-A'raf 7:156, interpretation of the meaning).

كَتَبَ عَلَىٰ نَفْسِهِ ٱلرَّحْمَةَ ۚ.

- *He has decreed upon Himself mercy.* (Al-An‘am 6:12, interpretation of the meaning).

These verses affirm that mercy is intrinsic to God's nature, not something given sparingly or conditionally. For vulnerable Muslim populations, this serves as a profound ethical and spiritual grounding: just as God's mercy encompasses all things, survivors and refugees are worthy of care, compassion, and validation. ‘Abdullah ibn Mughaffal (may Allāh be pleased with him) reported that the Prophet (ﷺ) said, “Allāh is compassionate and loves compassion. He gives for compassion what He goes not give for harshness” (Al-Adab Al-Mufrad). In another *ḥadīth*, it is narrated by Abdullah ibn Amr ibn al-'As (may Allāh be pleased with him) that the Prophet (ﷺ) said: “The Compassionate One has mercy on those who are merciful. If you show mercy to those who are on the earth, He Who is in the heaven will show mercy to you” (Abī Dāwūd). This *ḥadīth* establishes compassion as a divine and ethical obligation, not merely a personal virtue.

The therapist, embodying *raḥmah*, reflects this divine attribute in their approach, listening without judgement, acknowledging suffering, and providing a safe, supportive environment. This understanding reassures traumatic clients that their pain is recognised and that healing is not only possible but aligned with the compassionate ethos that underpins their faith. Therapists who embody *raḥmah* cultivate a therapeutic environment grounded in compassion, where survivors feel genuinely heard, validated, and supported. By listening without judgement and acknowledging the full scope of the survivor's trauma, emotional, psychological, physical, and spiritual, the therapist reassures clients that their suffering is recognised and valued. This approach not only facilitates trust and emotional safety but also integrates the survivor's faith into the healing process, reinforcing that recovery is both possible and consistent with the compassionate principles central to their religious and cultural framework. In essence, *raḥmah* guides the therapist to provide care that is empathetic, ethically grounded, and spiritually attuned.

The principle of *ʿadl* (justice) is central when working with vulnerable Muslim populations. In Islāmic thought, *ʿadl* is not merely fairness; it is a moral stance that requires recognising oppression (*ẓulm*) and refusing to allow harm to be concealed, normalised, or justified. Abu Dharr (may Allāh be pleased with him) quoted the Prophet (ﷺ) saying among what he narrated from Allāh (*Hadīth Qudsī*), the Most High that He has said, “O MY slaves, I have made oppression unlawful for myself, and I have made it unlawful among you, so do not oppress one another” (Muslim). Classical scholars, including Imām An-Nawawī, note that this divine prohibition establishes a binding ethical duty: oppression is never permissible, and justice is obligatory for all humans. When an abuse survivor enters the therapeutic encounter, the principle of justice shapes the therapist's responsibilities in several ways. First, *ʿadl* requires naming abuse as injustice.

In Islāmic thought, *ʿadl* is not merely fairness; it is a moral stance that requires recognising oppression (*ẓulm*) and refusing to allow harm to be concealed, normalised, or justified. An Islāmic therapist guided by *ʿadl* cannot participate in that distortion. In keeping with the Prophet's statements, the therapist acknowledges that in the case of domestic and intimate partner violence, abuse is a moral wrong, not a marital problem, a test to be endured, or a private family matter to be hidden. Second, a key aspect of *ʿadl* is ensuring that religious teachings are never used to justify or excuse harm. Upholding justice also involves making clear that Islām does not sanction harm, and no spiritual ideal justifies wrongdoing. For example, abuse survivors often struggle with religious interpretations that have been used to justify or excuse harm. Some may have internalised patriarchal readings of religious texts, or feel that their suffering is "Allāh's test" in ways that prevent them from seeking help. Therapists working in an Islāmic paradigm must navigate these sensitivities by respectfully challenging harmful beliefs without dismissing the client's faith. They may need to collaborate with Islāmic scholars or community leaders, or use psychoeducation to help survivors reframe religious narratives in a way that supports healing and empowers them.

Third, *ʿadl* calls the therapist to restore the vulnerable Muslims and survivors' sense of dignity and moral worth. Abuse often distorts a person's understanding of themselves, convincing them they deserved the harm or lacked value. Justice, in the Islāmic ethical sense, involves affirming their God-given *karāmah* (dignity) and supporting their right to safety, respect, and truth. Fourth, '*adl* means supporting the survivor's autonomy. Injustice often robs vulnerable individuals of their sense of control and self-determination; and justice helps to restore it. The therapist does not dictate or pressure decisions but offers clarity, validation, and honest ethical guidance, enabling the survivor to make choices from a place of strength rather than fear. Finally, *ʿadl* demands honesty and moral courage from the therapist. This includes gently correcting harmful interpretations or narratives, and being transparent about limits of confidentiality and safeguarding responsibilities. In this way, *ʿadl* becomes a living moral framework in the therapeutic relationship. It calls the Islāmic psychotherapist to stand with the survivor against oppression, honour their dignity, and ensure that the therapeutic space is one where truth, integrity, and justice are upheld without compromise.

Central to this work is *amānah*, the trust placed in the therapist. The vulnerable client 's story is treated as a sacred trust that must be held with integrity, confidentiality, and deep respect. Jabir bin Abdullah (may Allāh be pleased with him) narrated that the Messenger of Allāh () said: "When a man narrates a narration, then he looks around, then it is a trust" (Tirmidhī). This *hadīth* emphasises confidentiality and honouring the vulnerability shared in therapeutic spaces. One of the most pressing ethical dilemmas arises in respecting the autonomy and confidentiality of survivors of abuse and marginalised clients. In many cultural contexts, disclosure of abuse can carry immense stigma, fear of family or community backlash, or even spiritual guilt. Meta-ethnographic research findings illustrate that many Muslim women internalise shame or self-blame, and are wary of seeking help because of concerns about how their religious community might respond (Sharifnia et al.,

2025). Therefore, therapists must create a space of trust, ensuring privacy and confidentiality, and clarifying what will and will not be shared outside sessions, even when family involvement is culturally expected. This responsibility also requires avoiding any form of gaslighting, including narratives that shame the survivor or downplay their suffering. Instead, the therapist creates a space that respects the complexity of the survivor's experiences, acknowledging that their environment may have contributed to harm while also respecting the ways faith can offer meaning and comfort.

Human dignity (*karāmah*) forms another pillar of ethical conduct. The therapist must uphold the vulnerable survivor's God-given worth, safeguarding their autonomy and avoiding any paternalistic or coercive tendencies. Truthfulness (*ṣidq*) requires clarity in communication and transparency about professional boundaries, ensuring the therapeutic relationship is grounded in honesty. The legal Islāmic maxim *"lā ḍarar wa-lā ḍirār"* demands that therapy must not exacerbate guilt, shame, or self-blame. Narrated by bn 'Abbas (may Allāh be pleased with him), Allāh's Messenger (ﷺ) said: "There should neither be harming (of others without cause), nor reciprocating harm (between two parties)" (Ahmad and Ibn Majah). The principle of *lā ḍarar wa-lā dirār*, to cause no harm, reminds the therapist that even religious reflections must be offered with care, ensuring they do not intensify guilt or shame. This humility extends to the therapist's sense of their own limitations. Islāmic ethics encourage intellectual and spiritual humility, prompting the therapist to seek consultation or refer onward when the survivor's needs exceed their expertise.

In Islāmic psychotherapy, competence (*iḥsān*) is not merely a professional standard but a religious obligation, particularly when working with survivors of abuse and vulnerable clients. The concept of *iḥsān,* to act with excellence, moral integrity, and ethical intelligence, requires that the therapist operate strictly within the limits of their training and expertise. Abuse cases are often complex, layered, and highly sensitive; engaging beyond one's competence risks re-traumatising the survivor, violating trust (*amānah*), and failing to uphold justice (*ʿadl*). Classical Islāmic jurisprudence placed significant emphasis on the competence and accountability of physicians. According to modern scholarship, Muslim jurists required physicians to possess both sufficient theoretical knowledge (*maʿrifa*) and practical expertise (*professional excellence*) before practicing medicine (Ghaly, 2024). Ibn al-Qayyim's (2003) categorisation of the physician–patient relationship highlights the importance of competence, consent, and accountability, principles that are directly applicable to working ethically with survivors of abuse. Just as a physician is held responsible for negligence, exceeding authority, or administering harmful treatment, a therapist must work within the bounds of their training and expertise to avoid causing further harm.

Engaging with survivors without sufficient knowledge or consent, or applying interventions improperly, parallels the ethical breaches Ibn al-Qayyim warned against in medicine. Accountability, in this context, ensures that the survivor's well-being, dignity, and safety are prioritised, and that ethical standards, grounded in both professional integrity and Islāmic moral principles, are upheld. In essence, consent and competence, obtaining informed consent, and avoiding harm are critical to maintaining trust and providing compassionate, just, and ethically sound care to survivors. Ethical practice, in this context, involves ongoing education, careful supervision, and timely referrals to specialists when necessary, ensuring that survivors receive competent, safe, and compassionate care. Acting without sufficient knowledge or preparation is not only professionally negligent but also a breach of the Islāmic ethical duty to protect the well-being, dignity, and rights of those who have suffered harm.

Supporting survivors of abuse and those who are vulnerable in Muslim communities often extends beyond individual therapy. Addressing systemic challenges, such as community stigma and the scarcity of culturally sensitive service, is essential. Ethical Islāmic psychotherapy may therefore require therapists to engage in advocacy, collaborating with community organisations to create supportive environments. This systemic approach reflects Islāmic principles of justice (*'adl*) and care for the oppressed (*ma 'dūm 'alayhim*). This approach aligns with the concept of socially engaged spirituality, which applies spiritual principles to real-world issues such as poverty, discrimination, and conflict. Rothberg (1993) notes that it refers to the development of "spiritual qualities within the context of full involvement in social, political, and communal life" (p. 105). In therapy, this means assisting individuals not only with personal healing but also with understanding and navigating their roles within society, responding to injustice, and cultivating resilience. Through socially engaged spirituality, therapists uphold a commitment to fostering justice, compassion, and holistic healing that benefits both individuals and their wider communities. Taken together, these values form an ethical framework in which the Islāmic psychotherapist is not only a clinician but also a spiritual and moral guide, someone who embodies compassion, integrity, justice, and humility while safeguarding the dignity and trust of survivors of abuse.

9.6 Introduction to the Case Vignettes

The following case vignettes are presented to illustrate the ethical complexities encountered in Islāmic psychotherapy when working with survivors of domestic and intimate partner violence, particularly among refugee and marginalised Muslim women. These cases highlight how intersecting factors such as trauma history, migration status, cultural expectations, religious meaning-making, and structural vulnerability shape both client experiences and therapeutic decision-making. Each vignette foregrounds a distinct ethical dilemma that clinicians may face, including tensions between confidentiality and safety, autonomy and beneficence, and religious sensitivity versus the ethical responsibility to challenge harm. Together, these cases demonstrate how ethical principles do not operate in isolation but intersect dynamically within real-world clinical contexts. By engaging with these vignettes, practitioners are invited to reflect on their ethical reasoning, examine their positionality, and consider how Islāmic values can guide ethical decision-making in complex therapeutic situations.

9.6.1 Case Vignette 1: Confidentiality vs. Safety

Sorayah, a 34-year-old refugee, was referred to therapy by a community health clinic due to symptoms of anxiety, insomnia, and emotional detachment. During sessions, she revealed ongoing intimate partner violence, including threats and coercive control by her husband. Sorayah expressed deep fear of engaging with authorities, citing past persecution, and worried that disclosure could jeopardise her immigration status and lead to family separation. She explicitly requested that the therapist keep this information confidential and avoid involving external services. The therapist must balance respect for Sorayah's autonomy and confidentiality with the ethical and legal duty to protect her and her children from harm. Navigating mandatory reporting requirements while maintaining therapeutic trust and minimising retraumatisation presents a significant ethical challenge. Table 9.1 presents ethical reflection on case vignette 1.

Table 9.1 Case vignette 1: Ethical reflection

Reflective domain	Reflective practice questions
Limits of confidentiality	What are the limits of confidentiality in this case, and how can they be communicated clearly, transparently, and compassionately?
Autonomy and protection	How can respect for the client's autonomy be balanced with the ethical and legal duty to protect her and any dependents from harm?
Minimising retraumatisation	What steps can be taken to minimise retraumatisation if safeguarding procedures or mandatory reporting become necessary?
Trust and fear of authorities	How might fear of authorities, immigration insecurity, or past persecution shape the client's trust in the therapist and the therapeutic process?
Religious and cultural meaning-making	How might the client's religious and cultural framework influence her understanding of harm, responsibility, and help-seeking behaviours?
Multidisciplinary and community support	What multidisciplinary, legal, or community-based resources can be ethically engaged to support safety while preserving the client's dignity?
Therapist reflexivity	What assumptions, emotional reactions, or biases arise for the therapist when engaging with this vignette, and how might these affect clinical judgement?
Islāmic ethical foundations in practice	How can Islāmic ethical concepts such as *niyyah* (intention), *raḥmah* (compassion), *ʿadl* (justice), and *amānah* (trust) guide the therapist's stance and decision-making?

9.6.2 Case Vignette 2: Autonomy vs. Beneficence

Samira, a 29-year-old Muslim woman, sought therapy following repeated episodes of emotional and physical abuse by her spouse. She described feeling trapped due to financial dependence, community pressure to preserve marriage, and fear of bringing shame (*'ayb*) upon her family. Despite acknowledging the harm, Samira stated that leaving the relationship was not an option for her at this time. She requested emotional support and coping strategies rather than intervention aimed at separation or legal action. The therapist faces tension between respecting Samira's autonomous choices and the professional obligation to promote her well-being and safety. Ethical practice requires supporting Samira without endorsing harm, avoiding coercion, and continually assessing risk while empowering her with information and resources. Table 9.2 presents Ethical reflection on case vignette 2.

Table 9.2 Case vignette 2: Ethical reflection

Reflective domain	Reflective practice questions
Respecting autonomy without endorsing harm	How can the therapist support the client's expressed wish to remain in the relationship while clearly not endorsing ongoing harm or abuse?
Empowerment and agency	What does "empowerment" mean in this context, and how can it be fostered gradually and safely over time?
Risk assessment and monitoring	How can risk be assessed and continually monitored while respecting the client's autonomy and stated choices?
Psychoeducation and resource provision	How can the therapist offer psychoeducation and information about support services without pressuring the client toward separation or legal action?
Religious and cultural meaning-making	How might the client's religious and cultural framework shape her understanding of harm, responsibility, patience, and help-seeking?
Narratives of marriage and patience	In what ways might cultural or religious narratives surrounding marriage, endurance, and patience influence the therapist's clinical approach?
Therapist reflexivity	What personal assumptions, biases, or emotional reactions arise for the therapist when engaging with this vignette, and how might these affect clinical judgement?
Islāmic ethical foundations in practice	How can Islāmic ethical concepts such as niyyah (intention), *raḥmah* (compassion), *'adl* (justice), and *amānah* (trust) guide the therapist's stance and interventions?

9.6.3 Case Vignette 3: Religious Sensitivity vs. Challenging Harmful Narratives

Leyla, a 41-year-old refugee mother, presented with depressive symptoms and spiritual distress. She reported that her husband justified his abusive behaviour using selective religious interpretations emphasising obedience and patience. Leyla expressed guilt, believing her suffering reflected personal spiritual failure. She sought Islāmic psychotherapy but feared that challenging her husband's authority would be religiously inappropriate. The therapist must respectfully engage with Leyla's religious framework while ethically challenging distorted or abusive uses of religious texts. The dilemma involves maintaining cultural and religious sensitivity without reinforcing harmful narratives, ensuring that Islāmic principles of justice, compassion, and dignity are upheld within the therapeutic process. Table 9.3 presents Ethical reflection on case vignette 3.

Table 9.3 Case vignette 3: Ethical reflection

Reflective domain	Reflective practice questions
Religious interpretation and ethics	How would you differentiate between authentic Islāmic teachings and their misuse to justify abuse?
Ethical responsibility and harm	What ethical responsibilities arise when religious language contributes to a client's guilt, shame, or self-blame?
Therapeutic challenge and sensitivity	How can harmful interpretations be challenged respectfully without undermining the client's faith or spiritual identity?
Cultural and religious context	How might the client's religious and cultural framework influence her understanding of harm, responsibility, and help-seeking?
Islāmic ethical reframing	What role can Islāmic principles of justice (*ʿadl*), dignity (*karāmah*), and accountability play in reframing the client's experience?
Consultation and professional boundaries	When might consultation with religious scholars or culturally informed supervisors be appropriate or necessary?
Therapist reflexivity	What assumptions or emotional reactions do you notice in yourself when engaging with this vignette, and how might these influence your clinical judgement?
Islāmic ethical foundations in practice	How can Islāmic ethical concepts such as *niyyah* (intention), *raḥmah* (compassion), *ʿadl* (justice), and *amānah* (trust) inform your therapeutic stance and interventions?

9.7 Conclusion

Working with vulnerable Muslim populations in Islāmic psychotherapy demands a profoundly ethical and reflective approach. Therapists must overcome complex layers of trauma, cultural norms, spiritual meaning, and social marginalisation while maintaining compassion (*raḥmah*), justice (*ʿadl*), trust (*amānah*), and competence (*iḥsān*). Ethical practice involves not only addressing psychological distress but also validating the survivor's dignity, supporting autonomy, and challenging harmful interpretations of religion that may have been used to justify abuse. Additionally, therapists must remain aware of structural inequalities, Islāmophobia, and barriers to care that shape the lived experiences of survivors, refugees, and marginalised communities. By integrating psychological expertise with Islāmic ethical principles, therapists can provide culturally grounded, spiritually informed, and morally responsible care, promoting healing, resilience, and empowerment among those most vulnerable.

References

Abī Dāwūd. *Sunan Abi Dawud 4941*. In-book reference: Book 43, Hadith 169. English translation: Book 42, Hadith 4923. Sahih (Al-Albani). https://sunnah.com/abudawud:4941

Abdoli-Najmi, L., & Mirghafourvand, M. (2024). Impact of intimate partner violence on maternal functioning, depression, and anxiety among postpartum women: A cross-sectional study. *BMC Psychology, 12*, 57. https://doi.org/10.1186/s40359-024-01664-2

Abu-Ras, W. (2007). Cultural beliefs and utilization of services by Arab immigrant battered women. *Violence against Women, 13*(10), 1002–1028.

Abu-Ras, W., & Abu-Bader, S. H. (2008). The impact of the September 11, 2001, attacks on the well-being of Arab Americans in New York City. *Journal of Muslim Mental Health, 3*(2), 217–239.

Abu-Ras, W., & Abu-Bader, S. H. (2009). Risk factors for depression and posttraumatic stress disorder (PTSD): The case of Arab and Muslim Americans post-9/11. *Journal of Immigrant & Refugee Studies, 7*(4), 393–418.

Aday L. A. (1994). Health status of vulnerable populations. *Annual review of public health, 15*, 487–509.https://doi.org/10.1146/annurev.pu.15.050194.002415

Aflakseir, A., & Coleman, P. G. (2009). The influence of religious coping and religious orientation on mental wellbeing among Iranian Muslims. *Mental Health, Religion & Culture, 12*(5), 435–447.

Afrouz, R., Crisp, B. R., & Taket, A. (2020). Seeking help in domestic violence among Muslim women in Muslim-majority and non-Muslim-majority countries: A literature review. *Trauma, Violence & Abuse, 21*(3), 551–566. https://doi.org/10.1177/1524838018781102

Ahmad and Ibn Mājah. *Sunan Ibn Mājah. Book 7, Hadith 171*. English translation: Book 7, Hadith 924. Arabic reference: Book 7, Hadith 918. https://sunnah.com/bulugh/7/171

Ai, A. L., Peterson, C., & Huang, B. (2003). The effect of religious-spiritual coping on positive attitudes of adult Muslim refugees from Kosovo and Bosnia. *International Journal for the Psychology of Religion, 13*(1), 29–47. https://doi.org/10.1207/S15327582IJPR1301_04

Al-Adab Al-Mufrad. *Al-Adab Al-Mufrad 472*. In-book reference: Book 26, Hadith 11. English translation: Book 26, Hadith 472. https://sunnah.com/adab:472

Ali, P. A., & Ahmed, Z. (2023). Domestic violence and abuse: Impact on health of British Muslim women and factors affecting access to health. In S. Dogra (Ed.), *British Muslims, ethnicity and health inequalities* (pp. 161–184). Edinburgh University Press.

Aloud, N., & Rathur, A. (2009). Factors affecting attitudes toward seeking and using formal mental health and psychological services among Arab Muslim populations. *Journal of Muslim Mental Health, 4*(2), 79–103. https://doi.org/10.1080/15564900802487675

Amer, M. M., & Hovey, J. D. (2012). Anxiety and depression in a post-September 11 sample of Arabs in the USA. *Social Psychiatry and Psychiatric Epidemiology: The International Journal for Research in Social and Genetic Epidemiology and Mental Health Services, 47*(3), 409–418. https://doi.org/10.1007/s00127-011-0341-4

American Psychological Association. (2017). *Ethical principles of psychologists and code of conduct*. AmericanPsychological Association. https://www.apa.org/ethics/code

Auerbach, R. P. (2007). The role of psychological vulnerability in stress–psychopathology models. *Journal of Personality, 75*(6), 1239–1270. https://doi.org/10.1111/j.1467-6494.2007.00475.x

Barlow, D. H. (2002). *Anxiety and its disorders: The nature and treatment of anxiety and panic* (2nd ed.). Guilford Press.

Batool, S., & Abtahi, A. (2017). Psychosocial impact of childhood sexual abuse: Perspective of victims. *Journal of Arts and Social Sciences, 4*, 36–48.

Beauchamp, T. L., & Childress, J. F. (2019). *Principles of biomedical ethics* (8th ed.). Oxford University Press.

Bell, S., Forchuk, C., & Monari, E. N. (2024). Population needs: Vulnerable populations. In S. Roles & K. Kalia (Eds.), *The nurses' guide to psychotherapy* (pp. 197–212). Springer. https://doi.org/10.1007/978-981-97-4738-2_11

Bronstein, I., & Montgomery, P. (2011). Psychological distress in refugee children: A systematic review. *Clinical Child and Family Psychology Review, 14*(1), 44–56. https://doi.org/10.1007/s10567-010-0081-0

Brewin, C. R. (2011). The nature and significance of memory disturbance in posttraumatic stress disorder. *Clinical Psychology Review, 31*(1), 52–60. https://doi.org/10.1016/j.cpr.2010.09.004

Budhwani, H., & Hearld, K. R. (2017). Muslim women's experiences with stigma, abuse, and depression: results of a sample study conducted in the United States. *Journal of women's health (2002), 26*(5), 435–441. https://doi.org/10.1089/jwh.2016.5886

Carlsson, J., Sonne, C., Vindbjerg, E., & Mortensen, E. L. (2018). Stress management versus cognitive restructuring in trauma-affected refugees-A pragmatic randomised study. *Psychiatry Research, 266*, 116–123. https://doi.org/10.1016/j.psychres.2018.05.015

Cole, E. R. (2009). Intersectionality and research in psychology. *American Psychologist, 64*(3), 170–180. https://doi.org/10.1037/a0014564

Crenshaw, K. (1989). Demarginalizing the intersection of race and sex: A black feminist critique of antidiscrimination doctrine, feminist theory, and antiracist politics. *University of Chicago Legal Forum, 1989*(1), 139–167. https://chicagounbound.uchicago.edu/cgi/viewcontent.cgi?article=1052&context=uclf

Fazel, M., Wheeler, J., & Danesh, J. (2005). Prevalence of serious mental disorder in 7000 refugees resettled in western countries: A systematic review. *Lancet (London, England), 365*(9467), 1309–1314. https://doi.org/10.1016/S0140-6736(05)61027-6

Fazel, M., & Betancourt, T. S. (2018). Preventive mental health interventions for refugee children and adolescents in high-income settings. *The Lancet. Child & Adolescent Health, 2*(2), 121–132. https://doi.org/10.1016/S2352-4642(17)30147-5

Fisher, C. B. (2016). *Decoding the ethics code: A practical guide for psychologists* (4th ed.). Sage.

Ghaly, M. (2024). Islāmic ethico-legal perspectives on medical accountability in the age of artificial intelligence. In B. Solaiman & I. G. Cohen (Eds.), *Research handbook on health, AI and the law* (Chapter 14). Edward Elgar Publishing Ltd. https://www.ncbi.nlm.nih.gov/books/NBK613218/?utm_source=chatgpt.com

Gilbert, P. (2010). *Compassion focused therapy: Distinctive features*. Routledge.

Guruge, S., Khanlou, N., & Gastaldo, D. (2009). Intimate male partner violence in the migration process: Intersections of gender, race and class. *Journal of Advanced Nursing, 66*(12), 2524–2534. https://doi.org/10.1111/j.1365-2648.2009.05184.x

Harari, L., & Lee, C. (2021). Intersectionality in quantitative health disparities research: A systematic review of challenges and limitations in empirical studies. *Social Science & Medicine, 277*, Article 113876. https://doi.org/10.1016/j.socscimed.2021.113876

Haque, K. (2026). *Islāmically integrated psychotherapy and domestic abuse*. Routledge.

Hassan, G., Ventevogel, P., Jefee-Bahloul, H., Barkil-Oteo, A., & Kirmayer, L. J. (2016). Mental health and psychosocial wellbeing of Syrians affected by armed conflict. *Epidemiology and Psychiatric Sciences, 25*(2), 129–141.

Hassouneh, D., & Culley, E. (2008). The influence of gender role stereotyping on women's experiences of domestic violence. *Journal of Women's Health, 17*(3), 435–441.

Ibn al-Qayyim. (2003). *The Prophetic medicine; Al-Tibb al-Nabawī* (A. A. Abd el-Azeez, Ed., pp. 168–171). Dār al-Gadd al-Jadeed.

Ishtiaq, H., Batool, T. E., Mamoon, B., Majeed, A. I., Atta, M., Atta, A., & Masood, S. (2025). Mental health problems in Pakistani society as a consequence of violence and trauma: A case for better integration of care. *Cureus, 17*(5), Article e83486. https://doi.org/10.7759/cureus.83486

Ishtiaq, S., Qadir, F., & Fatima, S. (2020). Spiritual coping, resilience, and mental health among displaced Muslim refugees. *Journal of Immigrant and Minority Health, 22*(3), 505–512.

Istratii, R., & Ali, P. (2023). A scoping review on the role of religion in the experience of IPV and faith-based responses in community and counseling settings. *Journal of Psychology and Theology, 51*(2), 141–173.

Kennedy, A. C., & Prock, K. A. (2018). "I still feel like i am not normal": A review of the role of stigma and stigmatization among female survivors of child sexual abuse, sexual assault, and intimate partner violence. *Trauma, Violence & Abuse, 19*(5), 512–527. https://www.jstor.org/stable/26638234

Khawaja, N. G., White, K. M., Schweitzer, R., & Greenslade, J. (2008). Difficulties and coping strategies of Sudanese refugees: A qualitative approach. *Transcultural Psychiatry, 45*(3), 489–512. https://doi.org/10.1177/1363461508094678

Kunst, J. R., Tahir, H., Sam, D. L., & Ulleberg, P. (2012). Coping with Islamophobia: The effects of religious stigma on Muslim minorities' identity formation. *International Journal of Intercultural Relations, 36*(4), 518–532. https://doi.org/10.1016/j.ijintrel.2011.12.014

Malik, M., Munir, N., Ghani, U., & Ahmad, N. (2020). Domestic violence and its relationship with depression, anxiety and quality of life: A hidden dilemma of Pakistani women. *Pakistan Journal of Medical Sciences, 37*(1), 191–194. https://doi.org/10.12669/pjms.37.1.2893

Marley, C., & Mauki, B. (2019). Resilience and protective factors among refugee children post-migration to high-income countries: A systematic review. *European Journal of Public Health, 29*(4), 706–713. https://doi.org/10.1093/eurpub/cky232

Miller, K. E., & Rasmussen, A. (2017). The mental health of civilians displaced by armed conflict: An ecological model of refugee distress. *Epidemiology and Psychiatric Sciences, 26*(2), 129–138. https://doi.org/10.1017/S2045796016000172

Montero Orphanopoulos, C. (2025). Approaches to the concept of vulnerability in psychology. In *An interdisciplinary approach to vulnerability* (pp. 15–34). Springer. https://doi.org/10.1007/978-3-031-84412-6_2

Muslim. *Sunnah.com reference: Book 16, Hadith 58*. English translation. Book 16, Hadith 1537. Arabic reference: Book 16, Hadith 1494. https://sunnah.com/bulugh/16/58

Olcese, M., Cardinali, P., Madera, F., Camilleri, A. P., & Migliorini, L. (2023). Migration and community resilience: A scoping review. *International Journal of Intercultural Relations, 93*, Article 101924. https://doi.org/10.1016/j.ijintrel.2023.101924

Oyewuwo, O.B., Chaudhry, T., Mokhtar, H., Hashem, H., Friend, K., Mercado, E.,Tabahi, S., Berte, D., McGee, B., & Barqadle, K. (2024). American Muslim intimate partner violence study (AMIPV) data brief. Peaceful Families Project. https://www.peacefulfamilies.org/amipv.html

Padela, A. I., & Curlin, F. A. (2013). Religion and disparities: Considering the influences of Islam on the health of American Muslims. *Journal of Religion and Health, 52*(4), 1333–1345. https://doi.org/10.1007/s10943-012-9620-y

Porter, M., & Haslam, N. (2005). Predisplacement and postdisplacement factors associated with mental health of refugees and internally displaced persons: A meta-analysis. *JAMA, 294*(5), 602–612. https://doi.org/10.1001/jama.294.5.602

Rassool, G. Hussein,(2025). Islāmic Counselling & Psychotherapy. *An Introduction to Theory and Practice*. (2nded.). Routledge.

Rees, S., & Pease, B. (2007). Domestic violence in refugee families in Australia. *Journal of Immigrant & Refugee Studies, 5*(1), 1–19. https://doi.org/10.1300/J500v05n02_01

Rothberg, D. (1993). The crisis of modernity and the emergence of socially engaged spirituality. *ReVision, 15*(3), 105–114.

Sharifnia, A. M., Bulut, H., Ali, P., & Rogers, M. (2025). Muslim Women's Experiences of Domestic Violence andAbuse: A Meta-Ethnography of Global Evidence. *Trauma, violence & abuse, 26*(4), 694–711. https://doi.org/10.1177/15248380241286836

Silove, D., Ventevogel, P., & Rees, S. (2017). The contemporary refugee crisis: An overview of mental health challenges. *World Psychiatry : Official Journal of the World Psychiatric Association (WPA), 16*(2), 130–139. https://doi.org/10.1002/wps.20438

Steel, Z., Chey, T., Silove, D., Marnane, C., Bryant, R. A., & van Ommeren, M. (2009). Association of torture andother potentially traumatic events with mental health outcomes among populations exposed to mass conflict anddisplacement: a systematic review and meta-analysis. *JAMA, 302*(5), 537–549. https://doi.org/10.1001/jama.2009.1132

Tay, A.K. (2019) The Culture, Mental Health and Psychosocial Wellbeing of Rohingya Refugees: A SystematicReview. *Epidemiology and Psychiatric Sciences, 28*, 489–494.https://doi.org/10.1017/S2045796019000192

Tirmidhī. *Jami` at-Tirmidhi 1959*. In-book reference: Book 27, Hadith 65. English translation: Vol. 4, Book 1, Hadith 1959. Hasan (Darussalam). https://sunnah.com/tirmidhi:1959

Turan, J. M., Elafros, M. A., Logie, C. H., Banik, S., Turan, B., Crockett, K. B., Pescosolido, B., & Murray, S. M. (2019). Challenges and opportunities in examining and addressing intersectional stigma and health. *BMC Medicine, 17*(1), 7. https://doi.org/10.1186/s12916-018-1246-9

Vélez Agosto, N. M., & Almario-Zgheib, M. C. (2024). Multicultural therapy with vulnerable populations: A narrative case study. In S. Castaños-Cervantes, A. Ojeda García, & C. L. Reitz-Krueger (Eds.), *Working with vulnerable populations* (pp. 145–162). Springer. https://doi.org/10.1007/978-3-031-67710-6_10

World Health Organization. (2022). *WHO guidance on research methods for health emergency and disaster risk management* (Revised 2022). https://www.who.int/publications/i/item/9789240041826

Yako, R. M., & Biswas, B. (2014). "We came to this country for the future of our children. We have no future": Acculturative stress among Iraqi refugees in the United States. *International Journal of Intercultural Relations, 38*, 133–141. https://doi.org/10.1016/j.ijintrel.2013.08.003

Zempi, I., & Chakraborti, N. (2014). *Islamophobia, Victimisation and the Veil*. Palgrave Hate Studies.

Chapter 10
Ethical Challenges and Considerations in Technology-Based Psychotherapy

10.1 Introduction

The rapid expansion of digital platforms for psychotherapy has transformed the delivery of mental health services globally, providing clients with unprecedented access, flexibility, and convenience. Online therapy removes geographical barriers, allows for asynchronous communication, and can accommodate clients who may otherwise struggle to engage with traditional in-person services due to mobility, stigma, or time constraints. However, the convergence of online therapy and Islāmic principles presents unique ethical challenges that require careful management. Confidentiality must be safeguarded against digital breaches and private exposure. Quality of care involves delivering evidence-based therapy while respecting spiritual and cultural needs. Equity requires addressing disparities in technology access and client readiness. Informed consent should clearly explain both clinical and spiritual dimensions of therapy. Professional boundaries must be maintained to avoid blurring therapeutic and religious guidance. Therapists should ensure interventions are client-centred, culturally sensitive, and ethically robust. Overall, ethical practice demands vigilance, cultural competence, and integration of religious and clinical principles. This chapter explores the ethical concerns inherent in digital Islāmic psychotherapy, offering guidance on how to navigate issues of confidentiality, quality of care, equity, informed consent, and professional boundaries while remaining faithful to both Islāmic values and clinical standards.

G. H. Rassool, *Ethical Dilemmas in Islāmic Psychotherapy*,
https://doi.org/10.1007/978-3-032-26515-9_10

10.2 Concept of Online Therapy

Online therapy, also referred to as teletherapy, e-therapy, digital psychotherapy, or telepsychology, involves delivering mental health services remotely using technology. Mallen and Vogel (2005) define online counselling as "any delivery of mental or behavioural health services...by a licensed practitioner to a client in a non-face-to-face setting through distance communication technologies such as the telephone, asynchronous email, synchronous chat, and videoconference" (p. 764). Similarly, the Joint Task Force (2013) describes telepsychology as "psychological services delivered via telecommunication technologies, either synchronously or asynchronously, using tools such as phones, mobile devices, videoconferencing, email, text, or the internet" (p. 792). A wide variety of online modalities exist, including email, SMS/text, live chat, video, and audio sessions, each presenting unique benefits and challenges (UK Council for Psychotherapy [UKCP], 2021; British Association for Counselling and Psychotherapy [BACP], 2021). The term Online and Phone Therapy (OPT) specifically refers to counselling or psychotherapy delivered partially or wholly through technology such as phones, computers, tablets, or internet-enabled devices (BACP, 2021, p. 11).

The literature identifies both notable advantages and ethical concerns associated with online psychotherapy. Reported benefits include increased access to services and greater flexibility, cost-effectiveness, convenience, therapeutic benefits with the potential for enhanced communication, appropriateness for clients with mobility challenges or geographical constraints, and higher levels of user satisfaction (Chakrabarti, 2015; Deardorff, 2010; Stoll et al., 2020). However, ethical challenges persist, particularly in relation to privacy, confidentiality, and data security; communication limitations inherent in technology-mediated interactions; therapist competence and the need for specialised training; gaps in the existing research base; and the complexity of managing emergencies in remote contexts (du Preez et al., 2024; Stoll et al., 2020). As online psychotherapy continues to expand, clinicians must prioritise informed consent by clearly outlining potential benefits, limitations, and risks to clients (Cipolletta & Mocellin, 2018; du Preez et al., 2024; Stoll et al., 2020).

Despite these advantages, online psychotherapy also presents substantial ethical and practical challenges. Key concerns include safeguarding privacy and confidentiality, ensuring data security, and developing adequate technical competence and communication skills. Additional issues involve boundary management, maintaining therapeutic structure and control, and establishing a strong therapeutic alliance in virtual settings. Legal, practical, and systemic considerations such as cross-jurisdictional practice, insurance coverage, emergency protocols, and identity verification, require clear regulatory frameworks and further empirical investigation. Ongoing debates also address the equivalence of online and in-person therapy, professional liability, potential dehumanisation of care, client dependency, and the financial and security risks associated with digital platforms (Madej et al., 2016; Rutkowska et al., 2025; Stoll et al., 2020). Research findings show that some ethical dilemmas are unique to online therapy, like technological failures and data protection, while others overlap with face-to-face practice, such as maintaining relational quality and professional boundaries (Rutkowska et al., 2025). Video-based psychotherapy highlights key themes including applying traditional ethical principles online, addressing security and data protection, setting clear boundaries, and ensuring accessibility and appropriateness of interventions (du Preez et al., 2024; Stoll et al., 2020).

Professional guidelines provide further guidance for ethical and effective online practice. For instance, the UK Council for Psychotherapy (2021) guidelines aim to (1) raise practitioners' awareness of issues arising in online or remote work, (2) provide clinical guidance on assessment, risk, and safeguarding, and (3) outline general considerations for online practice, including work with children. Similarly, the British Association for Counselling and Psychotherapy (BACP, 2021) offers the OPT (Online and Phone Therapy) competence framework, emphasising safe, competent, and culturally sensitive online delivery. Overall, online psychotherapy functions as an umbrella term encompassing both synchronous and asynchronous modalities, with growing evidence supporting its reliability, effectiveness, and adaptability across diverse populations and settings (Chakrabarti, 2015).

10.3 Islāmic Ethical Challenges in Online Therapy

Online therapy brings with it certain ethical considerations in all forms of online psychotherapy and Islāmic psychotherapy. Mainstream online therapy is primarily guided by professional and legal codes of conduct, and these frameworks provide a secular ethical foundation that emphasises core principles, including client welfare, autonomy, confidentiality, non-maleficence, and beneficence. Decisions in mainstream practice are typically informed by empirical research, clinical evidence, and legal requirements. For instance, maintaining confidentiality may involve secure data storage and encrypted communication channels, with guidelines developed primarily to protect clients from harm and uphold professional accountability. The focus is on measurable outcomes, professional standards, and adherence to societal laws rather than spiritual or religious obligations.

In contrast, Islāmic online therapy integrates both professional ethical codes and religious moral principles, which serve as an additional layer of guidance. This ethical framework is guided by both professional ethical codes and Islāmic moral principles, including the Qur'ân and *Sunnah*. These primary sources, supplemented by scholarly consensus (*ijmā'*) and analogical reasoning (*qiyās*), provide the framework for ethical decision-making in Islāmic health care (Chamsi-Pasha & Albar, 2017). In practical terms, Islāmic online therapy requires that every therapeutic action be evaluated through a dual lens: its clinical appropriateness and its alignment with *Shari'ah*-compliant ethics. This dual responsibility adds depth and complexity to routine ethical decision-making. For instance, when ethical breaches occur, such as data leaks, insecure digital practices, or misuse of sensitive information, the consequences extend beyond professional accountability. In an Islāmic framework, such lapses also hold religious and moral significance, as they violate the trust placed in the therapist and contravene ethical duties before God. This sense of spiritual accountability elevates the ethical gravity of digital practice and reinforces the importance of safeguarding the client's dignity and well-being. Overall, while mainstream online therapy relies primarily on secular professional codes, legal standards, and evidence-based guidelines, Islāmic online therapy incorporates an additional spiritual and moral dimension. This ensures that therapeutic practice not only meets clinical and professional expectations but also respects the client's religious values, cultural context, and the sacred trust that underpins the therapeutic relationship.

10.3.1 Preservation of Life and Health in Islāmic Ethics

In Islāmic teachings, safeguarding human life and well-being is a fundamental moral imperative. The Qur'ân highlights this by declaring,

وَلَا تَقْتُلُوٓا۟ أَنفُسَكُمْ ۚ إِنَّ ٱللَّهَ كَانَ بِكُمْ رَحِيمًا.

- *And do not kill yourselves [or one another]. Indeed, Allāh is to you ever Merciful* (An-Nisa' 4:29 interpretation of the meaning)

This verse emphasises God's profound concern for safeguarding both physical and emotional well-being. Within this moral framework, online therapy emerges as a practical means of fulfilling the obligation to protect life and promote health. By offering digital access to care, individuals in remote locations, underserved communities, or those with mobility constraints can obtain psycho-spiritual support without delay, thereby removing many of the obstacles that typically hinder timely and essential treatment. In doing so, online psychotherapy not only improves the quality and reach of care but also contributes to preserving life, preventing harm, and enhancing overall well-being in accordance with Islāmic ethical principles.

In Islāmic jurisprudence, the *Maqāṣid al-Sharīʿah* (higher objectives of Islāmic law) provide a comprehensive framework aimed at ensuring the welfare of individuals and society. Among these core objectives is the preservation of life (*ḥifẓ al-nafs*) and the protection of health, which encompasses both physical and psychological dimensions. Online psychotherapy, whether delivered through digital or telehealth platform, aligns closely with these objectives. Since mental well-being is a vital component of holistic health in Islām, digital therapeutic services support individuals who may otherwise face barriers such as stigma, geographical distance, or limited mobility. By enabling timely access to mental health care, online therapy helps prevent harm, reduces risks such as self-harm or suicidal ideation, and strengthens overall community mental health, thereby fulfilling some of the key aims of the *Maqāṣid al-Sharīʿah*.

10.3.2 *Confidentiality and Privacy in Digital Islāmic Psychotherapy*

Confidentiality and privacy remain among the most pressing ethical challenges in digital Islāmic psychotherapy, requiring careful attention to both technological systems and human practices. The use of online tools, such as smartphones, web-based applications, and social media platform, exposes sensitive client information to risks including unauthorised access, data breaches, and weak digital security infrastructures (Gooding & Kariotis, 2021; Rubeis, 2021). Himmatun 'Aliah et al. (2024) emphasise the significant ethical implications of digital privacy within community counselling environments, noting that the potential leakage of counselling information can severely undermine client trust, with psychological and social consequences. The findings from research further indicate that many digital mental health platforms employ inconsistent data protection standards and insufficient privacy practices, heightening vulnerabilities for users (Gooding & Kariotis, 2021). Any breach of confidentiality can diminish trust, jeopardise client safety, and harm the therapeutic alliance. Beyond security risks, technological disruptions, such as internet outages, device malfunctions, or server failures, may also interrupt therapeutic sessions. Therapists must anticipate these challenges and outline alternative communication arrangements as part of the informed consent process.

Confidentiality in digital counselling is guided by several major ethical frameworks from professional associations. The American Psychological Association, Joint Task Force for the Development of Telepsychology Guidelines (APA) (2013) guidelines for telepsychology emphasise secure technology use, informed consent, and confidentiality protections tailored to digital service delivery. These principles guide psychologists in ethically adapting traditional standards to virtual environments. The British Association for Counselling and Psychotherapy (BACP) emphasises that practitioners must actively safeguard client information. Clause 55 outlines requirements such as informing clients about data use, ensuring confidentiality agreements with all data recipients, and complying with relevant legal and contractual obligations (BACP B, n.d.). The Psychotherapy and Counselling Federation of Australia (PACFA) stresses the need for modality-specific consent procedures when offering online therapy. Their guidance highlights the importance of explaining digital risks, using secure systems for communication and transactions, and maintaining clear documentation of the consent process (PACFA Ethics Committee, n.d.). Broader guidelines on digital therapy recommend robust digital security measures, including encryption and safe device use, alongside clear disclosure of online risks, crisis-management planning, and firm boundaries around electronic communication and session recordings (Psychology Town, 2024).

From an Islāmic perspective, confidentiality and privacy holds a central place within Islāmic ethics. It is a well-established principle rooted in the teachings and practices of the Qur'ân, the Prophet Muhammad (), his Companions (may Allāh be pleased with them), and the generations who followed with excellence. Allāh says in the Qur'ân.

.لًاوُئْسَمَ نَاكَ دَهْعَلْا نَّإِ ۖ دِهْعَلْابِ اوفُوْأَوَ

- *And fulfill [every] commitment. Indeed, the commitment is ever [that about which one will be] questioned.* (Al-Isra' 17:34, interpretation of the meaning).

.اهَلِهْأَ ىٰلَإِ تِانَامَلْأَا اودُّؤَتُ نأَ مْكُرُمُأْيَ للَّهَا نَّإِ

- *Indeed, Allāh commands that you should render back the trusts to whom they are due.* (An-Nisa' 4:58, interpretation of the meaning).

Ibn Kathir (2000) explains that Allāh commands believers to honour all promises and covenants, whether to Him or to others. Breaking a promise undermines trust, social harmony, and one's relationship with Allāh, while fulfilling them reflects piety, faith, and moral integrity. In Al-Isra' 17:34, every commitment, whether to people, organisations, or Allāh, carries responsibility, and all will be questioned on the Day of Judgment. Al-Qurtubi (n.d.) adds that covenants include contracts, agreements, promises, and moral obligations, and failing to uphold them incurs spiritual accountability. Maintaining promises demonstrates honesty, reliability, and God-consciousness, forming a core part of a believer's character. In essence, both scholars emphasise that fulfilling promises is a moral and spiritual duty, with accountability before Allāh, establishing a timeless principle of integrity and trustworthiness. So, if keeping confidentiality is obligatory, then disclosing them is *haram.*

It is narrated by Jabir ibn Abdullah (may Allāh be pleased with him) that the Prophet (ﷺ) said: "When a man tells something and then departs, it is a trust"(Abū Dāwūd). In this *ḥadīth*, the Prophet Muḥammad (ﷺ) affirms that meetings and gatherings are inherently confidential and grounded in mutual trust. It has been explained that the phrase *"then looks around"* refers to the speaker glancing to the right and left out of caution. The statement *"it is a trust"* means that the information becomes an *amānah* for the listener, obligating them to maintain confidentiality in accordance with the rulings of entrusted matters. Ibn Raslān clarifies that the speaker's cautious glancing signals to the listener that he fears others may overhear him and has intentionally chosen this person to confide in. This gesture functions as an unspoken instruction meaning: *"Listen to this and keep quiet about it because it is a trust (or a secret)"* (Cited in Islamqa, 2003). Islāmic ethics therefore teaches that information shared within a private setting should not be conveyed to others unless clear permission has been granted. ʿUmar ibn al-Khaṭṭāb (عنه الله رضي) reinforces this principle, stating that "If your brother mentions something to you in private, then walks away, it is an *amānah* (trust) even if he didn't instruct you not to inform anyone" (Ibn Muflih al-Maqdisi, 1996). It has been suggested that "Someone whose advice is sought is in a position of trust" (Shah Waliullah Dehlawi, n.d.). That is in therapeutic and counselling contexts, this means that the practitioner is entrusted with sensitive information and is ethically obligated to safeguard the client's privacy, act with integrity, and offer guidance with sincerity and responsibility. These narrations make it clear that confidentiality is a moral obligation, especially when information is conveyed with an expectation of privacy.

Therapists are responsible for educating clients about potential risks while collaborating to develop strategies that support continuity of care if online therapy is disrupted. Upholding electronic confidentiality also requires ongoing staff training, secure data-transmission protocols, and transparent policies concerning record retention and access (Gedge, 2002; Kanani & Regehr, 2003). In alignment with both professional and Islāmic ethical principles, digital platforms and practitioners must adopt rigorous security measures, including encryption, secure data storage, and restricted access protocols. Clear guidelines regarding data protection, informed consent, and contingency planning are essential. Adhering to these standards safeguards client privacy, reinforces trust, and fulfils the ethical responsibilities of contemporary psychotherapy within an Islāmic framework.

10.3.3 Informed Consent and Autonomy

Informed consent is fundamental to ethical practice and must be adapted for online therapy. Patients need to understand how their data will be used, the risks involved, and the limitations of the technology. This is especially important for mobile health apps and internet-based interventions, where clinical care can overlap with consumer-driven tools (Warrier et al., 2023). Ensuring patient autonomy requires that individuals can make fully informed decisions about using digital mental health technologies (Bauer et al., 2017; Fiske et al., 2019; Torous & Roberts, 2017). For minors and other vulnerable groups, additional safeguards must be observed, including parental consent and careful consideration of the child's developmental needs (Bolton, 2011).

Securing informed consent in online psychotherapy or counselling brings a distinct set of challenges. Because therapists cannot rely on the full range of verbal and non-verbal cues available in face-to-face settings, it becomes more difficult to determine whether a client genuinely understands the information provided and has the capacity to give valid consent (Harris & Birnbaum, 2015; Wiggins-Frame, 1998). This limitation is further compounded by individual factors such as a client's reading ability, cognitive functioning, cultural or linguistic background, and overall familiarity with digital communication platforms. Given these potential barriers, therapists must take extra care to deliver information in a clear, accessible, and culturally sensitive manner. This may include using simple language, checking for understanding, offering translations or visual aids, and providing opportunities for clients to ask questions before agreeing to treatment. By enhancing clarity and ensuring comprehension, therapists support clients in making truly informed decisions about whether to engage in online therapeutic services.

Evaluating a client's psychological state in an online setting introduces further ethical challenges. Therapists often have reduced ability to identify whether a client is impaired by psychoactive substances or experiencing cognitive or perceptual disturbances, as many subtle behavioural cues are less visible through digital communication. In addition, the consent procedures used by some online platforms reduce complex information to a simple checkbox, which can lead clients to approve terms without thoroughly reading or comprehending them. These constraints highlight the need for thoughtfully structured informed consent processes that actively protect client autonomy and understanding within digital counselling environments. In the context of digital Islāmic psychotherapy, clients may begin therapy without a clear grasp of how their personal information will be handled, what the therapeutic process entails, or the potential risks associated with the intervention. This makes it even more important for practitioners to communicate transparently and ensure that clients fully understand the nature and implications of the services being offered.

Islāmic psychoethics is founded on the understanding that human beings possess free will (*ikhtiyār*) and moral responsibility, qualities that enable them to fulfil their role as *khalīfah* (vicegerents) on earth. This freedom, however, operates within the moral framework of the *Sharīʿah,* whose purpose is to uphold human dignity, justice, and social well-being. Central to this worldview is the concept of *Hurriyat al-Ikhtiyār* (freedom of choice) and the responsibility that accompanies it. Islām views individuals as rational and discerning beings capable of making informed decisions about their actions. This capacity for choice is inseparable from the Qur'ânic principle of *taklīf* (moral accountability). In Islāmic theology, *taklīf* refers to the state of moral accountability placed upon every *mukallaf* (a person who has reached the necessary level of maturity, intellect, and awareness), to be held accountable for their actions. Such an individual is expected to use their God-given faculties of reason, intention, and discernment to navigate moral choices in accordance with divine guidance. The Qur'ān emphasises personal accountability, reminding believers that their actions ultimately benefit or harm their own souls:

مَّنْ عَمِلَ صَٰلِحًا فَلِنَفْسِهِۦ ۖ وَمَنْ أَسَآءَ فَعَلَيْهَا ۗ.

- *Whoever does righteousness-it is for his [own]soul; and whoever does evil [does so] against it.*(Fussilat 41:46, interpretation of the meaning).

This verse highlights a core Islāmic principle: every individual bears the consequences of their moral choices. Acts of righteousness spiritually benefit the person, while wrongdoing harms them. Consequently, the ability to comprehend information, assess alternatives, and make voluntary decisions is fundamental not only in Islāmic law and theology but also in ethical practice, including counselling and psychotherapy. Autonomy (*istiqlāl al-dhāt*) is a central value in Islāmic jurisprudence, especially in domains that require personal responsibility, informed decision-making, and voluntary participation, such as contracts, financial transactions, medical interventions, and family matters. Upholding an individual's capacity to make informed and voluntary choices is considered a key aspect of preserving human dignity (*karāmah Insāniyyah*), one of the primary objectives of the *Sharīʿah.* The preservation of human dignity (*karāmah insāniyyah*) is central to Islāmic teachings, and respecting a person's right to make informed, voluntary choices is part of safeguarding that dignity. Scholars also highlight that ethical decision-making requires clear understanding and consent, as actions taken under coercion or ignorance lack full moral and legal validity in Islāmic jurisprudence. Islāmic legal scholars stress that for agreement, whether social, financial, or medical, to be valid, they must be based on clarity, comprehension, and freedom from coercion (Syed, 2016, 2023). Consent that is uninformed, forced, or given under pressure is both ethically and legally invalid. This principle closely mirrors the modern concept of informed consent, which requires that individuals fully understand and voluntarily agree to any proposed action.

The teachings of the Prophet (ﷺ) further reinforce the significance of autonomy, demonstrating that the right to make informed, voluntary choices is a fundamental ethical obligation in Islām. It was narrated from Dawud bin Salih Al Madani that his father said: "I heard Abu Sa'eed Al-Khudri (may Allāh be pleased with him) say: "The Messenger of Allāh (ﷺ) said: 'Transactions may only be done by mutual consent'" (Ibn Majah). The significance of medical consent in Islām can be illustrated through a *hadīth* narrated by ʿĀ'ishah (may Allāh be pleased with her)." We poured medicine into the mouth of Allāh's Messenger (ﷺ) during his illness, and he pointed out to us intending to say, "Don't pour medicine into my mouth." We thought that his refusal was out of the aversion a patient usually has for medicine. When he improved and felt a bit better, he said (to us.) "Did not I forbid you to pour medicine into my mouth?" We said, "We thought (you did so) because of the aversion, one usually have for medicine." Allāh's Messenger (ﷺ) said, "There is none of you but will be forced to drink medicine, and I will watch you, except Al-`Abbas, for he did not witness this act of yours" (Bukhārī). This *hadīth* highlights a core principle of medical ethics in Islām: a patient's refusal of treatment must be respected, even when communicated through non-verbal signals. It also underlines that informed consent does not necessarily require written documentation; rather, it must be clearly understood, voluntarily given, and acknowledged before any intervention takes place (Al-Nawawi, 1972).

Freedom of belief is another core principle supported by the Qur'ān. Allāh says that.

لَآ إِكْرَاهَ فِى ٱلدِّينِ ۖ.

- *There is no compulsion in religion…*" (Al-Baqarah 2:256).

This verse emphasises that faith must arise from genuine conviction rather than external pressure or coercion. In ethical and therapeutic contexts, this principle reinforces the importance of voluntary choice and informed consent, ensuring that individuals are free to make decisions about their spiritual, emotional, and physical well-being without undue influence. Together with the concept of *karāmah*, it highlights Islām's commitment to upholding human dignity, personal autonomy, and the moral responsibility of each person to act in accordance with their conscience.

In the context of counselling or psychotherapy, including digital Islāmic therapy, these principles translate into ensuring that clients:

- Fully understand the nature and scope of the intervention.
- Are aware of their rights and responsibilities.
- Know the potential risks, benefits, and limits of confidentiality.
- Provide consent freely, without coercion, misunderstanding, or ambiguity.

Thus, Islāmic ethics not only supports but strengthens the requirement for clear, informed, and voluntary consent in therapeutic practice.

10.3.4 Gender Sensitivity and Boundaries

Islāmic teachings emphasise modesty (*ḥayā'*), respect, and the protection of personal boundaries, which have direct implications for therapeutic practice, particularly when providing culturally sensitive care. These norms guide appropriate interactions between individuals of different genders and inform expectations in professional settings. For instance, many Muslim clients may prefer therapists of the same gender to avoid discomfort or perceived impropriety in emotionally vulnerable contexts, whether in-person or through video sessions. In addition, Muslim clients may opt out of video sessions due to privacy or modesty concerns, preferring alternatives such as audio-only or text-based counselling. Respecting gender preferences and modesty is not only culturally sensitive but also an ethical obligation. Therapists must provide flexible options, ensuring interventions respect religious values while safeguarding psychological safety and therapeutic efficacy.

The digital environment presents unique challenges in maintaining professional boundaries, particularly regarding privacy, dual relationships, and client access. Online platforms can blur professional and personal boundaries. Clients may attempt to interact with therapists outside the formal therapeutic context, which risks compromising objectivity. Therapists' public online presence, through social media, blogs, or professional profile, can inadvertently invite client over-identification or boundary violations. Clients may also project expectations or emotional needs onto the therapist based on their online persona, complicating the therapeutic alliance. Therapists need to be aware of the personal information about themselves that is publicly accessible and establish clear boundaries in cyberspace, such as avoiding "friending" clients on social media. Using privacy settings on networking sites can help control the type of personal information that is visible to the public (Bolton, 2011).

In summary, gender-sensitive practices and cultural norms must be respected, particularly in Islāmic contexts. Therapists should consider client preferences regarding the gender of the therapist, communication modalities (video, audio, text), and adherence to Islāmic principles of modesty and privacy. At the same time, these considerations must be balanced so that care remains effective, evidence-based, and inclusive. By integrating ethical, cultural, and professional standards, digital Islāmic psychotherapists can provide safe, respectful, and culturally congruent care in online therapeutic settings.

10.3.5 Accessibility and Equity in Digital Islāmic Psychotherapy

Ensuring accessibility in digital Islāmic psychotherapy is not simply a technical consideration; it is an ethical obligation central to providing effective and compassionate care. In online therapeutic contexts, accessibility extends beyond the existence of a digital platform; it requires creating an environment in which individuals from diverse cultural, linguistic, socioeconomic, and ability backgrounds can meaningfully participate in the therapeutic process. This is especially important in Islāmic psychotherapy, where cultural congruence and spiritual sensitivity significantly shape the healing experience. Accessible design, therefore, becomes integral to both ethical practice and therapeutic effectiveness.

A major barrier to accessibility is the ongoing digital divide, which continues to restrict many individuals' ability to engage with online mental health services. Under-resourced communities may lack reliable internet access, up-to-date devices, or private spaces suitable for therapy. Others may have limited digital literacy or may be unaware that such services exist. Thus, the global scalability of digital psychotherapy can become paradoxical: although the service is widely available, it remains inaccessible to many who need it most. From an Islāmic ethical standpoint, addressing these disparities is a matter grounded in the principles of justice (*'adl*) and compassion (*raḥmah*). Digital services should be intentionally designed to promote inclusion by offering multilingual interfaces, culturally relevant content, and accommodations for individuals with disabilities.

10.3.6 Ethical Training and Competency Standards

The rapid expansion of digital technology in mental health care has far outpaced the development of ethical training and competency standards. Consequently, many clinicians find themselves using digital tools, such as text-based communication, videoconferencing platforms, and cloud-based data storage, without adequate preparation. Anthony (2014) offers one of the earliest comprehensive analyses of the skills required for competent practice in digital environments. She identifies a clear mismatch between traditional counselling education and the realities of contemporary digital practice. Crucially, she argues that digital literacy is now an essential component of ethical care; without it, practitioners are vulnerable to serious ethical risks, including breaches of confidentiality, boundary violations, and compromised therapeutic effectiveness. Her emphasis on dual-modality competence, the ability to work both online and offline, highlights how digital culture shapes all forms of therapeutic engagement.

The lack of adequate training increases the risk of ethical violations, unintentional harm, and legal complications. Lustgarten and Elhai (2018) emphasise the critical need for structured training programmes that prepare clinicians to navigate the ethical, legal, and technical challenges associated with digital mental health practice. Beyond clinical expertise, therapists must also develop robust technical competencies to ensure that online services are delivered securely, ethically, and effectively. The British Association for Counselling and Psychotherapy (BACP) (2021) underlines that competence is the cornerstone of safe and ethical online practice. Practitioners can protect both their professional integrity and their clients' well-being by providing online counselling only within the bounds of their expertise. Just as in face-to-face practice, ensuring competence in digital modalities is fundamental to good therapeutic practice and the ethical delivery of care.

10.4 Introduction to Case Vignettes

These case vignettes illustrate ethical challenges in delivering digital psychotherapy to clients within a culturally and spiritually sensitive framework, particularly in the context of Islāmic psychotherapy. With the rapid expansion of online mental health services, therapists increasingly encounter dilemmas related to confidentiality, informed consent, accessibility, and professional boundaries. Both vignettes highlight the intersection of professional ethics and Islāmic moral principles, demonstrating the importance of safeguarding human dignity, autonomy, and well-being. They serve as practical examples for clinicians in training to reflect on ethical decision-making, culturally sensitive interventions, and the integration of spiritual care in digital mental health services.

10.4.1 Case Vignette 1: Confidentiality and Informed Consent in Digital Psychotherapy

Ahmad is a 35-year-old Muslim man living in a remote area where in-person mental health services are unavailable. He presents with symptoms of anxiety and depression following a recent relocation, which was driven by family pressure. Due to geographic isolation, Ahmad seeks online psychotherapy. However, he expresses significant concerns about digital privacy, fearing that his personal information could be leaked or misused. Such a breach, he worries, might compromise his safety and damage his reputation within his close-knit community. Ahmad also voices unease about whether engaging in online therapy aligns with his spiritual practices, raising questions about the compatibility of telepsychology with his religious values.

The therapist faces a complex ethical dilemma in providing online therapy to Ahmad, requiring careful management of multiple responsibilities. They must ensure Ahmad fully comprehends the risks, protections, and limitations of digital therapy, maintaining informed consent and confidentiality while safeguarding

Table 10.1 Ethical reflection on case vignette 1

Ethical domain	Reflective questions
Confidentiality and digital ethics	–How should therapists explain the limits and safeguards of online confidentiality to clients like Ahmad?—What strategies can be used to mitigate risks of data breaches in telepsychology?—How would you ensure informed consent is fully understood in an online environment, particularly regarding confidentiality risks?—What digital security measures are ethically necessary to protect the client's privacy?
Cultural and spiritual considerations	–How might Ahmad's religious concerns shape the therapeutic process?—What approaches can therapists use to integrate spiritual sensitivity into online care?—How might cultural and spiritual considerations influence the client's willingness to engage in online therapy?
Access vs. Equity	–What ethical responsibilities do therapists have when clients have no alternative to online therapy?—How can practitioners ensure equitable access while respecting cultural and personal boundaries?
Therapeutic alliance	–How can trust be fostered in an online setting where privacy concerns are heightened?—What role does transparency play in maintaining therapeutic rapport?—How can therapists maintain professional boundaries and therapeutic alliance in telepsychology sessions?
Professional responsibility	–What guidelines or codes of ethics should inform the therapist's decision-making in telepsychology?—How can therapists balance legal requirements with culturally sensitive practice in remote contexts?—How can Islāmic ethical principles, such as *amānah* (trust) and *raḥmah* (compassion), guide online therapy practice?

sensitive information against potential data breaches. At the same time, the therapist must respect Ahmad's religious beliefs and integrate culturally and spiritually sensitive approaches into the therapeutic process. Additionally, the clinician must balance the necessity of providing accessible online care with the ethical imperative to minimise harm, uphold trust, and ensure that therapy is both safe and culturally responsive. Table 10.1 presents the ethical reflection on Case Vignette 1.

10.4.2 Case Vignette 2: Accessibility and Equity in Digital Islāmic Psychotherapy

Yusuf is a 17-year-old male refugee adolescent presenting with symptoms of post-traumatic stress disorder (PTSD) and social anxiety, with his refugee experiences intensifying feelings of isolation and vulnerability. Due to mobility restrictions, language barriers, and stigma within his community, Yusuf cannot access in-person therapy. He seeks online psychotherapy that is both culturally sensitive and spiritually aligned with his Islāmic faith. Yusuf's circumstances present multiple layers of vulnerability. As a 17-year-old refugee adolescent, he faces heightened risks of marginalisation and re-traumatisation. His limited digital literacy and restricted access to secure technology may hinder effective engagement in online therapy, while his need for therapy in a language he fully understands introduces challenges related to translation, cultural nuance, and establishing therapeutic rapport. Community stigma and fear of exposure make confidentiality and discretion especially critical, and his desire for care that aligns with Islāmic values requires the therapist to balance evidence-based clinical interventions with culturally and spiritually sensitive approaches.

The therapist must navigate the challenge of providing equitable and accessible care while addressing Yusuf's digital literacy, language requirements, and cultural preferences. This involves ensuring inclusion and fairness in telepsychology, safeguarding his confidentiality and safety in digital environments where breaches could have serious social consequences, and delivering therapy that respects his faith and cultural identity while remaining clinically effective. Table 10.2 presents the ethical reflection on Case Vignette 2.

10.5 Conclusion

Digital Islāmic psychotherapy presents an exciting challenge in integrating faith with mental health support. It offers significant opportunities to enhance accessibility, flexibility (Bloch-Atefi, 2025), and personalised mental health care. However, it also demands careful ethical reflection rooted in both Islāmic values and contemporary clinical standards. However, these benefits are accompanied by ethical challenges concerning privacy, informed consent, professional competency, and the protection of vulnerable populations. Therapists must remain vigilant, using secure platforms, adhering to professional and legal standards, maintaining transparency, and safeguarding client autonomy. The lesson to be learned from the Vastaamo breach (Looi et al., 2024) (see Chap. 6) is the critical importance of robust cybersecurity governance in mental health care, including strict adherence to privacy and data protection legislation, the use of comprehensive technical safeguards, and careful consideration of what sensitive information is recorded, alongside the need for timely communication and adequate support for affected patients in the event of a data breach. By addressing these ethical considerations, mental health professionals can leverage digital innovations while upholding the trust, effectiveness, and integrity of psychotherapy. Future development must prioritise inclusivity, integrity, and collaboration between scholars, clinicians, and technologists to ensure this field grows in a way that is spiritually grounded and clinically responsible.

Table 10.2 Ethical reflection on case vignette 2

Ethical/Clinical domain	Reflective questions
Confidentiality & digital ethics	–How would you ensure the client fully understands the risks and safeguards of online confidentiality?—What digital security measures are ethically necessary to protect the client's privacy?—How can therapists maintain professional boundaries and therapeutic alliance in online therapy?—What professional guidelines or codes inform ethical practice in telepsychology?
Cultural & spiritual sensitivity	–How might the client's religious or cultural concerns influence engagement and therapeutic approach?—How can Islāmic principles like *amānah* (trust) and *raḥmah* (compassion) guide online therapy practice?—How can spiritual and cultural values be integrated respectfully while maintaining evidence-based care?—What ethical challenges arise when balancing spiritual sensitivity with clinical interventions?
Access & equity	–How can therapists adapt telepsychology platforms for clients with limited digital literacy or technological access?—What strategies ensure that vulnerable populations, such as refugee adolescents, are not excluded from mental health care due to technological barriers?—How can therapists ensure equitable access while respecting cultural and personal boundaries?—How can Islāmic ethical principles such as *karāmah* (human dignity) and *ʿadl* (justice) inform equitable online care?
Language & communication	–How can therapists navigate language barriers while maintaining therapeutic rapport?—What role do interpreters or bilingual therapists play in ensuring culturally congruent care?—How can therapists confirm client understanding of informed consent in an online environment?
Confidentiality & community stigma	–What safeguards are necessary to protect client privacy in digital spaces?—How should therapists address the risk of stigma if therapy participation becomes known within the client's community?—How can trust be fostered when privacy concerns are heightened?
Adolescent & developmental considerations	–What unique considerations apply when providing online therapy to adolescents, particularly refugee minors?—How can therapists ensure developmental needs are met in digital therapeutic environments?—How might trauma history affect engagement, trust, and coping in online psychotherapy?

References

Abū Dāwūd. *Sunan Abi Dawud 4868*. In-book reference: Book 43, Hadith 96. English translation: Book 42, Hadith 4850. Hasan (Al-Albani). https://sunnah.com/abudawud:4868

Al-Nawawi, Y. S. (1972). *al-Minhaj: Sharh Sahih Muslim bin al-Hajjaj* (2nd ed.). Dar Ihya' al-Turath al-Arabi.

Al-Qurtubi. *Tafsîr An-Nisa' 4:58*. https://quran.com/ar/al-isra/34/tafsirs?utm_source=chatgpt.com

American Psychological Association, Joint Task Force for the Development of Telepsychology Guidelines. (2013). Guidelines for the practice of telepsychology. *American Psychologist, 68*(9), 791–800. https://www.apa.org/pubs/journals/features/amp-a0035001.pdf

Anthony, K. (2014). Training therapists to work effectively online and offline within digital culture. *British Journal of Guidance & Counselling, 43*(1), 36–42. https://doi.org/10.1080/03069885.2014.924617

Bauer, M., Glenn, T., Monteith, S., et al. (2017). Ethical perspectives on recommending digital technology for patients with mental illness. *International Journal of Bipolar Disorders, 5*, 6. https://doi.org/10.1186/s40345-017-0073-9

Bloch-Atefi, A. (2025). Balancing ethics and opportunities: The role of AI in psychotherapy and counselling. *Psychotherapy and Counselling Journal of Australia, 13*(1). https://doi.org/10.59158/001c.129884

Bolton, J. (2011). The ethical issues which must be addressed in online counselling. *Australian Counselling Research Journal, 11*(1), 1–15.

British Association for Counselling and Psychotherapy. (n.d.). *Ethical framework for the counselling professions: Confidentiality*. https://www.bacp.co.uk/events-and-resources/ethics-and-standards/ethical-framework-for-the-counselling-professions/confidentiality/

British Association for Counselling and Psychotherapy. (2021). *Online and phone therapy (OPT) competence framework: User guide*. BACP. https://www.bacp.co.uk/media/10850/bacp-online-and-phone-therapy-user-guide-feb21.pdf

Bukhārī. Sahih al-Bukhari 6897. In-book reference: Book 87, Hadith 36. USC-MSA web (English) reference: Vol. 9, Book 83, Hadith 35. https://sunnah.com/bukhari:6897

Chakrabarti, S. (2015). Usefulness of telepsychiatry: A critical evaluation of videoconferencing-based approaches. *World Journal of Psychiatry, 5*(3), 286–304.

Chamsi-Pasha, H., & Albar, M. A. (2017). Ethical Dilemmas at the End of Life: Islamic Perspective. *Journal ofreligion and health, 56*(2), 400–410. https://doi.org/10.1007/s10943-016-0181-3

Cipolletta, S., & Mocellin, D. (2018). Online counseling: An exploratory survey of Italian psychologists' attitudes towards new ways of interaction. *Psychotherapy Research : Journal of the Society for Psychotherapy Research, 28*(6), 909–924. https://doi.org/10.1080/10503307.2016.1259533

Deardorff, L. (2010). Online counseling: A literature review. *International Journal for the Advancement of Counselling, 32*(1), 14–29.

du Preez, E., van Kessel, K., & Webb, X. (2024). A systematic review of the ethical considerations of delivering video-based therapy. *Psychotherapy and Counselling Journal of Australia, 12*(1). https://doi.org/10.59158/001c.115608

Fiske, A., Henningsen, P., & Buyx, A. (2019). Your robot therapist will see you now: Ethical implications of embodied artificial intelligence in psychiatry, psychology, and psychotherapy. *Journal of Medical Internet Research, 21*(5), Article e13216. https://doi.org/10.2196/13216

Gedge, L. (2002). Online counselling and confidentiality: Practical considerations. *British Journal of Guidance & Counselling, 30*(3), 233–244.

Gooding, P., & Kariotis, T. (2021). Ethics and law in research on algorithmic and data-driven technology in mental health care: Scoping review. *JMIR Mental Health, 8*(6), Article e24668. https://doi.org/10.2196/24668

Harris, B., & Birnbaum, R. (2015). Ethical and legal implications on the use of technology in counselling. *Clinical Social Work Journal, 43*(2), 133–141.

Himmatun 'Aliah, V., Budiman, N., & Aulia Nadhirah, N. (2024). Digital privacy ethics issues: Counseling information leaks in community counseling settings. *Journal of Counseling and Psychology, 4*(1), 39–47. https://proceedings.uinsa.ac.id/index.php/ICONICS/article/view/3553/2289

Ibn Kathir. (2000). *Tafsir ibn Kathir* (Trans. J. Abualrub, N. Khitab, H. Khitab, A. Walker, M. Al-Jibali, & S. Ayoub). Darussalam Publishers and Distributors.

Ibn Majah. *Sunan Ibn Majah 2185.* In-book reference: Book 12, Hadith 49. English translation: Vol. 3, Book 12, Hadith 2185. Sahih (Darussalam). https://sunnah.com/ibnmajah:2185

Ibn Muflih al-Maqdisi, M. (1996). *Al-adab al-shar'iyyah wa al-minah al-mar'iyyah.* Dar al-Kutub al-'Ilmiyyah.

Islamqa. (2003). *What is the ruling on one who discloses secrets*? Question: 27190. In Tuhfat al-Ahwadhi. https://islamqa.info/en/answers/27190/what-is-the-ruling-on-one-who-discloses-secrets

Joint Task Force for the Development of Telepsychology Guidelines for Psychologists. (2013). Telepsychology guidelines. *Professional Psychology: Research and Practice, 44*(4), 397–403.

Kanani, K., & Regehr, C. (2003). Ethical considerations in online counselling. *Canadian Journal of Counselling, 37*(4), 274–287.

Looi, J. C., Allison, S., Bastiampillai, T., et al. (2024). Cybersecurity lessons from the Vastaamo psychotherapy data breach for psychiatrists and other mental healthcare providers. *Australasian Psychiatry, 33*(1), 106–110. https://doi.org/10.1177/10398562241291340

Lustgarten, S. D., & Elhai, J. D. (2018). Technology use in mental health practice and research: Legal and ethical risks. *Clinical Psychology: Science and Practice, 25*(2), Article e12234. https://doi.org/10.1111/cpsp.12234

Madej, A., Sendler, D., & Makara-Studzińska, M. (2016). *Online psychotherapy: Ethics challenges. Psychoterapia, 3*(178), 31–36.

Mallen, M. J., & Vogel, D. L. (2005). Online counselling: Review of relevant research. *Journal of Counselling Psychology, 52*(2), 695–700.

PACFA Ethics Committee. (n.d.). *Informed consent and confidentiality issues to be considered for online therapy.* https://pacfa.org.au

Psychology Town. (2024). *Navigating ethical issues in e-counselling: Best practices and guidelines.* https://psychology.town

Rutkowska, E., Furmańska, J., Marques, C. C., Martins, M. J., Lane, H., & Meixner, J. (2025). Psychotherapists' ethical dilemmas regarding online and face-to-face psychotherapy during the COVID-19 pandemic: Survey study. *Journal of Medical Internet Research, 27.* https://doi.org/10.2196/69154

Rubeis, G. (2021). E-mental health applications for depression: An evidence-based ethical analysis. *European Archives of Psychiatry and Clinical Neuroscience, 271*, 549–555. https://doi.org/10.1007/s00406-019-01093-y

Shah Waliullah Dehlawi. *Forty Hadith of Shah Waliullah Dehlawi.* Hadith 4, 40 Hadith Shah Waliullah. https://sunnah.com/shahwaliullah40:4

Stoll, J., Müller, J. A., & Trachsel, M. (2020). Ethical issues in online psychotherapy: A narrative review. *Frontiers in Psychiatry, 11*, 1–16. https://doi.org/10.3389/fpsyt.2020.00582

Syed, M. U. (2023, July 18). Compulsion in Islamic law. In J. L. Esposito (Ed.), *Oxford encyclopedia of Islamic law.* Oxford University Press. https://oxfordislamicstudies.com

Syed, M. U. (2016). *Coercion and responsibility in Islam: A study in ethics and law.* Oxford University Press.

Torous, J., & Roberts, L. W. (2017). The ethical use of mobile health technology in clinical psychiatry. *The Journal of Nervous and Mental Disease, 205*(1), 4–8. https://doi.org/10.1097/NMD.0000000000000596

UK Council for Psychotherapy. (2021). *Guidelines for working online or remotely.* https://www.psychotherapy.org.uk/media/jrohoner/ukcp-guidelines-for-working-online-or-remotely-v1.pdf

Warrier, U., Warrier, A., & Khandelwal, K. (2023). Ethical considerations in the use of artificial intelligence in mental health. *Egyptian Journal of Neurology, Psychiatry and Neurosurgery, 59*, 139. https://doi.org/10.1186/s41983-023-00735-2

Wiggins-Frame, M. (1998). The ethics of counseling via the Internet. *The Family Journal: Counseling and Therapy for Couples and Families, 5*(4), 328–330.

Chapter 11
Ethical Decision-Making in Islāmic Psychotherapy

11.1 Introduction

Islāmic psychotherapy exists at the intersection of psychological science and spiritual guidance, necessitating a comprehensive ethical framework that integrates professional mental health practices with the core moral and spiritual principles of Islām. Central to this framework is ethical decision-making, which provides clinicians with a structured approach to navigating complex dilemmas that may arise across diverse cultural, professional, religious, psycho-spiritual, and clinical contexts. By grounding therapeutic practice in both evidence-based psychology and Islāmic ethical values, therapists can ensure that their interventions are both clinically effective and spiritually sensitive. This process extends beyond ordinary decision-making, as it seeks to harmonise professional codes of ethics, Islāmic moral principles, and the multiple responsibilities of the therapist, including client well-being, professional integrity, and broader societal and cultural obligations, often in complex and uncertain circumstances.

This chapter outlines key ethical decision-making frameworks and proposes an Islāmic approach that therapists can utilise to guide their professional judgements in a variety of therapeutic contexts. The Ethical Dilemma Decision-Making Model for Islāmic psychotherapists (Rassool, 2025) uses *niyyah* (intention) to guide therapists in making decisions aligned with Islāmic values. It provides a culturally sensitive framework that integrates ethics, cultural awareness, and family considerations, while promoting self-reflection, consultation, and ongoing education to ensure ethical and competent care.

G. H. Rassool, *Ethical Dilemmas in Islāmic Psychotherapy*,
https://doi.org/10.1007/978-3-032-26515-9_11

11.2 Ethical Decision-Making Frameworks

Ethical decision-making frameworks are structured models that outline the processes individuals or professionals can follow to identify, analyse, and resolve ethical dilemmas. These frameworks prioritise key considerations such as client autonomy, confidentiality, non-maleficence (avoiding harm), beneficence, and justice. Although the models differ in emphasis, they share a common commitment to balancing client rights with professional responsibilities in ways that are culturally respectful and clinically appropriate. In essence, the findings of a study by Ricou et al. (2023) identified that the most common principles across psychotherapy ethics codes include confidentiality, competence, integrity, honesty, accuracy, and the ongoing development and awareness of professional competence. In contrast, principles mentioned less often are promoting client self-determination, extended responsibility, and social responsibility and ethical awareness. Key ethical principles, such as autonomy, beneficence, non-maleficence, fidelity, justice, veracity, and self-respect, are identified across major counselling and psychotherapy codes (American Counseling Association, 2014; British Association for Counselling & Psychotherapy, 2018). While there are some minor differences, these principles are generally consistent across frameworks.

Smith (2021) suggested that putting ethical principles into practice does not necessarily require a detailed formal framework. He cited the recommendation of the British Association for Counselling and Psychotherapy (2018), which advises practitioners to ask themselves, "Is this decision supported by these principles without contradiction?" If the answer is yes, the decision can be considered ethically sound; if not, it indicates a potential ethical issue that requires further reflection. In therapeutic practice, this means that therapists prioritise their ethical codes, professional standards, and legal responsibilities even when doing so is uncomfortable or may lead to challenging outcomes. Below, we explore five different ethical decision-making frameworks commonly used in mental health practice: Principle-based approach; Virtue ethics approach; Four-Quadrant approach; Utilitarianism approach; and Deontological approach.

11.2.1 Principle-Based Approach

The principle-based approach is one of the most widely recognised ethical frameworks in mental health, offering clear guidance for decision-making through key ethical principles. This approach, adapted from medical ethics, emphasises applying foundational principles to ensure responsible and ethical practice. This framework is widely used in health care, psychotherapy and counselling. In counselling and psychotherapy, four main principles, autonomy, beneficence, non-maleficence, and justice, are commonly applied. For example, when a client presents with a complex mental health issue, the therapist must:

- Respect autonomy by supporting the client's informed decision-making and self-determination regarding treatment choices.
- Promote beneficence by recommending interventions that are in the client's best interest and support psychological well-being.
- Avoid harm (non-maleficence) by ensuring that interventions do not exacerbate distress or lead to unintended negative consequences.
- Ensure justice by providing equitable access to care and treating clients fairly, regardless of background or circumstances.

These principles help therapists navigate ethical dilemmas in practice, providing a clear framework for balancing client needs, professional responsibilities, and ethical standards. As in health care, real-life therapeutic situations can be complex, requiring careful reflection, supervision, and collaboration with clients and colleagues to achieve the most ethical and effective outcomes.

Case example: Emma, a 32-year-old client, sought therapy to address severe anxiety associated with a career change. During therapy, the therapist encountered an ethical dilemma when Emma requested guidance. The dilemma centred on whether to focus on strategies that would reduce Emma's anxiety in the short term by encouraging avoidance, or to guide her toward interventions that might cause temporary discomfort but ultimately support her long-term personal and professional goals. To navigate this dilemma, the therapist applied the Principle-Based Approach by systematically considering core ethical principles. Emma's autonomy was respected by offering her multiple options and supporting informed decision-making. Beneficence was promoted through the recommendation of strategies aimed at improving her coping skills and overall well-being, while non-maleficence was upheld by carefully evaluating the potential emotional impact of each intervention to minimise harm. Additionally, the therapist ensured justice by providing fair and unbiased care throughout the therapeutic process. By integrating these principles, the therapist was able to support Emma effectively and ethically, balancing her immediate concerns with her long-term goals while maintaining professional standards.

11.2.2 Virtue Ethics Approach

Virtue ethics centres on the moral character, values, and personal qualities of the practitioner rather than relying primarily on rules, principles, or anticipated outcomes. Houser et al. (2006) emphasise that virtue ethics is not culturally neutral; understandings of virtue and their expression are shaped by the cultural context, worldview, and lived experiences of both the therapist and the client. Within this perspective, the therapist qualities such as empathy, compassion, honesty, integrity, humility, wisdom, and courage guide ethical decision-making beyond formal ethical codes or consequence-based reasoning. In psychotherapy, this framework encourages practitioners to reflect on whether their actions are consistent with the kind of caring and ethical professional they strive to be. Houser et al. (2006) argue that ethical decision-making is inherently relational, as the therapist's virtues interact dynamically with the client's cultural background, values, and needs, shaping how ethical dilemmas are understood and addressed. Rather than relying solely on professional codes, practitioners are encouraged to engage in ongoing self-reflection, critically examining their moral motivations, strengths, and limitations.

Virtue ethics places strong emphasis on the therapeutic relationship, proposing that ethical choices should arise from genuine concern for the client's well-being and deep respect for their experiences. Through case illustrations, Houser et al. (2006) demonstrate how virtue-based reasoning operates in real counselling situations, particularly where cultural values and ethical tensions intersect. They ultimately situate virtue ethics within a hermeneutic decision-making framework that balances universal professional principles with the moral particularities of culturally diverse contexts. Closely aligned with this perspective, relational ethics highlights authentic, respectful, and caring engagement within the therapeutic relationship as central to ethical practice (Mental Health Academy, 2024). Therapists guided by virtue and relational ethics prioritise trust, understanding, and client welfare over rigid rule-following, while still attending to ethical principles such as confidentiality. Ethical decisions are informed by the therapist's moral character and intention, guided by reflective questions such as *What would a compassionate, honest, and wise therapist do in this situation?* This integrated approach fosters moral development, relational awareness, and ethical integrity throughout clinical practice.

Case example: Adam, a 40-year-old client, sought therapy to address depression and feelings of social isolation. An ethical dilemma emerged when Adam began to rely heavily on the therapist for emotional support. The therapist was faced with the challenge of balancing increased emotional availability to meet Adam's immediate needs with the responsibility to maintain appropriate professional boundaries, in order to prevent dependency that could undermine Adam's long-term autonomy and social development.

The Virtue Ethics Model would guide the therapist to respond by prioritising moral character and relational responsibility rather than rigid rules. Drawing on virtues such as empathy, compassion, integrity, and practical wisdom, the therapist would offer emotional support while remaining mindful of professional boundaries. Through empathy and compassion, the therapist acknowledges Adam's loneliness and validates his emotional needs, while integrity and prudence guide the therapist to encourage Adam's independence and the development of supportive relationships outside of therapy. Ongoing self-reflection allows the therapist to monitor their intentions and actions, ensuring they are motivated by genuine concern for Adam's well-being rather than reinforcing dependency. By acting in accordance with virtuous character, the therapist maintains a supportive yet ethically sound therapeutic relationship that promotes Adam's long-term autonomy, personal growth, and social connection.

11.2.3 Four-Quadrant Approach

Although originally developed for medical ethics (Mental Health Academy, 2024), the four-quadrant approach can be effectively adapted for psychotherapy and counselling. The model offers a structured way for clinicians to consider the multiple dimensions involved in ethically complex situations. It divides the decision-making process into four key areas, as presented in Table 11.1

The Four-Quadrant Approach guides therapists in ethical decision-making by systematically evaluating multiple dimensions of a clinical situation. It considers clinical indications, ensuring that interventions are evidence-based and ethically justified; client preferences, respecting autonomy, values, cultural background, and goals; quality of life, assessing how decisions may impact the client's psychological, emotional, and relational well-being; and contextual features, including family dynamics, cultural norms, legal requirements, and organisational policies. By integrating these four areas, therapists can make balanced, ethically sound decisions that are both clinically appropriate and responsive to the client's individual needs and circumstances. By applying these four quadrants, therapists or counsellors can evaluate ethical dilemmas in a balanced and comprehensive manner. The approach supports thoughtful decision-making that integrates clinical judgement, client autonomy, contextual sensitivity, and the pursuit of the client's well-being.

Case example: A therapist is working with Maya, a 19-year-old university student experiencing depression and intense family pressure. During a session, Maya reveals she has been drinking heavily to cope and hints at occasional thoughts of "not wanting to be here," but insists she does not want anyone informed, fearing her parents' reaction. Using the Four-Quadrant Approach, the therapist addressing Maya's case systematically considers multiple dimensions of ethical decision-making. Clinical indications highlight the need to assess suicide risk and

Table 11.1 Four-Quadrant approach

Quadrant	Focus/Considerations	Key questions
Clinical indications	Evaluates whether the chosen intervention is consistent with evidence-based practice and professional standards	Is this approach clinically appropriate and ethically justified for this client?
Client preferences	Respects the client's autonomy, values, cultural background, and stated goals	What does the client want, and how can their preferences be honoured while maintaining ethical responsibility?
Quality of life	Considers how decisions or interventions affect the client's psychological, emotional, and relational well-being	How will this choice affect the client's overall quality of life, both inside and outside therapy?
Contextual features	Examines broader factors such as family dynamics, cultural norms, legal issues, and organisational policies	What external elements shape this situation, and how should they inform my ethical decision?

address harmful coping behaviours such as heavy drinking. Client preferences are respected by acknowledging Maya's desire for privacy and her cultural concerns about family disappointment. Quality of life considerations guide interventions that may be uncomfortable but aim to reduce long-term harm and enhance her safety and overall well-being. Contextual features such as legal obligations, university mental health policies, and cultural stigma are also taken into account. By balancing these four quadrants, the therapist collaboratively develops a safety plan with Maya, maintains confidentiality where possible, schedules close follow-up, and clearly communicates the limits of confidentiality, ensuring an ethically informed, culturally sensitive, and clinically appropriate response.

11.2.4 Utilitarianism Approach

Utilitarianism emphasises choosing the action that produces the greatest overall benefit or minimises harm for the most people. That is, it focuses on promoting the greatest overall happiness or minimising harm for the greatest number of people (Kilgour & Delaney, 2024).

Knapp (1999) suggested that the common use of utilitarian ethics is "On one level, many lay persons and psychologists are more or less utilitarian, although they might not have reflected in depth as to the foundations of their ethical beliefs" (p. 383). Knapp's (1999) observation highlights how utilitarian thinking often operates implicitly in everyday ethical decision-making, including within psychotherapy. His point suggests that both the general public and many clinicians may rely on outcome-focused reasoning, seeking the "greatest good" or least harm, without consciously identifying this as a philosophical stance. Rather than deliberately choosing utilitarianism, practitioners may default to it because it feels intuitive or pragmatic, especially in complex situations where consequences weigh heavily. In psychotherapy, this may arise when a therapist must balance the needs of an individual client with the safety of others. For example, if a client expresses violent intentions toward a third party, a utilitarian approach would guide the therapist to prioritise public safety over maintaining strict confidentiality. Although breaching confidentiality may strain the therapeutic relationship, it prevents greater potential harm to multiple people.

Case example: A therapist is treating Sam, who reveals increasing anger toward a former colleague and describes a specific plan to "get revenge soon." Using the utilitarianism approach, the therapist prioritises actions that produce the greatest overall benefit and minimise harm. In Sam's case, while maintaining confidentiality would protect his privacy, it could place others at serious risk. Applying a utilitarian lens, the therapist determines that preventing potential harm to others outweighs the duty to preserve confidentiality. They conduct a thorough risk assessment, notify appropriate authorities to protect potential victims, and continue working with Sam to manage his anger safely. This approach focuses on maximising overall safety and well-being for all parties involved, guiding ethical decision-making through the principle of the greatest good.

11.2.5 Deontological Approach

The deontological framework emphasises adherence to moral rules and duties, regardless of the consequences. Within this approach, an action is considered ethical if it aligns with moral or professional principles regardless of the consequences. In psychotherapy, this includes respecting client autonomy, maintaining honesty, and upholding confidentiality except in legally defined exceptions. For instance, even when a therapist strongly believes a client would benefit from involving family members, the therapist must honour the client's decision if they decline, as long as there is no risk of harm. A central strength of deontological ethics is that it lays moral responsibility within the individual's intentions and adherence to duty, rather than the unpredictability of outcomes (The Ethics Centre, 2016). This perspective is particularly valuable in therapeutic work, where consequences cannot always be foreseen and clinicians often operate under uncertainty. By focusing on intention, therapists are encouraged to act with integrity, honesty, and respect for ethical principles, even when the results of those actions may be complex or imperfect. However, this emphasis on intention also highlights a limitation; good intentions do not always guarantee good outcomes. Therefore, while deontology provides a stable and principled foundation for ethical decision-making, it benefits from being balanced with other frameworks that consider client welfare, context, and potential consequences.

Case example Maria, a 25-year-old client, discloses struggling with severe anxiety. The therapist suggests that involving a trusted family member might provide helpful support, but Maria firmly declines, citing cultural concerns and the desire for privacy. Applying the Deontological Approach, the therapist focuses on adhering to moral duties and principles rather than outcomes. In Maria's case, although involving a family member might benefit her therapy, the therapist respects her autonomy and informed consent, honouring her decision to maintain privacy due to cultural concerns. By upholding the duty to respect Maria's rights, the therapist continues therapy in line with her preferences, collaboratively developing coping strategies while maintaining trust and ethical integrity. This approach emphasises acting according to professional and moral obligations, ensuring that ethical principles guide decision-making regardless of potential consequences.

11.3 Models of Ethical Decision-Making

Psychotherapists regularly encounter complex ethical dilemmas, and relying solely on intuition, or what feels right, can increase risks to clients and undermine public trust. As Welfel (2016) notes, intuition alone may lead to ethical errors, highlighting the need for structured frameworks to support sound decision-making. To address this, several ethical decision-making models have been developed, each offering different perspectives and tools to help clinicians think critically,

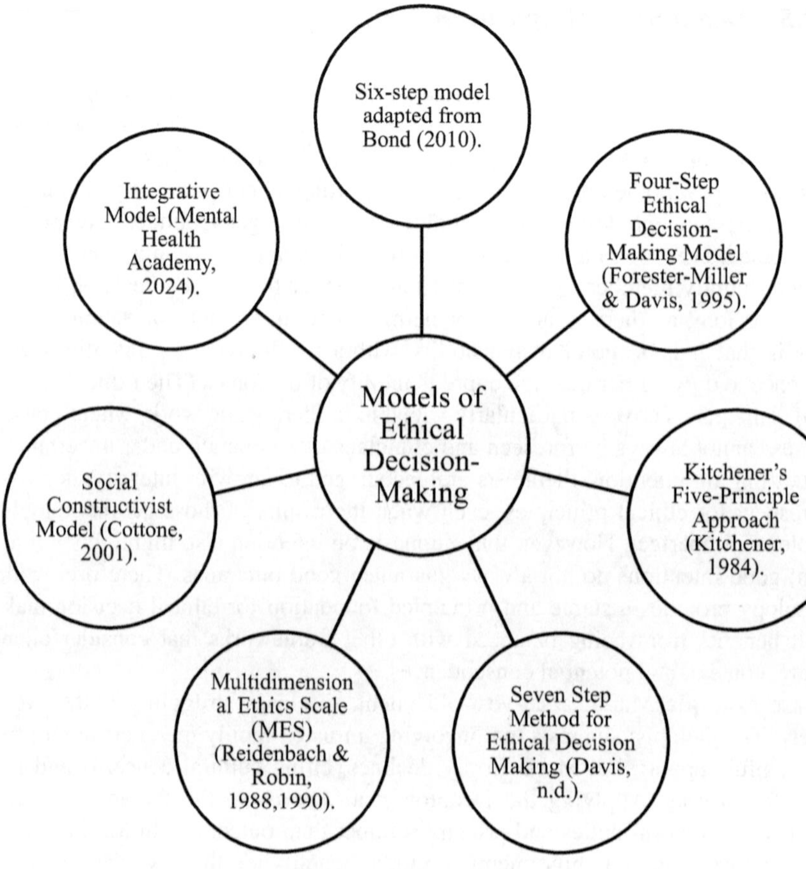

Fig. 11.1 Models of ethical decision-making

uphold ethical standards, and safeguard client welfare. These models guide therapists through a variety of challenges, including dilemmas involving spirituality and religion (Barnett & Johnson, 2011), boundary issues (Younggren & Gottlieb, 2004), and culturally complex scenarios. Importantly, as Corey et al. (2011) emphasise, no single model can account for every client or every situation, ethical decision-making requires flexibility, reflection, and professional judgement. Figure 11.1 outlines the models of ethical decision-making.

One commonly used process is the six-step model adapted from Bond (2010), which begins with eliciting a clear description of the dilemma and determining who is primarily facing it, the therapist, the client, or both. Practitioners are then encouraged to consult relevant professional codes, consider possible courses of action, choose the most ethically appropriate option, and finally implement and evaluate the decision. This structured approach ensures that decisions are accountable, well-reasoned, and grounded in ethical standards. Barnett and Teehan (2022) further emphasise prevention and preparation as core elements of ethical practice. They recommend that therapists stay well-informed about ethical codes, relevant legislation, and organisational policies, while also recognising that legal allowances do not automatically dictate ethical action. Practitioners are encouraged to clarify their own values, seek consultation when dilemmas arise, and maintain transparency with clients, particularly regarding personal beliefs or frameworks, such as Islāmic psychotherapy. Clear communication through informed consent and public-facing materials helps ensure that clients understand the nature of the services being offered and the values underpinning them.

Among the formal ethical decision-making models, the Four-Step Ethical Decision-Making Model by Forester-Miller and Davis (2016) provides a systematic, sequential approach. Therapists begin by identifying the ethical problem, apply relevant ethical guidelines, evaluate stakeholder perspectives and possible alternatives, and finally implement and review the chosen action. This model supports reflective, thorough, and methodical decision-making. Kitchener's Five-Principle Approach (1984) offers a principled framework grounded in autonomy, beneficence, non-maleficence, justice, and fidelity. Widely used in counselling psychology, this approach helps practitioners prioritise client welfare, fairness, and professional integrity. It provides a clear structure for balancing competing duties, particularly in situations where multiple ethical principles appear to conflict. For more multifaceted dilemmas, the Multidimensional Ethics Scale (MES) developed by Reidenbach and Robin (1988, 1990) encourages therapists to consider diverse sources of ethical guidance: societal norms, professional codes, personal moral values, client cultural values, and theoretical orientation. This wider lens enables nuanced, contextually responsive decisions that acknowledge both universal standards and individual differences. The Seven-Step Method (Davis, n.d.) expands on structured decision-making by guiding practitioners to clearly define the problem, gather relevant facts, identify stakeholders, generate multiple options, test each option, make a tentative choice, and then finalise the decision. This methodical sequence ensures that therapists extensively examine ethical dilemmas and make transparent, defensible decisions.

Alternatively, Cottone's (2001) Social Constructivist Model conceptualises ethical decision-making as a relational and collaborative process. Rather than focusing solely on internal reasoning, this model emphasises dialogue with clients, colleagues, and other stakeholders. Practitioners assess the relational dynamics, cultural context, and power structures at play, consult ethical guidelines and experts, and work toward consensus. This approach is particularly valuable in culturally diverse contexts, where meaning-making and ethical interpretation emerge through shared understanding. Finally, the Integrative Model (Mental Health Academy, 2024) weaves together multiple ethical perspectives to support holistic and culturally sensitive decision-making. The model begins with identifying ethical conflicts, exploring the client's cultural and contextual background, and considering the viewpoints of all affected parties. Therapists may consult literature, experts, or supervision to support the process. This model encourages clinicians to balance ethical principles, anticipated consequences, and relational awareness, resulting in decisions that are both ethically justified and clinically appropriate.

Together, these models equip mental health professionals with a diverse and flexible set of tools for navigating ethical dilemmas. While some frameworks prioritise structured analysis or core principles, others highlight relational, collaborative, or culturally responsive approaches. In practice, therapists often blend these models to match the complexity of the ethical issue, the client's cultural and personal context, and the expectations of professional standards. A summary of the key models is presented in Table 11.2.

Table 11.2 Models of ethical decision-making

Model	Key Features	Steps / Principles	Focus in Therapy
Six-Step Ethical Decision-Making Model (Bond, 2010)	Structured, stepwise; promotes accountability and reflection	Clarify the dilemma; Consult guidelines; Generate options; Evaluate ethically; Decide; Implement and review	Guides therapists in making well-reasoned, ethically sound decisions that balance client welfare, professional standards, and clinical judgment
Four-Step Ethical Decision-Making Model (Forester-Miller & Davis, 1995)	Systematic, structured approach	Identify the problem Apply ethical codes/standards Consider stakeholders & alternatives Implement & evaluate	Ensures all aspects of a dilemma are considered; encourages reflective and methodical decision-making
Kitchener's Five-Principle Approach (Kitchener, 1984)	Principle-based, ethical competence	Autonomy. Beneficence. Nonmaleficence. Justice. Fidelity	Guides counsellors to prioritise client welfare while maintaining professional integrity
Multidimensional Ethics Scale (MES) (Reidenbach & Robin, 1988,1990)	Holistic, multidimensional	Societal standards. Professional standards. Personal values. Client values. Theoretical orientation	Supports nuanced decision-making integrating legal, professional, personal, and client perspectives
Seven Step Method for Ethical Decision Making (Davis, n.d.)	Structured. Comprehensive. Stepwise	State the problem Gather and assess relevant facts in the case Identifying the stakeholders Develop list of at least five options Test options Make a tentative choice Make final choice	Provides a detailed, stepwise framework to systematically evaluate ethical dilemmas and make well-informed decisions

(continued)

Table 11.2 (continued)

Model	Key Features	Steps / Principles	Focus in Therapy
Social Constructivist Model (Cottone, 2001)	Collaborative, relational, consensus-oriented	Gather information from all parties involved (clients, colleagues, stakeholders) Assess the counsellor–client relationship and context Consult experts, literature, and ethical guidelines Negotiate and reach consensus Respond in a fair and ethically aligned manner	Focuses on building ethical decisions through relationships, dialogue, and consensus; emphasises cultural context, power dynamics, and collaborative problem-solving in therapy
Integrative Model (Mental Health Mental Health Academy, 2024)	Conflict identification, Cultural awareness, stakeholder perspectives	Identifies conflicting principles Considers the client's cultural and personal context Weighs the perspectives of possible stakeholders including the client's family	The focus of this is to guide ethical decision-making through a flexible, holistic approach stakeholders

11.4 Islāmic Ethical Dilemma Decision-Making Model

There is an increasing need for an Islāmic-oriented ethical decision-making model, as existing frameworks, though widely used and valuable, are primarily grounded in Western philosophical traditions and do not fully account for the moral, spiritual, and cultural foundations that shape the experiences of many Muslim clients and practitioners. Islāmic ethics incorporates not only universal principles such as justice, compassion, and the avoidance of harm, but also emphasises spiritual accountability, sincerity of intention (*niyyah*), and the holistic well-being of individuals and the wider community. In therapeutic settings, Muslim clients may present concerns shaped by religious beliefs, family dynamics, communal expectations, and cultural norms that secular ethical frameworks often do not adequately address. An Islāmic-oriented model therefore provides a culturally congruent and spiritually sensitive structure, guiding practitioners to make decisions that respect clients' values while maintaining professional integrity.

The *Islāmic Ethical Dilemma Decision-Making Model* (Rassool, 2025) was specifically developed to address ethical dilemmas in Islāmic psychotherapy. The model has been updated and adapted to incorporate contemporary clinical

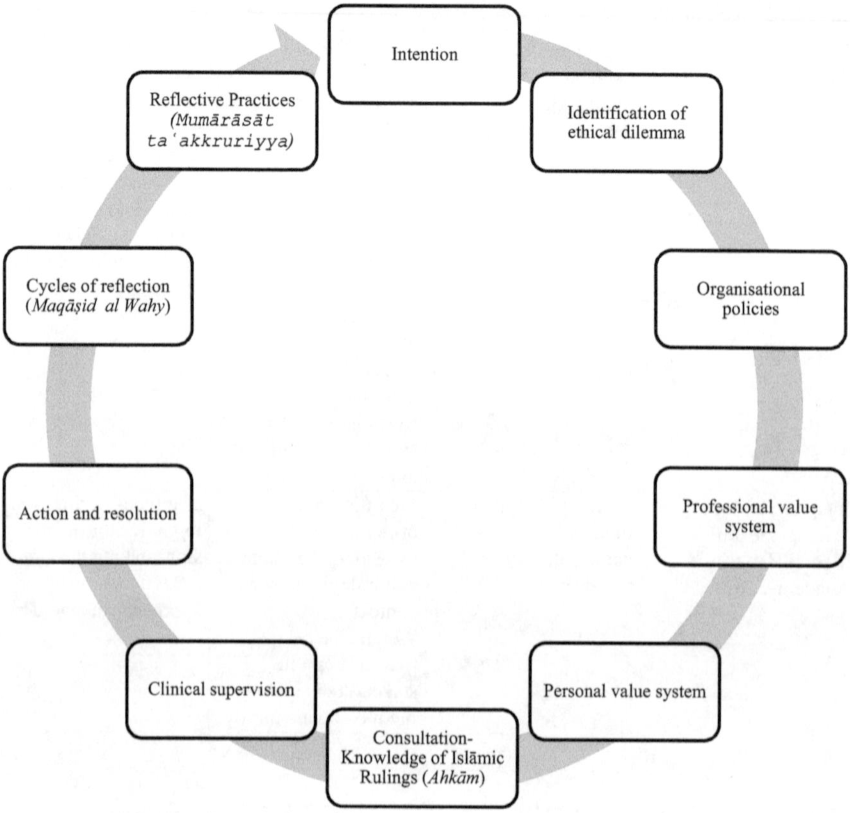

Fig. 11.2 The Islāmic ethical dilemma decision-making model

practices, cultural nuances, and professional standards, ensuring its relevance for therapists working in diverse Islāmic contexts. These enhancements increase the model's flexibility, allowing practitioners to integrate traditional Islāmic ethical principles with modern therapeutic approaches while preserving fidelity to both religious and professional guidelines. An overview of the updated model is presented in Fig. 11.2.

The rationale for this model stems from the recognition that Western ethical frameworks, while important, cannot fully capture the theological, spiritual, and cultural dimensions central to Muslim perspectives. Ethical decision-making in Islām is rooted in Qur'ānic teachings, Prophetic guidance, and the higher objectives of *Sharī'ah* (*Maqāṣid al-Sharī'ah*), which emphasise the protection and promotion of faith, life, intellect, lineage, and property. By integrating these principles, an Islāmic ethical model enables therapists to navigate dilemmas with a sense of divine accountability, holistic spirituality, and communal responsibility. It bridges professional ethical standards with Islāmic moral imperatives, ensuring therapeutic decisions are both clinically sound and religiously authentic. Such a framework is essential for supporting culturally attuned, spiritually informed, and ethically coherent practice among Muslim psychotherapists and for meeting the needs of Muslim clients seeking therapy within the context of their faith tradition.

The *Islāmic Ethical Dilemma Decision-Making Model* emphasises the importance of *niyyah* (نِيَّة, intention) as the foundational element. *Niyyah* serves as a moral and ethical compass, guiding therapists to make decisions aligned with Islāmic values and principles. It enables practitioners to navigate complex ethical dilemmas while prioritising client welfare and upholding Islāmic ethical standards. When confronted with ethical conflicts, therapists consciously reflect on their niyyah to ensure sincerity and purity in their actions. The first step in the Islāmic ethical dilemma decision-making process therapists is identifying the ethical problem. In this stage, therapists carefully examine situations to detect potential ethical conflicts in their practice. A common dilemma may arise when a client's requests or beliefs appear to conflict with Islāmic ethical guidelines. Organisational policies are integral within this framework, covering aspects such as confidentiality, informed consent, client rights, boundaries, and professional conduct. By adhering to these policies, therapists maintain professionalism, safeguard client welfare, and ensure consistent ethical practice. Organisational guidelines also clarify acceptable behaviours in challenging situations, such as dual relationships or client gifting, allowing therapists to protect client well-being while upholding essential professional boundaries.

The integration of the professional value system is another cornerstone of this model. It anchors therapists to established ethical standards and provides guidance for complex dilemmas. While professional codes (e.g., BACP, APA) outline broad ethical standards, they may not address every possible scenario. Therapists are therefore encouraged to exercise professional judgement alongside these codes. Barnett (2019) highlights that terms such as "reasonably, appropriate, and potentially within the Ethics Code are designed to allow practitioners to apply their judgment and adapt ethical principles to diverse situations" (p. 432). Therapists' personal value systems also play a crucial role. These systems, shaped by individual beliefs, ethical foundations, and principles, influence how dilemmas are assessed and resolved. In Islāmic psychotherapy, reflective practices on personal values help therapists reconcile potential conflicts between personal beliefs, professional ethics, and Islāmic teachings.

Consultation is a cornerstone of ethical decision-making in Islāmic psychotherapy, reflecting both professional and religious commitments. Therapists are encouraged to seek guidance from colleagues, clinical supervisors, or qualified Islāmic scholars when faced with complex ethical dilemmas. This collaborative approach ensures that multiple perspectives are considered, helps clarify ambiguous situations, and provides additional support in balancing professional obligations with Islāmic ethical principles. Clinical supervision, in particular, offers a structured setting to discuss cases, reflect on decision-making processes, evaluate potential actions, and receive feedback that aligns with both professional codes and Islāmic values. In Islāmic contexts, consultation extends beyond standard professional guidance to include knowledge of Islāmic rulings (*ahkām*). These rulings, derived from Qur'ānic teachings, Prophetic traditions (*Sunnah*), and the broader framework of *Sharīʿah*, provide clear guidance on moral and ethical conduct. Understanding *ahkām* allows therapists to assess ethical dilemmas through an Islāmic lens, ensuring that decisions are consistent with religious obligations, such as intentions (*niyyah*), communal responsibility, and the protection of clients' well-being. By integrating consultation with professionals and scholars, therapists can navigate the intersection of religious, cultural, and clinical considerations, making decisions that are ethically sound, culturally sensitive, and spiritually coherent. The "Action" and "Resolution" stages emphasise implementing and evaluating decisions. Therapists act in accordance with ethical deliberation, professional codes, organisational policies, and Islāmic principles. For example, in cases of confidentiality breaches, actions may include addressing the issue with the client, taking steps to prevent recurrence, and mitigating harm. The resolution stage involves assessing the outcomes to ensure ethical standards are upheld and the therapeutic relationship is maintained. Thorough documentation of decisions and actions is essential, providing legal protection, promoting transparency, and facilitating continuity of care.

The "Cycles of Reflection" stage underlines ongoing ethical growth, self-awareness, and continuous learning. Therapists critically reflect on their decisions, examining the interplay of ethical principles and the application of Islāmic values within the therapeutic context. Drawing from Jasser Auda's Maqāṣid Methodology (2021), this stage involves repeated, deep engagement with the higher objectives of *Sharīʿah* (*maqāṣid*), allowing therapists to evaluate not only explicit ethical rules but also the underlying values, intentions (*niyyah*), and broader communal and spiritual implications of their actions. Through these reflective cycles, therapists can dynamically assess and refine their ethical reasoning, ensuring that interventions remain both clinically effective and consistent with Islāmic moral and spiritual teachings. This approach fosters a continual process of ethical development, promoting culturally sensitive, spiritually informed, and ethically coherent practice in Islāmic psychotherapy.

Reflective practices (*Mumārāsāt taʿakkruriyya*) in Islāmic psychotherapy serve as a vital mechanism for enhancing ethical competence. By engaging in structured reflection, therapists critically examine the decisions they make, the ethical principles they apply, and the alignment of their actions with Islāmic values and spiritual teachings. This process helps therapists identify personal biases, cultural assumptions, or blind spots that may inadvertently influence their professional judgement. Moreover, reflective practice fosters ongoing professional growth by encouraging therapists to analyse past ethical dilemmas, evaluate the effectiveness of their chosen interventions, and consider alternative strategies for similar future situations. Through this continuous cycle of reflection, therapists become more adept at navigating complex ethical challenges while maintaining integrity, cultural sensitivity, and spiritual awareness. Ultimately, this iterative process embodies the ethical responsibility central to Islāmic psychotherapy, ensuring that therapeutic decisions not only adhere to professional and moral standards but also honour the holistic well-being of clients in line with Qur'ānic guidance, Prophetic teachings, and

Sharīʿah objectives (maqāṣid). Table 11.3 outlines the *Islāmic Ethical Dilemma Decision-Making Model.*

Overall, the Islāmic Ethical Dilemma Decision-Making Model offers a culturally sensitive, spiritually grounded, and holistic framework for navigating ethical challenges. By integrating Islāmic ethics, professional standards, personal reflection, consultation, and cultural awareness, therapists are equipped to manage real-world ethical dilemmas with integrity. Continuous reflection and education further strengthen ethical practice, ensuring culturally congruent and clinically sound care for Muslim clients.

11.5 Case Vignette

Yusuf, a 35-year-old Muslim man, seeks therapy for severe anxiety, marital difficulties, and financial stress. He discloses that his gambling has contributed to his current situation and is experiencing intrusive thoughts, including guilt and impulses to harm his business partner following a recent betrayal that led to significant financial loss. Yusuf is conflicted about whether to pursue legal action, confront his partner directly, or follow spiritual guidance and exercise patience in accordance with Islāmic teachings. He also worries about bringing dishonour to his family and community if his actions are perceived as aggressive or unethical. The therapist faces a complex ethical dilemma, needing to balance Yusuf's mental health and safety, the potential risk to others, legal responsibilities, and compliance with Islāmic ethical principles.

The therapist begins the process with intention (*niyyah*), reflecting on the sincerity of their motives and committing to act in a way that upholds Yusuf's well-being, promotes justice, compassion, empathy, prevents harm, and aligns with Islāmic ethical principles. Next, the ethical dilemma is clearly identified: Yusuf's potential risk to others, his mental health vulnerabilities, and his moral and religious concerns create a multifaceted ethical challenge. The therapist reviews organisational policies, ensuring adherence to confidentiality, risk management, mandated reporting obligations, and institutional guidelines for managing clients at risk of harm to self or others. The therapist applies their professional value system, prioritising beneficence, non-maleficence, justice, and respect for Yusuf's autonomy, while reflecting on their personal value system to ensure personal biases about aggression, gambling, and religious expectations do not influence the clinical approach. Recognising the need for faith-informed guidance, the therapist consults Islāmic rulings (*ahkām*), which stress the prohibition of harm (*la darar wa la dirar*), the importance of patience, ethical dispute resolution, and the accountability of intentions (*niyyah*) in decision-making.

To enhance clinical judgement, the therapist engages in clinical supervision, discussing risk management strategies, therapeutic interventions, and culturally and religiously sensitive approaches to addressing Yusuf's guilt, intrusive thoughts, and interpersonal conflicts. They then develop a concrete action and resolution plan in collaboration with Yusuf, which includes coping strategies

Table 11.3 Islāmic ethical dilemma decision-making model

Stage/Component	Key features	Steps/Principles	Focus in therapy
Niyyah (Intention)	Foundational moral compass; aligns actions with Islāmic values	Therapist reflects on their intention to act sincerely according to Islāmic principles	Guides ethical choices and prioritises client welfare while maintaining spiritual integrity
Identifying the ethical problem	Recognises dilemmas arising from conflicts between client needs, organisational policies, and Islāmic ethics	Assess situation carefully; note conflicts between client requests and Islāmic guidelines	Ensures therapists recognise ethical challenges early and respond appropriately
Organisational policies	Provides professional guidance for conduct, confidentiality, boundaries	Consult organisational rules on confidentiality, dual relationships, informed consent	Maintains consistency, protects client welfare, and upholds professional standards
Professional value system	Anchors decisions in established professional ethics	Reflect on ethical codes (APA, BACP) to guide decision-making	Ensures adherence to universal ethical standards while addressing specific dilemmas
Personal value system	Therapist's beliefs and principles inform decision-making	Reflect on personal biases, moral foundations, and alignment with Islāmic values	Supports self-awareness and integrity in ethical choices
Consultation & Supervision	Collaborative decision-making; multiple perspectives	Engage colleagues, supervisors, and qualified Islāmic scholars	Clarifies complex dilemmas, ensures alignment with professional and Islāmic principles
Action & resolution	Implementation of ethical decisions	Apply chosen action according to ethical, professional, and Islāmic standards; monitor outcomes	Resolves dilemmas while maintaining ethical integrity and therapeutic alliance
Cycles of reflection (*Maqāṣid al Wahy*)	Ongoing ethical growth, self-awareness, and dynamic moral reasoning	Reflect on decisions, ethical principles, application of Islāmic values; consider *Sharīʿah* objectives (*maqāṣid*)	Promotes culturally sensitive, spiritually informed, and ethically coherent practice in psychotherapy
Reflective Practices (*Mumārāsāt taʿakkruriyya*)	Structured reflection on decisions, principles, and alignment with Islāmic values	Critically analyse past ethical dilemmas, evaluate intervention effectiveness, identify biases, consider alternative strategies for future situations	Enhances ethical competence, spiritual awareness, cultural sensitivity, and ongoing professional growth; ensures decisions honour Qur'ānic guidance, Prophetic teachings, and *Sharīʿah* objectives (*maqāṣid*)

for intrusive thoughts, lawful and ethical ways to address the business conflict, management of gambling behaviour, and steps to maintain mental and spiritual well-being. Throughout the process, the therapist engages in cycles of reflection (*maqāṣid al-wahy*), evaluating each decision against the higher objectives of *Sharīʿah,* protecting life, intellect, property, and dignity to ensure ethical coherence, client safety, and the prevention of harm to others. Finally, reflective practices (*mumārāsāt taʿakkruriyya*) are applied, enabling the therapist to examine personal biases, assess the effectiveness of interventions, and refine ethical reasoning. This continuous reflection fosters professional growth and ensures that clinical decisions remain culturally sensitive, spiritually informed, and ethically robust. Table 11.4 presents the Islāmic Ethical Dilemma Decision-Making Checklist.

Table 11.4 Islāmic ethical dilemma decision-making checklist

Step	Focus	Guiding questions
Step 1	Identify the dilemma	• What is the ethical issue? • Does it involve autonomy, confidentiality, informed consent, professional boundaries, receiving gifts, or cultural/religious values?
Step 2	Gather relevant information	• What is the client's cultural, spiritual, and social context? • What do professional codes of ethics, organisational policies, and relevant local legal requirements require?
Step 3	Consult Islāmic sources and scholars/ Cycles of Reflection	• Cycles of reflection (Qur'ān and *Sunnah*)? • Which Qur'ānic principles are applicable? • What guidance is found in Prophetic traditions (*Sunnah* and *ḥadīth*)? How do *Maqāṣid al-Sharīʿah* (preservation of faith, life, intellect, lineage, and property) inform the situation? • How do *al-Qawāʿid al-Fiqhiyyah* (Islamic legal maxims) apply? Has consultation occurred with a qualified Islāmic scholar or jurist (*ʿālim*, *muftī*, or *fiqh* specialist), particularly in complex or high-risk cases?
Step 4	Balance competing values	• How can client autonomy be balanced with family or community expectations? • Are there tensions between Islāmic guidance and evidence-based practice? • How can these be ethically navigated?
Step 5	Seek supervision and professional consultation	• Has the dilemma been discussed with a clinical supervisor or peers? • Have diverse professional, cultural, and faith-informed perspectives been considered to minimise personal bias?
Step 6	Make and document the decision	• Is the decision clinically sound and ethically defensible? • Is it consistent with Islāmic ethical principles and professional standards? • Has the reasoning and decision-making process been clearly documented?
Step 7	Reflect and evaluate	• What was the outcome of the decision for the client and therapeutic process? • What lessons can be applied to future ethical practice?

11.6 Conclusion

There is a growing need for an Islāmic-oriented ethical decision-making model, as existing frameworks, though valuable, are largely rooted in Western philosophical traditions and may not fully address the moral, spiritual, and cultural dimensions central to Muslim clients and practitioners. Islāmic ethics combines universal principles such as justice, compassion, and non-maleficence with spiritual accountability, sincerity of intention (*niyyah*), and attention to the holistic well-being of individuals and communities. In therapeutic contexts, clients' concerns are often shaped by religious beliefs, family dynamics, communal expectations, and cultural norms that secular frameworks may overlook. An Islāmic-oriented model provides a culturally congruent and spiritually sensitive structure, enabling therapists to make ethical decisions that honour clients' values while upholding professional integrity. By integrating reflective practices and other structured approaches, such models offer a robust, faith-centred guide for navigating complex ethical dilemmas in psychotherapy.

References

American Counseling Association. (2014). *Ethical & professional standards*. https://www.counseling.org/knowledge-center/ethics

Auda, J. (2021). *Re-envisioning Islāmic scholarship: Maqāṣid methodology as a new approach*. Claritas Books & Maqasid Institute.

Barnett, J., & Teehan, D. (2022). Ethics and values in psychotherapy. *Psychotherapy Bulletin, 57*(2), 11–16.

Barnett, J. E., & Johnson, W. B. (2011). Integrating spirituality and religion into psychotherapy: Persistent dilemmas, ethical issues, and a proposed decisionmakingprocess. *Ethics & Behavior, 21*(2), 147–164. https://doi.org/10.1080/10508422.2011.551471

Barnett, J. E. (2019). The ethical practice of psychotherapy: Clearly within our reach.

Bond, T. (2010). *Standards & ethics for counselling in action*. Sage.

British Association for Counselling and Psychotherapy. (2018). *BACP ethical framework for the counselling professions*. https://www.bacp.co.uk/events-and-resources/ethics-and-standards/ethical-framework-for-the-counselling-professions/

Corey, G., Corey, M. S., & Callanan, P. (2011). *Issues and ethics in the helping professions*. Cengage Learning.

Cottone, R. R. (2001). A social constructivism model of ethical decision making in counseling. *Journal of Counseling & Development, 79*(1), 39–45.https://doi.org/10.1002/j.1556-6676.2001.tb01941.x

Davis, M. (n.d.). *Seven Step method for ethical decision-making*. online ethics center. https://doi.org/10.18130/dv34-4w94 adapted from Davis, M. (1999). *Ethics and the university* (pp. 166–167). Routledge.

Forester-Miller, H., & Davis, T. E. (2016). A practitioner's guide to ethical decision making. *American Counseling Association*.https://www.counseling.org/resources/aca-code-of-ethics.pdf

Houser, R., Wilczenski, F. L., & Ham, M. (2006). Virtue ethics and counselor decision makin *Culturally relevant ethical decision-making in counseling* (pp.11–18). Sage. https://doi.org/10.4135/9781452225838.n2

Kilgour, C., & Delaney, L. J. (2024). *Quality in healthcare: Assessing what we do.* The University of Queensland. https://doi.org/10.14264/4174bad

Kitchener, K. S. (1984). Intuition, critical evaluation and ethical principles: The foundation for ethical decisions in counseling psychology. *The CounselingPsychologist, 12*(3), 43–55. https://doi.org/10.1177/0011000084123005

Knapp, S. (1999). Utilitarianism and the ethics of professional psychologists. *Ethics & Behavior, 9*(4), 383–392. https://doi.org/10.1207/s15327019eb0904_7

Mental Health Academy. (2024, November 13). *Ethical decision-making in mental health.* Mental Health Academy. https://www.mentalhealthacademy.com.au/blog/ethical-decision-making-in-mental-health

Rassool, G. H. (2025). *Islāmic counselling & psychotherapy* (2nd ed.). Routledge.

Reidenbach, R., & Robin, D. (1988). Some initial steps toward improving the measurement of ethical evaluation of marketing activities. *J. Bus. Ethics, 7*, 871–879.

Reidenbach, R., & Robin, D. (1990). Toward the development of a multi-dimensional scale for improving evaluations of business ethics. *J. Bus. Ethics, 9*, 639–653. *Psychotherapy, 56*(4), 431–440. https://doi.org/10.1037/pst0000272

Ricou, M., Neto, D. D., Silva, A. N., & Marina, S. (2023). *Principios éticos en psicoterapia dentro de un amplio marco deontológico psicológico y médico: una comparación internacional* [Ethical principles in psychotherapy within a broad psychological and medical deontological framework: An international comparison]. *Quaderns de Psicologia, 25*(2), Article e1867. https://doi.org/10.5565/rev/qpsicologia.1867

Smith, W. (2021, July 30). *Ethics in counseling: The code + 10 common ethical issues.* PositivePsychology.com. https://positivepsychology.com/counseling-ethics-code/

The Ethics Centre. (2016, February 18). *Ethics explainer: Deontology.* https://ethics.org.au/ethics-explainer-deontology/

Welfel, E. R. (2016). *Ethics in counseling and psychotherapy: Standards, research, and emerging issues* (6th ed.). Cengage.

Younggren, J. N., & Gottlieb, M. C. (2004). Managing risk when contemplating multiple relationships. *Professional Psychology: Research and Practice, 35*(3), 255–260. https://doi.org/10.1037/0735-7028.35.3.255

Chapter 12
Toward an Islāmic Model of Clinical Supervision: Concept and Framework

12.1 Introduction

Islāmic psychotherapists, like their mainstream counterparts, are expected to practice independently with the professional skills required to deliver effective psychotherapy and counselling. They are accountable to both their clients and the profession, adhering to ethical standards, maintaining confidentiality, and engaging in continuous professional development to enhance their knowledge and competencies (Rassool, 2025). Such accountability and competence are essential for providing therapy that meets client needs while upholding professional and ethical standards. However, the lack of structured clinical supervision can hinder the development of clinical expertise in Islāmic psychotherapy (Rassool, 2021, 2025). Clinical supervision offers a roadmap for therapists to reflect on their practice, receive constructive feedback, and refine their skills. In Islāmic psychotherapy, supervision is particularly crucial as practitioners integrate Islāmic principles with therapeutic approaches. It also provides a forum to address ethical dilemmas that arise at the intersection of mental health practice and Islāmic values, ensuring care that is both clinically sound and spiritually informed.

A frequently overlooked aspect of Islāmic counselling and psychotherapy is the self-care and professional development of the practitioners themselves. Like all mental health professionals, Islāmic counsellors and psychotherapists are expected to operate autonomously, delivering safe, ethical, and effective interventions while remaining accountable to clients and professional standards. Beyond these foundational responsibilities, Islāmic practitioners face unique challenges, including balancing spiritual guidance, religious teachings, and culturally sensitive approaches while maintaining professional boundaries. Clinical supervision is therefore essential, not only for enhancing competence and ethical practice but also for supporting the emotional and spiritual well-being of the therapist. Despite its importance, literature on clinical supervision in Islāmic psychology and psychotherapy is

G. H. Rassool, *Ethical Dilemmas in Islāmic Psychotherapy*,
https://doi.org/10.1007/978-3-032-26515-9_12

limited, with only brief discussions found in Rassool (2021, 2025) and Ali (2021). Developing robust supervision frameworks is critical to equip Islāmic counsellors and psychotherapists to navigate ethical complexities, manage dual roles, and provide care that is spiritually grounded, culturally attuned, and psychologically effective, while safeguarding their own professional growth and resilience.

The aim of this chapter is to examine clinical supervision within Islāmic psychotherapy and its role in developing competent, ethical, and spiritually oriented practitioners. It examines the concept, purposes, forms, and models of supervision, highlighting both professional and reflective growth. The chapter discusses benefits such as enhanced clinical skills, ethical accountability, emotional support, and culturally responsive care. It proposes an Islāmic Clinical Supervision Model integrating spiritual-ethical, professional competence, reflective-development, and relational-interactive dimensions. Finally, it advocates structured training, organisational support, and research to strengthen supervision and improve client outcomes.

12.2 Concept of Clinical Supervision

The definitions of supervision are varied and often depend on the professional discipline, which can result in conflicting and sometimes contradictory interpretations. Negative connotations associated with supervision further complicate its understanding.

Bernard and Goodyear (1992) define clinical supervision as "This relationship is evaluative, extends over time and has the simultaneous purposes of enhancing the professional functioning of the more junior person and monitoring the quality of the professional services" (p. 8). This definition emphasises that clinical supervision is both evaluative and developmental, highlighting a sustained relationship in which the supervisor supports the professional growth of the junior practitioner while ensuring the quality of client services. Milne (2007) critiques earlier definitions, including Bernard and Goodyear (1992), for lacking precision and offers a more research-based alternative, defining clinical supervision as "The formal provision, by approved supervisors, of a relationship-based education and training that is work-focused and which manages, supports, develops and evaluates the work of colleague/s" (p. 437). In a more recent publication, Bernard and Goodyear (2019) describe clinical supervision as "an intervention provided by a more senior member of a profession to a more junior colleague or colleagues who typically (but not always) are members of that same profession. This relationship is evaluative and hierarchical, extends over time, and has the simultaneous purposes of enhancing the professional functioning of the more junior person(s); monitoring the quality of professional services offered to the clients that she, he, or they see; and serving as a gatekeeper for the particular profession the supervisee seeks to enter" (p. 9). Bernard and Goodyear's (2019) definition emphasises that clinical supervision is a structured, ongoing, and hierarchical relationship between a senior and junior professional. It highlights the dual purpose of supervision: developing the professional competence of the supervisee while ensuring the quality and ethical standards of client care. The inclusion of the gatekeeping role highlights the supervisor's responsibility in maintaining professional standards and safeguarding the integrity of the profession. Overall, the definition frames supervision as both developmental and evaluative, balancing mentorship with accountability.

Similarly, the Center for Substance Abuse Treatment (2009) defines clinical supervision as "a social influence process that occurs over time, in which the supervisor participates with supervisees to ensure quality clinical care. Effective supervisors observe, mentor, coach, evaluate, inspire, and create an atmosphere that promotes self-motivation, learning, and professional development." This definition highlights supervision as a relational and developmental process, not merely evaluative, emphasising the supervisor's multifaceted role in mentoring, coaching, and inspiring supervisees while fostering competence, confidence, and professional growth in clinical practice.

In summary, clinical supervision is a sustained, ongoing relationship between an clinically experienced supervisor and a junior supervisee, providing a structured framework for professional growth over time. It is both evaluative and developmental, aiming not only to enhance the professional functioning of the supervisee but also to monitor and ensure the quality of services delivered to clients. Supervision is work-focused and goal-oriented, centring on professional tasks, client care, and the development of clinical skills. In this process, supervisors play a mentoring and supportive role, offering guidance, feedback, coaching, and encouragement to foster competence, confidence, and overall professional growth. At the same time, supervision provides ethical and quality oversight, ensuring that practitioners adhere to professional standards and safeguarding both clients and the profession. Effective supervision is relational and socially influential, creating an environment that promotes self-reflection, learning, and motivation. Supervisors also fulfil a gatekeeping function, maintaining standards for entry into and ongoing practice within the profession.

12.3 Purpose of Clinical Supervision

Clinical supervision serves multiple interrelated purposes that are critical for maintaining the competence, well-being, and ethical practice of mental health professionals. One of the primary functions is enhancing professional functioning, where supervision is used to develop practitioners' skills, knowledge, and reflective capacity. This process allows supervisees to improve their clinical reasoning, ethical decision-making, and confidence in practice, ensuring that they are capable of delivering high-quality care to clients (Rothwell et al., 2019, 2021). By focusing on skill refinement and reflective practice, supervision fosters both the personal and professional growth of practitioners, helping them navigate the complexities of clinical work. A second essential purpose is monitoring the quality of services. Supervision functions as a safeguard to ensure that practitioners provide care that is safe, effective, and aligned with professional standards. By regularly evaluating clinical work, supervisors help maintain service quality and protect clients from substandard practice or potential harm (Rothwell et al., 2019). This evaluative aspect of supervision is particularly important in high-stakes environments, such as mental health and counselling settings, where ethical lapses or clinical errors can have significant consequences.

Another critical role of supervision is providing emotional and professional support. The safe space created through supervision allows practitioners to process the emotional demands of their work, reduce stress, and prevent burnout. Evidence indicates that supportive supervision not only promotes resilience but also enhances overall well-being among professionals (Rothwell et al., 2021; Yan, 2022). By fostering a safe and trusting environment, supervision enables practitioners to reflect on challenging cases, share concerns, and receive guidance, which contributes to sustained motivation and job satisfaction. Supervision also plays a vital role in facilitating continuing professional development. By encouraging reflection, providing feedback, and integrating new knowledge, supervision supports lifelong learning and the ongoing growth of professional competence (Rothwell et al., 2021). This function ensures that practitioners remain up to date with evolving clinical methods, evidence-based practices, and emerging ethical standards, which in turn enhances the quality of care delivered to clients.

Finally, supervision is instrumental in promoting accountability and ethical practice. When supervision is embedded within organisational structures, practitioners are held accountable for their clinical decisions and adherence to ethical codes. Evidence suggests that this accountability strengthens professional integrity and contributes to safer client care (Rothwell et al., 2021; Yan, 2022). Through this multidimensional oversight, supervision not only nurtures the development of practitioners but also safeguards clients, the profession, and the broader healthcare system.

In sum, clinical supervision is a complex, multifaceted process that integrates skill development, quality assurance, emotional support, ongoing learning, and ethical accountability. Together, these functions create a comprehensive framework that sustains professional competence, promotes practitioner well-being, and ensures high standards of care in clinical practice. Table 12.1 outlines the purpose of clinical supervision.

12.4 Forms of Supervision

There are many forms of clinical supervision: Self-reflection, One-to-One, co-supervision, group supervision and peer supervision. The One-to-One supervision and group supervision are common in mental health psychotherapy and counselling.

Table 12.1 Purpose of clinical supervision

Purpose of clinical supervision	Description/Evidence
Enhancing professional functioning	Develops practitioners' skills, knowledge, and reflective capacity. Improves clinical reasoning, ethical decision-making, and confidence in practice (Rothwell et al., 2019, 2021)
Monitoring quality of services	Ensures safe, effective, and ethical care. Maintains professional standards and protects clients from poor practice (Rothwell et al., 2019)
Providing emotional and professional support	Offers a structured space to process stress, reduce burnout, and sustain motivation. Supportive supervision enhances resilience and wellbeing (Rothwell et al., 2021; Yan, 2022)
Facilitating continuing professional development	Encourages reflection, feedback, and integration of new knowledge, supporting ongoing professional growth (Rothwell et al., 2021)
Promoting accountability and ethical practice	Embedding supervision into organizational structures holds practitioners accountable, strengthens adherence to ethical codes, and improves client safety (Rothwell et al., 2021; Yan, 2022)

12.4.1 Self-Reflection (Supervision)

Self-reflection is a structured, reflective process in which therapists actively monitor and evaluate their own clinical practice to enhance professional competence and ensure high-quality care. It enables practitioners to critically examine their decisions, identify potential biases, and align interventions with established best practices, especially in contexts where formal supervision is limited or unavailable (Lowe, 2000; Morrissette, 2001a, 2001b, 2013; Todd & Storm, 2014). While it fosters independence and prepares therapists for autonomous practice, self-reflection is most effective when combined with traditional supervisory methods, supporting ongoing professional development and ethical, competent practice. This practice can be understood as a form of "self-supervision in action," integral to both personal and professional growth, and applicable across diverse clinical contexts. Todd (1997) defines self-supervision as "a process whereby therapists self-monitor their therapeutic behaviour, comparing this behaviour with some model of more effective behaviour, with the intent of changing their behaviour to resemble this model closely" (p. 18). This definition underlines the intentional and reflective nature of self-reflection, emphasising the proactive evaluation of clinical behaviours against a model of effective practice. The aim is to encourage continuous professional growth, enhance clinical competence, and maintain accountability, particularly when formal supervision is limited.

Self-reflection is inherently personal, offering therapists the opportunity to explore their own thoughts, feelings, and actions through structured self-evaluation, which can itself be a therapeutic process. However, it should ideally be accompanied by other forms of supervision to ensure guidance, feedback, and external perspective. Crucial to all forms of self-reflection is the commitment to allocate sufficient time for reflection and the willingness to critically examine one's own clinical approach, guided by a "healthy internal supervisor" (Hawkins & Shohet, 2012). For a comprehensive overview of self-supervision models, see Basa (2018). In the context of self-supervision, the process can be understood as a form of guided reflection. At its core, self-supervision involves asking three fundamental questions:

- "What happened?
- So what?
- Now what?" (Driscoll, 2007).

First, the practitioner examines the events or interactions in their practice. Next, they reflect on the significance of these events, considering their emotional responses, insights, and any patterns that emerge. Finally, the practitioner uses these reflections to plan how they will respond or adapt their approach in future, similar clinical situations. This structured reflective process allows therapists to critically evaluate their own practice, foster professional growth, and enhance clinical competence independently.

12.4.2 One-To-One

This is the most common form of supervision that is given and received on an informal basis by practitioners in the helping profession. It is acknowledged that one-to-one clinical supervision will become a model in most branches of therapy but on a formal and regular basis. For example, a senior therapist provides clinical supervision to a drug and alcohol worker. Harper (2025) suggests that individual (one-to-one supervision) provides personalised guidance tailored to the supervisee's caseload, therapeutic style, and client needs. It offers a consistent and confidential space for exploring professional challenges, personal reactions, and countertransference, supporting both clinical and personal development. This type of supervision is often considered the most effective type of supervision for retaining practitioners, as it provides tailored guidance, a confidential space for reflection, and focused support that enhances professional development and job satisfaction (Cortis et al., 2021). The style of supervision should be person-centred, meaning it prioritises the supervisee's development needs rather than primarily serving the supervisor's or organisation's agenda (Edgar et al., 2023). While organisational goals remain important, supervision should primarily focus on the individual, ensuring that their growth, learning, and professional development are at the centre of the process.

12.4.3 Co-Supervision

Co-supervision in psychotherapy is a reciprocal process where two practitioners take turns acting as supervisor and supervisee. This model emphasises equality, shared responsibility, and mutual learning, rather than the hierarchical structure of traditional supervision (Hawkins & Shohet, 2012). While it does not replace formal supervision, it can serve as a valuable complement, especially for those seeking reflective dialogue, cultural sensitivity, and shared accountability. In practice, co-supervision often occurs informally, outside organisational systems, and is common among community-based therapists, independent practitioners, and peer groups. Sessions typically involve collaborative reflection, where each participant presents cases, dilemmas, or professional challenges. The co-supervisor helps explore these issues, offering feedback and guidance that promote deeper insight and critical thinking. Both practitioners share accountability for ethical standards, clinical quality, and ongoing professional development. Because the practice is flexible, participants can negotiate the frequency, format, and focus of their meetings to suit their needs.

Co-supervision offers several strengths. It fosters equality and mutual respect, encourages diverse perspectives, and provides emotional support that reduces the isolation often experienced in private or community practice. It is also cost-effective compared to traditional supervision. However, challenges exist. Alternating roles can create role ambiguity, and its informal nature may not meet organisational or licensing requirements. Without external oversight, there is also a risk of collusion, where difficult feedback is avoided. Finally, the quality of co-supervision depends heavily on the commitment and skill of both participants, which can vary.

12.4.4 Group Supervision

Group supervision is whereby a supervisor or consultant external to the agency or with a different orientation is responsible for the facilitation of the group. Group supervision involves several practitioners meeting routinely with a supervisor to discuss cases, share experiences, and learn collectively, fostering a supportive and collaborative professional community. An essential element of successful group supervision is having a skilled facilitator. This individual leads the discussion, promotes balanced participation, and helps the group remain centred on constructive feedback and practical solutions. The facilitator also works with supervisees to determine how presentation time is allocated. Through this structured process, the consultation group can develop case formulations and strategies that offer members fresh insights and actionable plans.

Group supervision provides supervisees with opportunities for mutual support, shared experiences, collaborative problem-solving, skill acquisition, focused skills training, enhanced interpersonal abilities, and increased self-awareness (MacKenzie, 1990). Central to this model is the dynamic interaction among group members. Bernard and Goodyear (1992) highlight several common focal points in group supervision, including didactic teaching, case conceptualisation, individual and group development, organisational factors, and issues that arise within supervisory relationships. Reynolds (2013) argues that group formats create an optimal environment for cultivating ethical repertoires. He attributes this to the capacity of groups to support active, multi-voiced dialogue about ethical matters, something that cannot be fully replicated in individual supervision. Learning in a group context also offers several unique advantages not typically available in one-to-one supervision. These include peer feedback, opportunities for social networking, exposure to multiple perspectives, observational learning, increased empathy, modelling and practicing constructive communication, developing presentation and public-speaking skills, and strengthening professional competencies (Valentino et al., 2016).

According to Geller (1994), group supervision enhances traditional supervision and effectively exposes students to group processes as mechanisms for learning, growth, and change. Additional benefits of group supervision over individual formats include cost-effectiveness in terms of time and resources, a supportive atmosphere, opportunities to test emotional and intuitive responses with others, access to diverse feedback from both peers and facilitators, and the advantage of drawing on a broad range of life experiences and group-based techniques. However, its limitations include the difficulty of replicating the dynamics of one-to-one sessions and the potential for group dynamics to dominate, leaving less time for focused attention on individual supervisees (Hawkins & Shohet, 2012).

12.5 Models of Clinical Supervision

Supervision models can be categorised based on their theoretical foundations, approaches, and purposes. For instance, developmental models draw on principles of developmental psychology and conceptualise supervision as a progressive, evolving process. They suggest that clinicians move through distinct stages, from novice to experienced practitioner—and that supervision should be adapted to correspond with each stage.

Supervision models can be classified according to their theoretical foundations, methodological approaches, and intended functions. Competency-based models emphasise the supervisee's skills and learning needs, employing strategies such as goal-setting, role-play, and modelling. Supervisory functions typically include teaching, consulting, and counselling, as illustrated in Bernard and Goodyear's Discrimination Model (2004) and Mead's Task-Oriented Model (1990). Treatment-based models focus on training supervisees in a specific theoretical orientation or evidence-based practice, such as cognitive-behavioural therapy, motivational interviewing, or psychodynamic therapy, with an emphasis on practical application. Developmental models conceptualise supervision as a progressive process in which clinicians advance through stages of growth shaped by context, assignments, and client populations. Examples include Stoltenberg and McNeill's Integrated Developmental Model (2011), Skovholt and Rønnestad's Life-Span Model (1992), and Stoltenberg and Delworth's (1987) three-stage framework, which highlights progression in self- and other-awareness, motivation, and autonomy. Integrative models combine multiple approaches, accounting for leadership style, treatment orientation, supervisee developmental stage, contextual factors, and both skill and affective growth. Bernard's Discrimination Model (1979) and Holloway's Systems Approach to Supervision (1995) exemplify this category. Emerging in the 1970s and 1980s, social role models emphasise the roles and tasks of the supervisor alongside the developmental stages of the supervisee. Hawkins and Shohet's Six-Focused Model (2000) is particularly influential, while Bernard and Goodyear's Discrimination Model (2019) also fits within this category. Although described as "a-theoretical," the latter highlights three supervisory roles, teacher, counsellor, and consultant, each of which can be applied across three distinct foci of supervision.

Psychotherapy-based models are grounded in established therapeutic frameworks such as psychodynamic or cognitive-behavioural approaches, illustrated by Frawley-O'Dea and Sarnat's (2001) Psychodynamic Model and Liese and Beck's (1997) Cognitive-Behavioural Model. Finally, supervision-specific models focus explicitly on the processes, tasks, structure, and supervisory relationship, as seen in Proctor's Three-Function Interactive Framework (1987) and the General Supervision Framework by Scaife and Scaife (1996). Collectively, these models highlight the diverse theoretical orientations and practical strategies that shape effective clinical supervision.

12.6 Clinical Supervision: Barriers and Evidence

Effective clinical and peer supervision consistently demonstrate a wide range of positive outcomes for practitioners, teams, and service delivery. Wheeler and Richards (2007), in a review for the British Association for Counselling and Psychotherapy, noted that while supervision is widely regarded as essential, empirical evidence supporting its direct impact on client outcomes and practitioner development remains limited. Their findings indicated tentative evidence across multiple domains, including supervisee self-efficacy, therapy outcomes, client satisfaction, and the development of counselling and psychotherapeutic skills. Additionally, supervision was preliminarily supported in enhancing self-awareness, transferring learning into clinical practice, and shaping the therapeutic process. Factors such as supervisor trustworthiness, the perceived safety of individual versus group supervision, and session timing were identified as influencing effectiveness. Despite methodological limitations, the review emphasised the need for more rigorous research and the careful integration of evidence into professional practice.

Contemporary research findings consistently highlight the value of clinical supervision as a core mechanism for sustaining and strengthening practitioner competence. Studies across counselling, psychology, and related fields indicate that supervision supports skill development, reflective practice, and adherence to ethical and professional standards (Borders et al., 2014; Falender & Shafranske, 2017; Gaete & Strong, 2017; Simpson-Southward et al., 2017). While causal pathways between supervision and client outcomes require further investigation, supervision remains foundational for professional development, quality assurance, and safe, effective practice in mental health services. Rothwell et al. (2019), in a systematic review of clinical and peer supervision outcomes, identified improved job satisfaction and staff retention as frequent benefits. High-quality, supportive supervision fosters a sense of value and support among employees, which enhances stability and encourages ongoing professional growth. Additionally, supervision promotes confidence, leadership, and professional skills, enabling practitioners to perform more effectively and take on decision-making and leadership responsibilities with assurance.

Recent research findings further confirm the positive impact of supervision on practitioner development. Schreyer et al. (2025), in a systematic review and meta-analysis, reported that supervision enhances supervisees' skills, self-efficacy, and reflective capacity, with some evidence of improved client outcomes, though effects were generally stronger for counsellor development than direct patient change. Zhu and Luke (2022) highlighted the importance of clear outcome measures, recommending systematic evaluation of supervisee growth, client progress, and the supervisory alliance. A mixed-methods study by Gönültaş et al. (2024) of first-time supervisees showed that supervision supports personal growth, professional identity, and counselling skills, increasing confidence and ethical awareness, particularly in early-career practitioners.

Clinical supervision also provides structured opportunities for reflection, critical thinking, and leadership development. Research findings across healthcare professions show that supervisory settings not only promote self-care, innovation, and overall well-being but also foster creativity, personal growth, professional confidence, reflective practice, resilience, ethical awareness, and professional identity formation, directly supporting counsellors' development and effective service delivery (Society for the Advancement of Psychotherapy, 2016); Rothwell et al., 2019; Rawatlal, 2023). Clinical supervision in healthcare has been shown to foster self-confidence, innovation, and professional development by promoting reflective practice, creativity, and professional identity formation, with practitioners reporting increased confidence and readiness for leadership roles (Yan, 2022). Group supervision creates a secure and supportive setting where practitioners can process emotions, exchange resources, and solve problems collaboratively, helping to lower stress and anxiety while peer support and empathetic guidance mitigate workplace pressures (Martin et al., 2022). In addition, supportive supervision promotes compliance with workplace policies, increases cultural competence, bolsters teamwork, and nurtures positive collegial relationships. It also facilitates professional reflection, effective communication, and collaborative problem-solving, ultimately enhancing the quality of service delivery (Martin et al., 2022). Supportive supervision promotes compliance with workplace policies, improves cultural awareness, strengthens teamwork, and cultivates positive collegial relationships. It also encourages professional reflection, effective communication, and collaborative problem-solving, which together enhance service delivery (Martin et al., 2021).

The effectiveness of clinical supervision is influenced by key enablers and barriers. Rothwell et al. (2021) identified enablers, including regular supervision in protected, private spaces, flexible delivery to meet supervisee needs, the ability to choose supervisors, and relationships grounded in trust, rapport, and cultural understanding. A clear and shared understanding of supervision's purpose, tailored to developmental needs and focused on enhancing knowledge and skills, further strengthens effectiveness. Supervisor training, feedback, and the use of multiple supervisors to address overlapping or conflicting demands also contribute positively. Conversely, barriers include limited time and space, lack of trust, unclear supervision goals, and inadequate organisational support, all of which can undermine supervision's impact.

Research findings also emphasise the negative consequences of inadequate supervision. Rodwell et al. (2014, 2017), in cross-sectional surveys of nurses in five Australian hospitals, found that abusive supervision, including personal attacks and social isolation, was associated with lower job satisfaction, higher psychological strain, and increased turnover intentions. Their findings emphasised the need for organisational support, zero-tolerance policies for antisocial behaviour, and robust reporting mechanisms. Similarly, Gibson et al. (2009) found that high work demands coupled with low supervisory support led to lower personal accomplishment scores, signalling increased burnout risk. Collectively, these studies demonstrate that insufficient supervision erodes staff well-being, increases turnover, and compromises overall care quality.

In summary, the evidence indicates that effective clinical supervision substantially enhances practitioner well-being, confidence, and competence while reducing stress and anxiety. It promotes job satisfaction, staff retention, leadership capacity, and critical thinking, while fostering culturally responsive, supportive work environments that improve teamwork and organisational functioning. Effective supervision is consistently linked to improved care quality, communication, and reflective practice, and in some cases, better patient outcomes. Regular supervision also provides culturally informed guidance, ensuring therapeutic work remains competent, sensitive, and aligned with Islāmic values. Research findings further indicate that experiences such as completing coursework, attending workshops, and receiving multicultural supervision are associated with counsellors' perceived competence in working with diverse populations (Olfert, 2006; Pope-Davis et al., 1995; Sodowsky et al., 1998). Table 12.2 presents the benefits and barriers to effective clinical and peer supervision.

Table 12.2 Benefits and barriers to effective clinical and peer supervision

Domain	Benefits of clinical and peer supervision	Barriers to effective supervision
Practitioner development	Enhanced clinical skills and competence; increased self-efficacy and confidence; development of professional identity; improved reflective capacity and critical thinking	Unclear supervision goals; inadequately trained supervisors; mismatch between supervisory approach and supervisee developmental needs
Wellbeing and retention	Reduced stress, anxiety, and burnout; increased job satisfaction and morale; improved staff retention and workforce stability	High workload and time constraints; infrequent or inconsistent supervision; lack of protected supervision time
Quality of practice and care	Improved ethical awareness and accountability; stronger adherence to professional standards; enhanced quality of service delivery	Limited organisational support; supervision framed as managerial rather than developmental
Reflective and learning processes	Effective transfer of learning into practice; increased self-awareness; support for innovation and creativity	Unsafe or judgmental supervisory environments; fear of evaluation or punitive consequences
Relational and team functioning	Stronger collegial relationships; improved teamwork and collaboration; peer support and shared problem-solving	Lack of trust and psychological safety; abusive or controlling supervisory behaviours
Leadership and professional growth	Development of leadership and decision-making skills; increased readiness for advanced roles; confidence in managing complex cases	Power imbalances; limited choice of supervisors
Cultural and ethical practice	Enhanced cultural competence and humility; support for culturally responsive and values-aligned practice, including Islāmic values	Lack of cultural understanding or sensitivity; absence of multicultural or faith-informed supervision

12.7 Toward an Islāmic Model of Clinical Supervision: Concept and Framework

Traditional supervision models are predominantly grounded in Western psychological theories, drawing on developmental, integrative, social role and competency-based frameworks. While these models provide structured approaches to supervisee growth and skill acquisition, they are largely informed by Western epistemological assumptions, ontological views of the self as primarily individualistic, and axiological priorities that emphasise technical competence and measurable outcomes. Consequently, they give limited attention to Islāmic epistemology, ontology, and axiology, which conceptualise knowledge as divinely informed, the human being as an integrated unity of body, mind, heart, and spirit, and ethical practice as inseparable from moral and spiritual accountability.

In Islāmic psychotherapy, clinical supervision cannot simply replicate Western clinical models. It must integrate spiritual, cultural, and ethical dimensions to ensure that professional development is both clinically sound and religiously authentic. There is limited literature on Islāmic clinical supervision or alternatives to secular Western models. Lekkeh et al. (2023) propose an alternative supervision model, termed WONDERFUL, which originates from Eastern contexts. This model challenges the dominance of WEIRD (Western, Educated, Industrialised, Rich, and Democratic) supervision frameworks by incorporating indigenous knowledge and culturally grounded healing practices. The authors argue that implementing this model in humanitarian settings, particularly in low- and middle-income countries (LMICs), has the potential to enhance clinical competence, reduce mental health challenges, and improve service user satisfaction. The WONDERFUL acronym stands for Western-originated, Needs-based, Decolonial, Exchange of knowledge and skills, Respectful and reflective, Flexible, Useful, Linking, and Collaboration, offering a culturally sensitive and comprehensive framework for supervision.

An Islāmic approach to clinical supervision integrates the spiritual, ethical, and professional dimensions of practice, drawing guidance from Qur'ânic teachings, *hadīth* and Islāmic ethical principles. This approach not only addresses clinical competence but also emphasises moral integrity, accountability, and the holistic development of the supervisee, ensuring that professional practice aligns with both ethical and spiritual values. Islāmic clinical supervision, in the context of this chapter, can be defined as a structured professional relationship in which a supervisor guides a supervisee's development in clinical knowledge, skills, and ethical practice while incorporating Islāmic values, principles, and spiritual awareness.

12.8 Islāmic Clinical Supervision Model

A proposed model for Islāmic clinical supervision can integrate traditional supervision practices with Islāmic ethical and spiritual principles. The model can be visualised in four interconnected layers, organised clearly from innermost (core) to outermost layer. Figure 12.1 shows the four dimensions of the Islāmic Clinical Supervision Model.

12.8.1 Spiritual-Ethical Dimension

At the heart of the Islāmic clinical supervision model lies the Spiritual-Ethical Dimension, which serves as the innermost core and moral foundation upon which

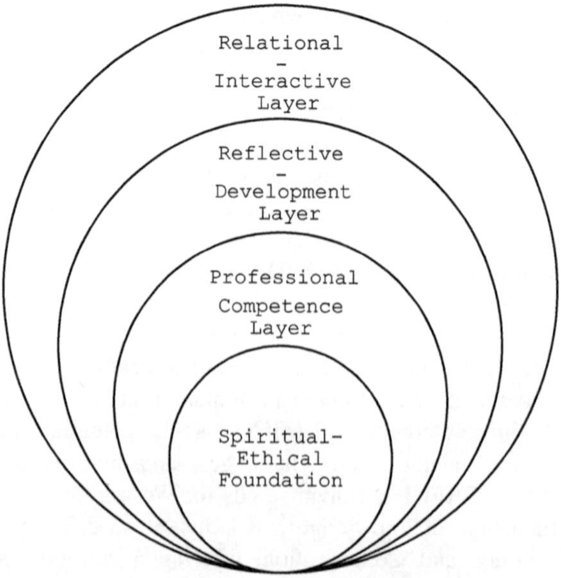

Fig. 12.1 Proposed Islāmic clinical supervision model

all other supervisory processes rest. This dimension is rooted in the *Tawḥīdic paradigm*, the Islāmic worldview that affirms the oneness of Allāh and the interconnectedness of all knowledge, actions, and ethical responsibilities under divine guidance. Within this framework, the supervisee's clinical decisions, professional conduct, and reflective practices are understood as expressions of spiritual accountability. Supervisees are encouraged to internalise essential Islāmic values such as justice, compassion, honesty, sincerity (*ikhlāṣ*), and accountability to Allāh, recognising that their therapeutic work reflects both personal integrity and spiritual responsibility.

Clinical supervisors, in turn, function as moral and spiritual models. They embody the ethical principles of Islām in their behaviour and use supervision as a space for fostering reflective practice regarding duties toward clients, colleagues, institutions, and the broader community. Their role extends beyond technical oversight; it includes guiding supervisees to recognise the spiritual significance of their professional responsibilities and to cultivate an ethical orientation aligned with Islāmic teachings. Through this integration of spiritual consciousness with professional guidance, the Spiritual-Ethical Dimension forms a stable anchor that shapes all aspects of clinical decision-making, professional behaviour, and interpersonal interactions within supervision. It nurtures a moral compass that promotes clinical competence while simultaneously supporting the supervisee's spiritual growth, ultimately contributing to holistic character development.

A profound illustration of this ethical foundation is found in the well-known *ḥadīth* narrated by ʿAbdullāh ibn ʿUmar (may Alah be pleased with him), in which the Prophet Muḥammad (ﷺ) states: "Each of you is a shepherd and each of you is responsible for his flock. The *imām* who is over the people is a shepherd and is responsible for his flock; a man is a shepherd in charge of the inhabitants of his household, and he is responsible for his flock; a woman is a shepherdess in charge of her husband's house and children and she is responsible for them; and a man's slave is a shepherd in charge of his master's property and he is responsible for it. So, each of you is a shepherd and each of you is responsible for his flock" (Bukhārī and Muslim). This *ḥadīth* provides a powerful theological and moral lens through which the responsibilities of clinical supervision can be understood. Just as the Prophet (ﷺ) describes every leader as a shepherd accountable for those under their care, the clinical supervisor is entrusted with the guidance, protection, and moral cultivation of supervisees in the master-apprentice system. This responsibility includes ensuring that supervisees develop the competence, ethical awareness, and professional integrity necessary for safe and effective clinical practice. In this context, leadership is not a position of authority but a role of service, characterised by humility, protection, and care.

The *ḥadīth* also highlights the notion of *amānah*, the sacred trust that every individual carries in their respective roles. Within clinical supervision, both supervisors and supervisees share this *amānah*. Supervisors bear the responsibility of ensuring that supervisees are prepared to carry out their therapeutic duties ethically and competently, while supervisees must uphold the welfare of their clients, honour professional boundaries, and commit to continual growth. This shared trust transforms supervision into a moral partnership, grounded in sincerity and accountability before Allāh. Furthermore, the layered examples within the *ḥadīth* reflect the different dimensions of responsibility within therapeutic work. The leader responsible for his people parallels the supervisor's duty toward supervisees; the individual responsible for their household mirrors the therapist's obligation toward clients; and the caretaker of a home reflects the clinician's responsibility for maintaining ethical boundaries and professionalism. These parallels reinforce the principle that ethical diligence and conscientiousness are required at every level of therapeutic practice.

Importantly, the *ḥadīth* also enriches the reflective aspect of supervision. It invites supervisees to critically examine whether they are fulfilling their responsibilities with integrity, whether their decisions align with Islāmic moral values, and whether they are aware of the influence they hold in the therapeutic relationship. This theological perspective deepens the Reflective-Development Dimension by emphasising that professional responsibility is inseparable from spiritual accountability. Ultimately, the message of the *ḥadīth* aligns directly with the *Tawḥīdic* paradigm: every action in clinical work carries spiritual significance, and every role is an arena for moral excellence. By integrating this prophetic teaching into the Spiritual-Ethical Dimension, Islāmic clinical supervision fosters practitioners who approach their work not merely as a technical or professional duty, but as an expression of worship, service (*khidmah*), and ethical excellence (*ihsān*). In doing so, it ensures that clinical competence is always intertwined with spiritual awareness and that the therapeutic role is carried out with both moral integrity and consciousness of divine accountability.

12.8.2 Professional Competence Dimension

Encircling the Spiritual-Ethical core, the Professional Competence Dimension emphasises the development of clinical skills, professional knowledge, and practical expertise within the framework of Islāmic ethical and spiritual principles. In this dimension, supervisees engage in structured activities such as case conceptualisation, clinical assessments, skills training, goal-setting, reflective exercises, and receiving constructive feedback. These activities enhance technical proficiency while promoting ethical decision-making, ensuring that clinical interventions are effective, culturally sensitive, and aligned with Islāmic moral values. This dimension also involves continuous evaluation of supervisee competencies, identifying strengths and areas for growth, and providing applied learning opportunities in real-world settings. Supervisors guide supervisees to integrate evidence-based practices with spiritual awareness, encouraging reflection on interventions that are both clinically appropriate and consistent with values such as justice, compassion, and accountability to Allāh. By combining technical skill development with ethical and spiritual consciousness, this layer ensures that clinical competence is inseparable from moral integrity and professional responsibility.

Within the Spiritual-Ethical Dimension, Islāmic clinical supervision places a strong emphasis on ethics that are not only aligned with professional codes, such as those of the APA or BACP, but also fully compliant with *Sharīʿah* principles. Supervisors play a crucial role in ensuring that therapeutic interventions and clinical practices do not conflict with Islāmic moral frameworks, such as upholding modesty, respecting family values, and honouring religious obligations. Ethical dilemmas are approached through a dual lens, integrating conventional clinical reasoning with *fiqh*-based perspectives, thereby creating a system of accountability that addresses both professional standards and spiritual responsibilities. This integration reinforces the *tawhīdic* principle of ultimate accountability to Allāh, guiding supervisees to make decisions that are morally, spiritually, and professionally sound.

12.8.3 Reflective-Development Dimension

The Reflective-Development Dimension acts as a bridge connecting professional competence with relational and ethical growth. This layer emphasises ongoing self-reflection, critical thinking, cycles of contemplation, and thoughtful analysis of professional experiences, ethical dilemmas, and clinical challenges, all situated within the Tawhīdic paradigm. Supervisees are guided to assess their actions, decisions, and interpersonal interactions not only through technical and clinical reasoning but also through Islāmic values such as justice, compassion, empathy, honesty, and accountability to Allāh. Through journaling, structured reflective exercises, skills development, guided discussions, and supervisor feedback, supervisees develop deeper self-awareness, recognise personal biases, and identify areas requiring both spiritual and professional enhancement. This dimension strengthens moral and ethical discernment, supporting supervisees as they navigate complex clinical situations while remaining aligned with Islāmic principles. By integrating spiritual contemplation with professional learning, this layer nurtures practitioners who are ethically responsible, spiritually grounded, and clinically skilled, promoting holistic growth across personal and professional domains.

An essential element of the Reflective-Development Dimension is the supervisee's capacity to recognise and meaningfully integrate the cultural diversity that exists across heterogeneous Muslim communities. Islāmic clinical supervision acknowledges that Muslims represent a wide range of cultural background, including Arab, South Asian, Southeast Asian, African, and Western Muslim contexts, each with its own traditions, ethnicity, languages, family structures, and community norms that shape clients' worldviews. Supervisees are encouraged to critically reflect on their own cultural assumptions and potential biases, as well as how their backgrounds influence their clinical judgements. Supervisors guide this reflective process by promoting cultural humility anchored in Islāmic values of justice, compassion, and respect for diversity. This ensures that therapists approach clients with sensitivity to local customs, community expectations, and religious-cultural dynamics. Case formulation within this dimension therefore incorporates sociocultural elements such as mental health stigma, communal identity, extended family involvement, and intergenerational relationships. By weaving these factors into reflective practice, supervisees develop a more comprehensive understanding of clients' lived realities. This culturally informed approach enhances the supervisee's ability to make decisions that honour both Islāmic principles and the cultural contexts in which clients live. Through this reflective engagement, the dimension cultivates practitioners who are not only competent and spiritually anchored but also culturally attuned, enabling them to provide care that is respectful, context-sensitive, and effective across diverse Muslim populations.

Another central feature of this dimension is the understanding that professional development in an Islāmic framework extends beyond technical skill acquisition to include the therapist's spiritual maturation and character formation. Supervision therefore encourages supervisees to embody God-consciousness (*taqwā*), humility *(tawāḍu')*, sincerity (*ikhlāṣ*), and a profound sense of moral responsibility, recognising that therapeutic work is both a clinical obligation and a spiritual trust (*amānah*). Through guided discussions, reflective exercises, cycles of reflection (Qur'ân and *Sunnah*) and supervisory feedback, supervisees are encouraged to examine not only how they practise but also who they are becoming in the process. They reflect on their intentions, emotional responses, and internal states, heightening awareness of how their spiritual orientation influences their therapeutic presence, ethical decision-making, and interactions with clients. This integrative perspective frames professional growth as a holistic journey in which clinical competence and spiritual development unfold in tandem. Supervisees come to view their work as an act of service (*khidmah*) and a responsibility before Allāh, ensuring that their interventions align with both evidence-based practice and Islāmic moral values. By fostering technical proficiency alongside spiritual virtues, this dimension shapes practitioners who embody integrity, compassion, and ethical excellence in their clinical roles.

12.8.4 Relational-Interactive Dimension

The outermost layer, the Relational-Interactive Dimension, encompasses the dynamic and collaborative relationship between supervisor and supervisee. This dimension emphasises mentorship, mutual respect, guidance, and ongoing support, providing the primary context in which professional skills, ethical principles, and spiritual development are integrated and applied. Interactions in this dimension are guided by key Islāmic values such as *adab* (proper conduct), *ihsān* (excellence in behaviour), *shura* (consultation), and *amānah* (trustworthiness), creating an environment that fosters collaboration, ethical accountability, and personal growth. In practice, this involves active dialogue, case discussions, collaborative problem-solving, feedback exchanges, and joint reflection on clinical experiences.

Supervisors serve not only as facilitators, teachers, and evaluators but also as mentors, role models, and spiritual guides, assisting supervisees in navigating ethical dilemmas and professional challenges while reinforcing Islāmic moral principles. By cultivating a safe, supportive, and respectful relationship, this layer enables supervisees to internalise professional competence, ethical conduct, and spiritual awareness simultaneously. It also promotes reciprocal learning, as supervisees contribute insights, perspectives, and cultural knowledge, creating a dynamic, interactive, and ethically grounded supervisory process. Table 12.2 provides a summary of the Islāmic Clinical Supervision Model.

12.9 Conclusion

For clinical supervision to maintain its role as an essential component of lifelong professional learning, it is crucial to establish standardised training pathways and clear clinical practice standards. At present, limited research directly examines how supervisee performance within supervision translates into measurable patient outcomes. This highlights the need for a shared, well-defined understanding of the goals, functions, and expectations of Islāmic clinical supervision in psychotherapy and counselling, While supervision has a more established presence in mental health and psychotherapy, it remains insufficiently developed within the Islāmic psychotherapy field. Ultimately, advancing clinical supervision in Islāmic psychotherapy depends on clinicians, educators, and managers working together to cultivate an organisational culture that values and sustains reflective learning and professional support (Rassool, 2021, 2025). It is anticipated that positioning clinical supervision as a structured developmental activity within the Islāmic psychotherapy and counselling sectors will encourage further research. Such research should not only evaluate the effectiveness of educational and supervisory programmes but also investigate whether enhanced professional competence resulting from supervision leads to demonstrable improvements in client care and treatment outcomes.

References

Ali, S. F. (2021, May 19). *Mastering mentoring series part two: Traditional versus emerging models*.https://muslimmentalhealth.com/mastering-mentoring-series-part-two-traditional-versus-emerging-models/

Basa, V. (2018). 'Self-supervision' in the therapeutic profession. *European Journal of Counselling Theory, Research and Practice, 2*, Article 6. https://www.nationalwellbeingservice.com/journals

Benshoff, J. M. (1993). Peer supervision in counsellor training. *Clinical Supervisor, 11*(2), 89–102.

Bernard, J. M. (1979). Supervisor training: A discrimination model. *Journal of Counseling & Development, 19*(1), 60–68. https://doi.org/10.1002/j.1556-6978.1979.tb00906.x

Bernard, J. M., & Goodyear, R. K. (1992). *Fundamentals of clinical supervision*. Allyn & Bacon.

Bernard, J. M. & Goodyear, R. K. (2004). *Fundamentals of Clinical Supervision*. Pearson Education.

Bernard, J. M., & Goodyear, R. K. (2019). *Fundamentals of clinical supervision*. Pearson

Borders, L. D., Glosoff, H. L., Welfare, L. E., Hays, D. G., DeKruyf, L., Fernando, D. M., & Page, B. (2014). Best practices in clinical supervision: Evolution of a counseling specialty. *The Clinical Supervisor, 33*(1), 26–44. https://doi.org/10.1080/07325223.2014.905225

Bukhārī and Muslim. *Mishkat al-Masabih 3685*. In-book reference: Book 18, Hadith 25. https://sunnah.com/mishkat:3685

Center for Substance Abuse Treatment. (2009). *Clinical supervision and professional development of the substance abuse counselor* (Treatment Improvement Protocol [TIP] Series 52, HHS Publication No. SMA 14–4435). Substance Abuse and Mental Health Services Administration.

Cortis, N., Seymour, K., Natalier, K., & Wendt, S. (2021). Which models of supervision help retain staff? Findings from Australia's domestic and family violence and sexual assault workforces. *Australian Social Work, 74*(1), 68–82. https://doi.org/10.1080/0312407X.2020.1798480

Devine, A., & Baxter, D. (1995). Introducing clinical supervision: A guide. *Nursing Standard, 9*(40), 32–34.

Driscoll, J. (2007). *Reflection: Principles and practice for healthcare professionals* (2nd ed.). Bailliere Tindall.

Edgar, D., Moroney, T., & Wilson, V. (2023). Clinical supervision: A mechanism to support person-centred practice? An integrative review of the literature. *Journal of Clinical Nursing, 32*(9–10), 1935–1951. https://doi.org/10.1111/jocn.16589

Falender, C. A., & Shafranske, E. P. (2017). Competency-based clinical supervision: Status, opportunities, tensions, and the future. *Australian Psychologist, 52*(2), 86–93. https://doi.org/10.1111/ap.12265

Frawley-O'Dea, M. G., & Sarnat, J. E. (2001). *The supervisory relationship: A contemporary psychodynamic approach*. Guilford Press.

Gaete, J., & Strong, T. (2017). Facilitating supervisees' developing competence through supervisory conversation. *Counselling Psychology Quarterly, 30*(2), 166–187. https://doi.org/10.1080/09515070.2016.1167013

Geller, C. (1994). Group supervision as a vehicle for teaching group work to students: Field instruction in a senior center. *Clinical Supervisor, 12*(1), 199–214.

Gibson, J. A., Grey, I. M., & Hastings, R. P. (2009). Supervisor support as a predictor of burnout and therapeutic self-efficacy in therapists working in ABA schools. *Journal of Autism and Developmental Disorders, 39*(7), 1024–1030.

Gönültaş, M., Meydan, B., & Sağkal, A. S. (2024). The examination of the counseling supervision effect on personal and professional development of first-time supervisees. *International Journal of Psychology and Educational Studies, 11*(4), 342–356.

Holloway, E. (1995). *Clinical supervision: A systems approach.* Sage Publications.

Hardy, G. E. (2017). How do we know what makes for "best practice" in clinical supervision for psychological therapists? A content analysis of supervisory models and approaches. *Clinical Psychology & Psychotherapy, 24*(6), 1228–1245. https://doi.org/10.1002/cpp.2084

Harper, K. (2025, June 19). *Exploring the different types of clinical supervision: Individual, dyadic, and group.* Insight Online. https://www.insight-online.ca/exploring-the-different-types-of-clinical-supervision/

Hawkins, P. & Shohet, R. (2000). *Supervision in the Helping Professions* (2nd ed.) . Buckingham Open UniversityPress

Hawkins, P., & Shohet, R. (2012). *Supervision in the helping professions* (4th edn). Open University Press.

Lekkeh, S. A., Faruk, M. O., Jahan, S., Beetar, A., Kurt, G., Wells, R., & Wong, S. (2023). Clinical supervision across Australia, Türkiye, Syria, and Bangladesh: From Weird to Wonderful. *Social Sciences, 12*(3), 170. https://doi.org/10.3390/socsci12030170

Liese, B. S., & Beck, J. S. (1997). Cognitive therapy supervision. In C. E. Watkins (Ed.), *Handbook of psychotherapy supervision.* Wiley.

Lowe, R. (2000). Supervising self-supervision: Constructive inquiry and embedded narratives in case consultation. *Journal of Marital and Family Therapy, 26*(4), 511–521. https://doi.org/10.1111/j.1752-0606.2000.tb00234.x

MacKenzie, K. R. (1990). *Introduction to time-limited group therapy.* American Psychiatric Press.

Martin, P., Lizarondo, L., Kumar, S., & Snowdon, D. (2021). Impact of clinical supervision on healthcare organisational outcomes: A mixed methods systematic review. *PLoS ONE, 16*(11), Article e0260156. https://doi.org/10.1371/journal.pone.0260156

Martin, P., Kumar, S., Tian, E., Argus, G., Kondalsamy-Chennakesavan, S., Lizarondo, L., Gurney, T., & Snowdon, D. (2022). Rebooting effective clinical supervision practices to support healthcare workers through and following the COVID-19 pandemic. *International Journal for Quality in Health Care, 34*(2), mzac030. https://doi.org/10.1093/intqhc/mzac030

Mead, D. E. (1990). *Effective supervision: A task-oriented model for the mental health professions.* Routledge.

Milne, D. (2007). An empirical definition of clinical supervision. *British Journal of Clinical Psychology, 46*(4), 437–447. https://doi.org/10.1348/014466507X197415

Morrissette, P. J. (2001). *Self-supervision: A primer for counsellors and helping professionals.* Brunner-Routledge.

Morrissette, P. J. (2001, 2013). *Self-supervision: A primer for counselors and human service professionals* (1st ed.). Routledge. (eBook published May 13, 2013).

Olfert, P. K. (2006) .*A critique of multicultural psychotherapy and counselling competencies and implications for counsellor education.* MA project, Campus Alberta Applied Psychology Psychotherapy and counselling Initiative, Calgary University. http://dtpr.lib.athabascau.ca/action/download.php?filename=caap/pamelaknelsenolfertProject.pdf, (accessed 20 December 2023).

Pope-Davis, D. B., Reynolds, A. L., Dings, J. G., & Nielson, D. (1995). Examining multicultural counseling competencies of graduate students in psychology. *Professional Psychology: Research and Practice, 26*(3), 322–329. https://doi.org/10.1037/0735-7028.26.3.322

Proctor, B. (1987). Supervision: A co-operative exercise in accountability. In M. Marken & M. Paynes (Eds.), *Enabling and ensuring: Supervision in practice.* National Youth Bureau and the council for Education and Training in Youth and Community work.

Rassool, G. Hussein. (2021). *Islāmic psychology: Human behaviour and experience from an Islāmi perspective.*Routledge.

Rassool, G. Hussein. (2025). *Islāmic counselling and psychotherapy: An introduction to theory and practice* (2nd ed.). Routledge.

Rawatlal, K. V. (2023). Towards well-being: Self-care in the supervisory space. In *Clinical supervision in South Africa* (pp. 101–114). Springer. https://doi.org/10.1007/978-3-031-41929-4_9

Reynolds, V. (2013). Centering ethics in group supervision: Fostering cultures of critique and safety. *The International Journal of Narrative Therapy and Community Work, 4*, 1–13.

Rodwell, J., Brunetto, Y., Demir, D., Shacklock, K., & Farr-Wharton, R. (2014). Abusive supervision and links to nurse intentions to quit. *Journal of Nursing Scholarship, 46*(5), 357–365.

Rodwell, J., McWilliams, J., & Gulyas, A. (2017). The impact of characteristics of nurses' relationships with their supervisor, engagement and trust, on performance behaviours and intent to quit. *Journal of Advanced Nursing, 73*(1), 190–200.

Rothwell, C., Kehoe, A., Farook, S., & Illin, J. (2019). *The characteristics of effective clinical and peer supervision in the workplace: A rapid evidence review* (Final report). https://www.hcpc-uk.org/globalassets/resources/reports/research/effective-clinical-and-peer-supervision-report.pdf

Rothwell, C., Kehoe, A., Farook, S. F., & Illin, J. (2021). Enablers and barriers to effective clinical supervision in the workplace: A rapid evidence review. *British Medical Journal Open, 11*, Article e052929. https://doi.org/10.1136/bmjopen-2021-052929

Scaife, J. (2019). *Supervision in clinical practice: A practitioner's guide* (3rd ed.). Routledge.

Scaife, J. A., & Scaife, J. M. (1996). A general supervision framework: Applications in teacher education. In J. Trafford (Ed.), *Learning to teach: Aspects of initial teacher education*. USDE Papers in Education.

Schreyer, B., Leithner, C., Eilers, R., Gossmann, K., & Rosner, R. (2025). The effects of clinical supervision on supervisees and patient outcomes in psychotherapy: A systematic review and meta-analysis. *Frontiers in Psychiatry, 16*. https://doi.org/10.3389/fpsyt.2025.1705578

Simpson-Southward, C., Waller, G., & Hardy, G. E. (2017). How do we know what makes for best practice in clinical supervision for psychological therapists? A content analysis of supervisory models and approaches. *Clinical psychology & psychotherapy, 24*(6), 1228–1245. https://doi.org/10.1002/cpp.2084

Skovholt, T. M., & Ronnestad, M. H. (1992). *The evolving professional self: Stages and theories in therapist and counselor development*. Wiley.

Society for the Advancement of Psychotherapy. (2016). *Guidelines for clinical supervision in health service psychology*. https://societyforpsychotherapy.org/guidelines-clinical-supervision-health-service-psychology/

Sodowsky, G. R., Kuo-Jackson, P. Y., Richardson, M. F., & Corey, A. T. (1998). Correlates of self-reported multicultural competencies: Therapist multicultural social desirability, race, social inadequacy, locus of control, racial ideology, and multicultural training. *Journal of Counseling Psychology, 45*(3), 256–264. https://doi.org/10.1037/0022-0167.45.3.256

Stoltenberg, C. D. & Delworth, U. (1987). *Supervising counselors and therapists: A developmental approach*. JosseyBass.

Stoltenberg, C. D., McNeill, B., & Delworth, U. (1998). *IDM supervision: An integrated developmental model for supervising counselors and therapists* (1st ed.). JosseyBass Publishers.

Stoltenberg, C. D., & McNeill, B. W. (2011). *IDM supervision: An integrative developmental model for supervisingcounselors and therapists* (3rd ed.). Routledge

Todd, T. C. (1997). Self-supervision as a universal supervisory goal. In T. C. Todd & C. L. Storm (Eds.), *The complete systematic supervisor: Contexts, philosophy, and pragmatics* (pp. 17–25). Allyn & Bacon.

Todd, T. C., & Storm, C. L. (2014). *The complete systemic supervisor: Context, philosophy and pragmatics* (2nd ed.). John Wiley & Sons, Ltd.

Valentino, A. L., LeBlanc, L. A., & Sellers, T. P. (2016). The benefits of group supervision and a recommended structure for implementation. *Behavior Analysis in Practice, 9*(4), 320–328. https://doi.org/10.1007/s40617-016-0138-8

Wheeler, S., & Richards, K. (2007). The impact of clinical supervision on counsellors and therapists, their practiceand their clients: A systematic review of the literature. *Counselling and Psychotherapy Research, 7*(1), 54–65.https://doi.org/10.1080/14733140601185274

Yan, C. C. (2022). Clinical supervision in the health professions: A literature review. *Journal of Learning Design and Leadership, 1*(1), 77–104.

Zhu, P., & Luke, M. M. (2022). A supervisory framework for systematically attending to outcomes in clinical supervision. *International Journal for the Advancement of Counselling, 44*(1), 94–111. https://doi.org/10.1007/s10447-021-09455-9

Chapter 13
The Formulation and Application of an Ethical Framework for Muslim Psychologists: The IAMP Code of Ethics

Hanan Dover

13.1 Introduction

Over several decades, psychological practice informed by Islāmic values has largely operated under general professional codes of ethics developed within secular epistemological frameworks (Khan, 2019; Rassool, 2025a). While these codes provide robust guidance for mainstream psychological practice, they often fail to address the ethical complexities that arise when psychotherapy is explicitly integrated with religious epistemology, communal norms, and spiritual meaning systems. Scholars of Islāmic psychology have long identified limitations in the secular framing of mental health, particularly its tendency to marginalise spiritual dimensions of human functioning (Rassool, 2024a). Early conceptualisations of Islāmic psychology and psychotherapy proposed integrative approaches grounded in the Qur'ân and *Sunnah* as a means of addressing behavioural and psychological distress holistically (as discussed in Khan, 2019). However, in the absence of a standardised ethical framework, practice remained largely dependent on the individual practitioner's integrity, theological literacy, and ethical discernment (Saifuddin, 2020).

This absence of a profession-specific ethical code has rendered Islāmic psychology and psychotherapy vulnerable to ethical ambiguity, epistemological inconsistency, and professional misrepresentation (Rassool, 2024c). The development of the International Association of Muslim Psychologists' (IAMP) Code of Ethics was therefore undertaken to establish clear ethical standards, define professional scope, and protect both clients and the emerging discipline itself (Dover, 2025). This chapter examines the formulation, theoretical grounding, and application of the International Association of Muslim Psychologists (IAMP) Code of Ethics.

Hanan Dover (Centre for Islamic Studies and Civilisation, Charles Sturt University, Somerton, Victoria, Australia) is the sole author of this chapter. Editorial review and substantive editing were conducted by Professor Dr. G.Hussein Rassool.

G. H. Rassool, *Ethical Dilemmas in Islāmic Psychotherapy*,
https://doi.org/10.1007/978-3-032-26515-9_13

13.2 Ethical Foundations: *Maqāṣid Al-Sharīʿah* and Bioethical Integration

The IAMP Code of Ethics is grounded in the *Maqāṣid al-Sharīʿah*, which articulate five overarching objectives of Islāmic law: the preservation of faith (*dīn*), life (*nafs*), intellect (*ʿaql*), lineage (*nasl*), and property (*māl*) (Rassool, 2025b; Rattani & Hyder, 2019). These objectives provide an ethical framework that guides decision-making in contexts where psychological, spiritual, and social considerations intersect. In parallel, the Code incorporates the four foundational principles of contemporary bioethics: autonomy, beneficence, non-maleficence, and justice (Hasan et al., 2025). Rather than adopting these principles in a value-neutral manner, the IAMP Code situates them within Islāmic moral theology.

Beneficence is understood through the concepts of *raḥmah* (compassion) and *iḥsān* (excellence), framing therapeutic care as a morally accountable act (Rassool, 2025c). Non-maleficence is grounded in the Islāmic legal maxim *lā ḍarar wa lā ḍirār*, obligating practitioners to prevent harm and exploitation (Rassool, 2025b). Justice (*ʿadl*) requires equitable access to care and active resistance to discrimination (Hasan et al., 2025). Autonomy is conceptualised relationally, recognising that decision-making within many Muslim contexts occurs through consultation (*shūrā*) and communal responsibility rather than radical individualism (Rassool, 2024a).

13.3 Authority, Scope, and Professional Standards

A defining contribution of the IAMP framework is its explicit articulation of professional authority and scope of practice. The IAMP Position Statement on Authority clarifies that ethical authority in Islāmic psychology requires dual competence in both psychological science and Islāmic knowledge (International Association of Muslim Psychologists [IAMP], 2026).

Formal psychological qualifications, including accredited undergraduate and postgraduate training, are identified as non-negotiable prerequisites for diagnosing mental health conditions or delivering psychological interventions (IAMP, 2026). The IAMP adopts this position on the importance of formal psychological qualifications: "To gain accreditation in IP [sic Islāmic Psychology], individuals must have a solid psychological foundation, as the field integrates established psychological science with Islāmic knowledge rather than serving merely as a spiritual or cultural add-on" (Haque, 2025). Competence within the field of Islāmic psychology is a vital area for continued development and may be understood as a dynamic, multifaceted, and interconnected construct encompassing knowledge, skills, attitudes, beliefs, and values grounded in an Islāmic paradigm (Rassool, 2023).

Rassool (2023) proposed a model that outlines four key domains in which psychotherapists must maintain competence throughout their professional development: Islāmic Ethics, Fundamental Competencies, Functional Competencies, and Developmental Competencies. A prerequisite for practice is formal academic training in psychology or a related discipline, such as clinical psychology, counselling psychology, or psychotherapy, accredited by a recognised academic institution. Beyond foundational psychological knowledge, Islāmic psychotherapists are also expected to possess a sound background in Islāmic studies (Khan, 2019; Rassool, 2023) and to have completed formal training in Islāmic psychotherapy or counselling through an accredited university programme. However, religious scholarship alone does not confer authority to practise psychology (Khan, 2019).

This distinction is critical in addressing increasing instances of misrepresentation within the field, where individuals without clinical training present spiritual guidance as psychological treatment, thereby placing clients at risk and undermining public trust (Rassool, 2024c).

13.4 Propriety, Supervision, and Ethical Research

The principle of propriety obliges psychologists to practice within the limits of their competence, engage in ongoing professional development, and seek supervision appropriate to integrated Islāmic practice (Rassool, 2025a). The IAMP Code emphasises that ethical competence includes the practitioner's capacity for self-regulation, reflective practice, and moral accountability (Dover, 2025). In relation to research, the Code aligns with Islāmic research ethics frameworks that prioritise intention (*niyyah*), benefit, and harm minimisation (Rattani & Hyder, 2019). Research lacking social value or ecological validity or exposing participants to disproportionate risk is considered ethically impermissible (Rassool, 2025b).

13.5 Confidentiality in Communal Contexts

Confidentiality poses particular ethical challenges in Muslim and collectivist communities, where overlapping social networks may increase the risk of inadvertent disclosure (Saifuddin, 2020). The IAMP Code reinforces heightened confidentiality obligations, informed by Qur'ânic principles emphasising the concealment of private matters and protection of dignity (Al-Hujurāt 49:12). Disclosure is permitted only when legally mandated or required to prevent serious harm, aligning Islāmic legal necessity (*ḍarūra*) with established psychological duty-to-warn principles (Rassool, 2025c).

13.6 Expanded Ethical Guidance for Practice

The IAMP Code provides expanded guidance for recurrent clinical dilemmas. These include culturally appropriate informed consent processes that protect a client's right to decline religious integration (Al-Baqarah 2:256; Dover, 2025), collaborative care with *imāms* or scholars under clear consent and role boundaries (IAMP, 2026), and gender-sensitive practice grounded in modesty and professional boundaries (Rassool, 2024a).

The Code also addresses religious struggles such as *waswasa*, requiring clinicians to distinguish intrusive thoughts associated with conditions such as obsessive–compulsive disorder from normative faith-based questioning (Khan, 2019; Rassool, 2024c). Additionally, ethical practice includes recognising and addressing the psychological impacts of Islamophobia, racism, and collective trauma, consistent with principles of justice and harm prevention (Salari & Larijani, 2021).

13.7 Integrity and Non-Exploitation

Integrity within the IAMP framework encompasses honesty, transparency, and the absolute prohibition of exploitation. Sexual, romantic, financial, or ideological exploitation of clients or supervisees is categorically prohibited, recognising the inherent power imbalance in therapeutic relationships (Dover, 2025; Rassool, 2025c).

13.8 Implementation Challenges

Despite its comprehensive scope, the IAMP Code faces implementation challenges, including a limited workforce trained in both Islāmic ethics and clinical psychology, and the scarcity of supervision models tailored to integrated practice (Rassool, 2024b). Further, empirical validation of Islāmic psychotherapeutic interventions remains constrained by limited research infrastructure (Salari & Larijani, 2021). The Code therefore emphasises international collaboration, supervision development, and research capacity-building as priorities for the field's continued growth (Dover, 2025).

13.9 Conclusion

The IAMP Code of Ethics represents a significant milestone in the professionalisation of Islāmic psychology. By grounding ethical standards in the *Maqāṣid al-Sharīʿah* while maintaining alignment with contemporary psychological science, the Code provides a coherent and rigorous ethical framework for practice (Dover, 2025). As the discipline evolves, practitioners are called to sustained self-reflection, humility, and the pursuit of *iḥsān*. The IAMP Code ensures that Islāmic psychology develops on an ethical and empirical foundation that respects human dignity, safeguards public trust, and serves the well-being of the *ummah*.

References

Dover, H. (2025). *IAMP code of ethics and expanded ethical guidelines* International Association of Muslim Psychologists.

Hasan, M., Khan, A., Hathi, M. B. A., & Salahudeen, S. M. (2025). The four principles in Islāmic and Western medical ethics: A scoping review. *The New Bioethics, 31*(2–4), 120–135. https://doi.org/10.1080/20502877.2025.2590274

Haque, A. (2025). *A guide to Islāmic psychology programs. A guide to Islāmic psychology programs.*

International Association of Muslim Psychologists. (2026). *Position statement on authority, scope, and professional standards in Islāmic psychology.*

Khan, N. A. (2019). *Discerning mental health in the medieval and modern Islāmic traditions: Traversing psychology, law, and ethics* [Master's thesis, Hartford Seminary]. ProQuest Dissertations Publishing.

Rassool, G. Hussein. (2023). *Islāmic psychology: The basics*. Routledge.

Rassool, G. Hussein. (2024a). Islāmic psychotherapy: Tackling challenges, employing strategies, cultivating competence. In *Islāmic psychotherapy* (pp. 359–367). Routledge. https://doi.org/10.4324/9781003453413-25

Rassool, G. Hussein. (2024b). Readiness for knowledge integration of Islāmic ethics and Islāmic psychology: An integrated research study. In G. H. Rassool (Ed.), *Advancing Islāmic psychology education* (pp. 61–83). Routledge. https://doi.org/10.4324/9781003329596-5

Rassool, G. Hussein. (2024c). Unveiling the role of the Islāmic psychotherapist: Exploring the nature and scope of psychotherapy. In *Islāmic psychotherapy* (pp. 35–50). Routledge. https://doi.org/10.4324/9781003453413-4

Rassool, G. Hussein. (2025a). Islāmic ethics related to counselling. In *Islāmic counselling and Psychotherapy: An introduction to theory and practice* (2nd ed., pp. 83–93). Routledge.

Rassool, G. H. (2025b). Principles of Islāmic ethics: Issues in conducting a research. In *Integrated Research in Islāmic psychotherapy* (pp. 35–46). Routledge. https://doi.org/10.4324/9781003346241-3

Rassool, G. Hussein. (2025c). The moral compass of Islāmic psychotherapists: Ethical considerations and responsibilities. In *Spiritual integration in Islāmic psychotherapy* (pp. 18–32). Routledge. https://doi.org/10.4324/9781003468219-2

Rattani, A., & Hyder, A. A. (2019). Developing an Islāmic research ethics framework. *Journal of Religion and Health, 58*(1), 74–86. https://doi.org/10.1007/s10943-017-0508-8

Saifuddin, A. (2020). Ethical code of Islāmic psychotherapy in Indonesia. *Buletin Psikologi, 28*(1), 85–98. https://doi.org/10.22146/buletinpsikologi.47661.

Salari, P., & Larijani, B. (2021). Publication trend in Islāmic medical ethics in Iran and the world: Designing a road. *Journal of Religion and Health, 60*(2), 941–960. https://doi.org/10.1007/s10943-020-01154-w

Chapter 14
Reflections and Future Directions

14.1 Introduction and Summary of Key Insights

The integration of Islāmic values into psychotherapy involves aligning clinical practice with ethical and moral principles derived from the Qur'ān, Sunnah, and *Maqāṣid al-Sharī 'ah* (objectives of Islāmic law). This approach encourages therapists to view clients holistically, considering their spiritual, emotional, and social dimensions. Concepts including *amānah* (trust), *raḥmah* (compassion), *'adl* (justice), *wasatiyyah* (moderation), and *maṣlaḥah* (well-being) provide a framework for ethical decision-making and culturally sensitive care. Such integrative approaches strengthen therapeutic engagement, trust, and outcomes, particularly for Muslim clients seeking care consistent with their religious beliefs.

Ethical conduct is therefore positioned as a cornerstone of Islāmic psychotherapy, framing it as a coherent and ethical paradigm rather than a loosely connected set of practices. The framework developed here underlines the interrelationship between spiritual, moral, and psychological dimensions of human experience, recognising ethics as central to both therapeutic intent (*niyyah*) and clinical practice. Within this paradigm, ethical decision-making is understood as a dynamic process informed by classical Islāmic source, Qur'ānic principles, prophetic guidance, and scholarly tradition, while also engaging rigorously with contemporary professional and regulatory standards. This integrated approach equips clinicians with a strong foundation for navigating complex ethical terrain in practice.

This chapter brings together the central themes and findings discussed throughout the book. It has explored the ethical dilemmas that arise in the practice of Islāmic psychotherapy, particularly the challenge of balancing faith, culture, and professional ethical standards. These issues have been examined in detail, showing that while the integration of Islāmic principles into psychotherapy offers clients meaningful opportunities for growth and deeper alignment with their faith, it also presents significant ethical questions. Among the most pressing are how therapists

G. H. Rassool, *Ethical Dilemmas in Islāmic Psychotherapy*,
https://doi.org/10.1007/978-3-032-26515-9_14

can respect the sacred dimensions of clients' beliefs while remaining accountable to professional codes of practice; how they can navigate complex matters of identity, morality, and cultural expectations without imposing personal values or compromising client autonomy; and how ethical frameworks, often shaped by Western traditions, can be reconciled with the moral and spiritual heritage of Islām.

Key insights emerging from this work highlight the importance of confidentiality, informed consent, and the careful balance between individual autonomy and communal or family values. They also emphasise the need for culturally responsive interventions and the thoughtful integration of Islāmic teachings into therapeutic practice. Distinctive challenges arise for Islāmic psychotherapists, particularly in contexts where family and community expectations exert strong influence. Boundaries and multiple professional roles add further complexity, as practitioners may be perceived as fulfilling functions such as *tarbiyah* (education), *irshād* (guidance), *tazkiyah* (spiritual purification), *da 'wah* (religious outreach), *taṭbīb* (healing), *shifā'* (curing), *wisāṭah* (mediation), *istiṭā 'ah* (empowerment), *ra 'āyah* (caretaking), and *naṣīḥah* (advising). Each of these roles carries distinct ethical implications for boundaries and professional responsibility.

14.2 Core Ethical Principles in Islāmic Psychotherapy

Ethical practice in Islāmic psychotherapy is best understood as a dynamic process that integrates professional responsibility with spiritual integrity. Qur'ānic principles, prophetic guidance, and the objectives of *Sharī 'ah* (*Maqāṣid al-Sharī 'ah*) provide a moral foundation, while professional codes of ethics ensure accountability and consistency in clinical care. Together, these frameworks encourage therapists to view clients holistically, considering their spiritual, emotional, and social dimensions. Concepts such as *raḥmah* (compassion), *'adl* (justice), *wasatiyyah* (moderation), and *maṣlaḥah* (well-being) offer guiding values for ethical decision-making and culturally sensitive care.

Ethical practice in Islāmic psychotherapy requires careful attention to both professional standards and religious guidance. Therapists must address dilemmas related to autonomy, informed consent, confidentiality, and dual or multiple relationships, while remaining aware of professional codes of ethics and the cultural and spiritual contexts in which they work. Ethical conduct is not limited to compliance with external regulations; it also involves cultivating moral awareness, empathy, and spiritual sensitivity in the therapeutic encounter. Practitioners often face distinctive challenges when working within Muslim communities. Autonomy and informed consent may be complicated by strong family or communal expectations, which can influence decision-making and therapeutic engagement. Boundaries are another area of concern, as therapists may be perceived as fulfilling multiple roles, such as educator (*tarbiyah*), guide (*irshād*), spiritual mentor (*tazkiyah*), or advisor (*naṣīḥah*). Each of these roles carries ethical implications that must be carefully managed to preserve professional responsibility and therapeutic integrity. The ethical challenges encountered in practice highlight the importance of supervision, ongoing education, and therapist self-reflection.

14.3 Lessons from Case Studies and Clinical Applications

The case studies and vignettes presented throughout this work illustrate the practical complexities of applying ethical principles in clinical settings. They reveal how therapists must often overcome tensions between personal, community, and religious values, while also addressing specific challenges that shape the therapeutic process. These examples highlight the delicate task of integrating spiritual interventions into psychotherapy without compromising professional boundaries or ethical responsibility. A recurring theme is the need for flexibility and critical thinking. Effective Islāmic psychotherapy requires therapists to adapt their approaches to the unique circumstances of each client, demonstrating sensitivity to religious identity, cultural background, and social context. At the same time, practitioners must remain vigilant in upholding professional standards, ensuring that interventions are both ethically sound and clinically appropriate.

The case material also highlights the importance of therapist self-awareness and reflective practice. By examining their own assumptions, values, and potential biases, therapists are better equipped to engage authentically with clients while safeguarding autonomy and dignity in congruence with Islāmic teachings. Consultation with peers and supervisors emerges as another vital resource, offering opportunities for dialogue, accountability, and shared wisdom in navigating complex ethical terrain. Taken together, these lessons affirm that ethical practice in Islāmic psychotherapy is not a matter of rigid adherence to rules but a dynamic process. It requires a balance of professional competence, cultural sensitivity, and spiritual integrity, enabling therapists to respond thoughtfully to the diverse realities of clients' lives.

14.4 New Changes in Implementing Ethical Standards in Islāmic Psychotherapy

14.4.1 Code of Ethics and Expanded Ethical Guidelines

Recent developments emphasise the need to move beyond informal practice toward codified ethical frameworks that integrate both professional codes of conduct and Islāmic moral principles. This milestone has been marked by the recent publication of the International Association of Muslim Psychologists (IAMP) Code of Ethics and Expanded Ethical Guidelines (2026). The document presents the Code of Ethics together with detailed guidelines, offering practical direction, illustrative examples, and policy-style recommendations to support implementation across both Muslim-majority and Muslim-minority contexts. In cases where local legislation imposes stricter requirements, the higher standard is applied. The Code articulates fundamental ethical principles and establishes clear standards to guide the conduct of practitioners and organisations. It emphasises respect for human dignity, the promotion of well-being, and the upholding of integrity as central pillars of practice. By combining universal ethical commitments with faith-informed guidance, the IAMP Code provides a comprehensive framework for ensuring that Islāmic psychotherapy is both professionally accountable and spiritually authentic.

14.4.2 Structured Training Programmes on Ethical Issues in Islāmic Psychotherapy

There is growing recognition of the importance of structured training programmes that explicitly address ethical issues unique to Islāmic psychotherapy. New efforts should be undertaken by curriculum developers to integrate the study of ethical dilemmas within educational programmes in Islāmic psychology and psychotherapy. Rather than treating ethics as a peripheral topic, training should integrate these issues as a central component of professional formation. This includes examining real-world case studies, exploring tensions between religious guidance and professional codes of practice, and addressing challenges such as client autonomy, confidentiality, informed consent, and boundary management.

By incorporating ethical dilemmas into the curriculum, students are encouraged to develop critical thinking, moral sensitivity, and spiritual awareness. Such training prepares future practitioners to navigate complex situations with integrity, balancing evidence-based psychological interventions with Qur'ānic principles, prophetic guidance, and the objectives of *Sharī 'ah*. It also fosters reflective practice and equips therapists to respond to diverse cultural and theological contexts with professionalism and compassion.

14.4.3 Islāmic Ethical Dilemma Decision-Making Model

The Islāmic Ethical Dilemma Decision-Making Model (Rassool, 2025) was developed to provide structured guidance for addressing ethical challenges in Islāmic psychotherapy. The model has now been updated and adapted to incorporate contemporary clinical practices, and professional standards, ensuring its relevance for therapists working in diverse Islāmic contexts. The rationale for this model lies in the recognition that Western ethical frameworks, though valuable, do not fully capture the theological, spiritual, and cultural dimensions central to Muslim perspectives. Ethical decision-making in Islām is rooted in Qur'ānic teachings, Prophetic guidance, and the higher objectives of *Sharīʿah* (*Maqāṣid al-Sharīʿah*), which emphasise the protection of faith, life, intellect, lineage, and property. By integrating these principles, the model enables therapists to approach dilemmas with divine accountability, holistic spirituality, and communal responsibility. This framework supports culturally attuned, spiritually informed, and ethically coherent practice, equipping Muslim psychotherapists to meet the needs of clients who seek care aligned with their faith tradition.

The implementation of the Islāmic Ethical Dilemma Decision-Making Model requires embedding it into both training and clinical practice so that therapists can systematically address ethical challenges with clarity and integrity. In education, curriculum developers should integrate the model into teaching modules through case studies, role-play, and reflective exercises, enabling students to practice navigating dilemmas step by step. In clinical settings, practitioners can apply the model as a structured guide, identifying dilemmas, consulting Qur'ānic principles and professional codes, balancing competing values, seeking supervision, and reflecting on outcomes, to ensure decisions remain both clinically relevant and based on an Islāmic perspective. Institutions and professional associations can further strengthen implementation by adopting the model into policy frameworks, supervision protocols, and peer consultation practices, thereby standardising ethical decision-making across diverse Muslim contexts.

14.4.4 Need for Clinical Supervision

Clinical supervision in Islāmic psychotherapy is increasingly being adapted to incorporate faith-sensitive frameworks, enabling clinical supervisors to help therapists resolve professional standards with religious obligations. This approach strengthens accountability and provides a safe, reflective space for practitioners to examine complex ethical dilemmas. Importantly, clinical supervision should not only be considered a best practice but also encouraged and mandated by professional associations associated with Islāmic psychology and psychotherapy, ensuring that therapists consistently uphold both ethical integrity and spiritual authenticity in their work.

14.5 Future Research Directions

Future research should prioritise the exploration of psychoethical dimensions and ethical dilemmas within faith-informed practice. Key areas include:

- Conduct empirical studies evaluating psychotherapeutic approaches that combine Islāmic ethical and spiritual principles with conventional therapy,

assessing outcomes such as psychospiritual well-being, ethical competence, professional integrity, and client satisfaction.
- Investigate the ethical dilemmas faced by therapists, including balancing individual autonomy with communal obligations, navigating dual relationships, and managing culturally or religiously specific conflicts.
- Develop assessment instruments and decision-making frameworks that are tailored to diverse Muslim populations and vulnerable populations, to support ethical and culturally informed clinical practice.
- Examine how values such as justice (*'adl*), sincerity (*ikhlāṣ*), trust (*amānah*), God-consciousness (*taqwā*), proper conduct (*adab*), and excellence (*iḥsān*) shape ethical reasoning, moral accountability, and supervisory guidance within clinical and educational settings.
- Conduct rigorous quantitative and qualitative studies to evaluate traditional, peer, and Islāmic-integrated supervision models, focusing on supervisee skill development, reflective capacity, professional competence, and client care.
- Explore how the integration of the Spiritual–Ethical Dimension of Islāmic supervision influences supervisees' ethical decision-making, management of confidentiality, dual relationships, and culturally specific dilemmas.
- Compare outcomes of faith-informed supervision with conventional models.
- Investigate the effectiveness of supervision in different Muslim cultural and organisational contexts.
- Develop culturally appropriate evaluation and feedback mechanisms aligned with *Sharī'ah* principles.
- Examine how supervision impacts sustained professional growth, moral and spiritual development, resilience, and client well-being over time.
- Assess whether enhanced ethical consciousness translates into improved clinical practice and reduced risk of ethical breaches.
- Study the effects of specialised training in Islāmic ethics, *fiqh*-based perspectives, and reflective practices on supervisory effectiveness.
- Examine how clinical supervisors function as moral and spiritual mentors, fostering ethical, clinical, and professional development in supervisees.

By focusing on these dimensions, future research can strengthen the evidence base for Islāmic psychotherapy, providing therapists with guidance on managing ethical dilemmas while respecting both professional standards and religious values.

14.6 Recommendations for Clinical Practice

To promote ethically and culturally informed practice, clinicians are encouraged to:

- Compliant with the International Association of Muslim Psychologists (IAMP) Code of Ethics and Expanded Ethical Guidelines (2026).

- Uphold confidentiality, informed consent, and client autonomy while considering community and religious values.
- Integrate Islāmic ethical and spiritual principles into therapy without compromising professional standards.
- Engage in ongoing supervision, consultation, and reflective practice to navigate complex ethical and cultural dilemmas.
- Develop culturally sensitive interventions tailored to the needs of diverse Muslim populations.
- Foster awareness of personal biases, values, and assumptions to provide non-judgemental, empathic care.

By following these recommendations, therapists can provide care that is both ethically sound and spiritually resonant, contributing to holistic client well-being.

14.7 Conclusion

This chapter has synthesised the lessons learned from integrating Islāmic values with contemporary psychotherapy, highlighting the importance of ethical awareness, cultural competence, and spiritual sensitivity in clinical practice. As the field of Islāmic psychotherapy continues to develop, ongoing research, the establishment of standardised frameworks, and dialogue between religious and psychological scholarship will be essential. Emerging modalities, such as telepsychology and online therapy, present new ethical dilemmas where personal, professional, and spiritual values may intersect or conflict. Preparing clinicians to navigate these challenges with ethical rigour and spiritual insight will be crucial. By embracing both moral responsibility and holistic care, therapists can support the well-being of Muslim clients while contributing to culturally and spiritually informed mental health practice.

References

International Association of Muslim Psychologists. (2026, January). *IAMP code of ethics and expanded ethical guidelines*. Author.

Rassool, G. H. (2025). *Islāmic counselling & psychotherapy* (2nd ed.). Routledge.

Index

G. Rassool, *Ethical Dilemmas in Islāmic Psychotherapy*,
https://doi.org/10.1007/978-3-032-26515-9

FSC
www.fsc.org
MIX
Papier | Fördert
gute Waldnutzung
FSC® C083411

Zeitfracht Medien GmbH
Ferdinand-Jühlke-Straße 7
99095 Erfurt, Deutschland
produktsicherheit@kolibri360.de